FOR DUMMIES
BESTSELLING BOOK SERIES

W9-ADJ-850

Investing Online For Dummies, 6th Edition

How to Get Started Investing Online

Are you the impatient type? Do you just want to get started right away? Here's a quick step-by-step list to get you going:

1. **Save your money.** You don't need much to get started investing, preferably $50 or more. Find an online broker with no minimum deposit, as described in Chapter 4.

2. **Learn the terms.** Investing is full of jargon. You'll need to know basic words just to get started. Get up to speed with Web sites like Investopedia (`www.investopedia.com`) and InvestorWords (`www.investorwords.com`) to make sure you have a good grasp of the language of online investing.

3. **Practice with fake money first.** Before you start playing around with your real money, take a dry run by entering stock trades using the Investing Online Resource Center's Investing Simulator Center (`www.investingonline.org/isc/index.html`). Next, test your investment strategy with fake money using online trading simulators like Icarra (`www.icarra.com`) or Zack's Simulator (`simulator.zacks.com/zacks/default.aspx`).

4. **Choose an online brokerage firm.** Your online broker should be your wingman when investing online, so pick one you like and can trust. No one broker is best for all investors. Be sure to read Chapter 4 to get in-depth help on how to pick an online brokerage. Also, pick the right type of account to meet your financial goal, as described in Chapter 3.

5. **Keep saving money.** You'll want to keep adding savings to your brokerage account so you can put more of your money to work.

6. **Study.** The steps above will get you online and investing online. But there's so much more to it if you want to be successful. Be sure you read the longer step-by-step list of how to get started investing online in Chapter 1.

Quick and Helpful Tips You May Not Know About

✔ **Quickest way to get stock information.** If you're in a hurry and want basic information about a stock, fast, hit the search engines. Enter a stock's ticker symbol into the search blank in all the popular search engines including Google (`www.google.com`), Live.com (`www.live.com`), and Ask (`www.ask.com`). You'll immediately get the basic information about the stock, including a chart of the stock price, price quote, and market value.

✔ **Instant access to MSN Money.** MSN Money is an excellent Web site, discussed many times in this book, that has an unfortunate address. You must type in, or set as a favorite, the long address `moneycentral.msn.com/investor/home.asp`. But here's a trick: Directly access MSN Money by typing in `www.investor.com`. Much easier, wouldn't you say?

✔ **Instant access to Yahoo Finance and Google Finance.** You can access these popular investing sites by visiting their front pages and clicking the appropriate links. But here's a better and more direct way. Just type `finance.yahoo.com` for Yahoo Finance and `finance.google.com` for Google Finance.

For Dummies: Bestselling Book Series for Beginners

MAR 2008

Investing Online For Dummies®, 6th Edition

Cheat Sheet

Protecting Your Money and Your Identity Online

When you're buying and selling investments online, it pays to be extra careful to make sure your personal and financial information doesn't get stolen by cyberthieves. At the very minimum, you should protect yourself by:

- **Locking down your computer.** You'll want to install antivirus software — software that protects your files from malicious code — on your computer at the very least. Better yet, be sure you install firewall software or enable the firewall software built into your operating system. A firewall puts a fence around your computer, letting you control what data comes in and what goes out.

- **Being extra careful of wireless connections.** If you're online using a public wireless Internet connection, you need to be especially cautious. Find out how to protect your wireless communications in Chapter 1.

- **Checking up on your brokerage.** Before you give money to anyone, be sure to run the broker or brokerage firm through the Financial Industry Regulatory Authority's online BrokerCheck tool (`www.finra.org`). This simple search will take only a few moments and will tell you if the broker or brokerage firm is permitted to sell you securities. Chapter 18 shows you how to do this.

- **Knowing what's reasonable.** You should have a grasp of what kind of returns you can expect from investments. You can get this knowledge by reading Chapter 1. Knowing what legitimate investments return will help you smell a sham a mile away. If someone promises "guaranteed" or "risk-free" returns that exceed the return of stocks, you know you're most likely being lied to.

- **Getting familiar with regulators' resources.** The Securities and Exchange Commission (`www.sec.gov`) offers free and tremendously helpful tools and tips to investors. Take the time to explore the site and you'll be a much better investor. A great place to start is by checking out brokers and financial advisers. It's easy. Just click on the Check Out Brokers & Advisers link on the right-hand side of the page under where it says Investor Information. And the North American Securities Administrators Association (`www.nasaa.org`) puts you in touch with your state regulator in two clicks. Just click the Contact Your Regulator link on the left-hand side and then click on your state on the map.

For Dummies: Bestselling Book Series for Beginners

Investing Online
FOR
DUMMIES®
6TH EDITION

by Matt Krantz

BICENTENNIAL
1807
⊕WILEY
2007
BICENTENNIAL

Wiley Publishing, Inc.

4/08

WI

Investing Online For Dummies,® 6th Edition

Published by
Wiley Publishing, Inc.
111 River Street
Hoboken, NJ 07030-5774
www.wiley.com

Copyright © 2008 by Wiley Publishing, Inc., Indianapolis, Indiana

Published by Wiley Publishing, Inc., Indianapolis, Indiana

Published simultaneously in Canada

WILEY

About the Author

Matt Krantz is a nationally known financial journalist who specializes on investing topics. He has been a writer for *USA TODAY* since 1999, where he covers financial markets and Wall Street, concentrating on developments affecting individual investors and their portfolios. His stories routinely signal trends that investors can profit from and sound warnings about potential scams and issues investors should be aware of.

In addition to covering markets for the print edition of *USA TODAY*, Matt writes a daily online investing column called "Ask Matt," which appears every trading day at USATODAY.com. He answers questions posed by the Web site's audience in an easy-to-understand manner. Readers often tell Matt he's the only one who has been able to finally solve investing questions they've sought answers to for years.

Matt has been investing since the 1980s and has studied dozens of investment techniques while forming his own. And as a financial journalist, Matt has interviewed some of the most famous and infamous investment minds in modern history. Before joining *USA TODAY*, Matt worked as a business and technology reporter for *Investor's Business Daily* and was a consultant with Ernst & Young prior to that.

He earned a bachelor's degree in business administration at Miami University in Oxford, Ohio. Unlike other business majors who just focused on accounting, finance, and investments, Matt took journalism classes on his own time. He was an editor of the campus newspaper and filed stories to several newspapers, including *The Cincinnati Enquirer*.

In addition to appearing on the print and online pages of *USA TODAY*, Matt's work has also been featured in *Men's Health* magazine. He has spoken for investing groups, including at the national convention of BetterInvesting and on *Nightly Business Report*, which airs on PBS.

Matt is based in *USA TODAY*'s Los Angeles bureau. When he's not writing, he's either spending time with his wife and young daughter, running, playing tennis, mountain biking, or surfing.

Dedication

This book is dedicated to my wife Nancy, who has supported and carried me throughout the entire project from the very beginning. During the bleary-eyed writing sessions sitting in front of the computer at 1 a.m., Nancy was always there to suggest that perfect word I couldn't think of, bring in fresh-cut strawberries, or read every single page. The book is also dedicated to my daughter, Leilani, who put up with a Dad who was almost as nervous about being a first-time book author as he was to be a first-time parent.

Author's Acknowledgments

Staring at a flashing cursor on a blank Microsoft Word window, knowing I needed to fill hundreds of pages in a few months, was an intimidating task. That's why all the support I received kept me going. My editors at *USA TODAY* supported the book from its genesis and encouraged me along the way. My assignment editor, David Craig, as well as other *USA TODAY* editors, including Rodney Brooks, Ray Goldbacher, Jim Henderson, John Hillkirk, Ken Paulson, Geri Coleman Tucker, and Kinsey Wilson, have supported this book or my development as a writer and reporter. Chris Woodyard, a fellow business reporter in *USA TODAY*'s Los Angeles bureau, has been a great source of ideas and daily encouragement. My wife, Nancy, continued her personal mission of stomping out every typo on the planet by reading every word in this book over my shoulder.

Wiley has been tremendous to work with as well, including Senior Acquisitions Editor Bob Woerner, Senior Project Editor Paul Levesque, and Copy Editor Virginia Sanders. Julie Huynh, technical editor, made sure the book was free of "dead links" by checking every URL. Big thanks to Matt Wagner, my literary agent, for thinking of me for the project and presenting it to me. Fane Lozman provided a hand by sharing his options expertise. Thanks to my mom and dad for instilling, at a very young age, a curiosity in investing, writing, and computers (and for buying me my first computer well before having a PC was common). And thanks to my grandparents for teaching me the power of saving and investing.

Publisher's Acknowledgments

We're proud of this book; please send us your comments through our online registration form located at `www.dummies.com/register/`.

Some of the people who helped bring this book to market include the following:

Acquisitions, Editorial, and Media Development

Senior Project Editor: Paul Levesque

Senior Acquisitions Editor: Bob Woerner

Copy Editor: Virginia Sanders

Technical Editor: Julie Huynh

Editorial Manager: Leah Cameron

Media Development Project Manager: Laura Moss-Hollister

Media Development Assistant Producer: Angela Denny

Editorial Assistant: Amanda Foxworth

Sr. Editorial Assistant: Cherie Case

Cartoons: Rich Tennant (`www.the5thwave.com`)

Composition Services

Project Coordinator: Katherine Key

Layout and Graphics: Claudia Bell, Reuben W. Davis, Joyce Haughey, Melissa K. Jester, Ronald Terry, Christine Williams

Proofreaders: David Faust, Evelyn W. Still

Indexer: Slivoskey Indexing Services

Anniversary Logo Design: Richard Pacifico

Publishing and Editorial for Technology Dummies

Richard Swadley, Vice President and Executive Group Publisher

Andy Cummings, Vice President and Publisher

Mary Bednarek, Executive Acquisitions Director

Mary C. Corder, Editorial Director

Publishing for Consumer Dummies

Diane Graves Steele, Vice President and Publisher

Joyce Pepple, Acquisitions Director

Composition Services

Gerry Fahey, Vice President of Production Services

Debbie Stailey, Director of Composition Services

Contents at a Glance

Table of Contents

Bonus Chapters on the Web Site BC1

Introduction

You might be wondering why you need a book like this one to help you invest online. After all, if you're looking for information about investing online, you can certainly type **"investing online"** into a search engine and get thousands of search results.

But that's the problem. You'll get thousands of search results. Some of the sites you'll find using a search engine might have secret agendas and push financial products hazardous to your goals. Yet other sites offered up by a search engine might be filled with bad information that isn't correct, causing you to unknowingly make poor investment decisions. Worse yet, you might stumble on fraudulent Web sites determined to steal your identity or money. Sure, you might find some good Web sites through a Web search, but how can you tell the good from the bad when you get hundreds, if not thousands of results?

Along came *Investing Online For Dummies,* 6th Edition. This book is here to act as a down-to-Earth guide for getting started with online investing. I steer you clear of unnecessary investing gobbledygook, and I point you to resources that you can trust. I've already done all the mucking through the thousands of investing Web sites to find good ones — there's no reason you should have to do so as well!

About This Book

Investing Online For Dummies has been completely rewritten in this sixth edition to be your intelligent guide through this often confusing and constantly changing world of investing online. As the author, I can share the tricks, tips, and secrets I've learned from a career writing about online investing for readers just like you. This book can save you the trouble of fumbling through the Internet looking for the best online resources. I'm in the fortunate position of knowing what kind of information you're looking for thanks to what I do. Not only am I a markets reporter for USA TODAY, but each day I answer investing questions e-mailed to me through my daily online "Ask Matt" column at USATODAY.com. I've answered thousands of reader questions. That puts me in the position of knowing what questions most investors, and perhaps you, tend to have. Much of the wisdom I've picked up writing about investing and answering readers' questions is presented in this book.

Don't worry, *Investing Online For Dummies* isn't just a directory of Web sites that robotically lists hundreds of Web site addresses and leaves it up to you to look everything up. Those directory-type books, I've found, tend to be frustrating for investors looking for a road map and some handholding to get started investing online. Instead, I've taken special care to bake in principles about investing first and then show you how to use the Internet and your computer to boost your success.

This book doesn't attempt to highlight every single investing Web site, but instead, it focuses on the best ones. Most of the sites I've selected have been around long enough to prove to be reliable and accurate. And because this book's purpose is to help you make and save money, not spend it, it sticks mainly to Web sites that are free. When a site requires a subscription, I let you know so you can decide whether the fee is worthwhile.

I have one big caveat. Keep in mind as you enter the addresses of some of the Web pages that the Internet is so fast-changing, you might encounter a link or two that no longer works. Don't assume the site has gone to Internet heaven. Try entering the name of the site into a search engine using techniques described in the first part of the book. More times than not, you'll find the site is still online but has just changed its address slightly. Similarly, even if a Web page isn't quite how I describe it, the page might have been changed, so you might have to ditch my instructions and play around to find how what's different.

Who Invests Online?

Online investing isn't just an interesting niche for techies and day traders. More than 9 million households will trade online in 2007, estimates market research firm Forrester Research.* And that number is expected to soar by more than 30% and hit 12 million households by 2011 as long as the stock market posts moderate gains, Forrester says. Online stock trading has taken off so much that it was named the 18th top "eureka" moment since 1982 by USA TODAY, ahead of disposable contacts, TiVo, and home satellite TV.

Research has found out several things about online investors:

- **They're young.** Generation Y (ages 18 to 26) and Generation X (ages 27 to 40) are big online investors with 19% of the group reporting they've invested online at some point in 2005, Forrester says, citing the most recent data available. That's nearly double the 10% of boomers (ages 41

*"US Online Trading Forecast: 2006 to 2011", Forrester Research, Inc., February 2007."

to 61) and seniors (aged 61 and higher) who have traded online, Forrester says.

- ✔ **They're wealthy.** Investing online won't necessarily make you rich, but many of the rich do invest online. More than 20% of affluent households, with $1 million in assets, traded online, and 15% of households with assets between $100,000 and $999,999 traded online in 2005, Forrester says, citing its most recent data.

- ✔ **They're Web savvy.** The longer people have Internet access, the more interested they get in investing online. Although only 2% of households that had online access for just a year traded online in 2006, 16% of households that had online access for eight years or more did, Forrester says. And more people are becoming Web savvy. Forrester estimates that as of 2007 76% of U.S. households are online at least once a month, up from 57% in 2000.

Foolish Assumptions

No matter your skill or experience level with investing, you can get something out of *Investing Online For Dummies*. I assume some readers haven't invested in anything other than baseball cards or Pez dispensers and have no clue of where to even start. If that describes you, the first part of the book is custom made for you and takes extra care to step through all the key points in as much plain English as possible. (When I have no choice but to use investing jargon, I tell you what it means.) But I also assume more advanced investors might pick this book up too, looking to discover a few things. The book takes on more advanced topics as you progress through it and carefully selects online resources that will add new tools to your investing toolbox.

Conventions Used in This Book

I want to help you get the information you need as fast as possible. To help you, I use several conventions:

- ✔ Monofont is used to signal a Web address. This is important since there are so many Web addresses in the book.

- ✔ *Italics* signal that a word is a unique and important term for online investors.

- ✔ **Boldfaced** words make the key terms and phrases in bulleted and numbered lists jump out and grab your attention.

> ✔ Sidebars, text separated from the rest of the type in gray boxes, are interesting but slightly tangential to the subject at hand. Sidebars are generally fun and optional reading. You won't miss anything critical if you skip the sidebars. If you choose to read the sidebars, though, I think you'll be glad you did.

How the Book Is Organized

All the chapters in this book are self-contained and can be read by themselves. That means you shouldn't read *Investing Online For Dummies* like you would *War and Peace,* and hopefully you won't fall asleep as much as you would if you read *War and Peace,* either. Jump around. Flip through. Scan the index and find topics you've been dying to read about for years. And don't fear that you'll get in over your head if you read the back of the book first. If there are concepts you need to know at any point, I carefully added references to those pages in the book so you can jump around. This book is a reference, and you shouldn't feel as if you need to suffer through topics you already know or don't care to know. With that said, though, the book is assembled in a logical order. My goal is to start simple and then ramp things up as the book goes on.

The book is divided into four parts.

Part 1: Getting Started Investing Online

If you like the idea of investing online but haven't the foggiest on where to start, this part is for you. You find everything you need to know to get up and running with online investing, ranging from mastering the terminology to getting your computer set up for online trading. I help you decide what kind of account to open and explain how to pick an online broker. After reading the chapters in this part, you should have a good idea of what's entailed in investing online and what kinds of returns you can expect.

Part 11: Using Online Investing Resources

Ever see a campy science fiction movie? More often than not, the plot involves some sort of computer that ends up ruling humans. If you've ever seen people struggling with and cursing at their computers, that sci-fi nightmare isn't all that far-fetched. This part lets you turn the tables on the Machine and put the Internet to work for you, rather than getting worked over by the Internet. I show you how to get your computer to help you design the perfect portfolio for you and even help you locate mutual funds and exchange-traded funds that fit your strategy.

Part III: Maximizing Investment Knowledge

If you've ever wondered why mutual fund managers get paid the big bucks and what they do all day, you can find out in this part. Part III delves into some advanced topics such as how to pick investments and study company's financials. What's unique about this part, however, is that it shows you how to do these advanced analyses using your computer and the Internet.

Part IV: The Part of Tens

These final and short chapters wrap up many of the basic lessons illustrated throughout the book in easy-to-digest nuggets. You'll find ways to avoid making the 10 most common online investment mistakes as well as ways to protect your money and identity online.

Bonus Chapters on the Web Site: Alternative Investing Strategies

There's so much to cover in this book, I couldn't stuff it all in. No worries. A few offbeat — but still important — investments are covered in this part and made available to you online at www.dummies.com/go/iofd. Don't think this part isn't as important because it's only online. This part covers international investing, which is something that belongs in almost all investors' portfolios. You can also find information on how to read online stock charts and study initial public offerings. And, for good measure, I take the time to answer questions that seem to enter the minds of nearly all online investors at some point or another.

Icons Used in This Book

When you're flipping through this book, you might notice several icons that catch your attention. That's done on purpose. I use several distinct icons to alert you to sections of the book that stand out. Those icons are

These icons highlight info that you should etch on the top of your brain and never forget, even when you're getting caught up in the excitement of investing online.

Read these sections to quickly pick up insider secrets that can boost your success when investing online.

Some of the things covered in the book get a bit hairy and complicated. This icon flags such sections for two reasons. First, you may decide to avoid the headache and skip over them — the info isn't vital. Second, the icon is a heads-up that the paragraph is probably loaded with investment jargon. Don't be embarrassed if you need to read the section a second or third time. Hey, you didn't want this book to be too easy, did you?

Avoid the landmines scattered throughout Wall Street that can decimate your good intentions at building wealth with these sections.

Where to Go from Here

If you're a new investor or just getting started investing online, you might consider starting from the beginning. That way, you'll be ready for some of the more advanced topics I introduce later in the book. If you've already been investing online, have a strategy you think is working for you, and are pleased with your online broker, you might skip to Part II. And if you're dying to know about a specific topic, there's nothing wrong with looking up those terms in the index and flipping to the appropriate pages.

Part I
Getting Started Investing Online

"The first thing you should know about investing online is that when you see the exploding bomb icon appear, it's just your browser crashing—not your portfolio."

In this part . . .

The idea of investing online is irresistible to most investors. Low trading commissions, cutting out high-price brokers, and gaining tremendous financial control are all possible with online investing. What's not to like, right?

The trouble, though, for many investors is how to get started. Investing online is laden with enough jargon and Web sites to send some beginners running. Consider this part to be your user's manual on how to get started investing online. You discover everything you need to know to get yourself and your computer ready to pick, buy, and sell investments online. I go over all the key terms you need to know to set up investment accounts, pick a broker, and get started. Even more importantly, you discover the main ways to invest online and quickly gain the wisdom of more experienced investors. You also find the answers to two of the most commonly asked questions investors ask me: "How do I get started investing online?" and "How much money do I need to invest online?"

Chapter 1

Getting Yourself Ready for Online Investing

In This Chapter

▶ Analyzing your budget and determining how much you can invest

▶ Taking the basic steps to get started

▶ Understanding what returns and risks you can expect from investing

▶ Getting to know your personal taste for risk

▶ Understanding your approach to investing: Passive versus active

▶ Finding resources online that will help you stick with a strategy

*I*f you've ever watched a baby learn to walk, you've seen how cautious humans are by nature. Babies will hold themselves against a wall and scoot along before actually going toe-to-toe with gravity and trying to walk. That skepticism stays with most people as they get older. Before doing something risky, you probably think good and hard about what you stand to gain and what you might lose. Surprisingly, many online investors, especially those just starting out, lose that innate sense of risk and reward. They chase after the biggest possible returns without considering the sleepless nights they'll suffer through as those investments swing up and down. Some start buying investments they've heard others made money on without considering whether those investments are appropriate for them. Worst of all, some fall prey to fraudsters who promise huge returns in get-rich-quick schemes.

So, I've decided to start from the top and make sure the basics are covered. You discover what you can expect to gain from investing online — and at what risk — so you can decide whether this is for you. You also find out how to analyze your monthly budget so you have cash to invest in the first place. Lastly, you find what kind of investor you are by using online tools that measure your taste for risk. After you've gotten to know your inner investor better, you can start thinking about forming an online investment plan that won't give you an ulcer.

Why Investing Online Is Worth Your While

Investing used to be easy. Your friend would recommend a broker. You'd give your money to the broker and hope for the best. But today, thanks to the explosion of Web-based investment information and low-cost online trading, you get to work a lot harder by taking charge of your investments. Lucky you! So, is the additional work worth it? In my opinion, taking the time to figure out to invest online *is* worthwhile because

- **Investing online saves you money.** Online trading is much less expensive than dealing with a broker. You'll save tons on commissions and fees. (Say, why not invest that money you saved?)

- **Investing online gives you more control.** Instead of entrusting someone else to reach your financial goals, you'll be personally involved. It's up to you to find out about all the investments at your disposal, but you'll also be free to make decisions.

- **Investing online eliminates conflicts of interest.** By figuring out how to invest and doing it yourself, you won't have to worry about being given advice that might be in your advisors' best interest and not yours.

Getting Started

I can't tell you how many investors just starting out write me and ask the exact same question. Maybe it's the same question running through your head right now: "I want to invest but where do I start?"

Getting started in investing seems so overwhelming that some get confused and wind up giving up and doing nothing. Others get taken in by promises of gigantic returns and enroll in seminars, subscribe to stock-picking newsletters, or agree to invest in odd assets like payphones, only to be disappointed. Others assume that all they need to do is open a brokerage account and start madly buying stocks. But as you'll notice if you look at the Table of Contents or flip ahead in this book, I don't talk about picking a broker and opening an account until Chapter 4. You have many tasks to do before then.

But don't let that fact intimidate you. Check out my easy-to-follow list of things you'll need to do to get started. Follow these directions, and you'll be ready to open an online brokerage account and start trading:

1. **Decide how much you can save and invest.**

   You can't invest if you don't have any money, and you won't have any money if you don't save. No matter how much you earn, you need to set aside some money to start investing. (Think saving is impossible? I show you computer and online tools later in this chapter that can help you build up savings that you can invest.)

2. **Master the terms.**

The world of investing has its own language. I help you to understand investingese now so you don't get confused in the middle of a trade when you're asked to make a decision about something you've never heard of. (Chapter 2 has more on the language of online investing.)

3. **Familiarize yourself with the risks and returns of investing.**

You wouldn't jump out of an airplane without knowing the risks, right? Don't jump into investing without knowing what to expect, either. Luckily, online resources I show you later in this chapter and in Chapter 8 can help you get a feel for how markets have performed over the past 100 years. By understanding how stocks, bonds, and other investments have done, you'll know what is a reasonable return and set your goals appropriately.

I can't stress how important this step is. Investors who know how investments move don't panic — they keep their cool. Panic is your worst enemy because it has a way of talking you into doing things you'll regret later.

4. **Get a feel for how much risk you can take.**

People all have different goals for their money. You might already have a home and a car, in which case you're probably most interested in saving for retirement or building an estate for your heirs. Or perhaps you're starting a family and hope to buy a house within a year. These two scenarios call for very different tastes for risks and *time horizons* (how long you'd be comfortable investing money before you need it). You need to know what your taste for risk is before you can invest. I show you how to measure your taste for risk later in this chapter.

5. **Understand the difference between being an active and passive investor.**

Some investors want to outsmart the market by darting in and out of stocks at just the right times. Others think doing that is impossible and don't want the hassle of trying. At the end of this chapter, you find out how to distinguish between these two types of investors, active and passive, so that you're in a better position to choose which one you are.

6. **Find out how to turn your computer into a trading station.**

If you have a computer on your desk and a connection to the Internet, you have all you need to turn it into a source of constant market information. You just need to know where to look, which you find out in Chapter 2.

The danger of doing nothing

After reading through the 11 steps for getting started, you might be wondering whether you've taken on more than you bargained for. Stick with it. The worst thing you can do now is put this book down, tell yourself you'll worry about investing later, and do nothing.

Doing nothing is extremely costly because you lose money if you don't invest. Seriously. Even if you stuffed your cash under a mattress and didn't spend a dime, each year that money becomes worth, on average, 3% less due to inflation. Suppose you won $1 million in the lottery and stuffed it in a hole in your backyard with the plan of taking it out in 30 years to pay for your retirement. In 30 years, all 1 million greenbacks would still be there, but they'd only buy $400,000 worth of goods. InflationData (www.inflationdata.com) has many online tools that show inflation drives up the costs of goods and services.

Even if you put your extra cash in a savings account, you're not doing much better. Because savings accounts usually let you get the money anytime, they pay low levels of interest, around 1 to 2%. Even high-yield savings accounts and Certificates of Deposit (CDs) typically pay only slightly higher interest than the level of inflation, meaning you're barely keeping up and not getting ahead. To be successful, you need to move money you don't need for a while out of savings and into investments. Investments have the potential to generate much higher returns.

7. **Take a dry run.**

   Don't laugh. Many professional money managers have told me they got their starts by pretending to pick stocks and tracking how they would have done. It's a great way to see whether your strategy might work, before potentially losing your shirt. You can even do this online, which I cover in Chapter 2.

8. **Choose the type of account you'll use.**

   You can do your investing from all sorts of accounts, all with different advantages and disadvantages. I cover them a little in this chapter and go into more detail in Chapter 3.

9. **Set up an online brokerage account.**

   At last, the moment you've been waiting for: opening an online account. After you've tackled the preceding steps, you're ready to get going. This important step is covered in Chapter 4.

10. **Understand the different ways to place trades and enter orders.**

    I explain in Chapter 5 about the many different ways to buy and sell stocks, each with very different end results. (You also need to understand the tax ramifications of selling stocks, which I cover in Chapter 3.)

11. **Boost your knowledge.**

    After you have the basics down, you're ready to tackle the later parts of the book, where I cover advanced investing topics. This involves picking an asset allocation (covered in Chapter 9), researching stocks to buy and knowing when to sell (covered in Chapter 13), and evaluating more exotic investments (the stuff you find in the chapters contained in the bonus chapters on the Web).

Measuring How Much You Can Afford to Invest

Online investing can help you accomplish some great things. It can help you pay for a child's college tuition, buy the house you've been eyeing, retire, or travel to the moon. Okay, maybe not the last one. But you get the idea. Investing helps your money grow faster than inflation. And by investing online, you can profit even more by reducing the commissions and fees you must pay to different advisors and brokers.

One thing online investing cannot do is make something out of nothing. To make money investing online, you have to save money first. Don't get frustrated, though, because you don't need as much to get started as you might fear. If you have a job or source of income, building up ample seed money isn't too hard.

Turning yourself into a big saver

If you want to be an investor, you must find ways to spend less money now so you can save the excess. That means you must retrain yourself from being a consumer to being an investor. Many beginning investors have trouble getting past this point because being a consumer is so easy. Consumers buy assets that they can use and enjoy, but almost all of those assets lose value over time. Cars, electronic gadgets, and clothing are all examples of things consumers "invest" their money in. You don't even have to have money to spend — plenty of credit card companies will gladly loan it to you. Consumers fall into this spending pattern vortex and end up living paycheck-to-paycheck with nothing left to invest.

Investors, on the other hand, find ways to put off current consumption. Instead of spending money, they invest it into building businesses or goods and services that will earn money, rather than deplete it. The three main types of investments are stocks, bonds, and real estate, although there are others that I cover in the later chapters.

Scouring the Web for savings help

Even fastidious savers have unavoidable basic expenses. Investors, though, find ways to be smart about even these routine costs. These sites can help:

✔ **Feed The Pig** (www.feedthepig.com) urges you to stop wasting money and offers tips to help you get out of debt by cutting excess spending. The site can calculate how to get out of debt and even how much you can save by packing a lunch instead of buying one.

✔ **Get Rich Slowly** (www.getrichslowly.org) provides tips, calculators, and online tools to help you save more so you can invest more.

✔ **The Consumerist** (www.consumerist.com), offers tips to educate consumers. It explains how to play hardball with service providers, like cell phone companies, that sock you with monthly fees.

Here are a few things you can do now to help you change from being a consumer to an investor:

✔ **Start with what you can manage by putting aside a little each month.**

✔ **Keep increasing what you put aside.** If you do it gradually, you won't feel the sting of a suddenly pinched pocket.

✔ **Hunt for deals and use coupons and discounts.** Put aside the saved money.

✔ **Buy only what you need.** Don't be fooled into buying things you don't need because they're on sale.

Using personal finance software

The word *budget* is a real turnoff. It conjures up images of sitting at the kitchen table with stacks of crumpled-up receipts, trying to figure out where all your money went. As an investor who prefers to do things online, this image probably isn't too appealing.

It's worth your while to find other ways to see how much money is coming in and how much is going out. Fortunately, you have a painless option available: *personal finance software,* which helps you track your spending and investments.

Take a look at these two big names in personal finance software:

- ✔ **Microsoft Money** (www.microsoft.com/money) is a great tool for measuring how much money you can afford to invest. It helps you determine how much money you spend, where it goes, and how much excess you accumulate each month that you can channel into investing. You can view the results in charts, such as the one in Figure 1-1. Money can also create a budget for you, essentially at the push of a button. The software alerts you if you're spending more on a certain category than you budgeted for. The biggest gripe against the software is that you have to get your transactions into it first. You can type them in by hand, which is kind of a pain, or you can download them from your credit card company or bank. Money also costs you $30 for the Deluxe edition. My advice: Don't run out and buy it. First, download the free trial that lets you test Money 2007 for three months.

- ✔ **Intuit's Quicken** (www.quicken.com), like Money, is an outstanding tool for tracking where all your money goes. Its 2007 version introduced a home page that shows you at a glance where your money is going. It also offers a version for Macintosh. It costs $50 for the Deluxe edition. Quicken, like Money, warns you if you're spending too much on certain types of items.

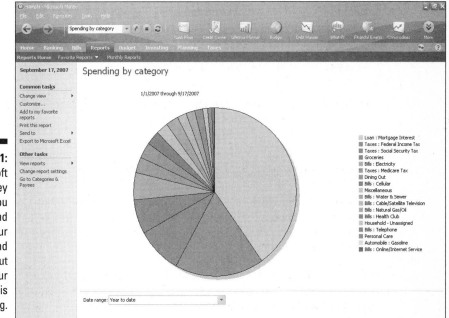

Figure 1-1: Microsoft Money allows you to slice and dice your budget and find out where your money is going.

Both Quicken and Money do more than help you set and stick to a budget. Both help you with more advanced topics, such as managing your portfolio and taxes — stuff I cover later in this book.

Not sure whether you'd like Money or Quicken? It's really a personal decision, but if some expert opinions might sway you one way or another, you'd be happy to know that both Money and Quicken are reviewed each year at technology Web site CNET.com. The 2007 review can be found here: `http://reviews.cnet.com/4520-9239_7-6631482-1.html`. Reviews from other sites are compiled at ConsumerSearch.com (`www.consumersearch.com/www/software/accounting_software/index.html`).

Money and Quicken might be the big kids on the block, but they aren't alone. Be sure to check out these other options (some of which are free!):

- **Moneydance** (`www.moneydance.com`) comes in versions for Windows, Macintosh, and Linux. If you're already using Money or Quicken, no worries — Moneydance can translate your files. It's comparably priced at $30 and offers a trial that lets you use the software until you hit 100 transactions.

- **Money Manager Ex** (`www.thezeal.com/software/index.php?Money_Manager_Ex`) tries to make the power of software like Money and Quicken free. It's *open-source* personal finance software, programmed by hobbyists and offered to the public as a service. If you like it, you can donate to the programmers who have created it.

- **Buddi** (`http://buddi.sourceforge.net/en`) is another free option. But unlike the other personal finance software, Buddi is designed to track budgets and spending, not investment portfolios.

- **PearBudget** (`www.pearbudget.com`) is free budgeting software that works in Microsoft Excel or other popular spreadsheet programs. The software tracks your costs and tells you whether you're sticking with the plan.

Microsoft also provides several helpful budgeting spreadsheets, which you can find by entering the word *budget* in the search field of the Microsoft Office Templates home page (`http://office.microsoft.com/en-us/templates/default.aspx`). The Web site It's Your Money (`www.mdmproofing.com/iym/excel.htm`) also provides several spreadsheets to help you manage your money.

Perusing personal finance Web sites

Before you can put personal finance software to work, you often need to download and install it on your computer. You then need to spend some time figuring out how to actually use it. If that's exactly the kind of thing that scared you away from making a budget in the first place, you might want to consider *personal finance Web sites*. Personal finance Web sites' main benefits include the fact they let you see your information from any PC connected to the Internet, and you generally don't have to install software to make them work. Here are a few to check out:

- ✔ **Mvelopes Personal** (www.mvelopes.com) will be your spending cop that tells you you're spending too much. Mvelopes is a Web-based spending tracker that tries to be the digital version of envelope-based budgeting. Rather than stuffing cash in envelopes set aside for certain expenses, Mvelopes lets you decide before you get a paycheck how much you're willing to spend in certain categories (such as dining out) and plan your spending for the month. As the month progresses, you download all your spending from banks and credit card companies and subtract each transaction from the envelopes you set aside. That way, if you're spending too much on restaurants, for instance, you know to cut back or to skimp in other areas. It also comes with some electronic bill payment services. It's not a cheap tool, though, and will set you back $130 a year, although you can consider the 30-day free trial or a two-year plan for $190.

- ✔ **Wesabe** (www.wesabe.com) lets you enter your budget and track it. But it has a twist: Other Wesabe users can see where your money is going and offer suggestions on ways to save more. It's free, too, which saves you some money right away.

- ✔ **Geezeo** (www.geezeo.com) is designed for people who want to track their spending, but are more likely to have a cell phone than sit in front of a computer. With your permission, the site pulls down your account balances from all your financial institutions. That way, when you're shopping, you can send a text message to Geezeo and get a message back showing all your account balances. Hopefully that will remind you to not spend money you don't have. Other users also offer tips on the Web site on how to save money.

Personal finance information sites don't track your transactions, but they're still able to give you the big picture. The following sites are worth checking out:

- ✔ **The Financial Planning Association's Life Events & Financial Decisions** (http://fpanet.org/public/tools/lifeevents/?WT.svl=2) lets you click on financial goals, like "becoming established," and get advice.

- ✔ **Smartaboutmoney.org** (www.smartaboutmoney.org) provides various tips on how to save more and boost your financial strength.

✔ **U.S. Financial Literacy and Education Commission** (www.mymoney.gov) is a government-run site that steps you through everything from saving more to avoiding frauds. It's also a good directory of useful information available from other government agencies.

Many financial information Web sites are designed for older investors who are looking for information on homes, kids, and retirement. If you're a parent hoping your kids will be more responsible with money, check out Young Money (www.youngmoney.com). You can find advice that's more targeted for young adults, such as managing credit card debt or avoiding campus scams.

Saving with Web-based savings calculators

If personal finance software or sites seem too much like a chore or too Big Brotherish, you might consider Web-based tools that measure how much you could save, in theory, based on a few parameters that you enter.

✔ **MSN Money's Savings Calculator** (www.moneycentral.msn.com/Investor/calcs/n_savapp/main.asp) asks you a series of questions to help you analyze your spending and find out how much you can save, how long it'll take you to save a certain amount, how much you must save to meet a goal or how long it will take to save $1 million.

✔ **Young Money's Home Budget Calculator** (www.youngmoney.com/calculators/personal_finance_calculators/home_budget) helps you break down where all your money is going so you can determine how much you can save. It steps you through all your major expenses and helps you find ways to waste less.

✔ **Bankrate.com's Saving for a Goal Calculator** (www.bankrate.com/brm/calc/savecalc.asp) asks you what you're saving for, be it college or buying a car. It then breaks down your financial objective and tells you how much you need to save to meet said objective.

✔ **Financial Industry Regulatory Authority's (FINRA) Savings Calculator** (http://apps.finra.org/investor_Information/Calculators/nasd/SavingsCalc.aspx) lets you enter different combinations of variables such as how much you've saved already and how much additional money you intend to save. It then gives you a realistic estimate of how much you can expect to save.

✔ **USATODAY.com's The Real Person's Budget** (www.usatoday.com/money/perfi/basics/2005-04-21-real-budget-story_x.htm) was developed by a personal finance advisor to help you interactively figure out where your money is going.

Relying on the residual method

Are you the kind of person who has no idea how much money you have until you take out a wad of twenties from the ATM and check the balance on the receipt? If so, you're probably not the budgeting type, and the preceding options are too strict. For you, the best option might be to open a savings account with your bank or open a high-yield savings account and transfer in money you know you won't need. Watch the savings account over the months and find out how much it grows. That will give you a good idea of how much you could save without even feeling it. You can find out where you can get a high rate of interest on your savings from Bankrate.com (www.bankrate. com/brm/rate/highyieldmma.asp?prodtype=chksav).

Using Web-based goal savings calculators

All the preceding methods help you determine how much you can save. But the following sites help you determine how much you *should* save to reach specific goals:

- **Vanguard's retirement calculator** (https://flagship.vanguard. com/VGApp/hnw/planningeducation/retirement/PEdRetInvSet YrSavGoalsContent.jsp) helps you figure out how much you should save by measuring how much you will need. The site prompts you to enter how much you make and how long you have until retirement to help you figure out how much you need to save. Vanguard offers similar tools to help you decide how much you need to save for other goals, such as paying for a child's college.

- **T. Rowe Price's Retirement Income Calculator** (www3.troweprice. com/ric/RIC) uses advanced computerized modeling to show you how much you need to save no matter what the stock market does. It runs your variables through a "Monte Carlo simulation," which simulates what happens to your savings no matter what and gives you the odds you'll have enough money. It has similar tools to help you decide how much you need to save to retire, including a Retirement Planning Worksheet (www.troweprice.com/common/indexHtml3/0,0,htmlid= 902,00.html?scn=T._Rowe_Price_Calcul&rfpgid=8278).

- **Nationwide's RetirAbility Check** (www.nationwide.com/nw/nrri/ index.htm?wtgo=retirability) asks you some questions and then rates your ability to retire when and how you plan to. It also suggests tips on improving your odds of saving as much as you hope.

- **Financial Calculators** (www.financialcalculators.com) can help you calculate just about any financial goal you might have — from buying a home to saving for college.

Being prepared for emergencies

When creating your budget and moving money from savings to an investment account, be sure to keep an emergency fund. This is money that's readily available in case of an emergency, stored in an account you can access immediately, such as a bank savings account. A decent guideline is to always have enough cash handy that you could pay at least six months of living expenses. Add up how much you spend each month on necessities such as housing (rent or mortgage and property taxes), food, utilities, and transportation. Multiply by six to get a general idea how much you should have for emergencies.

Deciding How You Plan to Save

After you've determined how much you need to save and how much you can save, you need to put your plan in action. The way you do this really depends on how good you are at handling your money and saving. The different methods include:

- **Automatic withdrawals:** Ever hear the cliché, "pay yourself first"? It's a trite saying that actually makes sense. The idea is that before you go shopping for that big-screen TV or start feeling rich after payday, you should set money aside for savings. Some people have the discipline to do this themselves, but many do not. For those people, the best option is to set up *automatic withdrawals,* which is a way of giving a brokerage firm or bank permission to automatically extract money once a month. When the money is out of your hands, you won't be tempted to spend it.

- **Retirement plans:** If your goal is investing for retirement, you want to find out what retirement savings plans are available to you. If you're an employee, you might have access to a 401(k) plan. And if you're self-employed, you might consider various individual retirement accounts (also known as IRAs). When you're starting to invest, taking advantage of available retirement plans is usually your best bet. I cover this in more detail in Chapter 3.

- **On your own:** If you have money left over after paying all your bills, don't let it sit in a savings account. Leaving cash in a low-interest-bearing account is like giving a bank a cheap loan. Put your money to work for you. Brokers make it easy for you to get money to them via electronic transfers.

Want to Be a Successful Investor? Start Now!

The greatest force all investors have is time. Don't waste it. The sooner you start to save and invest, the more likely you will be successful. To explain, take the example of five people, each of whom want to have $1 million in the bank by the time they retire at age 65. The first investor starts when she is 20, followed by a 30-year-old, 40-year-old, 50-year-old, and 60-year-old. Assuming each investor starts with nothing and averages 10% returns each year (more on this later), Table 1-1 describes how much each must save per month to reach his or her goals.

Table 1-1	How Much Each Must Save to Get $1 Million, Part I
An Investor Who Is	*Must Invest This Much Each Month to Have $1 Million at 65*
20 years old	$95.40
30 years old	$263.40
40 years old	$753.67
50 years old	$2,412.72
60 years old	$12,913.71

See, youth has its advantages. A 20-year-old who saves less than $100 a month will end up with the same amount of money as a 60-year-old who squirrels away $12,914 a month or $154,968 a year! That's largely due to the fact that money that's invested early has more time to brew. And over time, the money snowballs and *compounds,* which is a concept I cover later in this chapter.

Learning the Lingo

Just about any profession, hobby, or pursuit has its own lingo. Car fanatics, chess players, and computer hobbyists have terms of art that they seem to learn through osmosis. Online investing is no different. Many terms, like stocks and bonds, you might have heard but not completely understood. As you read through this book and browse the Web sites I mention, you'll probably periodically stumble on unfamiliar words.

Don't expect a standard dictionary to help much. Investing terms can be so specialized and precise that old Webster might not be a big help. Fortunately, a number of excellent online investing glossaries explain in detail what investing terms mean. Here are few for you to check out:

- ✔ **Investopedia** (`www.investopedia.com`) has one of the most comprehensive databases of investing terms out there, with more than 5,000 entries. The site not only covers the basics, but explains advanced terms in great detail as well. It's also fully searchable so you don't waste time getting the answer.

- ✔ **Yahoo! Financial Glossary** (`http://biz.yahoo.com/f/g`) is all about quick answers. The database, written by Campbell Harvey, a professor of finance at Duke University, explains most basic investment terms in one or two sentences.

- ✔ **InvestorWords** (`www.investorwords.com`) has a fully searchable database of investment terms, but it also makes the dictionary a bit more interesting with unique features like a "term of the day" and a summary of terms that have recently rewritten definitions.

- ✔ **Investor Glossary** (`www.investorglossary.com`) covers all the basics but also attempts to describe some slang terms in the industry, such as an investing philosophy known as *the Dogs of the Dow*.

Setting Your Expectations

Have you ever talked to a professional investor or financial advisor? One of the first things they'll tell you is how much experience they have. I can't tell you how many times I've been told, "I've been on Wall Street 30 years. I've seen it all."

Some of that is certainly old-fashioned bragging. But these claims are common because in investing, experience does count. It's easy to say you could endure a bear market until you're watching white-knuckled and sweating bullets as your nest egg shrivels from $100,000 to $80,000 or $70,000. Experience brings perspective, which is very important.

But if you're new to investing, don't despair. Online tools can help you acquire the brain of a grizzled Wall Street sage. And don't forget that I'm here to set you straight as well. In fact, I'm set to start talking about how much you can expect to make from investing. And you'll be hearing a great deal about a little something called the *rate of return*.

Keeping up with the rate of return

Don't let the term *rate of return* scare you. It's the most basic concept in investing, and you can master it. Just remember that it's the amount, measured as a percent, that your investment increases in value in a certain period of time. If you have a savings account, you understand the concept already. If you put $100 in a bank account paying 4.5% interest, you know that by the end of the year you will have received $4.50 in interest. You earned a 4.5% annual rate of return. Rates of return are useful in investing because they work as a report card to tell investors how well an investment is doing, no matter how much they have invested.

You can calculate rates of return yourself with the following:

- ✔ **A formula:** Subtract an asset's previous value from its current value and divide the difference by the asset's previous value and multiply by 100. If a stock rises from $15 a share to $32, you would calculate the rate of return by first subtracting 15 from 32 to get 17. Next, divide 17 by 15 and multiply by 100. The rate of return is 113.3%.

- ✔ **Financial calculators:** You can use the Hewlett-Packard 12c that financial types always carry. If you have this calculator, you can learn how to crunch a rate of return with this easy-to-follow tutorial (www.hp.com/calculators/training/cbt/12c_platinum.html).

- ✔ **Microsoft's Excel spreadsheet software:** This software, which is available on most computers, calculates rates of return fairly easily. You can find out how with the instructions at www.office.microsoft.com/en-us/excel/HP011225061033.aspx.

- ✔ **Financial Web sites:** Many handy sites can calculate rates of return for you, including www.moneychimp.com/calculator/discount_rate_calculator.htm.

When you calculate the rate of return for a portfolio you've added money to or taken money from, you must take an extra step. I explain how to do that in Chapter 8.

The power of compounding

Famous physicist Albert Einstein once called *compounding* the most powerful force in the universe. Compounding is when money you invest earns a return and then that return also earns a return. (Dizzy yet?) When you leave money invested for a long time, the power of compounding kicks in.

Imagine you've deposited $100 in an account that pays 4.5% in interest a year. In the first year, you'd earn $4.50 in interest, which brings your balance to

$104.50. But in the second year, you'd earn interest of $4.70. Why? Because you've earned 4.5% on the $4.50 in interest you earned. The longer you're invested, the more time your money has to compound.

You can enter your own information and see how powerful a force compounding is here: www.dinkytown.net/java/CompoundSavings.html.

Compounding works on your side to fight against inflation and taxes. Financial data and news provider Bloomberg has a Web-based calculator (www.bloomberg.com/invest/calculators/returns.html) that tells you whether your rate of return is putting you ahead.

Determining How Much You Can Expect to Profit

Why bother investing online? To make money, of course. But how much do you want to make? Understanding what you can expect to earn is where you need to start. Whenever you hear about an investment and what kinds of returns it promises, you should be able to mentally compare it with the kinds of returns you can expect from stocks, bonds, and other investments. That way you know whether the returns you're being promised are too good to be true.

How do you do this? By relying on the hard work of academics who have done some heavy lifting. Academics and market research firms have ranked investments by how well they've done over the years. And I'm not just talking a few years, but for decades — in many cases, going back to the 1920s and earlier. The amount of work that's gone into measuring historical rates of returns is staggering, but if you're using online resources, you're just a click away from finding out how most types of assets have done.

What you expect to earn is a number that will affect most of your investment decisions, usually rather dramatically. The following table is a revised version of Table 1-1 — the one that showed how five different people could expect to save $1 million. Table 1-2 looks at how much they must save to make their goal changes based on how much they think they will earn from their investments.

Table 1-2	How Much Each Must Save to Get $1 Million, Part II		
An Investor Who Is	*Must Invest This Much Each Month If He Earns 5%*	*Must Invest This Much Each Month If He Earns 10%*	*Must Invest This Much Each Month If He Earns 15%*
20 years old	$493.48	$95.40	$15.28
30 years old	$880.21	$263.40	$68.13
40 years old	$1,679	$753.67	$308.31
50 years old	$3,741	$2,412.72	$1,495.87
60 years old	$14,704.57	$12,913.71	$11,289.93

The 20-year-old must save nearly $500 a month extra if she thinks she will earn only 5% a year from her investments instead of 15%. But even scarier, if she saves $15.28 thinking she'll earn 15% a year, but earns only 5%, she'll have just $30,963 instead of the $1 million she was counting on.

Studying the past

If someone asks you how stocks are doing, he often means how much they went up or down that day. Financial TV stations reinforce this preoccupation with the here-and-now by scrolling second-by-second moves in stock prices across the bottom of the screen.

But, second-by-second moves in stocks don't really tell you much. If a stock goes down a bit, and a company didn't report news, did anything really change during that second? Watching short-term movements of stock prices doesn't mean much in the overall scheme of things.

To understand how investments behave, it's more helpful to analyze their movements over as many years as you can. That way, recessions are blended with boom times to get you to a real, smooth average. Doing this requires the painstaking method of processing dozens of annual returns of stocks and analyzing the data. Luckily, some academics and industry pioneers have done much of the work for you, and you can access their findings if you know where to look. And I just happen to know a few places where you can start your search:

✔ **Bogle Financial Market Research** (www.vanguard.com/bogle_site/bogle_home.html) is the Web site maintained by the founder of Vanguard, John C. Bogle. Bogle revolutionized the investment industry by creating the world's largest index mutual fund, the Vanguard 500, which is designed to mirror the performance of the stock market index.

Stock market indexes, such as the Standard & Poor's 500 and Dow Jones industrial average, are benchmarks that let you track how the market is doing.

Bogle's site is invaluable because he explains that the market, on average, returns about 10% a year. That benchmark will be very important later as you evaluate different stocks. Indexes are covered in more detail in Chapter 8.

✔ **Russell's Web site** (www.russell.com) lets you look up how all types of stocks, ranging from small to large in addition to bonds, have done over the years. There's a handy color-coded sheet that shows you how they've all done every year since 1996 here: www.russell.com/ indexes/PDF/Styleperformance.pdf.

✔ **Kenneth R. French's Web site and Eugene Fama's Web site (respectively)**

http://mba.tuck.dartmouth.edu/pages/faculty/ken.french/data_library.html #HistBenchmarks

http://gsbportal.chicagogsb.edu/portal//server.pt/gateway/PTARGS_0_0_314_ 215_0_43/http%3B/gsbportal.chicagogsb.edu/Facultycourse/Portlet/Faculty Detail.aspx?&min_year=20064&max_year=20073&person_id=159486

These sites are complicated but worth the effort. French, a professor at Dartmouth, along with University of Chicago's Eugene Fama, revolutionized investing with an analysis that found three things that move stocks: what the general market is doing, how big the company is, and how pricey the shares are. Both keep statistics on their sites on how stocks move.

✔ **Index Funds Advisors** (www.ifa.com) compiles much of the research done by Fama and French and helps explain it in plain language. You can order a colorful book from the site, called *Index Funds: The 12-Step Program for Active Investors,* by Mark T. Hebner (IFA). The book explains how different types of stocks perform long term and how much you can expect to gain. It also shows long-term returns of bonds. You can download the book for free if you take the site's Risk Capacity Survey, explained later in this chapter.

✔ **Robert Shiller's Web site** (www.econ.yale.edu/~shiller) contains exhaustive data on how markets have done over the long term. You can view the data and make your own conclusions. Shiller is a well-known economics professor at Yale University.

✔ **Standard & Poor's Web site** (www2.standardandpoors.com/ portal/site/sp/en/us/page.topic/indices_500/2,3,2,2,0, 0,0,0,0,0,0,0,0,0,0,0.html) contains a full record of the returns from the Standard & Poor's 500 index going back for decades. This is invaluable data because you can understand how markets tend to move, instead of worrying about things that have never happened. Go to the Data tab to find the S&P 500 index historical returns. Open the Excel file and scroll down the annual total returns page. You can get an idea of how volatile stocks can be, but also what returns are possible if you stay invested.

✔ **MSN Money** (`http://moneycentral.msn.com`) lets you download the stock trading history of most investments. Figure 1-2 shows the long-term gain of the S&P 500 index, provided by MSN Money. These steps show you how to generate this kind of chart for any stock:

1. **Enter the ticker symbol of the investment you're interested and click the Go button.**

2. **Click Historical under the Charts heading on the left side to bring up the stock chart.**

3. **Click the Download the MSN Money Investment Toolbox link.**

4. **Select Download MSN Money Investment Toolbox. If you don't see the chart, install the ActiveX Control for the Investment Toolbox. After installation, you should see a Download Complete chart.**

5. **Proceed and click the I See Chart link, which pulls up the one-year chart.**

6. **Select the All Dates option from the period down-down menu option then select yearly.**

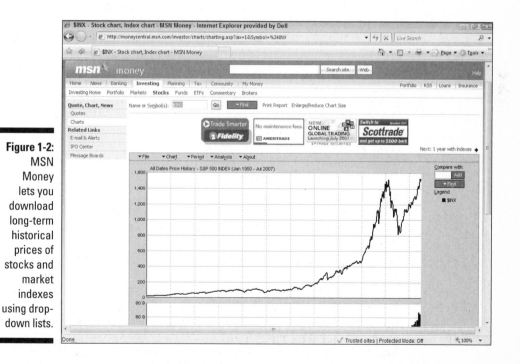

Figure 1-2: MSN Money lets you download long-term historical prices of stocks and market indexes using drop-down lists.

If you have trouble installing the MSN Money Investment Toolbox, you can get free help. From the front page of MSN Money, scroll down and click the Help link at the very bottom-right corner of the page. A sidebar appears. Type **MSN Money Toolbox** in the search field, click the green arrow, and then click the MSN Money Investment Toolbox Doesn't Install link.

Don't get too hung up if you don't understand everything on these sites. Several get pretty sophisticated, especially Fama and French's. Just scan through the annual returns so you can get a general feel for how markets behave over time — the idea here is for you to gain perspective, not cram for an econ Ph.D.

What the past tells you about the future

Exhaustive studies of markets have shown us that stocks, in general, return about 10% a year. Through the years, 10% returns have been the benchmark for long-term performance, making it a good measuring stick for you and something to help you keep your bearings. But long-term studies of securities also show that, to get higher returns, you usually must also accept more risk. Table 1-3 shows how investors must often accept more risk to get a higher return.

Table 1-3	No Pain, No Gain	
Investment	*Average Annual Return*	*Relative Risk*
Stocks	10.3% (based on S&P 500 since 1926)	Riskiest
Corporate bonds	6.8%	Moderately risky
Treasury bills (loans to the U.S. government that come due in a year or less)	3.8%	Least risky

Source: Global Financial Data, Inc.

Don't make the mistake of thinking that investing in stocks guarantees you a 10% return every year, like a savings account. That's not the case. Stocks are risky and tend to move in erratic patterns, and they test your confidence with sudden drops. In fact, each year stocks typically posted somewhere between a loss of 9% and a gain of 29.9%, according to IFA.com. And get this, since 1926, the Standard & Poor's 500 index has gained between 10.0% and 10.9% only four times and returned 10% only once, in 1966. Don't let short-term swings in stocks derail your long-term plan. Be aware ahead of time of the fact that markets move in violent ways. That way you won't be tempted to do something that you'll regret later. Volatility is the price you must pay to get returns.

Why knowing the past is valuable

By studying how investments have done, you get an idea, on average, of what to expect. This gives you perspective that lets you not only decide whether an investment is worthwhile but also gives you a B.S. meter. If you get a flyer in the mail talking up a "promising new company" that's expected to generate 10% returns, walk away. Why would you take a chance on a shaky company if you can expect the same return by investing in a lower-risk, diversified index fund? Similarly, a return that's much higher than 10% must be much riskier, no matter what the flyer says.

Table 1-4 shows you just how crazy the market's movements can be in the short term, using the 50-year history of the popular Standard & Poor's 500 index:

Table 1-4	Wild Days for the S&P 500
Event	*Amount*
Number of days up	6,608 (average gain 0.63%)
Number of days down	5,900 (average loss 0.64%)
Best one-day percentage gain	Oct. 21, 1987 up 9.1%
Worst one-day percentage loss	Oct. 19, 1987, −20.5%
Best year	1958, up 38.1%
Worst year	1974, −29.7%
Best month	October 1974, 16.3%
Worst month	October 1987, −21.8%

Source: www2.standardandpoors.com/spf/pdf/index/022807_AnniversaryRelease1.pdf

Gut-Check Time: How Much Risk Can You Take?

It's time to get a grip — a grip on how much you can invest, that is. Most beginning investors are so interested in finding stocks that make them rich overnight that they lose sight of risk. But academic studies show that risk and return go hand in hand. That's why you need to know how much risk you can stomach before you start looking for investments and buying them online.

Several excellent online tools can help you get a handle on how much of a financial thrill seeker you are. Most are structured like interviews that ask you a number of questions and help you decide what kind of investor you are. These are kind of like personality tests for your investment taste. I cover several of these in more detail in Chapter 9, where I discuss how to create an investing road map, called an *asset allocation*. For now, these questionnaires are worthwhile to take right away so you can understand what kind of investor you are.

- ✔ **Vanguard's Investor Questionnaire** (`https://flagship.vanguard.com/VGApp/hnw/FundsInvQuestionnaire`) asks you ten salient questions to determine how much of a risk taker you are with your money. It determines what your ideal asset allocation is. Take note of the breakdown. The closer to 100% that Vanguard recommends you put in stocks, the more risk-tolerant you are, and the closer to 100% in bonds, the less risk-tolerant you are.

- ✔ **Index Funds Advisors Risk Capacity Survey** (`www.ifa.com/SurveyNET/index.aspx`) offers a quick risk survey that will tell you what kind of investor you are after answering just five questions. You can also find a complete risk capacity survey that hits you with a few dozen questions. Whichever you choose, the survey will characterize what kind of investor you are and even display a painting that portrays your risk tolerance.

- ✔ **SmartMoney Asset Allocator** (`www.smartmoney.com/oneasset`) couldn't be much easier to use. You slide a variety of bars to indicate your financial goals, ranging from your desire to leave money for heirs to the number of years to retirement. The site will then give you a general breakdown of where you should invest your money based on your risk preference.

Passive or Active? Deciding What Kind of Investor You Plan to Be

Investing might not seem controversial, but it shouldn't surprise you that anytime you're talking about money, people have some strong opinions about the right way to do things. The first way investors categorize themselves is by whether they are passive or active. Because these two approaches are so different, the following sections help you think about what they are and which camp you see yourself in. Where you stand will not only affect which broker is best for you, as discussed in Chapter 4, but also will affect which chapters in this book appeal to you most.

How to know if you're a passive investor

Passive investors don't try to beat the stock market. They merely try to keep up with it by owning all the stocks in an *index*. An index is a basket of stocks that mirrors the market. Passive investors are happy matching the market's performance, knowing that they can boost their real returns with a few techniques I discuss in Chapter 9.

You know you're a passive investor if you like the following ideas:

- ✔ **Not picking individual stocks:** These investors buy large baskets of stocks that mirror the performance of popular stock indexes like the Dow Jones industrial average or Standard & Poor's 500 so that they don't worry about whether a small upstart company they invested in will release its new product on time and whether it will be well received.

- ✔ **Owning mutual and exchange-traded funds:** Because passive investors aren't looking for the next Microsoft, they buy mutual and exchange-traded funds that buy hundreds of stocks. (I cover mutual and exchange-traded funds in more detail in Chapters 10 and 11, respectively.)

- ✔ **Reducing taxes:** Passive investors tend to buy investments and forget about them until many years later when they need the money. This can be lucrative because by holding onto diversified investments for a long time and not selling them, passive investors can postpone when they have to pay capital gains taxes. (I cover capital gains taxes in more detail in Chapter 3.)

- ✔ **Not stressing about stocks' daily, monthly, or even annual movements:** Passive investors tend to buy index mutual funds and forget about them. They don't need to sit in front of financial TV shows, read magazines, or worry about where stocks are moving. They're invested for the long term, and everything else is just noise to them.

Sites for passive investors to start with

One of the toughest things about being a passive investor is sitting still during a bull market when everyone else seems to be making more than you. Yes, you might be able to turn off the TV, but inevitably you'll bump into someone who brags about his or her giant gains and laughs at you for being satisfied with 10% market returns.

When that happens, it's even more important to stick with your philosophy. Following the crowd at this moment will undermine the value of your strategy. That's why even passive investors are well served going to Web sites where other passive investors congregate:

✔ **Diehards** (www.diehards.org) is an electronic water cooler for fans of Vanguard index funds and passive investors to meet, encourage, and advise each other. They call themselves Bogleheads in honor of the founder of Vanguard, John Bogle.

✔ **Indextown** (www.indextown.com) is a blog written for investors who believe in the long-term success of buying mutual funds tied to indexes.

✔ **The Arithmetic of Active Management** (www.stanford.edu/~wf sharpe/art/active/active.htm) is a reprint of an article by an early proponent of passive investing, William Sharpe, who explains why active investing will never win.

✔ **Vanguard's Web site** (www.vanguard.com) contains many helpful stories about the power of index investing and offers them for free, even if you don't have an account.

✔ **Mad Money Machine** (www.madmoneymachine.com) is an Internet radio show that tries to make the seemingly boring world of passive investing more exciting. The host, Paul Douglas Boyer, weaves jokes, music, and facts in a way to keep you investing passively.

How to know if you're an active investor

Active investors almost feel sorry for passive investors. Why would anyone be satisfied just matching the stock market and not even try to do better? Active investors feel that if you're smart enough and willing to spend time doing homework, you can exceed 10% annual returns. Active investors also find investing to be thrilling, almost like a hobby. Some active investors try to find undervalued stocks and hold them until they're discovered by other investors. Another class of active investors are short-term traders, who bounce in and out of stocks trying to get quick gains.

You're an active investor if you . . .

✔ **Think long-term averages of stocks are meaningless.** Active investors believe they can spot winning companies no one knows about yet, buy their shares at just the right time, and sell them for a profit.

✔ **Are willing to spend large amounts of time searching for stocks.** These are the investors who sit in front of financial TV shows, analyze stocks that look undervalued, and do all sorts of prospecting trying to find gems.

✔ **Believe they can hire mutual fund managers who can beat the market.** Some active investors think that there are certain talented mutual fund managers out there and that if they just give their money to those managers, they'll win.

- ✔ **Suspect certain types of stocks aren't priced correctly and that many investors make bad decisions.** Active investors believe they can out-smart the masses and routinely capitalize on the mistakes of the great unwashed.

- ✔ **Understand the risks.** Most active traders underperform index funds, some without even realizing it. Before deciding to be an active trader, be sure to test out your skills with online simulations, as described in Chapter 2, or make sure you're measuring your performance correctly, as described in Chapter 8. If you're losing money picking stocks, stop doing it. Be sure to know how dangerous active investing can be to your portfolio by reading a warning from the Securities and Exchange Commission here: `http://sec.gov/investor/pubs/online tips.htm`.

Many investors try, but very few are able to consistently beat the market. Consider Bill Miller, portfolio manager for the Legg Mason Value Trust mutual fund. Miller had beaten the market for 15 years and turned into a poster child for active investors and proof that beating the market was possible if you were smart enough. But even Miller's streak came to an end in 2006. That's when his Legg Mason Value Trust fund didn't just trail the market, it lagged by a mile, returning just 5.9% while the market gained 15.8%. Active investors lost their hero, but there will certainly be another hot manager to take his place.

Sites for the active investor to start with

Ever hear of someone trying to learn a foreign language by moving to the country and picking it up through "immersion"? The idea is that by just being around the language, and through the necessity of buying food or finding the restroom, they eventually get proficient.

If you're interested in active investing, you can do the same thing by hitting Web sites that are common hangouts for active investors. By lurking on these sites, you can pick up how these types of investors find stocks that interest them and trade on them. These sites will show you the great pains active investors go through in their attempt to beat the market. A few to start looking at include the following:

- ✔ **Yahoo! Finance** (`http://finance.yahoo.com`) is the finance section of this general purpose portal and a great resource for all investors. But it contains several elements of particular interest to active investors, such as the Investing Ideas section near the bottom of the page. Here you can find stocks of interest to active investors for certain reasons.

The site also offers active chat rooms on almost every stock under the Message Board heading on the left-hand side of the page. I talk about chat rooms in more detail in Chapter 7.

✔ **TheStreet.com** (`www.thestreet.com`) collects trading ideas and tips from writers mainly looking for quick moving stocks and other investments.

✔ **TradingMarkets** (`www.tradingmarkets.com`) explores the details of complicated trading philosophies. The site highlights stocks that have moved up or down by a large amount, which is usually something that catches the attention of traders.

Chapter 2

Getting Your PC Ready for Online Investing

*Y*ou live in a do-it-yourself world. You're expected to fill your own gas tank at the service station, refill your own soda at the fast-food restaurant, and book your own airline tickets. It's the same story with investing. If you want to reach your financial goals and retire comfortably, it's up to you to make it happen. The age of employers looking after their workers' futures with pensions is vanishing and being replaced with do-it-yourself retirement plans like 401(k)s.

If you ask for help, you're almost always pointed to the Internet and told to look it up or do your own research. That sounds reasonable, except that the Internet is a massive collection of Web pages, and you can find dozens if not hundreds of sources for investing advice, much of which is conflicting or, worse, wrong. No wonder many investors throw their hands up in utter frustration.

That's where this chapter comes in. In Chapter 1, I fill you in on what it takes to prepare yourself to be an online investor. Here in Chapter 2, it's time to prepare your computer for online investing and make it a tool that quickly provides you with the answers you need. This chapter helps you tweak your computer until it's like your personal investing workstation. It'll feel as comfortable to you as an old leather chair. And by using mostly free online resources, you'll save yourself some money in the process.

I escort you through the morass of financial Web sites and show you which ones you need to know. You find out what types of investing information are available online and how to access what you need from your computer. You also find out how to use online simulation sites that let you take a dry run investing with fake money to make sure you know what you're doing before using real money.

Turning Your PC into a Trading Station

When you think of a stock trading floor, you probably picture a room full of traders wearing brightly colored jackets throwing papers around and yelling out market orders. Some of that drama still exists on the New York Stock Exchange floor and in the Chicago futures markets, but it's largely a throwback from the old days.

Today, trading floors I've walked through look more like insurance offices. They have rows of desks with computers not unlike the one that's probably sitting on your desk. Professional traders do have an advantage: Many have high-end trading systems and software that costs thousands of dollars a month. That might be beyond your price range, but you might be amazed at how much market information you can get, for free or for little money, if you know where to go.

Using favorites to put data at your fingertips

The easiest way to turn your computer into a market monitoring station is by *bookmarking* or creating *favorites* to key sites with data you need. Favorites (also sometimes called bookmarks) are links in your Internet browser that let you quickly reach a Web page when you need it, without typing a long Web site address. Most Internet browsers have this capability, and they all work slightly differently. But just so you have an idea, if you're using Microsoft's Internet Explorer 7, you can create favorites by doing the following:

1. **Navigate to the Web site you're interested in saving.**

2. **Click the Favorites icon (the little gold star with the plus sign) in the upper-left corner of the screen.**

   You can see the star in Figure 2-1.

3. **Choose Add to Favorites.**

   An Add a Favorite dialog box pops up.

Add to Favorites icon

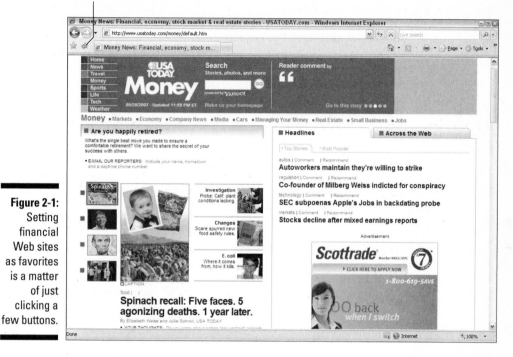

Figure 2-1:
Setting
financial
Web sites
as favorites
is a matter
of just
clicking a
few buttons.

4. **Give the site a name you can remember.**

   Most sites will do this for you.

5. **In the Create In space, choose the Favorite folder you want to put the Favorite into.**

   If you want to put this Favorite in a separate folder, you can create a folder by clicking the New Folder button. If you're not sure, just use the default Favorite folder.

6. **Click the Add button.**

If you want to access that address again, click the Favorites Center icon (the little gold star without the plus sign) and scroll down until you see the title of the page you're interested in.

Compiling a list of must-watch sites

So you know how to create favorites. But what sites are worth creating *as* favorites? My suggestion is to take a page from the professionals and try to replicate the data they're most interested in. Most professional trading workstations are set up so that they can take on five distinct tasks:

- ✔ Tracking the market's every move
- ✔ Monitoring news that has the potential to affect stock prices
- ✔ Checking in on Wall Street chatter
- ✔ Accessing company financial statements and regulatory filings
- ✔ Executing trades

Create separate favorite folders for all five functions and then fill them up with the sites I recommend in the rest of this chapter.

Tracking the Market's Every Move

You're probably hoping to study the market and find ways to score big and fast. Hey, everyone wants to get rich quick. Just remember that making money by darting in and out of stocks is extremely tough to do, and most investors, online or not, will be better off forming a long-term investment strategy and sticking with it. The difference between long-term investing (the in-it-for-the-long-haul approach, called *passive* investing) and short-term trading (the darting-in-and-out way of doing things, called *active* investing) is discussed in Chapter 1, where I also give you the tools necessary for figuring out how to decide which approach is best for you.

No matter what kind of investor you plan to be, watching real-time stock movements is fascinating. Watching rapid price moves with stock prices dancing around and flashing on the computer screen is a guilty pleasure and a source of entertainment for some investors.

You can find a great deal of overlap among online investing resources. Many of the following sites do more than what I highlight here. Explore the different sites and see whether certain ones suit you best.

There's no shortage of places where you can get stock quotes and see the value of popular market indexes such as the Dow Jones industrial average, Standard & Poor's 500, and NASDAQ composite index. That's why you can afford to demand more from Web sites if they're going to earn a position as one of your favorites. In Chapter 6, I list multiple sites best suited for tracking specific parts of the market. But the next section has a quick list that can help you get started creating general purpose online investing favorites. The sites listed here make the cut because they not only provide stock quotes, but also go a step further by being the best at a certain aspect of tracking the market.

When you look up a stock quote on many sites, you'll usually see three quotes: the *last sale,* the *bid,* and the *ask.* The last sale is what you probably think of as the quote and is what runs in newspaper listings and on Web sites. That's the price at which a buyer and seller agreed to a transaction. The bid, though, is the highest price other investors are willing to pay for the stock. The ask is the lowest price investors who own the stock are willing to sell it for.

Getting price quotes on markets and stocks

Nearly any site will give you stock quotes for the day, including the financial news Web sites discussed later in this chapter. But a few sites deserve special mention because they make it easy to get stock quotes for days in the past. And because they deserve special mention, they're getting it right here:

- ✔ **MSN Money** (www.moneycentral.msn.com/investor/home.asp) is one of the best sites on the Web for online investing information and will be mentioned several times in the book. For looking up prices of stocks and market indexes, it's hard to beat because it's fast and gives you everything you need, ranging from the stock's closing price to how much trading activity there was to when dividends (cash payments) were paid to investors. You can also see how the stock moved each minute of the day in real time, which is unusual for consumer stock sites. Most financial Web sites let you get quotes only on a 15-minute delay. And if you don't know the stock's ticker symbol, MSN Money lets you look it up quickly by using the symbol lookup feature.

    As part of the quote pages, you also see how the stock rates on MSN Money's StockScouter rating, with 10 being the best and 1 the worst. If you click the full report, you can see all the things that go into the rating, and you might discover a few things about the stock.

    One of the greatest strengths of MSN Money is that the site makes it incredibly easy to download and analyze historical data. You can find complete instructions on how to set up your computer in Chapter 1.

- ✔ **Yahoo! Finance** (http://finance.yahoo.com) lets you download historical data, too. Enter a stock symbol and click the Get Quotes button. Then, in the left column, click the Historical Prices link. You will see a page with a table of dates and the stock's prices on those dates. In the Set Date Range area near the top, you can pick a range of dates you'd like stock prices for. Below the table (scroll down a bit) is a link to Download to Spreadsheet.

- ✔ **DownloadQuotes** (www.downloadquotes.com) lets you download the end of day values of dozens of U.S. and foreign market indexes as well as individual stocks. Many of the site's areas are free.

Knowing your exchanges

When you get a stock quote from most Web sites, you also see what exchange the stock trades on. This is important information. Most stocks typically trade on one of three major exchanges in the U.S.: the New York Stock Exchange (NYSE), the NASDAQ, and the American Stock Exchange. The NYSE and the NASDAQ are by far the largest and are the exchanges for the biggest companies in the world.

There are other places where stocks trade, besides the NYSE and NASDAQ. There are foreign exchanges (which I cover in more detail in Bonus Chapter 1 on the Web) and informal marketplaces such as the Pink Sheets and OTC

Bulletin Board. Many beginning online investors are attracted to the Pink Sheets and Bulletin Board stocks due to their low share prices and high volatility, which is why they're called penny stocks or microcap stocks. But buying stocks on the Pink Sheets and Bulletin Board can be very risky. The Pink Sheets and Bulletin Board don't have the same oversight of their stocks, making them popular with fraudsters. You can read the Securities and Exchange Commission warnings to investors about these stocks here: `www.sec.gov/investor/pubs/microcap stock.htm`.

Slicing and dicing the markets

Although quite a few market indexes exist — I discuss many of them in Chapter 8 — there are some major market benchmarks *all* online investors need to be familiar with. These are the ones so commonly discussed that they need to be part of your investor vocabulary. Table 2-1 presents them in all their market-dominating glory:

Table 2-1	Key Market Indexes
Index Name	*What It Measures*
Dow Jones industrial Average	Thirty big, industrial companies. When investors hear about "the market," more often than not they think of the Dow.
Standard & Poor's 500	Big companies, including 500 of the nation's most well-known stocks. Moves very similarly to the Dow, even though it includes more stocks.
NASDAQ Composite Index	Stocks that trade on the NASDAQ Stock Market. It tends to closely track technology stocks.

Index Name	What It Measures
DJ Wilshire 5000	The entire stock market. Contains all significant stocks from the largest to the smallest.
Russell 2000	Small-company stocks. Tends to be more volatile than indexes that track large companies — the S&P 500, for example.

Nearly all financial Web sites let you track all the indexes listed in the table. Yahoo! Finance (http://finance.yahoo.com), though, makes it easy to monitor how different slices of the markets are doing, such as foreign stocks, specific industry sectors and bonds. The Yahoo! Finance Web site offers a couple of different ways for you to dig beyond the market indexes, as the following list makes clear:

- ✔ **Get a quick read on all U.S. market indexes.** To see how all the key U.S. market indexes are doing, click the View More Indices link on the left side of the page under the Market Summary heading. You can then see many market indexes by clicking the different tabs, such as Dow Jones, NASDAQ, and S&P under the Major U.S. Indices heading.

- ✔ **Get a run-down of how foreign stocks are doing.** If you click the View More Indices link and then click the World link on the left side, you can monitor just about any foreign market you'd care to track. Bonus Chapter 1 on the Web tells you more about investing in international stocks.

- ✔ **Get a summary of industry performances.** Back on the main Yahoo! Finance page, hover your cursor over the Investing tab and click the Industries link. When the Industry Center page appears, click the link for the industry you're interested in.

Yahoo! Finance makes tracking market indexes easy so you don't have to memorize or look up cryptic codes for indexes. You can find more tips about industries in Chapter 6.

Don't confuse stocks with indexes. Stocks are shares in individual companies, such as General Electric or Exxon Mobil. The prices of stocks reflect how much you would have to pay for a share of the stock. Indexes, on the other hand, are mathematical formulas that tell you how much a collection of stocks have changed in value. When the Dow Jones industrial average, which contains 30 stocks, hits 13,000, that doesn't mean you can buy it for $13,000. It's just a number that represents relative value.

How the Dow's value is calculated

Market indexes, such as the Dow, are priced not by traders, but by calculators. Mathematical formulas analyze the movements of the stocks contained inside an index to arrive at the value of the index. To get the value of the Dow, for instance, the prices of the 30 stocks in the indexes are multiplied by a *divisor* and added together. The divisor is used to smooth out interruptions that would be caused if stocks were replaced in the index for different reasons. (You can always look up the divisor of the Dow here: `www.djindexes.com/mdsidx/index.cfm?event=showAvgOverview&averageSelection=G`.) You can read more about indexes in Chapter 8.

Your crystal ball: Predicting how the day will begin

Some investors like to get a jump start on the trading day by watching the *futures market*. The futures market is an auction for future contracts, which are financial obligations allowing their buyers and sellers to lock in prices for commodities and other assets in the future. The futures market allows investors to bet how much certain assets will be worth minutes, day, weeks, or years from today. Futures are commonly used with commodities, such as energy and food, as described in more detail in Chapter 6.

You can see what the futures market is saying about stocks, too. Financial news and data company Bloomberg gives investors a sneak peak on how stocks could open the next trading day. On its Futures page (`www.bloomberg.com/markets/stocks/futures.html`), you can see how traders who apparently don't have anything better to do are betting after the stock market is closed how major market indexes around the world will open. If you're the kind of person who doesn't like surprises, it's an easy way to see how investors are behaving even when the market centers are closed.

Getting company descriptions

Professional investors like to bone up on what a company does, who's in charge, and how profitable it is without pouring through dozens of industry reports. You can get the same kind of quick snapshot information with online company descriptions. All the main investing sites I discuss have sections that describe the business a company is in. Here are a couple more sites worth checking out:

✔ **BusinessWeek:** (www.businessweek.com) This site, which I discuss at more length later in this chapter, offers in-depth profiles on companies. Just enter the stock's ticker symbol in the Stock Lookup text box — nestled under the Market Info heading — and you can find all the vital information about the company ranging from the names of its management to a description of what it does. You can also see a comprehensive tear sheet of company information based on data from S&P's high-end system called Capital IQ.

✔ **Hoovers:** (www.hoovers.com) Enter a company name, and you'll not only find out just about everything you'd need to know about the company, but also a detailed history. You can find hundreds of industry profiles that give you a view of the competitive landscape the company finds itself in. Some of the features on the site are free, but for others you must subscribe.

Keeping tabs on commodities

I have more on the exciting world of commodities — such as the oil, lumber, and coal that companies use to make their products — in Chapter 6, but if you can't wait until then, check out the following Web sites:

✔ **Bloomberg** (www.bloomberg.com/markets/commodities/cfutures.html) has a professional-grade site that lets you watch movements in just about any commodity that you can imagine, including gold, silver, and platinum. Interested in hog bellies? Yes, you can see the price. This data is necessary if you want to invest in commodities directly. Still, even if you don't buy or sell commodities, they're good to watch. For instance, if you own shares of Starbucks, wouldn't you want to know what the price of coffee is doing?

✔ **Chicago Board of Trade** (www.cbot.com) lists prices on many of the major commodities such as corn, soybeans, wheat, and ethanol. I describe this site (and commodities-centric sites) in more detail in Chapter 6.

Tracking bonds and U.S. Treasuries

A *bond* is an IOU issued by a government, a company, or another borrower. An owner of a bond is entitled to receive the borrowed funds when they're paid back by a certain time in the future at a predetermined interest rate. Even if you have no interest in investing in bonds, you still should know what rates are doing. After all, if you could invest in bonds issued by the Federal government that come due in 30 years, called Treasury bonds, and get 9% annual returns guaranteed, wouldn't you be a bit less enthusiastic about a risky stock that you think will return only 10%? The U.S. government sells other Treasuries, including Treasury bills (T-bills) that generally come due in a year or less and Treasury notes (T-notes) that come due in longer than a year but in ten years or less. I provide more details in Chapter 6 on how bond yields affect stock prices, but a few sites to start you out with include the following:

- ✔ **Bloomberg** (www.bloomberg.com/markets/rates/index.html) makes tracking bonds very easy. Bloomberg lets you, at a glance, see the yields on just about any major bond or Treasury you can imagine.

- ✔ **Federal Reserve Bank** (www.federalreserve.gov/fomc/funds rate.htm) is the online presence for "the Fed," as it's affectionately called. The Fed is in charge of strongly influencing *short-term* interest rates, including the federal funds rate. That's typically the rate banks lend money stored at the Fed to other banks overnight. No, you can't borrow at that rate, but it's very important to watch this interest rate because it affects long-term interest rates, which you *can* borrow at. You can see what the federal funds rate has been at the Fed's site, as shown in Figure 2-2. Traders buy and sell long-term Treasuries and set interest rates based in large part on where short-term rates are or where they're expected to be.

Figure 2-2: The Fed's Web site makes it easy to track important interest rates.

> **The Federal Reserve Board**
>
> **Open Market Operations**
>
> Open market operations--purchases and sales of U.S. Treasury and federal agency securities-- are the Federal Reserve's principal tool for implementing monetary policy. The short-term objective for open market operations is specified by the Federal Open Market Committee (FOMC). This objective can be a desired quantity of reserves or a desired price (the federal funds rate). The federal funds rate is the interest rate at which depository institutions lend balances at the Federal Reserve to other depository institutions overnight.
>
> The Federal Reserve's objective for open market operations has varied over the years. During the 1980s, the focus gradually shifted toward attaining a specified level of the federal funds rate, a process that was largely complete by the end of the decade. Beginning in 1994, the FOMC began announcing changes in its policy stance, and in 1995 it began to explicitly state its target level for the federal funds rate. Since February 2000, the statement issued by the FOMC shortly after each of its meetings usually has included the Committee's assessment of the risks to the attainment of its long-run goals of price stability and sustainable economic growth.
>
> For more information on open market operations, see the article in the *Federal Reserve Bulletin* (102 KB PDF).
>
> **Intended federal funds rate**
> Change and level, 1990 to present
>
> | Date | Change (basis points) | | Level (percent) |
> |------|----------|----------|------|
> | | Increase | Decrease | |

If you'd like to find out more about how the Fed affects the nation's money supply, the Federal Reserve Bank of Kansas City maintains a useful and simple site on the topic — designed for teens and college students, but useful for any investor — at `www.federalreserve education.org/Fed101`.

Monitoring Market-Moving News

Ever see a biotech stock skyrocket after the company announced a break-through treatment? Tech stocks routinely jump in price on the debut of popular new gadgets or software. That's the power of news — often called *market-moving news* in this sort of case. Markets are constantly taking in and digesting all sorts of developments and changes, both good and bad. And to stay on top of these developments, you'll want to set a few leading financial news sites as favorites. The following sections explore the different kinds of financial news sites in greater detail.

Financial Web sites

Many of the financial sites mentioned earlier in the chapter are also great places to get market-moving news. Yahoo! Finance and MSN Money pick up stories written by wire services on the markets and on individual stocks, making them helpful resources. Bloomberg covers just about every type of traditional investment you can imagine, thanks to its network of reporters. Others I haven't mentioned include the following:

- **Google News** (`http://news.google.com`) has a business section that pulls in important financial stories in one place. Its best feature is the ability to search for news based on very precise criteria, including keywords, the date the story appeared, or the geographic location of the news.

- **Briefing.com** (`www.briefing.com`) is similar to the kind of data services professional investors use to follow news. In fact, most of Briefing.com's service is for large traders and investors who pay for its platinum or trader services. Still, the site recently made some of its content available, for free, to regular investors. Just click the Free Content button in the box on the left side labeled Investor, as shown in Figure 2-3. You can find running commentary on market-moving news and events. Briefing.com's market wrap-up is a great way to find out what's behind the market's day-to-day swings so you can see how any random event can have a big effect on stocks.

Figure 2-3:
Briefing.
com
provides
many free
resources
to online
investors.

✔ **MarketWatch** (www.marketwatch.com) is a comprehensive site for all the business news you'll need. The site attempts to separate itself from the competition, though, by providing columns from various financial writers who opine about everything from companies' accounting practices to technology. MarketWatch has an attractive feature that lets you instruct it to e-mail you articles of interest. You can also have it send you an e-mail if a stock moves by a certain amount.

✔ **BigCharts.com** (www.bigcharts.com) is a service of MarketWatch dedicated to serving up graphical information about the markets. The best aspect of the site is the set of BigReports lists that show you, at a glance, what the biggest movers on Wall Street were that day in terms of price or percentage price change.

✔ **MotleyFool** (www.fool.com) has a little something for everyone. There's content for the active trader, including stock tips galore, as well as tricks and techniques on how to deeply analyze companies' financial statements. Passive investors, though, will appreciate the more general personal finance stories.

✔ **Reuters** (http://today.reuters.com/investing/defaultUS. aspx) makes high-end systems used by many professional traders. And it has put many of the same tools into your hands. If you enter a ticker symbol under the Stocks and Mutual Funds heading, you can see advanced statistics about the stock, including things like *dividend yields* and key ratios. (Don't worry. I cover all this advanced stuff in Chapters 14 and 15.)

Do you speak ticker symbol?

Nearly every financial Web site is centered on the ticker symbol. These are the two-, three-, or four-letter abbreviations used to symbolize stocks or investments. Originally, ticker symbols were used so brokers could quickly read a *ticker tape,* a scrolling printout of stocks and prices. But the symbol has taken on a new use in the online era, so much so that most sites have an empty text box at the top where you enter the symbol first, click a button and then get sent to another part of the site where you're handed all the information pertaining to that stock on a silver platter.

Ticker symbols have become so popular that investors sometimes use them instead of a company's name. And sometimes companies have fun with their symbols to make them more memorable. In 2006, for instance, motorcycle maker Harley-Davidson changed its symbol from the boring HDI to the more exciting HOG, the nickname for its rumbling bikes. Other fun ticker symbols include:

Ticker	*Company*
BUD	Anheuser-Busch
CAKE	Cheesecake Factory
HOT	Starwood Hotels
LUV	Southwest Airlines
SHOE	Shoe Pavilion
WOOF	VCA Antech (a veterinary company)
SAM	Boston Beer

There's one other thing to keep in mind regarding stock symbols. You used to be able to tell whether a stock traded on the NASDAQ or the New York Stock Exchange just by looking at the symbol. For many years, NASDAQ stocks traded with a symbol with four letters, such as INTC for Intel and MSFT for Microsoft. But that changed in 2007 when NASDAQ began issuing symbols of one, two, and three letters to its member companies. Delta Financial was the first NASDAQ stock to have three letters, with its symbol DFS.

Many financial Web sites and news stories use the terms *bullish* and *bearish.* When investors are bullish, they think the stock market is going to go up. And when investors are bearish, they think stocks will go down.

Traditional financial news sites

Many of the financial news providers you might already be familiar with from newspapers, magazines, and TV also provide data useful to investors online, including the following:

✔ **USA TODAY's Money section** (`http://money.usatoday.com`) at USATODAY.com delivers the business news that affects you (disclosure: I'm a full-time reporter at USA TODAY). You can find not only the breaking news stories from wire services, but also enterprise stories you won't find anywhere else on beats ranging from markets to business travel and cars. You can find extensive personal finance and mutual fund coverage. And if you have any specific investing questions, check out my online column, Ask Matt, where you can e-mail me questions, and I'll publish the answer. You can read the answer to questions Ask Matt readers have asked at the archive here: `www.usatoday.com/money/perfi/columnist/krantz/index.htm`.

The site also has an interesting stock-rating service. By entering a stock ticker symbol, you can see how aggressive or conservative an investment in that stock would be according to the USA TODAY Stock Meter. Figure 2-4 shows the Stock Meter rating for General Electric.

✔ **The Wall Street Journal Online** (`www.wsj.com`) is a source of breaking financial news. You might be familiar with the print edition of the Wall Street Journal; this is the online version. This site charges for much of its content.

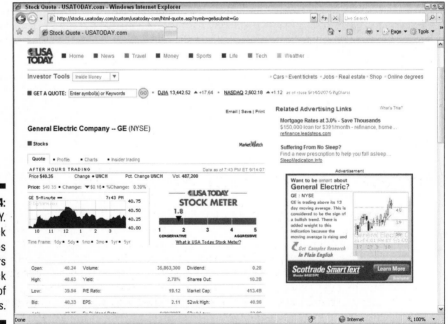

Figure 2-4: USATODAY.com's Stock Meter gives investors a quick analysis of stocks.

- ✔ **Financial Times** (www.FT.com) is a London-based business publication, so it provides a unique spin on business events here. It's a good source of merger announcements.

- ✔ **CNBC** (www.cnbc.com) updated its Web site in 2006, and now the financial TV channel's online presence offers many of the same things as other financial news sites. What makes it unique is that it lets you view segments that aired on CNBC that you might have missed. The segments are streamed in your browser, saving you the trouble of having to be in front of your TV.

- ✔ **BusinessWeek.com** (www.businessweek.com) is a stand-out site for investors, largely due to the fact that it's owned by McGraw-Hill, which also owns Standard & Poor's. The site offers some truly professional-level tools that are worth your while. On the Investing tab, you can find an interesting feature called the Interactive Stock Report. (You probably have to scroll down to find it.) This feature steps you through the details of an S&P stock research report on a certain stock each week.

- ✔ **CNN Money** (http://cnn.money.com) has a good mix of breaking financial news and general personal financial help. It contains specialized information on markets, technology, jobs, personal finance, and real estate.

- ✔ **Investor's Business Daily** (www.investors.com) is largely geared for active investors and allows subscribers to read the next day's paper early. The site also has tools to help you find stocks that are outperforming the rest of the stock market.

- ✔ **Barron's** (www.barrons.com) is a weekly publication written mainly for more advanced investors. Most of the features are available only to subscribers. Subscribers to the Wall Street Journal's Web site get a cut on Barron's online site because both are owned by Dow Jones.

Checking In on Wall Street Chatter

Rumor and innuendo are key parts to traders' lives. Because stock prices are highly sensitive in the short run to what other traders and investors are saying about a stock, traders make it their business to follow any murmur. As an individual investor, you're somewhat at a disadvantage in this department because you don't have portfolio managers of giant mutual funds calling you and telling you what they're hearing. But you can use chat rooms, which I cover in more detail in Chapter 7, or online blogs and podcasts if you're interested in the scuttlebutt.

If you're a passive investor, you probably couldn't care less about rumors. Even so, you can take advantage of blogs and chat rooms that are dedicated to index investing. Just remember that these are casual and sometimes unreliable ways to keep up with the market chatter on various topics.

Beware of rumors

Investors can't help themselves when it comes to rumors. And sometimes certain blogs and podcasts only feed your innate desire to get the inside scoop on an investment about to explode in value. Investment rumors are kind of like celebrity gossip: You're probably better off ignoring it, but sometimes it's impossible to resist. Just remember that making investment decisions based on rumors is usually a very bad idea.

Even giant stocks can get swept up in rumors and result in pain for gullible investors. Here's

an example: On June 8, 2007, U.S. Steel, one of the world's largest producers of steel, saw its stock price soar 8% to $125.05. The move created more than $1 billion in shareholder wealth overnight. And it was all because of rumors and speculation the company was going to be bought. But investors that piled in were sorry when it turned out the rumor wasn't true. In the following two trading days, the stock crumbled more than 9%, erasing the entire gain, and then some.

Everyone is an expert: Checking in with blogs

Thanks to low-cost computers and Internet connections, just about anyone with an opinion and a keyboard can profess their view of investments to the world. Some of these opinions are worth listening to, but many are not. One popular vehicle for sharing opinions is a *blog* (short for Web log), which is a sort of online journal. Blogs can vary greatly in quality. Some are the modern-day equivalent of a crazy person on the street corner yelling at anyone who walks by, whereas other blogs are thoughtful and well-informed. It's *buyer beware* with blogs, and you have to decide whether the person is worth listening to. Ask yourself what the blogger's track record is and how the blogger makes money.

Finding blogs

With so many blogs out there, sometimes the toughest part can be finding them. Here are several ways that you can locate them:

- ✔ **General search engines:** All the leading search engines, including Google, Yahoo!, Live.com, and Ask.com, let you search much of the blogging world. If it's a major blog, you're likely to find it just by searching this way: Just enter the word **investing** in Ask.com, for instance, and you can find general-interest finance blogs. Yahoo! Finance (http://finance.yahoo.com) also has a directory of financial blogs that makes the searching easier. Just enter a stock symbol and, when the page for that particular stock appears, click the Financial Blogs link under the News & Info heading on the left side of the page. (I discuss how to turn search engines into your investment tools later in this chapter.)

✔ **Blog search tools:** Some search engines are tuned with the express purpose of helping you locate blogs. One popular option is Google's Blog Search (http://blogsearch.google.com). Just enter investment terms you're interested in, and you get a list of the sites that meet your criteria. Instant Bull (http://instantbull.com) keeps a list of popular financial blogs. You can access the list by clicking the Blogs link in the top-left corner of the window.

✔ **Community sites:** Sites such as MySpace (www.myspace.com) and Windows Live Spaces (http://spaces.live.com) are best known as places for musicians to promote their latest albums and for families to share photos with each other. But some financial blogs are also lurking on these community sites. To find them, just log into the site and search for the words *financial, money, investing,* and *stocks.*

✔ **Mainstream media:** Almost all of the news sites have some of their writers penning blogs as well. Many blogs are available via Really Simple Syndication, (RSS), which I explain in the later section, "Getting your computer to do the work: RSS feeds."

Getting in tune with podcasts

Next time you see someone listening to an iPod or a Zune with earphone cords dangling from his ears, don't assume he's rocking out. He might be researching stocks or learning about investing. A *podcast* is an audio broadcast that's transferred electronically over the Internet to your computer or MP3 player — they're like radio shows for the Internet age. Like blogs, podcasts are often done by amateurs, so the same need for caution applies. But also like blogs, some podcasts are done by major media.

Finding podcasts

It's easy to find a radio or TV station: Just turn on the radio and start flipping. But finding podcasts takes a little more doing. It's not difficult, though, if you try these different methods:

✔ **Podcast search engines:** Most of the major online search companies have special online tools to help you pinpoint podcasts. AOL's Search Podcast (`http://podcast.search.aol.com`) lets you enter search terms and then get a giant list of podcasts that meet your requirements. The Yahoo! Podcasts search is available at `http://podcasts.yahoo.com`. Blubrry (`www.blubrry.com`) is another popular podcast search site.

✔ **Financial podcast search engines:** StreetIQ (`www.streetiq.com`) is a quick and easy place to go if you're only looking for financial and investing podcasts. Not only can you search by topic, but you can enter a ticker symbol and find out any podcast that has mentioned the investment you're interested in.

✔ **Podcast directories:** Are the podcast search engines giving you too many results? Try a podcast directory, which are online directories, much like the Yellow Pages, where editors sort podcasts by subject area. Podcast.net (`www.podcast.net`) keeps a comprehensive list of podcasts, including one on investment. Other directories worth looking into include Podcast Alley (`www.podcastalley.com`) and Podcast.com (`http://podcast.com`).

✔ **Audio software:** Apple's iTunes software (`www.apple.com/itunes`), for instance, has an excellent podcast search function as part of its Tunes Store, which you can access from the Store link. Click the Podcasts link and then click Business and you can scroll through hundreds of available podcasts, including some from mainstream outlets like BusinessWeek, CNBC and National Public Radio. Winamp (`www.winamp.com`) and Yahoo! Music Jukebox (`http://music.yahoo.com/jukebox`) can also help you find podcasts.

✔ **Directly from the site:** If you enjoy a Web site or blog, take a close look because you might find that it offers podcasts. For instance, if you've decided you want to be a passive investor (see Chapter 1) and enjoy reading IFA.com, click the IFA iTunes Audio Podcasts link on the site's front page, and your iTunes software automatically displays a list of all the site's available podcasts. If you don't have iTunes installed on your computer, you're prompted to install the software. In other cases, you can click a Listen to This Podcast link of some kind directly from the site's page and download it or listen immediately without leaving your browser.

Listening to podcasts

You can listen to most podcasts in three ways:

✔ **Listen on the site.**

You can listen to most podcasts by clicking a link, usually labeled Listen, directly on the site.

✔ **Download.**

Some podcasts let you click a Download button or, with Windows PCs, right-click the Listen" link and download them.

✔ **Subscribe.**

You can install special software that will search your favorite podcasts and automatically download new episodes when they're available. An option for both Windows and Mac users is downloading and installing Apple's iTunes software (www.itunes.com). iTunes handles all aspects of listening to podcasts, ranging from finding podcasts to subscribing to them so that they're automatically downloaded to your computer. Another choice is Yahoo! Music Jukebox (http://music.yahoo.com/jukebox).

Specialized podcasting software programs are also available. If you're running Windows on your computer, you can download and install Juice (http://juicereceiver.sourceforge.net) or Doppler (www.dopplerradio.net). A Macintosh version of Juice is also available.

Some podcasts let you download episodes using Really Simple Syndication, (RSS) links. I explain how to do this in the next section.

Getting your computer to do the work: RSS feeds

If you want to read investing news, read blogs, or listen to podcasts, you can use the Favorites feature of your Web browser to bookmark a bunch of the sites I mention in this chapter and then methodically make your way down your Favorites list at your leisure. But some savvy online investors don't have time for that, so they use something called Really Simple Syndication, or *RSS feeds*. RSS feeds are kind of like notices sent out by some blogs, podcasts, and news sites to let the world know that something new is available. If you use RSS feeds, you subscribe to a news Web site, blog, or podcast, and the news comes to you.

It's easy to get started. First you need to have a way to receive the RSS feeds. There are three main ways to do this:

✔ **Install an RSS reader.** An RSS reader lets you tell the computer what Web sites you'd like to subscribe to., The RSS reader software then pulls the feeds containing articles from all the different news sites you've chosen and presents them all to you in one page. Because RSS readers are software, the RSS articles the reader downloads are stored on your hard drive so you can read them later, even if you're not connected to the Internet.

FeedDemon (`www.newsgator.com/Individuals/FeedDemon`) is one example of an RSS reader. You can also find specialized RSS reader software programs, such as Investor Vista (`www.investorvista.com`), designed with the needs of online investors in mind. These types of readers, including FeedDemon, are usually not free and can cost about $30.

✔ **Subscribe to a Web-based RSS aggregator.** An *aggregator* creates a tailor-made page with all the RSS feeds you've requested. So, rather than logging onto individual sites, you log onto this one site that has dutifully pulled in all the RSS feeds you've subscribed to. A popular RSS aggregator is NewsGator Online (`www.newsgator.com`).

Some aggregators require you to be connected to the Internet to read your RSS feeds. Google Reader (`www.google.com/reader`), however, allows you to download some of the RSS content if you install the separate Google Gears plug-in (`http://gears.google.com`).

The biggest advantage of RSS aggregators is that they're usually free.

✔ **Use your Web browser.** If you're like me, you like to install as little software on your computer as you can get away with, and you don't like signing up for all kinds of Web services. If that describes you, you might consider checking to see whether your Internet browser supports RSS. The latest version of Internet Explorer, version 7, makes it pretty easy. Go to the Web site you'd like to subscribe to and click the orange RSS feed icon, usually located to the right of the home icon on the menu bar. You see a list of all the available RSS feeds from the site, like the one in Figure 2-5. Click the Subscribe to This Feed icon, which looks like a gold star with a green plus sign. A dialog box pops up, letting you name the feed and click Subscribe. After you subscribe, you just click the Favorites Center icon (a gold star without a green plus sign) and select the Feeds tab, and you see a list of all the updates that were pulled down for you. You can download Internet Explorer here: `www.microsoft.com/windows/products/winfamily/ie/default.mspx`.

For more options, check the Yahoo! list of RSS readers and aggregators at

`http://dir.yahoo.com/Computers_and_Internet/Data_Formats/XML__eXtensible_Markup_Language_/RSS/RSS_Readers_and_Aggregators`

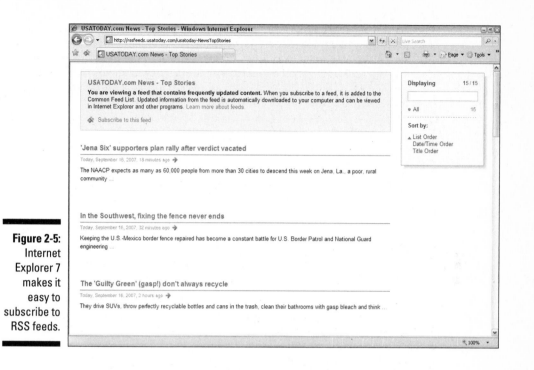

Figure 2-5:
Internet
Explorer 7
makes it
easy to
subscribe to
RSS feeds.

After you get your RSS software, Web-based reader, or browser set up, it's easy to start getting RSS feeds. Just navigate to your favorite investing sites and look for links that say "RSS Feed" or "XML" and click them. Your reader, aggregator, or browser then gives you instructions on how to subscribe.

Keeping Tabs on the Regulators

Professional traders' computers also keep close tabs on regulatory filings from companies. Regulatory filings are often the best, if not the only, data that investors get directly from a company. If companies make any significant announcements, they're required to notify the appropriate government watchdogs, which in most cases is the Securities and Exchange Commission.

I cover these important documents and what they contain in more detail in Chapter 12, but for now, it's important for you to know how to monitor these documents and quickly find them online. You can get regulatory filings online through

✔ **The company's Web site:** Most provide a section with their complete reports.

✔ **Financial sites and portals:** Most of the sites I list earlier in the chapter provide links to the documents.

✔ **Aggregation sites:** These sites, such as EdgarScan (http://edgar scan.pwcglobal.com/servlets/edgarscan), parse the filings from companies and make them easy to find and download for free. SEC Info (www.secinfo.com) sorts all the regulatory filings into easy-to-understand categories. There are also pay-for services, such as FreeEdgar (http://freeedgar.com). It's funny, I know, that a site called Free-Edgar isn't free. But it and other pay services go a step further and might even send you an e-mail the second a company files a report. Depending on your needs, those might be worth your money.

✔ **Securities and Exchange Commission:** (www.sec.gov) For most investors, the free SEC site has as much info as any sane person would ever want, and it isn't too difficult to navigate, to boot.

In fact, the Securities and Exchange Commission site is so easy to navigate that I'm going to show you how to do it right now. To find company regulatory filings, follow these steps:

1. **Point your Web browser to www.sec.gov.**

   The SEC site makes an appearance.

2. **In the Filings and Forms (EDGAR) section, click the Search for Company Filings link.**

   The Search the EDGAR Database page appears.

3. **On the Search the EDGAR Database page, under the General Purpose Searches, click the Companies & Other Filers link.**

   The EDGAR Company Search page appears.

4. **Enter the company's name or ticker symbol into the appropriate box and then click the Find Companies button.**

   There's no need to do anything with the Ownership Forms radio buttons, so you can leave them set on the default.

   You see a giant list of company filings in the order they were filed, as shown in Figure 2-6.

   It's an intimidating list that's hardly user-friendly because the forms are distinguished only by their *form,* which is regulatory code for the types of information the documents contain. Table 2-2 gives you the skinny on what the various form codes mean. I don't include all the form codes because there are so many. Several of the form codes are for documents you either don't need to worry about or can get the data more easily elsewhere, including when officers of the company sell stock.

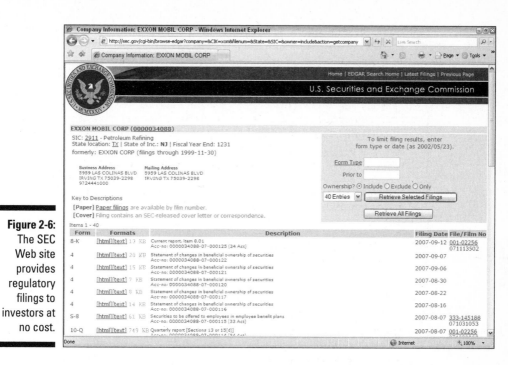

Figure 2-6:
The SEC
Web site
provides
regulatory
filings to
investors at
no cost.

Table 2-2	SEC Forms You Can Use
Form Code	**What It Contains**
8-K	A news flash from the company. 8-Ks can contain just about anything that's considered "material" or important to investors, ranging from the resignation of a top official to news of the win of a new customer.
10-Q	The company's quarterly report. This form displays all the information a company is required to provide to investors each quarter. You can find the key financial statements, such as the income statement and balance sheet, which are covered in more detail in Chapter 12.
10-K	The company's year-end report. This is one of the most important documents a company creates. It gives you a summary of everything that happened during the year, including comments from management and financial statements that have been checked, or *audited,* by the company's accounting firm.
DEF 14 and DEF 14A	The company's proxy statement. Contains all the important company information that's subject to shareholder approval and scrutiny. Most proxies contain everything that's up for a vote at the shareholder meeting, ranging from board members up for election, pay packages and other perks, and pending lawsuits. If you're going to read any document, it's this one.

Companies don't make their regulatory filings easy to read. You have to be part lawyer, part investor, and part investment banker to read between the lines in these often cryptic statements. I cover the basics in Chapter 12 and teach you how to pick apart 10-Ks, 10-Qs, and DEF 14s. But other online resources can help, including

- ✔ **Footnoted.org** (www.footnoted.org), a business blog which studies proxies and pinpoints things that smell fishy.

- ✔ **The AAO Weblog** (www.accountingobserver.com/blog), which is published by well-known accounting watchdog, Jack Ciesielski, who is trained to find suspicious things in company filings.

- ✔ **Major mainstream media** also pick the proxy statements apart and find things that stand out. USA TODAY, for instance, analyzed proxy statements for 2006 for an article you can find at www.usatoday.com/money/companies/2007-04-16-ceo-compensation-usat_N.htm.

Executing Trades

With all this talk about researching and analyzing, don't forget what job No. 1 is: buying or selling investments. You need to either log onto the Web site of your broker or download special software from your brokers that will handle the trades. I go over the dizzying number of choices you have for online brokers in Chapter 4.

Searching the Internet High and Low

If you're not able to find what you're looking for by using the tips and techniques in the preceding sections, it might be time to hit the main Web search engines. Some of the most popular search engines include

- ✔ **Google:** (www.google.com) Definitely the biggest and most popular Web search engine; so much so that investors often say they'll *google* a stock. Because the site is so clean and Zen-like, it has the benefit of being very easy to use.

- ✔ **Live.com:** (www.live.com) Microsoft's attempt to come up with a Google killer, Live.com has a few advantages for online investors, including the ability to tailor the Web site to your tastes.

- ✔ **Yahoo!:** (www.yahoo.com) Yahoo! is a good place for investors to search because it has two types of searches: keyword and directory. As with Google and Live.com, you can enter so-called *keywords* to search for. But if you're not quite sure what the right keywords are, look at the tabs above the Search text box and find the More menu there. Click the More menu, choose the Directory option, and then watch in amazement as the entire World Wide Web is put into categories for you. From there, you can drill down in search of what you're looking for. For instance, click the Business and Economy category and the directory will help you find blogs and other business resources. There's also a Finance and Investment category that pinpoints sites on precise topics ranging from brokerages to bonds and initial public offerings.

✔ **Ask:** (www.ask.com) I guess when you're #2 in your category — or #4 or #7 or #17 — you do try harder. Ask.com has been trying hard to steal traffic from the bigger search engines with different whistles and bells. One interesting feature is the ability to put your cursor over a search result with a binocular icon and see a tiny version of the page pop up, without actually clicking the link.

Keeping the Bad Guys Out: Securing Your PC

If you're going to use your computer to process your investing and banking tasks, you'd better lock it down. Cyber criminals have gotten sophisticated and have targeted online investors in hopes of gaining control of a person's account and stealing money.

Please, don't let such concerns scare you off from investing online. After all, cars get broken into, and you still drive. It's just that you must take certain precautions to make it harder for the bad guys to get into your PC, such as

✔ **Installing antivirus software:** If a sinister code designed to wreak havoc on your computer gets on your machine, it can be a real hassle. Viruses can corrupt system files and make your computer unreliable or unusable. Antivirus software is the easy solution. It runs in the background and looks at any program that tries to run on your computer and stops the program if it tries to do something improper.

Many antivirus software programs are available, including

- *Commercial:* Antivirus programs from McAfee (www.mcafee.com), Symantec (www.symantec.com), and TrendMicro (http://us.trendmicro.com) are popular. But these will cost you.

- *Free versions:* Another option is to download and install a free antivirus software program, such as AVG Free (http://free.grisoft.com).

✔ **Installing antispyware software:** Spyware is software that attaches itself to your computer without your permission and runs behind the scenes. It's especially sinister because it might forward personal information to a third-party, usually for marketing purposes. AVG (`http://free.grisoft.com`) offers free Anti-Spyware software, but countless others are available. Just search for the word *spyware* at Download.com (`www.download.com`) and see which ones work for you. Many are free.

✔ **Using firewalls:** A firewall is an electronic barrier that (selectively) separates you from the Internet at large. A proper firewall is like a moat around a castle — only traffic that you lower the drawbridge for can get in.

- *Built-in:* If you have Microsoft Vista, you have a firewall turned on by default. Windows XP has a built-in firewall, too, but you have to make the extra effort and turn it on. Just call up the Run dialog box (choose Start⇨Run), type **Firewall.cpl**, click OK, click the General tab in the dialog box that appears, and then select the On (recommended) option.

- *Router:* The other way to protect your computer with a firewall is to install a router. A router is a small box that sits between your computer and the wall jack that connects you to the Internet. Many routers work like a software firewall and can even make your computer invisible to other computers. Depending on your router, you might need to enable the firewall. Check the router's instructions to find out how.

- *Third-party software:* A number of companies make firewall software, some of which is free. ZoneAlarm Pro (`www.zonealarm.com`) is one option, which costs $30. Comodo Free Firewall (`www.personalfirewall.comodo.com`), you guessed it, is free.

✔ **Installing all-in-one security:** If the idea of installing three different levels of security (antivirus/antispyware/firewall) seems complicated, check out the available all-in-one answers. Microsoft offers Windows Live OneCare (`http://onecare.live.com`), and Symantec has Norton 360 (`www.symantec.com/norton360`).

Mastering the Basics with Online Tutorials and Simulations

Online investing is like Vegas in that there are no do-overs. If you invest all your money in a speculative company that goes belly up, you lose your money. Period. Don't expect the government to bail you out and don't think you can sue the company to get your money back. It's gone. That's why if you're new to investing, you might want to try the tutorials and simulations I discuss in the following sections before using real money.

Online tutorials

Before you jump into any risky activity, it's worthwhile to take a deep breath, relax, and make absolutely sure you understand how the process works. Several excellent online tutorials can step you through the process ahead of time to make sure you know what to expect. If you're just starting out, it's not a bad idea to run through one of the following:

✔ **Investing Online Resource Center:** (www.investingonline.org) Here's a site that all online investors should check out. It's separated into two halves: one part for beginners and one for more advanced online investors. Beginning investors should take the quiz to measure whether they're ready for the real world of investing and then read through the Eight Things You Should Know section. More advanced investors should view the Real Cost of Daytrading tutorial that steps you through the dangers of rapid-fire trading.

✔ **Investing 101 at Investopedia:** (http://investopedia.com/university/beginner) A great primer of what you can expect, it's worth running through to make sure you have all the basics down. Figure 2-7 shows you what this page looks like.

Figure 2-7: Investopedia's Investing 101 steps investors through most of the things they need to know.

- ✔ **Motley Fool's Investing Basics:** (www.fool.com/school/basics/basics.htm) This section of the popular Motley Fool site covers everything from getting started investing online to analyzing stocks — something I cover in more detail in Chapter 13.

- ✔ **The Investor's Clearinghouse:** (www.investoreducation.org) Here you find links to online resources on all sorts of investing topics, ranging from ways to research investments to finding investing help. An affiliated site, Help For Investors.org (www.helpforinvestors.org), provides even more tips.

- ✔ **American Association of Individual Investors:** (www.aaii.com) This site provides some free resources to investors including a virtual Investor Classroom that teaches the basics.

- ✔ **Path to Investing:** (www.pathtoinvesting.org) Here you can find tutorials and calculators to help you make sure you know what you're in for when you start investing online.

Be careful about which online tutorials you read and pay attention to. Many so-called tutorials are thinly guised pitches for investment professionals trying to get you to hire them. Some also promote specialized trading techniques with the purpose of getting you to buy books, video tapes, and other materials.

Simulations

Online games, or simulations, let you buy and sell real stocks using only funny money. Online simulations are a good idea for investors because they let you get a taste for investing before you commit to a strategy.

A few simulators you can try out include

- ✔ **Icarra** (www.icarra.com) is a powerful portfolio tracking software program that's so addictive, you might keep playing even after you set up an online trading account and invest for real. As you enter buys and sells, Icarra carefully tracks the performance of your stocks and tells you how you're doing. Even more interesting, though, is that you can view other members' portfolios and share your own.

You don't know "Jack"

An interesting feature about Icarra, the truly addictive investment-simulator program, is that investors can create portfolios that mirror famous investors' strategies and see how they turn out. One member created a portfolio suspected to be similar to that of Vanguard founder Jack Bogle using press reports of his holdings. You can also find portfolios in Icarra that mirror the portfolio of Warren Buffett and those recommended by David Swensen, the successful manager of Yale's massive endowment fund.

✔ **Zacks' Simulator** (`http://simulator.zacks.com/zacks/default.aspx`) lets you enter your buys and sells, and it ranks you against the others playing the game. The site, shown in Figure 2-8, adds a bit of a community feel by allowing the different people, who compete for a prize purse of $100,000, to post blogs describing their strategies.

✔ **Investopedia Stock Simulator** (`http://simulator.investopedia.com`) starts you with $100,000 in funny money and lets you invest in any way you choose, including some advanced techniques I cover in Chapter 5.

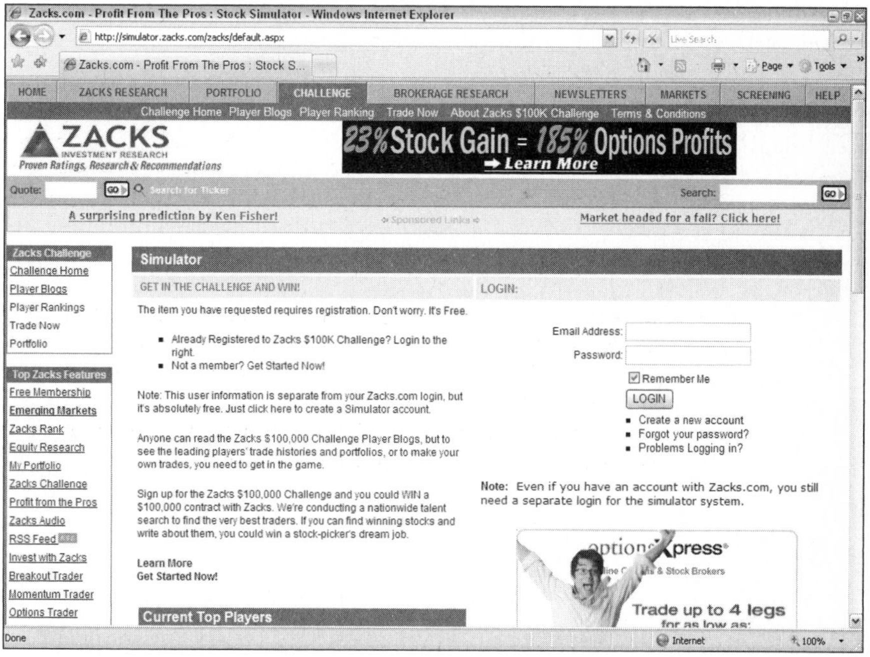

Figure 2-8: Zacks' Simulator lets you try your hand investing online with play money before putting your own money on the line.

- ✔ **BullPoo.com** (`http://bullpoo.com`) starts you with a virtual portfolio of $1 million to invest. It's similar to social networking investing sites, discussed in Chapter 7, except that those track real trades.

- ✔ **Marketocracy** (`www.marketocracy.com`) has a free service called Run A Fund that lets you pretend you're a money manager. It tracks your performance and ranks your investing prowess.

- ✔ **HedgeStop** (`www.hedgestop.com`) starts you with $50 million in play money and then lets you get to work investing. You can invest alone or create a team with friends. Your results are tracked and ranked.

Chapter 3

Choosing the Best Account Type for You

In This Chapter

▶ Understanding how different brokerage accounts are taxed

▶ Distinguishing between taxable accounts and tax-deferred accounts

▶ Knowing the different ways brokers can assign ownership to accounts

▶ Understanding the advantages and disadvantages of 401(k)s and IRAs

▶ Finding out about ways to cut the tax bite when saving for college

*O*nline investors tend to be do-it-yourself types, so it's unlikely that they'll have tax consultants on retainer just waiting to handle any tax issues they might have. No, many online investors are big on going it alone, which can be rewarding as long as such investors become tax-savvy, especially when it comes to how taxes on the different accounts vary.

In this chapter, I explain how investments are taxed and discuss ways in which picking the right kind of account can cut your tax bill. You'll want to understand the differences between the three main types of accounts — taxable, retirement, and education savings — before you sign up with an online broker. I also show how online tools can help you track and reduce your taxes. Finally, I step you through the different types of tax-advantaged accounts that can help you reach long-term goals such as saving for your child's college education or for your retirement.

Knowing How Different Accounts Are Taxed

Brokerage accounts might all seem the same; after all, they're just holding tanks for investments. Different types of brokerage accounts, though, look very different to the government. Thanks to the unbelievable complexity of the tax code, you can use three main types of accounts to hold your investments: taxable, retirement, and education savings accounts.

Taxable accounts

Taxable accounts are the standard accounts that come to mind when you think about investing online. Taxable accounts are very *liquid,* meaning you can easily access the money without paying special penalties. But that flexibility comes at a cost: taxes. When stocks you own in taxable accounts go up, or *appreciate,* and you sell them, you owe capital gains taxes on your profit that tax year. (*Capital gains* are gains you've made on the capital — cash — you've invested. Pretty simple, huh?) And if the stocks issue you cash payments, or *dividends,* you owe tax on those, too. I discuss how capital gains and dividends are taxed in the section entitled "Plain Vanilla: The Taxable Brokerage Account," later in this chapter.

Retirement accounts

Retirement is one of the largest and most intimidating things you must save for.

The bright side is that special *retirement accounts* make saving easier. It's a good thing, because company pensions are vanishing. That leaves retirement planning up to you. I explain the different types of retirement plans available to most people — and which ones could make the most sense for you — later in this chapter. The key retirement accounts to be aware of are

- **401(k)s** are typically retirement plans sponsored by a company. Oftentimes the company will match the employee's contributions. 401(k) plans allow you to delay when you must pay taxes on your contributions and investment gains.

- **Traditional individual retirement accounts or arrangements (IRAs)** are available to anyone below the age of 70½ who earn enough money to qualify and wants to delay when taxes are due on retirement savings. Your contributions might also be tax deductible if you're not covered by a company retirement plan or don't exceed income limits. You can look up the current limits on the Internal Revenue Services' Web site (www.irs.gov/publications/p590/ch01.html#d0e1025).

- **Roth IRAs** are retirement savings accounts that let you put in money that's already been taxed so it can grow and never be taxed again.

- **Other popular retirement plans** include simplified employee pension (SEP) accounts, 403(b) plans for employees of tax-exempt entities, and Keogh plans, which each have different advantages and disadvantages. I cover IRA-like SEPs in more detail later in this chapter.

Check out the "Retirement Accounts: Knowing Your 401(k)s from Your IRAs" section, later in this chapter, for more on your retirement plan options.

Education savings accounts

The cost of a college education keeps soaring. In 2007, the tuition and fees for a four-year public college degree cost $27,100, and a private college cost and $103,000, says Savingforcollege.com (www.savingforcollege.com/tutorial101/the_real_cost_of_higher_education.php), citing data from The College Board. And it gets worse: Tuition prices go up faster each year, 6% on average, than prices on almost anything else you'd buy, including stamps, eggs, and milk. If you factor in the 6% annual rate at which tuition fees are increasing, in 18 years the tab for a public college will hit $77,200, and it'll reach $294,100 for a private one. Online investors can get help from two types of *education savings accounts:*

- ✔ **529 plans** are very financially attractive state-sponsored education savings accounts. They can be used to shield money earmarked for college or to prepay college tuition fees to lock in today's price.

- ✔ **Coverdell Education Savings Accounts** are more restrictive than some education savings accounts, but they have the huge benefit that the money can be used to pay for elementary and secondary school as well.

I explain the different types of education savings accounts and how you can use online resources to maximize your tax savings in the "Going Back to School with Education Savings Accounts" section, later in this chapter.

Plain Vanilla: The Taxable Brokerage Account

If you want to talk intelligently about tax-advantaged accounts — accounts that are sheltered in some way for some period or other from the Internal Revenue Service — you would be well-served if you boned up on how regular taxable accounts are handled. It's hard to see why retirement accounts are such a boon for investors if you have no idea to what extent investments are usually taxed by Uncle Sam.

I give you online tools to help you crunch the numbers, but first, it's important to understand the basics of how the taxes work. Commit these basics to memory so you can think about any tax consequences before you place a trade in a taxable account. Keep in mind that these are just the basics, and the rules can change slightly for people in different situations. If taxes are your primary concern with investing, consult with books on the topic or with a tax professional. (I can, of course, recommend *Taxes 2007 For Dummies,* by Eric Tyson, David Silverman, and Margaret Munro.)

You have a taxable event in a taxable brokerage account when one of two things occurs:

- ✔ **Capital appreciation:** Imagine that you hit a veritable investing home run by buying a share of stock for $10 that soars to $100. When you sell the stock, that $90 per share gain is called *capital appreciation* or a *realized capital gain*. If you hold onto the stock and don't sell it, it's considered an *unrealized capital gain*. And with an unrealized capital gain, because you haven't actually cashed in the stock, you haven't profited in the eyes of the government and don't owe taxes. But the second you sell, everything changes. Your gain turns into a taxable one subject to rules I discuss shortly.

- ✔ **Dividends:** You probably remember dividends from the Chance card in the *Monopoly* board game. *Dividends* are cash payments made by companies when they're making so much money they don't know what to do with it. The only thing they can think of is returning it to the shareholders. That way, shareholders can reinvest the cash rather than it piling up in the company's bank account.

  I show you how to find out how much cash a company has on hand in Chapter 12, and in Chapter 13, I show you how to find stocks that pay fat dividends.

Capital appreciation is a fine thing to write about, and I do get to it eventually — right after the next section, to be precise — but dividends have that Somebody-Is-Sending-Me-Money-without-My-Really-Understanding-Why appeal, so I'm going to dive right in and talk about them first.

The importance of dividends

Dividends usually won't make you rich overnight, but don't think they're just for widows and orphans. Dividends accounted for about one-third of the Standard & Poor's 500 index 10% *total return* in its more than 50 years of existence. Total return measures your percentage gain on a stock resulting from both stock-price gains and dividends.

If you're not getting dividends, you could be missing out. Table 3-1 shows what stocks in the S&P 500 have returned each year since 2000 and the percentage that came from dividends. You'll notice dividends helped make up for losses in years when stocks declined in value.

Table 3-1	The Importance of Dividends			
Year	**Price Change**	**Total Return**	**Dividend**	**% of Return from Dividends**
2006	13.6%	2.2%	15.8%	13.8%
2005	3.0%	1.9%	4.9%	38.9%
2004	9.0%	1.9%	10.9%	17.3%
2003	26.4%	2.3%	28.7%	8.0%
2002	−23.4%	1.3%	−22.1%	N/A
2001	−13.0%	1.2%	−11.9%	N/A
2000	−10.1%	1.0%	−9.1%	N/A

Source: www2.standardandpoors.com/spf/xls/index/MONTHLY.xls

Dividends are paid based on how many shares you have. If a company declares a $1 per share dividend, and you own 100 shares, you will receive $100. To help compare the sizes of dividends, investors generally talk about the dividend yield. A dividend yield tells you how much return you're getting in the form of a dividend; in other words, how big the dividend is relative to what you've invested.

You can calculate a stock's dividend yield by dividing the annual dividend by the stock's price. But you can also get it from almost every financial Web site explained in Chapter 2. Reuters, for example, has an extensive database of dividend information. To get a company's dividend yield, here's what you do:

1. **Go to Reuters's Investing main page at** `http://today.reuters.com/investing/defaultUS.aspx.`

2. **Scroll down to the Stocks & Mutual Funds section and enter a ticker symbol in the Ticker Symbol field.**

3. **Click the Ratios link in the left column and click Go.**

   In the Dividends table, shown in Figure 3-1 using General Electric as an example, you can see what a company's dividend yield is now and what it was on average over the past five years. You can also see what kind of dividend yields other companies in the industry pay.

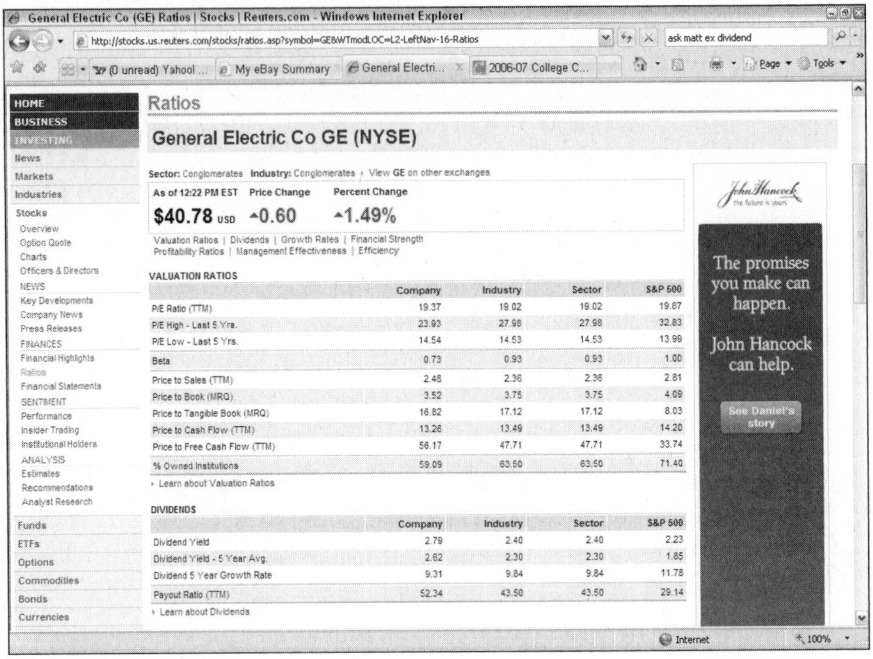

Figure 3-1:
Reuters lets
you find out
how much
of a
dividend a
stock pays
and how it
compares to
its industry.

Table 3-2 shows what kinds of dividends are typical in various industries.

Table 3-2	Dividends That Industries Pay
Industry	**Five-Year Average Dividend Yield**
Real estate operations	4.8%
Electric utilities	3.6%
Major drugs	2.5%
Conglomerates	2.3%
Software and programming	1.5%

Source: http://today.reuters.com/investing/defaultUS.aspx

Some online brokers and companies that sell their shares to investors directly allow you to use dividends paid by a stock to buy more shares of the stock. These programs are called dividend reinvestment plans (DRIPs). If you're interested in these plans, keep them in mind when evaluating brokers, as described in Chapter 4.

How capital gains are taxed

When you sell a stock held in a taxable account that has appreciated in value, you usually have taxes to pay. Generally, such *capital gains taxes,* as they are referred to, are calculated based on how long you owned the stock a period of time known as the *holding period.* There are two holding periods:

- **Short-term:** That's the type of capital gain you have if you sell a stock after owning it for one year or less. You want to avoid these gains if you can because you're taxed at the ordinary income tax rate, which as I explain shortly, is one of the highest tax percentages.

- **Long-term:** That's the type of capital gain result if you sell a stock after holding it for more than one year. These gains qualify for a special discount on taxes, as described a little later.

You must own a stock for *over* one year for it to be considered a long-term capital gain. If you buy a stock on March 3, 2007 and sell it on March 3, 2008 for a profit, that is considered a short-term capital gain. Also, an important thing to remember is that the holding period clock starts the day after you buy the stock and stops the day you sell it. Selling even one day too soon can be a costly mistake.

The high tax price of being short-term

If you're interested in cutting your tax bill in a taxable account, you want to reduce, as much as possible, the number of stocks you sell that you've owned for only a year or less because they're taxed at your ordinary income tax levels. You can look up your ordinary income tax bracket from the Internal Revenue Service (www.irs.gov/formspubs/article/0,, id=164272,00.html). But just to give you an idea, the tax brackets for 2007 are shown in Table 3-3.

Table 3-3	Federal Tax Rates for 2007	
If You're Single and Earn Between	*If You're Married and File a Joint Return with Income Between*	*Your Short-Term Capital Gains Are Taxed At*
$0 and $7,825	$0 and $15,650	10%
$7,825 and $31,850	$15,650 and $63,700	15%
$31,850 and $77,100	$63,700 and $128,500	25%

continued

Table 3-3 *(continued)*

If You're Single and Earn Between	If You're Married and File a Joint Return with Income Between	Your Short-Term Capital Gains Are Taxed At
$77,100 and $160,850	$128,500 and $195,850	28%
$160,850 and $349,700	$195,850 and $349,700	33%
$359,700 and beyond	$349,700 and beyond	35%

Source: Internal Revenue Service

Need an example? How about this one. Remember the stock I mention earlier that went from $10 to $100 a share (for a $90 per share gain)? Say the investor had $50,000 in taxable income that year and sold the stock after owning it for just three months. The investor's gain would fall from $90 to $67.50 after paying $22.50 in taxes.

How long-term capital gains are taxed

By owning stocks for more than a year, gains are taxed at what's known as the *maximum capital gain rate.* The rate you pay on long-term capital gains varies based on your normal tax bracket, but such rates are almost always much lower than your ordinary income tax rate. Long-term capital gains rates, though, can change dramatically due to political pressure, as explained by financial Web site Bankrate (www.bankrate.com/brm/itax/tips/20010305a.asp). Table 3-4 shows the maximum capital gain rates for 2007 for typical investments such as stocks and bonds.

Table 3-4	Maximum Capital Gain Rate
If Your Regular Tax Rate Is	*Your Maximum Capital Gain Rate Is*
25% or higher	15%
Lower than 25%	5%

Source: Internal Revenue Service (www.irs.gov/publications/p550/ch04.html#d0e14996)

I'm trying to save you time (and money!) by providing you with all the IRS tax brackets. But you can look them up yourself online at www.irs.gov/formspubs.

When you can win from your losses

If you're like most investors, you beat yourself up anytime you sell a stock for a loss. Nobody likes to lose money when the whole point of investing is to make it. But if there's a plus to suffering a loss, it comes at tax time. The IRS allows you to use capital losses to offset your capital gains and possibly your regular income. If your losses exceed your gains, you have a net capital loss to report on Schedule D, which can even cut your taxable income each year. This IRS rule presents several tax strategies that can cut your tax bill. The guidelines, when it comes to using losses to cut your capital gains taxes, include the following:

- ✔ **Use losses to avoid short-term gains.** Make it your goal to never have a short-term capital gain. If you sell a winning stock you've owned for a year or less, go through your portfolio, find a loser and sell it. (You can even use losses from stocks you've owned for more than a year to offset short-term capital gains.) If your long-term loss is greater than your short-term gain, the gain vanishes, and you have a *net long-term loss* instead. You can deduct up to $3,000 ($1,500 if you're married and file separately) from your regular taxable income. Not a bad deal.

  For example, imagine that you scored a $1,000 profit from a high-flying stock you owned for a month. Normally, you'd have to pay $280 in taxes because it's a short-term gain. But you can pay no tax if you sell a stock at a loss of $1,000 by the end of the tax year. You get the entire $1,000 from the first sale, and you offload a bummer of a stock at the same time. Win-win!

- ✔ **Dump your losers.** If you have losing stocks in your portfolio that you've lost hope in, sell them so you at least get a tax break. Tax rules allow you to deduct up to $3,000 a year in capital losses from your regular income. It's a decent way to get out of a stock you're tired of and cut your tax bill.

- ✔ **Don't forget tax-loss carryovers.** What if your net loss is greater than the annual limit of $3,000? Do you lose the deduction? Not at all; you just have to spread it out. You can carryover capital losses to your future tax returns until you use them up. Edward Jones (www.edwardjones.com/cgi/getHTML.cgi?page=/USA/resources/tax/transactions/capital_gains.html) provides detailed information about how to carry over capital losses.

Don't think you can sell a stock you're losing money on, take the loss for tax purposes, and just buy it back. The IRS's "wash sale" rule prohibits this. If you sell a stock or mutual fund for a loss, you're not allowed to deduct the loss if you bought that investment or one that's "substantially identical" within 30 days before or 30 days after the sale. To avoid triggering the wash sale rule, you must wait 31 days after the sale to buy the investment back. Here are two sites that can help you understand the complexities of the wash sale rules:

- ✔ **Fairmark** (www.fairmark.com/capgain/wash) provides a detailed description of wash sale rules and ways to avoid getting tripped up by this tax trap. (See Figure 3-2.)
- ✔ **The Securities and Exchange Commission** (www.sec.gov/answers/wash.htm) also provides guidance on wash sales.

What to do with your worthless stock?

Selling your losers is usually pretty straightforward: You swallow your pride, sell the stock, and take your tax loss. But sometimes it's not that easy. Periodically, companies crash so badly their stocks are *delisted* from the exchange, such as the New York Stock Exchange or NASDAQ, where they traded when you bought them. This happened to both Enron and Delta Air Lines. They become what's called a *worthless security*.

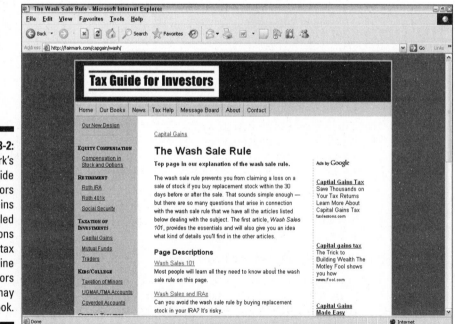

Figure 3-2: Fairmark's Tax Guide for Investors contains detailed descriptions of tax traps online investors may overlook.

You can still deduct the loss on a stock even if the shares aren't available for trading anymore. But the IRS is pretty clear about what you need to do. In most cases, even when a stock is delisted, it still trades on informal markets such as the Pink Sheets. It's best to sell the stock there so you can recognize the loss and have a paper trail. It's often best to sell this way, even though some online brokers charge slightly higher commissions because proving something is worthless without being able to sell it can be difficult. If you can't sell the stock, you must prove it's worth less than a penny per share. Additional rules say that you can deduct your loss from a worthless stock only in the year it became worthless. If you didn't realize a stock wasn't worth anything until the year after it lost its value, you have to file an amended return for the year the stock became worthless.

Using technology to measure your capital gain

Taxes can have a dramatic effect on your online investing success, so you need to be aware of the rules. Most online brokerages won't stop you from placing a trade that could hurt you when tax time rolls around. It's up to you to manage your tax picture. And it's also up to you to track your capital gains.

You might think "Easier said than done," but keeping track of your capital gains isn't that complicated. Essentially, if you know the following about all your investment transactions, you have what you need to keep tabs on your capital gains:

- ✔ **The date you bought the investment.**

- ✔ **The amount you paid to buy it, which is known as your *cost basis*.** You can calculate this by multiplying the stock price you paid times the number of shares you bought and then adding the commission you paid for the stock. All that added up together is your cost basis.

   For example, say you bought 100 shares of ABC for $50 and paid a $5 commission. Your basis is $5,005. You get that by multiplying the cost of the stock with the number of shares ($50 times 100 shares) and then adding the $5 commission.

- ✔ **The date you sold the investment.**

- ✔ **The amount you received for selling it, or your *proceeds*.** You can calculate this by multiplying the stock price you sold at times the number of shares you sold, minus the commission you had to pay.

   Imagine now that you sold your 100 shares of ABC for $100 and paid a $5 commission. The amount of your proceeds is $9,995. You get that by multiplying the price of the stock by the number of shares ($50 times 100 shares) and then subtracting the $5 commission.

Pay no capital-gains taxes?

It almost seems too good to be true. Could it be the government is cutting the capital gains tax to 0%? The answer is yes and no. Congress approved a bill that cut long-term capital gains taxes for many tax-payers through 2010. And, between 2008 and 2010, the long-term capital gains rate for some investors falls to nothing from 5%. The lower rate affects only long-term capital gains because short-term gains are taxed at your ordinary income rate.

Before you start writing a thank-you letter to the IRS, though, you should know that there are some heavy restrictions. The 0% long-term tax rate applies only to people in the bottom two tax brackets, which means in 2007 you'd have to have less than $31,850 in taxable income as a single person or less than $63,700 for a married couple filing jointly to qualify. Those cutoffs will rise a little in 2008 to adjust for inflation.

The following chart shows how much long-term capital gains taxes are scheduled to fall for those who qualify:

If Your Regular Tax Rate Is	2007 Capital Gains Rate	2008 Capital Gains Rate	2009 Capital Gains Rate
10%	5%	0%	0%
15%	5%	0%	0%
25% to 35%	15%	15%	15%

At tax time, you must then report all your capital gains on Schedule D. For more help on this, check out the current *Taxes For Dummies* book (Wiley Publishing) or check out what the IRS says about sales and trades of investment at www.irs.gov/publications/p550/ch04.html#d0e9488.

Because you're an online investor, you're probably loath to actually use a pencil and paper to keep track of all this information. Luckily, you have several alternatives:

✔ **Personal finance software:** These programs, including Microsoft Money and Intuit's Quicken (discussed at more length in Chapter 1), keep track of everything you need to file Schedule D. Both can also transfer all the data the government requires directly into tax-preparation software, such as H&R Block's TaxCut or Intuit's TurboTax. Both software programs also print out a capital gains worksheet you can give to your tax preparer.

✔ **Portfolio tracking sites:** Several of the Web-based portfolio-monitoring sites discussed in Chapter 8 can help you track everything you need to calculate your taxes. ClearStation (http://clearstation.etrade.com) can even help generate the tax form required by the IRS.

- **Online brokers' Web sites:** Such sites often track when you bought investments, how much you paid, and when you sold them. Nearly all online brokerages have a place on their Web sites where you can see your realized and unrealized gains. And at the end of the year, most online brokerages mail you a document showing all your trades and your basis.

- **Online capital gains calculators and sites** let you enter your stock buys and sells and help calculate your net capital gains or losses and carry-overs. SmartMoney.com offers a helpful calculator that does this (check it out at (www.smartmoney.com/tax/capital/index.cfm?story= capitalgains), as do MoneyChimp (www.moneychimp.com/ features/capgain.htm) and Quicken.com(www.quicken.com/ taxes/capgains).

- **Specialized online sites dedicated to optimizing your tax strategy** might make sense if you have a particularly complicated situation. For instance, GainsKeeper (www.gainskeeper.com) is a professional-level online service that helps you track your trades, tally your cost basis in stocks, and find ways to reduce your taxes. (Figure 3-3 shows the GainsKeeper site.) If you're an extremely active trader, the tax rules and keeping track of everything can get complicated, so software like this can be helpful. The system isn't free; it'll cost you at least $70 a year. Before signing up, though, check with your broker — some offer discounted subscriptions.

Figure 3-3: Gains Keeper is a dedicated Web site to help you find ways to optimize your tax strategy when it comes to investing.

Measuring your capital gains if you've lost your records

I know you meticulously track all of your investments and trading records. But in the off case you just can't find how much you paid for a stock, you can still figure out your basis by using the Internet as long as you know when you bought it. You can use the historical charting, as described in Chapter 2, to look back into time and see where the stock was trading the day you bought it.

Here's how:

1. **Log in to MSN Money (`http://moneycentral.msn.com/investor`) and enter the stock symbol in the Symbols text box on the main toolbar.**

2. **Click the Historical link under the Charts link.**

3. **Install the MSN Money Investment Toolbox software, as described in Chapter 1.**

   This software is easy to install. But if you don't want to bother or can't get it to install, skip to the Tip icon immediately following these steps.

4. **Select Custom from the Period pull-down menu at the top of the chart.**

5. **Enter the date you bought the stock in the From field and the date you sold it on the To field; then choose the Daily option under Display Detail and click OK.**

6. **Place you cursor on the first date in the chart, like the one you see in Figure 3-4, and click.**

   At the top of the chart, you see the price the stock traded at the day you bought it. Add the commission you paid to the stock price, and you have your cost basis.

7. **Place your cursor on the last date on the chart and click.**

   At the top of the chart, you see the price the stock traded the day you sold it.

8. **Use the information and follow the previous instructions on how to calculate your capital gain or loss.**

   The data you got from MSN Money are also what you need to fill out Schedule D.

If you're unable to install MSN Money Investment Toolbox, follow Steps 1 and 2 in the preceding list. Then scroll down to the bottom-left side of the page and enter the dates you bought and sold the stock under the Custom Date Range heading. Drag your cursor to the left to get the stock price on the date you bought the stock. Drag your cursor to the right to get the stock price on the date you sold.

Figure 3-4:
MSN
Money
allows you
to look at
what a
stock's price
was in a
date in the
past to help
you figure
out your
tax bill.

How dividends are taxed

Thanks to the Jobs and Growth Tax Relief Reconciliation Act of 2003, dividends caught a big-time tax break. Dividends that meet certain criteria are considered *qualified* and are taxed at the same favorable rate as long-term capital gains, as discussed in the previous section. That was a huge break, because prior to that, dividends were taxed at the typically much higher short-term capital gains rate. But, to get the lower tax treatment, dividends must be

✔ **Qualified:** Dividends from most companies that trade on U.S. exchanges are qualified. There are important exceptions, though, including some dividends paid by *real-estate investment trusts,* or REITs, which typically own commercial real estate such as apartment buildings and strip malls. Also keep in mind that dividends paid by money market accounts and many bond funds don't qualify either because they're considered interest.

The Fairmark.com Web site (`www.fairmark.com/mutual/ordinary.htm`) has a set of tools that can help you decide what kinds of dividends you have and how they're taxed.

✔ **Paid to a shareholder who holds the stock for the right amount of time:** To qualify for the lower rates, you must own the stock for a long enough time. The IRS says you must own the stock more than 60 days during the 121-day period starting 60 days before the stock's *ex-dividend date.* The ex-dividend date is the day a new investor who bought the stock is no longer entitled to dividend declared by the company. For more information on this, Fidelity.com (`http://personal.fidelity.com/planning/tax/distributions/qdi.shtml.cvsr`) has a section that explains qualified dividends. The Securities and Exchange Commission (`www.sec.gov/answers/dividen.htm`) explains the ex-dividend date.

Investors who buy investments and hold them for a long time get a huge tax advantage over short-term traders. By holding stocks, you can put off the time when you have to pay tax on your gains. That allows your entire, untaxed ball of cash to snowball tax deferred. But, even long-term investors have to pay taxes on dividends each year.

Retirement Accounts: Knowing Your 401 (k)s from Your IRAs

If you made your way through the previous section, you have a pretty good sense of just how complicated taxes can get when dealing with regular taxable brokerage accounts. The tax burden creates bookkeeping work for you when

---

Until death do you part: Ownership of taxable accounts

When you set up an online brokerage account, you'll be asked whose name it should be put in. This seemingly mundane question can have serious tax consequences. Sorry to be morbid here, but death is the event that makes the way you possess an account very important. The following are the main types of accounts and how each affects your tax situation in the event of your (timely or untimely) demise:

✔ **Individual accounts** are the common standard account. You are named the owner, and on your death, the assets go to your estate.

✔ **Joint tenants with rights of survivorship** gives each owner an entire stake. That

means if one owner dies, the assets transfer directly to the other owners.

✔ **Tenants in common** lets you slice up an account, by percentage, among different owners. When you die, your percentage of ownership passes to your estate.

✔ **Community property** is a method of ownership available only in states that allow it. This allows a married couple to equally own assets. The Internal Revenue Service (`www.irs.gov/pub/irs-pdf/p555.pdf`) recognizes nine community property states: Arizona, California, Idaho, Louisiana, Nevada, New Mexico, Texas, Washington, and Wisconsin. Alaska residents can choose to have community property treatment.

you buy or sell a stock (bad enough) and it also eats into your returns (even worse). Being forced to pay taxes frequently means that the amount of capital you can invest gets whittled away, hurting your ultimate performance. That's the beauty of retirement accounts. Just remember that the downside to retirement accounts is you might get socked with penalties if you take money out before you retire.

In this section, I describe the main types of retirement accounts. The tax rules are complex and not exactly as fascinating as the latest Dan Brown novel. If you just want the bottom line, many financial advisors recommend just doing the following:

1. **Open a 401(k) if your employer matches your contributions. Put in at least enough to get the match.**

2. **If you have money left over and qualify, open a Roth IRA. Most online brokers, discussed in Chapter 4, can open a Roth IRA for you.**

If you'd rather use online tools to help you decide what to do, check out the following sites:

- ✔ **Morningstar** (http://screen.morningstar.com/ira/ira calculator.html?tsection=tollsiracal) has a calculator that helps you pick the right retirement accounts for you. There are plenty of online resources dedicated to retirement issues.

- ✔ **Kiplinger.com** has a retirement center at (www.kiplinger.com/you retirement) where you can determine what accounts are best for you. If you're confused, some online brokers have financial advisors that can help you decide, which you can read about in Chapter 4.

- ✔ **360 Degrees of Financial Literacy** (www.360financialliteracy. org/Life+Stages/Retirement) is maintained by the American Institute of Certified Public Accountants. The site, shown in Figure 3-5, features advanced online tools that can help you make sure you're saving enough for retirement and using the right types of accounts.

- ✔ **Hugh's Mortgage and Financial Calculators** (www.hughchou.org/calc) provides a number of free online calculators that crunch complex financial problems. There's a complete section on retirement savings with several helpful tools.

- ✔ **FIRECalc** (http://firecalc.com) uses an advanced computerized model to help you determine how much you must save to retire. It bases its forecasts using real historical data.

The biggest downside to 401(k)s and most IRA accounts is that you get hit with a steep 10% penalty for taking money out before you turn 59½, unless you qualify for some exceptions. And you must start taking money out of a traditional IRA (not the Roth) when you turn 70½ years old.

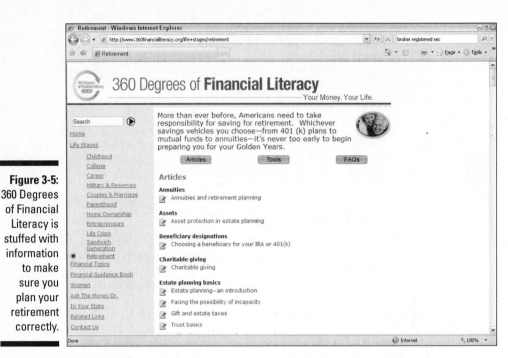

Figure 3-5: 360 Degrees of Financial Literacy is stuffed with information to make sure you plan your retirement correctly.

It's important that you understand all the catches, so I recommend doing a little 401(k)/IRA homework by checking out the following Web sites for complete descriptions of the different types of retirement plans:

- ✔ **Vanguard** (`https://flagship.vanguard.com/VGApp/hnw/accounttypes/retirement/ATSCompareIRAsContent.jsp`) contains an easy-to-follow chart that explains the advantages of disadvantages of traditional IRAs and Roth IRAs.

- ✔ **Investopedia** (`www.investopedia.com/terms/1/401kplan.asp`) describes 401(k) plans in addition to a new type of 401(k) called the Roth 401(k)

Anytime you use an account that lets you deduct contributions following the Don't Pay Tax Now/Pay It Later principle — any 401(k) plan, for example — you have to pay the ordinary income tax rate when you withdraw cash. Don't let this discourage you, though, because retirement accounts still provide tax savings to most investors.

401(k)s: A great place to get started

If your employer offers a 401(k) plan or the equivalent for public-service employees called the 403(b), don't pass it up. Thanks to the advantages retirement accounts offer to employees and employers, the 401(k) has been extremely popular.

If your company offers a 401(k) and makes matching contributions, that's the first account you should open. Passing up on a company match is like turning away free money. Just be sure this is money you're not going to need until you retire.

Most 401(k) plans let you contribute up to $15,000 for 2007 and $15,500 for 2008. If you're 50 years old or older, you can kick in an extra $5,000 as a catch-up contribution. For more details on 401(k) plans, check out *401(k)s For Dummies,* by Ted Benna and Brenda Watson Newmann (Wiley Publishing).

Managing your 401(k) plan online

Just because your 401(k) is tucked away and invested for your retirement doesn't mean you can't manage it online. You have several ways to tune and tweak your 401(k), including

- ✔ **The plan administrators' site:** Most 401(k) plans are easily accessible on a Web site. From here, you can set all the variables that matter most. You can instruct your company to withhold a set amount of money from your pay, decide which mutual funds you want to invest in, and shift money between mutual funds. You'll need to contact your company's human resources department to find out how to access the account.

- ✔ **401(k) education sites:** Sites such as 401(k) Day (www.401kday.org) help you take a more active role in making sure you'll have enough dough for your golden years. The site has an annual retirement checkup to tell you if you're on track and a 401(k) calculator to help you pick the right 401(k) strategy. Another similar site is 401k.org (www.401k.org), run by the Profit Sharing/401(k) Council of America, which also provides information (www.psca.org).

- ✔ **Regulators' sites:** These sites let you know your rights and the employer's obligations. Most retirement plans are overseen by the Department of Labor, which maintains extensive resources at www.dol.gov/dol/topic/retirement/typesofplans.htm.

Most employers require that you work for them for at least a year and that you be 21 or older before you can sign up for their 401(k) plans. But other than that, 401(k) plans vary between companies. Some 401(k) plans let you borrow money and pay interest to yourself. And in 2006, a few employers began offering Roth 401(k) plans, which combine the benefits of 401(k)s with Roth IRAs, which you can read about in the next section.

Getting in tune with IRAs

Practically everyone can fund an IRA if they have the money. But they're especially attractive if you don't have access to a 401(k) at work (perhaps because you're self-employed) or if the 401(k) at your company doesn't offer a match. IRAs, like 401(k)s, offer big benefits when you're saving for retirement. The Investor's Clearinghouse (www.investoreducation.org/IRAs) provides links to online resources to help you decide if an IRA will work for you.

Several types of IRA(s) exist, but you should really concern yourself only with the big three:

- ✔ **Traditional IRAs** are available to anyone. They're a great place to save money for retirement because you can put away $4,000 a year in 2007 and $5,000 in 2008, and even more if you're over 50 years old.

  Capital gains and dividends in a traditional IRA aren't taxed until you take out the money. And, you might be able to deduct your contributions if you're not covered by a company-sponsored retirement plan. If you or your spouse are covered by a company plan, the amount you can deduct is reduced based on much how you earn. The rules get complicated, but Vanguard has an excellent primer at https://flagship.vanguard. com/VGApp/hnw/accounttypes/retirement/ATSTradIRAWho ContributeContent.jsp that explains how much you may contribute.

  Even if you can't deduct your contribution, a traditional IRA might still make sense for you. A nondeductible IRA can be a great place to stash investments that generate nonqualified dividends and interest such as REITs and bonds.

- ✔ **SEP IRAs** are designed for owners of small businesses, employees of small businesses, and people who work for themselves. They're easy to set up and allow employers, including self-employed people, to contribute up to 25% of compensation to a limit of $45,000 in 2007. Vanguard provides more information about these plans at https://flagship.vanguard. com/VGApp/hnw/accounttypes/retirement/ATSSEPIRAOverview Content.jsp.

✔ **Roth IRAs** are one of the best things going, and if you can open one, you should. With Roth IRAs, you pay now and play later. You can't deduct contributions when you make them, but you can take out the money in the future tax-free if you're at least 59½ years old and owned the account for five years or longer. And unlike traditional IRAs, you're not required to take out the money at a certain age, allowing you to pass the giant, tax-free nest egg to your kids. Just imagine the power of compounding on an investment sitting untaxed for nearly two lifetimes. It doesn't get much better than that.

Roth IRAs are generally best if you think your tax rate will be higher in the future when you retire. It's impossible to know what Congress will do with tax rates in the future. But that's why many financial advisors say it's better to go with a Roth, lock in the rates now, and protect yourself from the risk of higher tax rates later.

Setting up an IRA

After you've made your decision about what type of retirement account you're interested in, be it a traditional IRA, Roth IRA, or SEP IRA, you need to find a broker to set it up. Nearly all the online brokers are equipped to set up all of these accounts. But before signing up, make sure there are

✔ **No extra fees or higher commissions:** In fact, online brokers might cut you special deals on your IRA accounts. This is something to look for when evaluating online brokers, as described in Chapter 4.

✔ **Plenty of low-cost investments to choose from:** Most brokerages let you invest in both individual stocks and mutual funds with IRA accounts.

Okay, so you've decided on a plan for saving for retirement and you've picked the type of accounts best suited for that plan. But how much do you need to save? Most of the preceding sites help you answer that question. The Choose to Save site (www.choosetosave.org/ballpark) takes a simplified approach by giving you a Ballpark Estimate of how much you'll need. And Analyze Now! (www.analyzenow.com) provides a Free Programs section stuffed with spreadsheets that can help you answer many of the questions you need to be asking yourself. In fact, the site even has an Investment Manager spreadsheet that can help you choose the right kind of accounts for planning your retirement.

Should you turn your traditional IRA into a Roth?

Do you have a traditional IRA and wish you had a Roth? Some tax payers can convert their traditional IRA to a Roth. Before doing that, though, you should consult several online resources, including

✔ **General sources,** such as Motley Fool (`www.fool.com/investing/small-cap/2004/12/03/roth-ira-conversion considerations.aspx`), provide guidelines where a conversion would make sense.

✔ **Comparison Web sites** help you know what you stand to gain or lose from the transformation. The rules surrounding Roth and traditional IRAs are complex. If you're not sure about anything, check out Vanguard's comparison site at `https://flagship.vanguard.com/VGApp/hnw/accounttypes/retirement/ATSCompareIRAs Content.jsp`.

✔ **Conversion calculators** take all your information and crunch the numbers and tell you whether you can, or should, make the leap. DinkyTown (`www.dinkytown.net/java/RothTransfer.html`), Washington Mutual (`www.wamu.com/personal/accountchoices/retirement/rothiraconversion/default.asp`), MoneyChimp (`www.moneychimp.com/articles/rothira/rothcalc.htm`), and Roth IRA (`www.rothira.com`) are a few. Most of the calculators, such as the MoneyChimp version shown in the figure, are easy to follow.

Going Back to School with Education Savings Accounts

Several special types of education savings accounts provide lucrative tax breaks, giving you a fighting chance to keep up with college costs. You need any help you can get because tuition costs rise at about twice the rate of most consumer goods.

The two main types of education savings accounts are the 529 plan and the Coverdell. Both 529s and Coverdell accounts work much like the Roth IRA, discussed in the previous section, in that you put after-tax dollars into the accounts and watch them grow tax-free. You can take out the money, without paying any tax, as long as you use the cash to pay for qualified education expenses. The Internal Revenue Service (www.irs.gov/publications/p970/ch08.html) describes qualified education expenses as "tuition, fees, books, supplies and equipment required for enrollment or attendance" to an eligible school. "Reasonable" room and board costs are also included for students that go to school at least half-time.

Three numbers you need to know: 529

When saving for college, it's tough to beat the 529. These are college savings plans typically run by states or educational institutions. The plans have several extremely positive attributes, such as

- ✔ **Tax savings:** As the earlier example describes, the tax savings from 529 plans makes them worthwhile. The tax savings can be even sweeter in some states that let you deduct your contributions to the state plan from your income.

- ✔ **Control:** Even though your child is the beneficiary of the money, you remain the owner. That's an important distinction because it means if Junior decides to run off and join the circus, he can't get the 529 money.

529 plans don't just have to be used for a kid. Open one for yourself if you're thinking about going back to school. And don't worry, your money won't be wasted if your child gets a scholarship. You can change the beneficiary to anyone else you want or even use the money to pay for more schooling for yourself. The downside is there are penalties to pay if you take the money out and don't use it to pay for college.

- ✔ **Availability and flexibility:** Unlike most other tax-advantaged accounts, which are mired with complex rules and restrictions, anyone can have a 529 account. There are limits to how much you can contribute, but they're generous, allowing you to contribute up to $12,000 a year in 2007 without triggering estate tax issues. For information on the limits, Forbes has a helpful estate planning section at (`www.forbes.com/finance/taxes estates`). And if you want more of an overview, check out *Estate Planning For Dummies,* by Brian Caverly and Jordan Simon (Wiley Publishing).

✔ **Lots of options:** Every state offers at least one 529 plan, and you can invest in any state's plan even if your child won't go to school in that state. So even if you invest in Utah's 529 plan, you can still use the money if your child wants to go to University of California, Los Angeles in California.

✔ **Something for everyone:** Some states, but not all, offer two types of 529 plans: *prepaid* and *savings.* With prepaid plans, you transfer the investment risk to the state by agreeing to pay the current price of a college education and essentially locking in the price. With savings plans, you contribute any amount you want and try to grow it by choosing wise investments. If you save and invest wisely with a 529 savings plan, you could make enough to pay for your kid's college and maybe part of a grandkid's, too.

Getting up to speed on 529 plans online

Some of the great things about 529 plans are that they're easy to sign up for, you can fund them without worrying about tax laws for the most part, and the investments are pretty much preselected. The biggest decision you must make is whether you'll opt for a plan offered by your state or go for one in another state.

Always evaluate and consider your own state's 529 plan before looking elsewhere. If your state lets you deduct contributions to its 529 plan, that might be a compelling feature you won't want to miss out on.

Here are the primary ways to research and find out about 529 plans:

✔ **College savings information sites:** Savingforcollege.com (`www.saving forcollege.com`) is a supersite when it comes to all things about college savings. You can find tutorials galore that show you how to pick a plan, decide which state's 529 plan is best for you, compare different 529 plans and fees and even provide links to the plans so you can sign up. College Savings Plans Network (`www.collegesavings.org`) helps you sort through the various options for saving for college. FinAid.org (`http://finaid.org/savings`) primarily deals with financial aid, but it also has resources on savings plans.

✔ **The states' 529 plan sites:** Each 529 plan runs its own Web site that gives you all the details on how much you can contribute, what your investment options are, what the fees are, and other things you need to know. The best way to find links to states' plans is through the Savingforcollege.com site, although Table 3-5 contains links to some plans.

Table 3-5	Web Site Addresses for Some States' 529 Plans	
State	**Plan Name**	**Web Address**
California	ScholarShare College Savings Plan	`www.scholarshare.com`
Iowa	College Savings Iowa	`www.collegesavings iowa.com`
New York	New York's 529 College Savings Program – Direct Plan	`www.nysaves.org`
Ohio	Ohio College Advantage 529 Savings Plan	`www.college advantage.com`
Oregon	Oregon College Savings Plan	`www.oregoncollege savings.com`
Texas	Tomorrow's College Investment Plan	`www.enterprise529.com`
Utah	Utah Educational Savings Plan	`www.uesp.org`

✔ **Broker or mutual fund's sites:** Some states' 529 plans are administered by large brokerage or mutual fund companies. In those cases, you can find out more about the plans directly from the administration companies. Vanguard, for instance, handles Nevada's Vanguard 529 College Savings Plan and Iowa's College Savings Iowa 529 plan. You can find out about both plans, and 529 plans in general, at Vanguard (`https://flagship.vanguard.com/VGApp/hnw/accounttypes/college/ATS529CollegeOVContent.jsp`). Fidelity operates California's plan and also offers a national plan. You can read about those plans at `http://personal.fidelity.com/planning/college/content/fidelity_managed_529_plans.shtml.cvsr?refhp=pr&ut=A17`.

✔ **529 ratings and analysis sites:** You can find additional commentary from sites that make it their business to rank 529 plans. Some examples include 529Ratings.com (`www.529Ratings.com`) and CNNMoney.com (`www.cnnmoney.com`), which routinely rate 529 plans. You can find additional information at the College & Education section of Yahoo! Finance (`http://finance.yahoo.com/college-education`) and from the Financial Industry Regulatory Authority (FINRA) regulatory body (`www.finra.org/RulesRegulation/IssueCenter/p006293`). FINRA is one of the regulatory bodies that oversees 529 plans along with the Municipal Securities Rulemaking Board (`www.msrb.org/msrb1/mfs/default.asp`). Figure 3-6 shows the FINRA site.

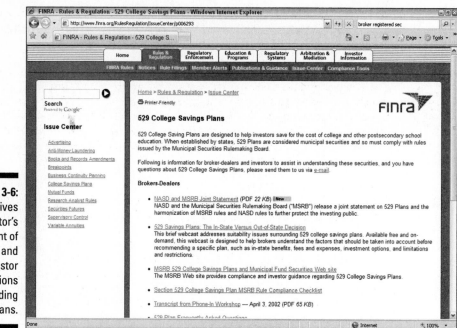

Figure 3-6:
FINRA gives
a regulator's
point of
view and
investor
suggestions
regarding
529 plans.

Understanding 529 fees

As great as 529 plans are, there are fees and charges to be familiar with. When evaluating plans, you want to see how the fee structures will affect your contributions and account balance to determine which are the best. The fees you need to know about include

- **Enrollment fees** are upfront fees some 529 plans charge to set up your account. Most 529s don't charge these, and you should try not to pay them if you can help it.

- **Account maintenance fees** are charged on an ongoing basis just to track and handle your account. These fees are a little more common than enrollment fees.

- **Program maintenance fees** are charged by almost all 529 plans to cover the costs of running the 529. These fees generally run between 0.1% of assets to 1.1%.

- **Fees charged by funds owned by the 529 plan** are also common. Say you invest in the Utah 529 plan, which invests in Vanguard funds. Those Vanguard funds themselves have fees that you must pay. These fees tend to be less than 1% of assets.

FINRA (http://apps.finra.org/investor_Information/Smart/ 529/Calc/529_Analyzer.asp) maintains a Web site that can help you weigh all the different fees and choose the plan best for you.

You might worry your child may have trouble getting financial aid if you stuff a ton of money into a 529 plan. Don't worry. It's not a big concern because the formula used for financial aid doesn't heavily factor in 529 plans. All that means, though, is that 529s do count a bit. If you want to keep the 529 completely out of the formula, you can legally name your child's grandparent as the owner of the account. That way the 529 won't count against your child's financial aid application at all.

Living in the 529's shadow: The Coverdell

529s get most of the attention, and for good reason: They're a great tax shelter for money needed to pay for education. But Coverdell accounts have one giant advantage over 529s: You can use money from a Coverdell to pay for kindergarten, primary school, and secondary school, in addition to college. 529s can be used only for college costs. Even so, Coverdell accounts have several drawbacks, including

- ✔ Contributions are limited to $2,000 a year.
- ✔ You can't earn too much income or you can't make the full contribution.
- ✔ Contributions aren't allowed after the beneficiary turns 18 years old.

You can find out about Coverdell accounts, and whether they fit your needs better than a 529, at www.savingforcollege.com.

Chapter 4

Connecting with an Online Broker

. . . .

. . . .

*I*n this chapter, I dive through the offers from all the major online brokerages to pinpoint which ones fit your needs. Why can't I save you the trouble and just tell you which broker is the best? It's not that easy. Choosing "the best" brokerage is like choosing the most beautiful painting in an art museum. Everyone has an opinion based on what is most important to him or her. When choosing a broker, if you're most interested in dirt-cheap commissions and don't care much for service, you have one set of brokers to pick from. If you're looking for access to physical branches staffed with live people who can help you choose stocks or navigate the Web site, you have an entirely different set of candidates.

You might think you don't need this chapter because you like a certain broker's ads on TV or have a cousin who swears by his online broker. But don't under-estimate the benefits that will accrue for you if you thoroughly research your broker options — face it, your broker is the gatekeeper to your money, and picking the right one will partly determine how successful you are as an investor.

Finding the Best Broker for You

People are constantly looking for the "best" of everything. Photography buffs pour through magazines and Web sites looking for the best camera, com-muters seek the best car, and parents search for the best stroller. Similarly, investors are on a constant quest for the best online broker. But just as differ-ent cameras, cars, and strollers fit different people's needs, the same is true with brokerages. As I explain in the previous three chapters, investors have different goals, taste for risk, and resources. And that's why one person's broker can be perfect for him or her, but completely wrong for you.

Not thoroughly researching your broker is a mistake. The fact that people often rush to pick an online broker might explain why many aren't happy with their choice: During 2006, 41% of online investors had a problem with their brokers, says rating service J.D. Power. That's up from 37% in 2005 and 27% in 2004.

Main factors to consider

Brokers differ from one another in nine main ways. If you're aware of these nine things and understand what you're looking for, you can quickly eliminate brokers that don't fit your needs. The factors to consider are

- ✔ **Commissions:** Perhaps the most important consideration for many investors is the price charged for executing trades, known as the *commission.* I discuss fees at length later in the chapter.

- ✔ **Availability of advice:** One way brokers separate themselves is whether or not they give you any help picking investments. On one end of the spectrum are the *full-service traditional brokers* that are all about giving you personalized attention. Not only will they pick stocks for you, but they'll also pour you coffee and serve you donuts when you visit them in their fancy offices. If you're not interested in paying for such niceties, the *self-service brokers* are happy to oblige. Self-service brokers give you the tools you need, and then you're pretty much on your own. A few brokers fit somewhere between full service and self service.

- ✔ **Access to an office:** Some brokers exist only in cyberspace. It's up to you to have your own computer and Internet connection. But others have branch offices in certain cities and allow customers to stop in, do some trading, and sometimes take classes and fraternize with other investors. You may think having access to a branch office will be important to you; after all, you're an online investor. Still, rating service J.D. Power found the 41% of online investors who have access to branch offices tend to be happier with their online brokers. Go figure.

- ✔ **Other banking services:** A brokerage account doesn't have to be a financial island. Some brokerage firms let you move money from your trading account into other types of accounts, such as high-yield savings or checking accounts. Some also provide ATM cards or credit cards.

- ✔ **Speed of execution:** When you click Buy or Sell on the Web site, it doesn't mean the trade is done. Your order snakes its way from your computer to other traders on Wall Street, where it is filled. Some brokerages have spent a great deal of effort giving you the fastest path to other traders. That's generally beneficial because it means you get a price that reflects the true value of the stock you're buying or selling. Depending on your strategy, you might not want your orders piling up in a bin, waiting to get filled. Speed of execution is tracked by broker-rating services, discussed later in this chapter, in the section "Finding Out What Reviewers Think."

✔ **Customer service:** Do you have a question about your account or about making a trade? When you do, you'll need to reach the broker and ask it. The levels of service vary wildly. Some brokers have customer service reps available at your beck and call either in offices or on the phone. Others let you e-mail a question and wait for an answer.

✔ **Site reliability:** No one wants to be in the position of finding a promising investment only to discover that his or her online brokerage is down for repair. Some brokerages have focused on limiting system downtime, which might be important to you if you trade many times a day. Again, this is something brokerage-rating services measure.

✔ **Access to advanced stock-buying tools:** Some brokerage sites are pretty bare-bones because they assume the investors already have the software and tools they need. Other brokerages, though, provide comprehensive tools that can track your tax liabilities, help you go prospecting for stocks, or monitor market movements or breaking news.

✔ **Ease of use:** Online brokers geared for people new to online investing or who plan to trade very infrequently are minimalist and have as few buttons as possible. They're the Zen of trading. But those aimed for hyperactive traders who click Buy and Sell so many times they have calluses on their fingers tend to give investors dozens of options allowing them to do some advanced stuff. You place a buy order when you want to own a stock and a sell order when you want to unload it.

"Gotchas" to watch out for

Brokerage firms often have confusing commission structures to fool you into thinking you'll pay less than you ultimately do. Make sure you check to see whether the firm charges extra for certain types of orders, such as limit orders (I discuss limit orders in Chapter 5) or mutual funds. Some brokers zing you with fees or inflate commissions if you don't keep a balance of a certain size. Some brokers also charge you for switching to another broker. Always check before signing up for covert fees. The "Avoiding Hidden Fees" section later in the chapter will help you spot things to watch out for.

Separating the Types of Brokerages

Choosing a brokerage firm might seem intimidating, but it's really no different than picking a restaurant. There are fast-food restaurants, where you have to walk up to the counter, place your order, put on your own ketchup and mustard, and find a place to sit. Then there are full-service restaurants where you're seated and pampered by dressed-up waiters who bring everything at your command and even clean the bread crumbs away when you're done.

The same goes for brokerages. Self-service brokers give you everything you need to get the job done and let you have at it. Because you're doing much of the work yourself, unless you ask for help, self-service brokers tend to have the lowest commissions. Self-service brokers are commonly grouped in three baskets: deep discounters, discounters, and premium discounters. Then there are the full-service traditional brokerages, which hold your hand through the whole process, down to suggesting investments, analyzing your portfolio, and offering estate-planning services. Remember that these are general brokerage types, and sometimes the lines blur a bit because some self-service brokers, especially the discounters and premium discounters, let you buy advice from them if you ask.

If you can't find a page on the broker's site that lists all its fees, commissions, and other charges in less than three mouse clicks from the home page, look elsewhere. I've found that brokers that bury fees do so for a reason.

How do you decide what you need? It's really a matter of deciding ahead of time how often you intend to trade, what types of investments you plan to buy, and how long you'll hold them. It's difficult to know this in advance, but there are ways to figure it out. For instance, did you perform the trading simulations I mention in Chapter 2? If so, how often did you trade? Next, familiarize yourself with the four types of online brokers: deep discount, discount, premium discount, and full-service traditional. Read the following descriptions and see what you can expect to get at each level. Decide whether the extra whistles and bells are worth the extra cost. To make things easy, the key stats are summarized in charts after each section. I include the standard commissions to give you the most realistic scenario for each broker.

Double-check brokers' fees before signing up — they change frequently. Also remember some brokers might charge lower commissions if you pay a monthly subscription fee, meet certain balance thresholds, or hold other types of accounts in addition to the brokerage account.

Deep discounters: Trading for $5 or less

These are the Wal-Marts and Home Depots of the brokerage world. When you sign up for a deep discounter, you're on your own. But if you know what you're doing, that's a good thing because you don't have to worry about getting pestered by a financial advisor trying to pitch stocks you have no interest in. And you'll get all the basics that you truly need, such as year-end tax statements, company information mailed to your door (if you choose paper delivery), basic access to stock quotes and research, and the ability to buy and sell stocks and other investments. But the real beauty of these brokers is their sweet, low price: Because they don't offer niceties like branches, they can have the lowest commissions, usually $5 a trade or less. Leaders include

✔ **BUYandHOLD** is pitching for investors looking for an all-you-can eat buffet of trading. For $14.99 a month, you can place as many trades as you like, or for $6.99 a month you can place two free trades. The trades aren't done immediately at those prices, but instead, in one of three trading sessions during the day. Real-time trades will cost you $15 apiece.

✔ **ShareBuilder** is trying to prove that deep discounters aren't just for active traders. You can buy stocks for $4. ShareBuilder caters to beginners, though. The site tries to keep things simple by allowing you to enter the dollar amount you want to spend buying stock, not the number of shares, as many brokerages do. There are some sacrifices, though. The discounted $4 orders aren't executed immediately, but rather, pooled and filled once a week. This is a deal killer if you're a *day trader* — someone trying to jump in and out of stocks several times a day to make a quick profit. If you want to buy a stock immediately, the commission jumps to $15.95. And be sure you're not planning on selling much because the commission for sell orders is also $15.95.

✔ **SogoInvest's** $3-a-trade offer fits snugly between Zecco, discussed below, and TradeKing. Its biggest advantage for some investors is that it offers discounted commissions in exchange for a subscription fee. That might make sense if you trade enough. For instance, if you pay $10 a month, you get a $1 break on trades, making the fee $2. Just make sure you trade at least 11 times a month, or you're wasting your money on this offer. Also, the brokerage nickels and dimes on a few things, such as charging $3 for paper statements. You must keep at least $2,500 in your account.

✔ **TradeKing** aims to give investors a few more niceties than other deep discounters, such as the ability to write checks against cash balances of $1,000, access to company news and research reports and a straightforward flat-fee commission of $4.95. It's geared largely for active investors who might exceed trading limits imposed by free offers from Zecco and want instant access to customer support on the phone. It's also targeted for heavy investors in options and offers a tool on its Web site, called the Profit + Loss Calculator, that graphs an options strategy and helps determine its success. There is no minimum account balance.

✔ **Zecco's** $0 commission is hard to beat if price is what matters most to you. Trades are free as long as you place fewer than ten trades a month and maintain an account balance of $2,500. Even if you use up all the freebies or have less than $2,500 in your account, trades are just $4.50. If you trade options (more advanced investments that I discuss in Chapter 5), you can save money here too with prices of $4.50 a trade and $0.50 per contract. And like brokerages that charge much higher commissions, Zecco will even move, or *sweep,* your uninvested cash into a high-yield checking account if you ask it to. It's not just for rich folks, either. In 2007, Zecco cut its minimum investment from $2,500 to $0.

As for the downsides, some extras (the ability to write checks against cash in your account, for example) cost you. And the free commissions do not apply to mutual funds, which cost $10 to buy and sell. You can view many of Zecco's offerings from its main page, as shown in Figure 4-1.

Table 4-1 sums up the main differences between the deep discounters.

Table 4-1	Deep Discounters		
Broker	**Web Address**	**Commission**	**Minimum to Open an Account**
BUYandHOLD	`www.buyand hold.com`	$6.99 a month fees (includes two free trades)	None
ShareBuilder	`www.share` `builder.com`	$4.00 to buy and $15.95 to sell	None
SogoInvest	`www.sogo invest.com`	$3.00	$2,500
TradeKing	`www.trade king.com`	$4.95	None
Zecco.com	`www.zecco. com`	$0, limit 10 a day and 40 a month	None

Figure 4-1: Zecco's Web site makes it very clear it's offering free trades.

Beginning investors always ask me how much money they need to start and where they can get started investing online. You can start with next to nothing with brokers that have no minimum deposit requirements, such as Share Builder and TradeKing. TradeKing will even reimburse you for fees your old broker might charge if you switch. If you're the kind of person who can't seem to save money until you've sent your cash off to a bank or brokerage, these are great places to start. Also, Zecco is hard to beat for beginners because all your money works for you rather than being siphoned off to pay commissions.

Discounters: Trading for $5.01 to $13

If the thought of being completely on your own makes you nervous but you're not willing to give up low-cost commissions, the discount brokers sit in the sweet spot for you. These brokers suit most investors ranging from beginners to the more advanced because they generally offer some advice (if you ask for it), and many have offices in most major cities. Even if you're not looking for advice, the discounters are still appealing because they load their Web sites with advanced tools to help do-it-yourself investors of all levels. Some provide access to advanced trading tools, real-time stock quotes, or special computer programs that let you enter trades just as fast as the traders on Wall Street. These extras come with slightly higher commissions, about $5.01 to $13, but still might be worthwhile based on your style of investing. Most discounters also offer price breaks if you're a hyperactive trader. The names to know here are

- ✔ **Charles Schwab** tries to be the Toyota Camry of brokers: not flashy or exotic in any one area but practical and pleasing to the bulk of investors. Its $12.95-per-trade commissions aren't the cheapest, but for that price, the broker adds services that might be valuable, whether you're looking for help or want to be left to your own devices. Do-it-yourselfers might like Schwab's Equity Ratings, a computerized system that evaluates stocks and assigns them letter-grade scores from A to F. It also provides access to Wall Street research and a full suite of banking services, including high interest rates paid on cash sitting in your account. But if you decide later you need more help, Schwab offers mutual funds designed to fit very specific needs in addition to making consultants available to give you personalized advice. If you're not going to use all these extra services, though, the higher commission might not be worth it. You can see the site in Figure 4-2.

- ✔ **E*Trade** has a reputation as being an innovator in the industry and seems to be always looking for ways to separate itself from others. E*Trade has long targeted active traders with computer software, such as MarketTrader, which lets you enter trades that will trigger automatically based on rules you set ahead of time. That way, you can buy and sell stocks even if you're not sitting in front of your computer. But E*Trade has things for beginners, too, such as access to stock research from six providers and the ability to shift cash to a checking or high-yield savings account. The commissions range from $6.99 to $12.99 based on your account balance and how often you trade.

The biggest strike against this broker is that it charges an account service fee of $40 per quarter, unless you meet one of several requirements, such as keeping at least $10,000 worth of cash and stocks in your brokerage account, trading at least once every three months, or having other accounts at E*Trade.

✔ **OptionsXpress,** as its name implies, is focused on investors who like to trade options. I explain options in more detail in the next chapter, but for now, suffice it to say that they're financial instruments that let investors either reduce risk or turbocharge their returns. Options trades can get mind-numbingly complicated, and some are best-known by exotic names like butterflies, straddles, and strangles. OptionsXpress helps traders place these complex trades with easy-to-follow Web screens and systems to help track the profit or loss.

This brokerage is clearly geared for active traders. Stock trades start at $9.95, but only if you make nine or more trades in a quarter. Otherwise, it jumps up to $14.95.

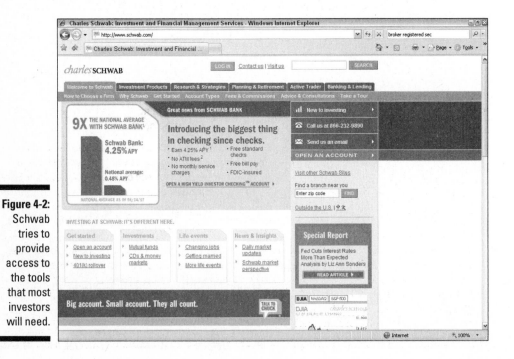

Figure 4-2: Schwab tries to provide access to the tools that most investors will need.

✔ **Scottrade** tries to undercut the big three (Schwab, E*Trade, and TD Ameritrade) on price but not service. Its $7 commissions are considerably less, but you still get access to branches, and it also has a separate service for active traders. It even throws in access to free software that shows real-time stock quotes, something you'd usually get only from more expensive brokers. Scottrade's Web site is relatively plain, which can be an advantage or a disadvantage depending on your goals.

✔ **TD Ameritrade's** earliest customers were active traders looking for low commissions. Some aspects of the brokerage's roots are still visible, especially the flat $9.99-per-trade commission no matter how many shares you buy or sell. (Other brokers, such as Schwab, charge extra if you buy more than 1,000 shares.) Investors who trade frequently during the day also like TD Ameritrade's bonus PC software trading tools, like the Streamer Suite and Strategy Desk, which let you see second-by-second stock price movements or test trading strategies and analyze how they would have done. The biggest knock against TD Ameritrade, though, has been that it has traditionally paid low rates of return on cash sitting in your account, especially if your balance is less than $10,000.

Are free trades really free?

When anything claims to be "free" in online investing, your defenses should go up instantly. Bank of America, Wells Fargo, and Zecco.com all promise free trades to investors. Be on guard and evaluate all the stipulations, though, before assuming these free offers are best for you. (See the section on hidden fees later in this chapter). The first thing to remember when looking at free brokerages: Don't overlook what interest rate will be paid on cash sitting in your account. Not paying attention to interest rates could wipe out any savings you think you're getting from free trades.

Here's what I mean. Say you trade five times a year and normally leave about $10,000 of uninvested cash in your account. If trades are free, it's true, your commission costs would be zero. But you still could be overpaying if you're not getting a high rate of return on your uninvested cash. In fact, you'd be $385 better off paying

$12.95 a trade if you get 4.5% interest on cash sitting in your account.

I've come up with a formula that takes the guess work out of "free" trades:

1. **Multiply the number of trades you do each year by the commission. Save this number.**

2. **Multiply the amount of uninvested cash you expect to keep in your account by the interest rate you will collect. Divide this number by 100 and save the result.**

3. **Subtract the answer from Step 2 from the answer from Step 1.**

This formula shows you how much the commissions are costing you: The lower the number, the better. If you're choosing between a couple of brokers, crunch this formula and choose the broker with the lowest (or negative) number.

✔ **thinkorswim** isn't as well known as some of the other brokers, but with $9.95 commissions, it's worth a look. The brokerage makes itself a little different by offering to pay for your Internet connection, up to $39.95 a month, if you trade 40 times or more a month. It also offers three free mutual fund transactions a month. It targets the options investors by letting them buy stock for a commission of just a nickel if it's part of an options strategy (more on this when I talk about options in the next chapter). Needless to say, this broker is for active stock and options traders only.

Check out Table 4-2 for an overview of what the different discounters have to offer.

Table 4-2		Discounters	
Broker	**Web Address**	**Commission**	**Minimum to Open an Account**
Charles Schwab	www.schwab.com	$12.95 for the first 1,000 shares of a stock	$1,000
E*Trade	www.etrade.com	$12.99 if you have less than $50,000 in your accounts	$1,000
OptionsXpress	www.options xpress.com	$14.95	None
Scottrade	www.scot trade.com	$7.00	$500
TD Ameritrade	www.td ameritrade. com	$9.99	None
thinkorswim	www.thinkor swim.com	$9.95	$500

Premium discounters: Trading for $13 or more

Premium online brokers aren't trying to win your business by tempting you with rock-bottom commissions. They're not the cheapest, and you can expect to pay $13 or more for stock trades. But they attempt to justify their higher cost with the prospect of a more rewarding trading experience, ranging from a better designed Web site to eliminating maddening system outages. If you're going to pay the extra dough, just make sure you're getting premium service or you're wasting your money. The premium online brokers include

✔ **Ameriprise** is all about the advice. If you're looking for access to professional help for all your financial questions, open an account with Ameriprise and expect to get calls from financial planners offering help. You can also get extras like American Express Gold Cards and discounts on home equity lines of credit. If these extras sound reassuring, it might be worth the relatively higher $19.95 commission. But if it sounds like opening the door to telemarketers, this isn't the brokerage for you, because trades are relatively pricey and there is a $20 quarterly account fee unless you meet requirements.

✔ **Bank of America** might not be what you think of as a stockbroker, but it's one of the large banks aggressively boosting its brokerage services. Traditionally, banks have targeted the well heeled with personal bankers who pick out investments like personal shoppers pick out ties for rich executives. But Bank of America has added self-service brokerage fees with reasonable commissions starting at $14. And you can get 30 free trades a month if you keep at least $25,000 with the bank in a deposit account. As your account grows, you have access to the wealth management services offered by the bank. Be careful, though, because the bank will hit you with a $50 fee twice a year if you don't have other accounts with it.

✔ **Fidelity** gets good marks for making its Web site (see Figure 4-3) easy to navigate and getting trades through quickly, according to a study by Keynote, an Internet rating service. But again, it's not going to win a price war at $19.95, unless you trade 120 times a year, when the commission falls to a more competitive $8.

✔ **Vanguard** gets bragging rights after winning top online brokerage rating from J.D. Power in 2006 — *despite* its higher-than-average $25 trading commissions for stocks. Vanguard's site came out on the top for speed, the quality of customer service, and availability to help customers navigate the site and make investment decisions. Remember, Vanguard's stock brokerage offering is separate from the account that lets you buy and sell Vanguard mutual funds, which I cover later. Just keep in mind that Vanguard isn't the cheapest option, and it also charges some investors a $30 yearly fee.

✔ **Wells Fargo** is another bank following the model of using brokerage services to tempt customers to put more money in its hands. Wells Fargo's self-service stock commissions start at $19.95. But if you keep at least $25,000 in your accounts, you can get up to 100 free trades a year. The Wells Fargo plan is a bit better than Bank of America's in that the $25,000 doesn't have to be sitting in a deposit account, like a savings account, but also includes the value of the stocks in your portfolio. But falling short of the $25,000 balance can be costly, resulting in a $25 a month fee.

Figure 4-3: Fidelity's site is designed to be easy to operate by both stock traders and mutual fund investors.

Table 4-3 shows you how the pricier outfits differ from one another.

Table 4-3	Premium Online Brokers		
Broker	**Web Address**	**Commission**	**Minimum to Open an Account**
Ameriprise	www.ameriprise.com	$19.95	$500
Bank of America	www.bankofamerica.com	$0 if requirements are met, otherwise $14.00	$25,000 for free trading offer, otherwise none.
Fidelity	www.fidelity.com	$19.95	$2,500
Vanguard	www.vanguard.com	$25.00	$3,000
Wells Fargo	www.wellsfargo.com	$0 if requirements are met, otherwise $19.95	$1,000

Full-service traditional

Because you're reading *Online Investing For Dummies,* chances are good that you're a do-it-yourself kind of investor or one looking for minimal handholding. But maybe after reading the preceding descriptions, you're looking for even more help. That's when you might consider a full-service traditional broker.

Full-service brokers pride themselves on being part of your team of "people" who you call on routinely for advice, like your real estate agent, housekeeper, and mechanic. The top full-service traditional brokerages are the Wall Street firms you've probably heard of, such as Merrill Lynch (shown in Figure 4-4), Wachovia, Smith Barney, Edward Jones, Morgan Stanley, and UBS. And by now, most can legitimately call themselves online brokerages because they have Web sites that let you view your accounts. Services that these firms provide include

✔ **Constant stock recommendations:** Most big Wall Street firms have famous strategists and analysts who think big thoughts and come up with stock tips. The brokers then spread those tips to you.

Figure 4-4: Merrill Lynch provides online tools to online investors as part of its Total Merrill service.

✔ **Access to initial public offerings:** When companies go public, they first sell their shares to large Wall Street investment banks. Those shares, especially if the initial public offering is expected to be popular, are often a sought-after commodity because they have the chance to pop in value the first day. If you're an active customer with these firms' brokerage divisions, you might get a shot at buying these shares at the IPO price. (You find more on IPOs in Bonus Chapter 2 on the Web site associated with this book.)

✔ **Availability of other financial services:** If you're a customer with a full-service traditional brokerage, you might get extra financial services, such as help with your taxes or estate planning.

But before you get too excited about the extra services that traditional full-service brokers may provide, there are also downsides to consider, such as

✔ **High cost:** Wall Street firms have to pay for those fancy offices you're enjoying somehow. The fees tend to be higher, and you might pay a lofty commission for each trade or pay a percentage of your assets.

✔ **Uneven treatment:** Remember that it's unlikely you'll end up being Merrill Lynch's best customer, so don't expect to get the real goods. For instance, when shares of the next truly promising IPO are doled out, if you're not a top customer or famous, you probably won't get shares anyway. (Fees and rates can vary, too, which is why I didn't even bother coming up with a table comparing fee structures for the full-service traditional brokerage crowd.)

✔ **Potential for conflicts:** Because brokers are often paid by commission, they might have an incentive to urge you to trade more frequently than you might like.

Be skeptical if a friend or family member recommends a broker to you. Many brokerage firms give customers checks for $50 or more or dozens of free trades if someone they refer signs up. I'm not telling you that you can't trust your friends. Just know that people recommending their broker might have a motive other than telling you which broker is best for you.

Avoiding Hidden Fees

The stock trade commission is likely the fee you'll pay the most often, so it's wise to pay the most attention to it. But don't think it's the only fee. Brokers often charge a host of other fees, which, depending on your circumstance, can add up fast. You should look for a page that discloses these fees, like the one shown in Figure 4-5. Here are some common hidden fees you should be aware of:

- ✔ **Maintenance fees** are monthly, quarterly, or annual fees some brokers charge you just to have an account with them. Don't pay maintenance fees. Period. If you're paying them, you're probably at the wrong broker for you. Most brokers exempt you from paying maintenance fees if you meet certain requirements. If you can't meet them, switch to a different broker.

- ✔ **Transfer fees** are charged when you want to part ways with your broker. Expect to get nicked with a $50 or higher fee, which brokers charge supposedly to cover their cost of shipping all your stock holdings and transferring cash to your new broker. The only way to avoid this charge is selling all the stocks in the old account and then writing a check to the new broker drawn on your old account. But this might not work. Keep in mind that you'll incur commissions for every stock you sell, and tax considerations might cost you well over $50. Refer to Chapter 3 for a refresher on capital gains taxes. Some brokers, including TradeKing, don't charge a transfer fee.

- ✔ **Certificate fees** are charged if you want your broker to mail you the actual physical stock certificates you own. It's usually a $50 or higher charge.

- ✔ **Check-writing fees** range dramatically from broker to broker. Some charge you an annual fee to have the privilege to write checks against your account. Others give you a certain number of free checks and charge only if you write rubber checks that bounce.

- ✔ **Special orders** are added fees if you trade more than a set number of shares. Most brokers also charge extra for placing so-called *limit* orders — trades in which you set the price you're willing to accept. Limit orders are covered in more detail in the next chapter.

- ✔ **Margin fees** are interest charges resulting from borrowing money from the broker to buy investments with. Buying on margin is only for the most risk-ready investors, and I explain why in Chapter 5.

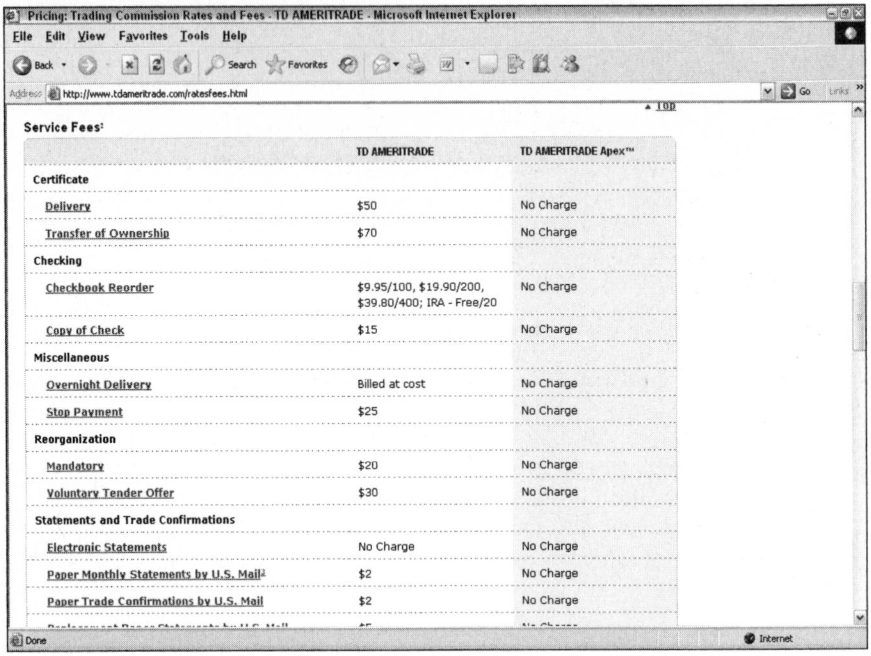

Figure 4-5:
TD
Ameritrade
discloses
all its
miscella-
neous fees
on a Service
Fees page.

Finding Out What Reviewers Think

It can be overwhelming to parse through all the brokers' commissions because there appear to be more moving parts than in a Swiss watch. Minimum requirements and fees vary, and it's hard to know how fast a broker's Web site will be until you actually sign up and try it. Luckily, some professional reviewers have kicked the tires for you. Different rating services and publications that evaluate brokers each year include

✔ **ConsumerSearch.com:** These folks review the reviews, compiling what other rating services, Web sites, and publications say about everything from toasters to cars to, yes, discount online brokers. The site, shown in Figure 4-6, also has a comprehensive section that ranks the reviews of online brokers and summarizes their findings.

✔ **J.D. Power:** Although it's best known for rating cars, J.D. Power also evaluates both online and full-service traditional brokers every year. It rates brokers based on several criteria, including cost, customer service, how quickly trades are completed, Web site design, data that's provided, and overall satisfaction. Read the latest reviews at `www.jdpower.com/finance/ratings/online_investment/index.asp`.

Figure 4-6:
Consumer-
Search is a
good place
to research
online
brokers
since it
compiles
reviewers'
reviews.

✔ **SmartMoney.com:** SmartMoney not only reviews the brokers but it also provides tools on its Web site to help you decide which is best for you. Its findings are available at www.smartmoney.com/brokers.

✔ **Barron's:** A Wall Street fixture since the 1920's, Barron's keeps an eye out for online brokers that serve sophisticated investors best. You'll have to subscribe, though, to read the stories online. An online subscription costs $79 a year. Barron's Online is available at http://online.barrons.com/public/main.

✔ **Gomez:** It certainly hasn't been around as long as Barron's, but Gomez *does* bring a bit of science to the process by measuring brokerages' speed and their likelihood to keep running even during hectic days on Wall Street. It rates them by constantly measuring the number of seconds you have to wait for the Web site to respond to commands, how often the system is down for maintenance, and generally how reliable it is. You can view the updated results at www.gomez.com/products/viewbenchmark.php?btype=3.

Is Your Money Safe? Checking Out Your Broker

When you're about to hand over your life's savings to a broker, especially one with no offices, you want to make sure it's a reputable outfit. Unlike bank savings accounts, brokerages have no government guarantee. But there are still some safeguards.

Your first layer of protection comes from the Securities Investor Protection Corporation (SIPC). The SIPC was formed by Congress in 1970 to protect investors by promising to help recover and return cash to investors if their brokerage closes due to bankruptcy. If cash or stock mysteriously goes missing in your account, the SIPC might help you recover the funds. The SIPC has helped in the recovery of $15.7 billion for 626,000 investors since it was formed. If a brokerage fails and doesn't have enough money to repay customers, the SIPC will cover up to $500,000 per customer. You should always check whether a broker is an SIPC member by logging on to www.sipc.org. In addition, some brokers carry additional insurance to protect customer assets beyond $500,000. All the brokers mentioned in this chapter are SIPC members.

Next, make sure your broker is has the appropriate approval from regulatory bodies to buy and sell investments. You wouldn't let someone who isn't a doctor remove your appendix, right? You should also make sure your broker is registered to be a broker. You can do this using the Financial Industry Regulatory Authority (FINRA) BrokerCheck at www.finra.org. You can access Broker Check by clicking the FINRA BrokerCheck link on the top left of the page. BrokerCheck tells you whether the brokerage is registered with this important regulatory body and whether the registration is current. Each state also keeps tabs on brokerages serving customers in their regions. State regulators are coordinated by the North American Securities Administrators Association, which provides access to the public at www.nasaa.org.

Lastly, you want to know whether the broker you're considering has been disciplined recently. You can access this info in the Rules & Regulation tab at the top of the screen at www.finra.org and also at a system maintained by the New York Stock Exchange's Disciplinary Action database at www.nyse.com/DiscAxn/discAxnIndex.html. And the ultimate watchdog on Wall Street is the U.S. Securities and Exchange Commission, which maintains records on brokers at www.sec.gov and provides tips to investors looking to check out their brokers at sec.gov/investor/brokers.htm.

Cutting the Cord: Wireless Trading

If the idea of checking up on your portfolio and placing trades while sipping margaritas by the pool appeals to you, get a life. Well, okay, sometimes you *do* need to check up on your account even when you're not sitting behind a computer at your desk. To help, plenty of brokers are providing wireless access to account information so customers can access their portfolios at any time, be it from a BlackBerry, Treo, or other wireless devices. You have several ways to accomplish this:

✔ **From a laptop:** Most laptops are equipped with wireless capabilities. If your laptop is set up for wireless access, using popular Wi-Fi technology, you can get online at thousands of locations that offer wireless internet connections, called Wi-Fi hotspots. Some hotspots available across the country are free to use, and you can find them by using this site: `www.wifi freespot.com`. You can also connect using Wi-Fi services that charge access fees, including those in Starbucks, Barnes and Noble, and Borders locations that are part of the T-Mobile network. If you try to go online in any of these places, you will be prompted by a sign-up screen to give a credit card number and pay. You can also sign up ahead of time at home or find out where this widespread network is available here: `http://hotspot.t-mobile.com`.

✔ **From a cell phone or PDA:** Several online brokers reformat their Web pages so they appear on the small screen of cell phones and BlackBerries. Just open the wireless browser in your Web-enabled phone, BlackBerry, Treo, or Windows Mobile device and type the address of the broker. Most brokers, such as E*Trade, will detect you're accessing them from a phone and reformat the pages automatically. Others, such as thinkorswim, require you to go to a special Web site from your phone. (In thinkorswim's case, that site is `www.tosmobile.com`.)

Pay Attention to Where Your Cash Is Parked: Money-Market Funds

You're an online investor, right? So why would you care about money that you haven't invested? It turns out that one of the biggest secrets in the brokerage world is what happens to cash sitting in your account that's not invested. Don't underestimate how important this is. If you have $10,000 in cash in your account waiting to be invested, that's worth $450 a year at a 4.5% rate.

A word about wireless security

Security is a serious concern when dealing with your money, and I discuss how to keep your money safe in more detail in Chapters 2 and 18. But when you access your stock data wirelessly, especially from a public area, you need to pay special attention to security. Here are three ways to do just that:

1. **Make sure your data are encrypted.**

   Most Internet browsers let you know whether the data is being encrypted, or scrambled. If you're using Microsoft's Internet Explorer 7, you can check by looking for the icon of a gold padlock. The gold padlock icon usually appears to the right of the address bar when a Web site asks for potentially sensitive information, such as account numbers, or when the Web site address begins with https (*s* stands for secure) rather than the usual http. When you see a gold padlock icon, that's a signal to you that the data is being scrambled to make it harder for the guy sitting next to you at Starbucks to read your information. Your computer and Windows then scramble your data. The data is then decrypted, or unscrambled, by the Web site.

   You can click the gold padlock icon to get more information about the security of the Web site. Be sure to select the check box that pops up to confirm that the site's certificate, or identification, lists the name of your brokerage firm. If the gold padlock doesn't appear, that might mean the site uses a different method of securing data, which is something you should ask your broker about.

   The padlock safeguard is a big help, but even scrambling isn't 100% secure. To be

extra safe, look for Internet Explorer's address bar to turn green, which validates the connection is safe, although not all online brokers support this yet.

2. **Use virtual private network (VPN) software.**

   A VPN is a technology used to protect your data from snoops over the Internet. Some Internet Service Providers (ISPs) offer this service to customers, or if you're using your work laptop, a VPN might be installed already. You might also consider subscribing to a VPN service, such as JiWire's Hotspot Helper, which costs $24.95 a year. You can read about it at www.jiwire.com/hotspot-helper.htm.

3. **Consider digital security keyfobs.**

   Some brokers, such as E*Trade, provide keyfobs that digitally display a new 6-digit code every minute. The idea here is that you'd then take that code and use it (in addition to your username and password) to log in to the Web site. The added wrinkle of an always changing code makes it extremely unlikely that a hacker could break into your accounts.

   Be sure to ask your broker what kind of protection it gives you if a hacker gets into your account. E*Trade, for instance, will cover the entire loss. Also, TD Ameritrade (www.tdameritrade.com/secrity/index.html) provides a very detailed guide to all the things you can do to protect your computer when investing online. You don't need to be a TD Ameritrade customer to use the site. The site also provides tips if you use browsers other than Internet Explorer.

Which is my way of telling you that, before choosing an online broker, you want to be absolutely sure what rate of interest your uninvested cash will get and how it's handled. Ideally, you want a *sweep* account. With a sweep account, idle cash is automatically scooped up and put into a money-market account. It's ideal because you don't have to do anything, and you're certain your money is working for you. Just make sure your money is being swept into a money market that pays an interest rate that is competitive with the going market rate. Schwab (www.schwab.com) and Ameriprise (www.ameriprise.com) are two brokers that offer this. Some brokers offer it only if you ask for it, such as Zecco (www.zecco.com). There's usually no additional charge.

Buying Stocks and Mutual Funds Without a Broker

Can you be an online investor without a broker? Sure. Some investors want to buy stocks but don't want to bother with a broker. There's nothing that says you need to have a broker to buy and sell stocks or mutual funds.

Stocks: Direct investments

Direct investments are where you buy the stock straight from the company. Many large companies, such as Coca-Cola, Procter & Gamble (P&G), and Walt Disney, will allow you to buy and sell your stock with them and avoid a broker. Many direct investment programs are connected with dividend re-investment plans (DRIPs), where the companies let you use dividend payments to buy, or reinvest, additional shares.

If you're interested in going with a direct investment program, you can visit the investor-relations section of the company's Web site to see whether it offers one. P&G, for instance, has an elaborate Shareholder Investment Program that lets you buy as little as $250 in stock and will even reinvest the dividends. You can read about this program (shown in Figure 4-7) at www.pg.com/investors/purchaseplan.jhtml.

The other way to find direct investment programs is through directory services, such as www.directinvesting.com. Just enter the symbol of the company you're interested in, and you can see if the company offers a direct investment plan.

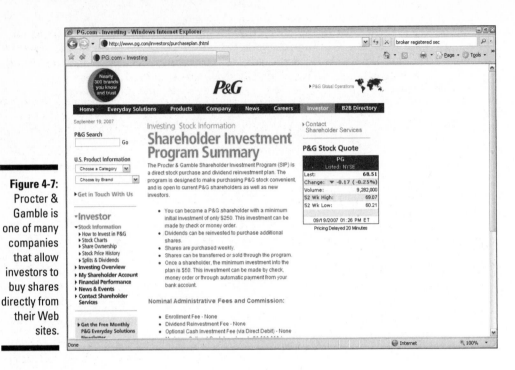

Figure 4-7:
Procter & Gamble is one of many companies that allow investors to buy shares directly from their Web sites.

Here are the upsides to direct investing:

- ✔ **Potential commission savings:** The fees charged by direct investment programs can be lower than what some brokers charge. P&G, for instance, charges $1 for investments plus a 2-cents-per-share charge if you buy the stock using money from your bank account and just $2.50 plus 2 cents per share if you mail a check.

- ✔ **Dividend reinvestments:** Dividends can be reinvested for free. If you're with a broker, you would often need to incur a commission to reinvest a dividend into the company stock.

As you might suspect, direct investing has some downsides:

- ✔ **Not free:** Some companies even charge commissions that exceed what deep discount brokerages charge. For instance, P&G charges $10 to sell stock. There are also loads of additional fees. P&G charges a 5% quarterly fee, up to $1.25, for plan maintenance.

- ✔ **Setup fees:** Although opening a brokerage account is usually free, some direct investment plans charge a fee to get started. P&G, for instance, charges $7.50.

✔ **Limited universe:** By using direct investment plans, you're narrowing your universe of possible investments to the hundreds of the largely older, blue-chip companies that offer these programs. That means you miss out on younger or small companies.

✔ **Administrative hassles:** With direct investment plans, you need to manage all your separate accounts, which could be a pain if you have ten or more investments. You also won't get access to any of the tax assistance or research the brokers provide.

Mutual funds: Straight from the mutual fund company

Mutual funds gather money from many investors and use the cash to invest in a basket of assets. When you buy a mutual fund, you're joining a pool with other investors that own assets, rather than owning the assets yourself. You can read more about mutual funds in Chapter 10.

Nearly all brokers let you buy and sell mutual funds in addition to stocks and other investments. And sometimes trading in mutual funds can make sense, especially if it's free. Most brokers have a list of "transaction-free" mutual funds you can buy and sell for no charge. Schwab, for instance, lets you buy and sell more than 2,000 mutual funds that are part of its OneSource program at no cost.

But, if you're not going to buy from the transaction-free lists, you're wasting your money buying mutual funds this way. Schwab, for instance, charges $49.95 to buy or sell a mutual fund not on its list. Don't let your broker's commission schedule determine which mutual funds you buy.

One of the best things about mutual funds is that you can buy them with no transaction fee if you deal directly with the mutual fund company. This can be a tremendous advantage, especially if you're making frequent and regular investments into a fund. After you figure out what fund you want to buy, log on to the mutual fund company's Web site, open an account, and buy it. You'll save yourself some cash.

When opening an account with a mutual fund company to buy a mutual fund, be sure to open a *mutual fund* account, not a brokerage account. Several mutual fund companies, including Vanguard and Fidelity, offer brokerage accounts in addition to mutual fund accounts, and the fees are completely different.

Opening and Setting Up Your Account

After you've made the decision about which broker to go with, the hard work is done. All you need to do to get started is open an account and get your cash to the broker. You can do this online or through the mail. If you're comfortable doing this online, which I imagine you are because you're reading *Investing Online For Dummies*, the online route is definitely the way to go because the cash can be transferred from your bank account and you can be up-and-running in a few hours or days. Signing up by mailing in a check and application, on the other hand, could take weeks.

 If you'd like to practice setting up an account before signing up for real, check out the demonstration at www.investingonline.org. But, to be honest, that's probably not really necessary because the process is very straightforward.

The checklist of what you need to know

The biggest button on most broker's Web site is the Open an Account or Start Now button, so you won't have trouble finding it. Typically, that's all you need to click to launch the area of the Web site that will set up your account. (If you want to sign up through the mail, click a link to download the necessary forms.)

Typically, you need to know three things to complete the application:

- ✔ **The kind of account you want to create:** This is usually a cash account or margin account. I cover margin accounts in more detail in Chapter 5.

- ✔ **The number of people associated with this account:** Is this just for you or for you and a spouse? This will determine whether you create an individual or joint account. You can review this in Chapter 3.

- ✔ **The tax status of the account:** Is this a taxable account or a tax-deferred account such as an IRA or a fund for college? You can review the differences in Chapter 3.

 Most brokers waive maintenance fees if you're opening an IRA account because they figure you'll keep your money with them for quite some time. Many also waive the minimum deposits. For these reasons, if you're just starting out with online investing, you might consider opening a retirement account first.

The checklist of what you need to have

You need these bits of info if you want to set up an account:

- ✔ **Identification,** such as a driver's license or government issued ID card.

- ✔ **A Social Security Number** is necessary, of course. If you're creating a joint account, you'll also need the Social Security Number of the person you're setting the account up with. This is used for tax reporting purposes.

- ✔ **The bank statement of the financial institution** from which you'll transfer money. This contains the account and banking routing numbers you'll need to instruct the broker to get your cash. Keep in mind some brokers won't let you open an account with electronically transferred money if you're depositing less than $500. In those cases, you need to mail a check.

- ✔ **The address of your employer** if you're an officer, director, or large shareholder of a publicly traded company.

See, that wasn't hard. And here's the best part: Now that you've entered all your information and funded your account, you're all set to start investing.

Chapter 5

Getting It Done: How to Enter and Execute Trades

In This Chapter

▶ Understanding the different ways your broker can hold your shares

▶ Differentiating between different types of orders

▶ Finding data about options

▶ Using put and call options

▶ Appreciating the upsides and downsides to trading after hours

▶ Knowing the potential reward and risks of buying on margin

*A*ll the theory in the world about online investing won't do you a bit of good if you can't seal the deal and *execute* your trades. Trade execution is the process of logging in to your online broker and buying or selling investments. You might be wondering what's so hard about buying a stock: Just log in to the online broker's Web site and click the Buy button. And in some cases, you're right. But sometimes you want to be a little more exacting. There are ways to tailor your buys and sells so your broker carries out the transaction precisely how you want it handled. For instance, you might want to buy a stock only if it falls below $25, or you might want your broker to automatically sell shares if they fall below a certain price.

In this chapter, I start at the beginning and go over all the ways you can hold your stock and how that decision affects how your trades are executed. Then, I'll go over the main ways to enter orders — ranging from market orders to limit orders — and talk about the advantages and costs of each. For the adventurous types, this chapter examines buying investments using borrowed money, called buying on margin, and also the risks and return of trading after hours. I then discuss the basics of options, which present unique ways for you to boost your returns or cut your losses, depending on how you use them.

Understanding How Stock Trades and Shares Are Handled

When you buy or sell a share of stock online, you click a few buttons and everything is done. In a few seconds, if even that long, you'll often have a confirmation sitting in the messages section of your online broker's Web site or in your e-mail box. The *confirmation* is a memo showing you what stock you bought or sold, the number of shares involved, and the price at which the trade was executed.

But perhaps unbeknownst to you, after you clicked the Buy button, your trade wiggled its way through countless computer networks where buyers and sellers competed for your order to buy stock until it was ultimately *executed* or filled. You might never need to know how this works, much like you might never need to know what's going on under the hood of your car, but it's an important part of investing online. So, the following sections describe a day in the life of a trade that's on its way from being an order on your computer screen to a done deal.

Ways you can hold your investments

The biggest factor influencing how your investments will actually make their way to Wall Street depends on how you hold your shares. The three main types are

- ✔ **Street name ownership** is the most common with most online brokers. It's so common that unless you tell your online broker to do otherwise, your broker will assume you want your shares owned in street name.

- ✔ **Holding paper stock certificates** is the old-school way of owning stocks. It's generally not a good idea for the reasons I outline in the section "Paper certificate ownership," a little later. If you insist on paper certificates, you just have to let your online broker know so it can mail them to you. Generally, despite the few advantages, this isn't a great idea.

- ✔ **Direct registration** is when the company issuing the stock holds your stock for you but lists you, not your broker, as the owner. If you buy stock through a direct stock purchase plan, as discussed in Chapter 4, this is a common form of ownership.

Street name ownership

If you're not sure how to hold your shares, street name ownership is probably your best bet. For most investors, the advantages of this form of ownership outweigh the few negatives.

Shares kept in street name are listed on the books of the company in your broker's name, not yours. The broker then lists you as the owner of the shares on its books. That might seem scary, I know, but you do have safeguards against broker fraud, as described in Chapter 4.

Street name ownership has several advantages:

- ✔ **Easy handling of dividends:** Dividends paid by companies you own stock in are sent directly to your online broker, which then deposits them to your account. For online investors used to doing almost everything on a Web site, this is a huge advantage and saves you from having to deposit dividend checks in your bank's ATM or mailing them to your broker.

- ✔ **Central source of company documents:** If you're like most online investors, you'll probably own shares of several companies. When you own the stock in street name, all the paper correspondence sent out by the companies first goes to your broker. The broker then forwards it to you. This situation has a giant advantage, especially if you move often: You can just let your broker know where you live and not worry about missing important documents.

  Your broker can also help make sure you get everything that's due to you. Periodically, a company you invested in years ago is sued or forced by regulators to make payments to past investors. If you own the stock in street name, you can be certain to receive these old payments, even if you're living somewhere else, because your broker will forward the checks.

- ✔ **Security:** It's up to the brokerage to safeguard your stock. And that's a good thing because getting paper stock certificates replaced, if you lose them, can be a hassle.

- ✔ **Easy to sell:** If your online broker has your shares on hand, you can sell them anytime you want without having to mail in a paper certificate first. That saves you time and postage, not to mention the worry about sending an important document through the mail.

Sounds great, right? But, street name ownership does come with a few disadvantages:

- ✔ **Potential delays in dividend payments:** Some brokers are quicker about crediting dividends to your account than others. You might have to wait a few days to actually receive a dividend after it was paid by the company.

- ✔ **Hassle if your broker fails:** Getting stock certificates transferred back to your name might be harder if your brokerage become insolvent.

Paper certificate ownership

Maybe the cons of street ownership are enough to make you consider Route #2 — the paper certificate option. I can tell you that the advantages to paper certificate ownership include the following:

✓ **Cutting out the middleman:** Company materials come straight to you. This can speed up the time it takes to get some documents.

✓ **Using certificates as loan collateral:** When you have the actual certificates, you might have a little easier time using the stock value to secure a loan.

✓ **Having actual certificates makes it easier to give them as gifts or for display:** A paper certificate can be framed and given to young investors as a present. There's something nice about having an item to wrap.

✓ **Being in control:** With the certificates in your possession, you know where they are and can decide who can have them.

In all honesty, though, I have to tell you that the main disadvantages to paper certificate ownership far outweigh the advantages. The disadvantages of paper certificate ownership include the following:

✓ **Difficulty in selling:** You might not be able to sell the stock as quickly as you'd like. Paper certificates must be mailed to your broker or to the company or a firm it hires to handle such matters before the stock can be sold.

✓ **Burden of keeping your contact information current with the company:** It's up to you to make sure the company has your current address.

✓ **Responsibility for safekeeping the certificates:** It's up to you to keep the paper certificates safe. You'll probably have to spend money to get a safe deposit box or at least lock the paper stock certificates up in your home somewhere. And when you send them through the mail, you will need to insure them in case they get lost. Some financial institutions recommend insuring mailed certificates for 2% of the market value, for reasons I explain later in this chapter.

If you decide to hold paper certificates rather than listing them in street name, don't lose them. Getting lost paper certificates replaced can be a hassle and somewhat costly. If the unfortunate event does occur, though, here's what to do to try to make it right:

1. **Call or e-mail your broker or the company's transfer agent and explain what happened.**

   Transfer agents are firms that companies hire to handle the processing of shares. The transfer agent will likely ask you to say how you lost the shares in a written report.

2. **Buy an indemnity bond with the help of your transfer agent.**

   An indemnity bond protects the company that issued the lost stock in case someone tries to cash it in later. Indemnity bonds usually cost up to 2% of the market value of the stock you lost.

For more details on what to do if you lose a stock certificate, the Securities and Exchange Commission maintains advice at www.sec.gov/answers/lostcert.htm.

Direct registration

If all my talk about the hassles of losing paper certificates makes you long for another way of owning stock, you can always go for direct registration. You get several advantages from having direct registration, including

✔ Company correspondence coming straight to you

✔ Being able to sell shares without mailing certificates to your broker

✔ Not having to worry about keeping the certificates safe

Direct registration has two main downsides:

✔ **Inability to sell shares immediately:** Selling shares you hold in direct registration almost always takes longer than you might think. You may instruct the company to sell the shares, but your request is generally put into a pool and executed at set times in the future, such as later in the day, week, or month. You may also sell your shares by instructing the company's transfer agent to electronically send the stock to your online broker. (A transfer agent is a firm hired by a company to track its shareholders and record transactions.) The transfer process can take a few days, so the price might change by the time you're able to sell the stock.

✔ **Pool of stock choices is somewhat reduced:** Most companies offer direct registration, but not all. Many of the stocks you want to buy might not offer direct registration.

A second in the life of a trade

When you buy or sell a stock on your online broker's site, your order is usually filled in seconds. But, before that transaction is completed, in milliseconds your order snakes its way through an advanced security trading system that has taken decades to build. Just a few years ago, it could take about 12 seconds for a trade to go from your desk to the floor of the New York Stock Exchange and back. But now that most of the steps have been computerized, it takes about a second. Using NASDAQ as an example, here's what happens in the one second it takes to execute an online trade:

1. You enter your order with your online broker.

2. The order is placed in a database.

3. The database checks all the different markets that trade the stock and looks for the best price. The different markets might include the NASDAQ and New York Stock Exchange in addition to electronic communications networks (ECNs). ECNs are computerized networks that connect buyers and sellers of stocks.

4. The market that successfully matched the buyer and seller sends a confirmation to both parties' brokers.

Buying paper stock certificates online

Due to the disadvantages listed elsewhere in this chapter, it doesn't make much sense to hold paper stock certificates for the shares in your portfolio. But some investors still like to buy paper stock certificates for gifts. Some folks collect old stock certificates much like you'd collect stamps or coins. There's even a word for the art of collecting stock certificates: *scripophily*. If this interests you, check out these online services that let you buy paper stock certificates:

✔ **OneShare.com** (www.oneshare.com) and **Frame A Stock** (www.frameastock.com) are single-share sales sites that understand the lost art and beauty of many stock certificates. Both let you buy a share of stock in companies which have certificates that are popular with individual investors. Both of these services even frame the certificates for you. The sites make it easy to find the perfect stock for the need. You can sort through the available certificates based on the occasion, recipient, or interest. For men, OneShare recommends Harley Davidson and Boston Beer, and for women it suggests Tiffany and Coach. Some certificates are also popular due to the artwork on them, with Disney being the best example.

Just be forewarned that you'll pay much more to acquire stock this way than through an online broker. In addition to the share price and framing fees, there's also a $39 transfer fee to acquire the stock. A $38 a share stock might easily cost nearly $130 by the time all the fees are added.

✔ **eBay** (www.ebay.com), not surprisingly, is a source for paper certificates. But because eBay isn't licensed to sell securities like stocks, it has to be careful about what kinds of certificates its members sell; otherwise, eBay risks running afoul of securities law. Only two types of stock certificates may be sold on eBay. The first type concerns old or collectible certificates of defunct companies, such as old railroads or Internet companies. The other type that may be sold on eBay are single-share stock certificates packaged as gifts and marked as being nontransferable. eBay requires that these certificates sell for at least twice the current market value of the stock as evidence they're priced based on their keepsake value.

✔ Certificate collection sites such as **Scripophily.net** (www.scripophily.net) provide prices on some hard-to-find certificates. Even if you're not a collector, it's interesting to see what some of the certificates go for when they're popular with collectors. Some Standard Oil stock certificates, personally signed by John D. Rockefeller, for instance, sell for $3,000 or more. Pixar stock certificates, decorated with characters from Toy Story like Buzz Lightyear, were a hot commodity when the company was bought by Disney. Old shares of Playboy were popular for their, um, artwork, because the company's certificates used to display some, let's say, assets. The old certificates have become even more sought after since Playboy's new certificates were changed to be more PG. The old shares sell for $300 or more, which is greater than the share price of the company. And some infamous companies, like Enron, also have collectible value even though the companies themselves have largely vanished, as shown in the following figure.

continued

5. The order and the price are reported to the regulatory bodies that over-see trading activity so they can be displayed to all investors.

6. NASDAQ stores a record of the trade in case regulators want to study past transactions.

7. NASDAQ sends a contract to the broker who sold the shares and the broker who bought them.

After all that is completed, the brokers have three days, called *T+3,* to actually exchange the cash and shares. Then the money or shares are officially in your account.

ECNs: You have been assimilated

Back in the heyday of day trading in the late 1990s, many investors believed they could go toe-to-toe with the biggest trading houses in the world. That feeling stems from the creation of trading networks called ECNs and their approval by regulators in 1997. ECNs promised to level the trading field by letting individual investors trade directly with each other, rather than going through *market makers* on the NYSE or specialists on the NASDAQ. Market makers and specialists are middlemen of sorts. They're traders that get special privileges to information in exchange for making sure trading is going smoothly.

Several handfuls of ECNs cropped up to cut out the middlemen. The biggest were Instinet, Brut, and Archipelago. Day traders would sign up for these ECNs and trade with each other. But because ECNs were so efficient and fast at matching buyers and sellers, they also caught on with big institutional investors needing to move massive blocks of stock. ECNs got so popular that the exchanges began losing some trading volume. If you can't beat them, buy them. The NYSE's parent company, NYSE Euronext, bought Archipelago (now called NYSE ARCA) in 2005. NASDAQ bought Brut in September 2004 and in 2005 acquired Inet, which was formed from the combination of Instinet with another ECN, called Island.

What does all this mean for online investors today? Now the distinction between the ECNs and the NYSE and NASDAQ is less, err, distinctive. They're so closely tied together that if you enter a stock order online, your broker is required to check the prices on ECNs to see whether that's where it can get the best price. If you can get a better price through an ECN rather than through an exchange, that's where your trade will occur. Some brokers let you choose where you want your order filled through something called *direct routing*. If your account is set up for direct routing, you can instruct the broker to execute the exchange or ECN of your choice, which is usually NYSE ARCA or Inet.

Direct routing is a bad idea for most online investors. Online brokers have sophisticated computers that shop your order to all the top markets automatically. They're required by regulators to get you the best available price. If you direct-route your order, you lose this advantage and most likely will wind up paying more. If there's an advantage to direct routing, I don't know what it is.

Getting It Done: Executing Your Trades

If you're buying something from a regular store, say a new computer, you can either buy it or not. End of discussion. But in more casual marketplaces, such as flea markets or garage sales, where prices are fluid and changing, there's a strategy to buying and selling things. It might surprise you that buying stock is more like a flea market than shopping at your local Wal-Mart, where prices are set. Because investments are priced in real time through active bidding between buyers and sellers, there are techniques to buying and selling.

Types of orders

When dealing with investments, you have five main ways to buy or sell them online:

- ✓ **Market orders** are the most common types of orders and the ones you will probably use the most. This is where you tell your broker to sell your shares at the best price someone is willing to pay right now or buy shares at the price currently being offered. Because these orders are executed almost immediately and are straightforward, they typically have the lowest commissions. (In Chapter 4, where I discuss different online brokers' commissions, I concentrate on market orders because they're the most common.)

- ✓ **Limit orders** let you be pickier about the price you're willing to take for a stock you're selling or the price you're willing to pay if you're buying. With a limit order, you tell your online broker the price you're willing to take if you're selling stocks and the price you're willing to pay if you're buying. The order will execute only if your price, or something better, is reached.

  For example, imagine you own 100 shares of ABC, which are trading for $50 a share. The stock has been on a tear, but you're convinced it will fall dramatically soon, by your estimate to $30. You could just sell the stock outright with a market order, but you don't want to because you're a bit greedy and don't want to miss out on any gains in case you're wrong. A limit order could be the answer. Here, you'd instruct your broker to sell the stock if it fell to $45 a share. If you're right, and the stock falls to $45 a share, your online broker will sell as many shares as possible at that price. You can also set a time limit on limit orders and tell your broker to let them expire after a few days or weeks.

  The precision of limit orders can be a shortcoming, too. Limit orders are filled only at the price you set. If the stock falls further than the price you set, the broker might be able to sell only some of the shares, or none, at the price you set. If that happens, you're stuck with the stock. In the preceding example, if ABC opened for trading and plunged straight to $25, never stopping at $45, you will still be holding the stock. This is a serious limitation that can give you a false sense of security.

- ✓ **Stop market orders** are similar to limit orders in that they let you set a price you want to buy or sell shares at. They have a very important difference, though, that addresses some of the shortcomings of limit orders. When a stock hits the price you designed, the order converts into a market order and executes immediately.

Imagine again that you have 100 shares of ABC, which are trading for $50 a share. But this time, you enter a stop market order for $45. And again, you wake up to find the stock plunged instantly to $25. This time, though, all your stock would have been sold. But, maybe not at $45. Your online broker will sell the shares at whatever the price was the moment your order converted to a market order, which in this case could have been $25.

✔ **Stop limit orders** are like stop market orders, but they're designed to cure the danger your shares will be blindly unloaded when a stock is moving. Stop limit orders are very customizable. First, you can set the *activation price.* When the activation price is hit, the order turns into a limit order with the limit price you've set.

Okay, ABC is trading for $50 a share when you enter a stop limit order with an activation price of $45 and a limit price of $35. It would work like this: Again, you wake up to find the stock plunged instantly to $25. This time, your broker would turn your order into a limit order after it fell below $45. When the stock fell to $35, the broker would try to fill orders at that price if possible. Most likely, though, you'd still be stuck with shares. But unlike with the stop market order, you would not dump the shares when they fell as low as $25.

✔ **Trailing stops** are a way to keep up with the times. With regular limit orders, they're either executed or they expire. Trailing stop orders get around this problem by letting you tell your broker to sell a stock if it falls by a certain number of points or a percentage.

If you're buying and selling individual stocks, trailing stops can be a good idea. Even before you buy a stock, you should have an idea of how far you'll let it fall before you cut your losses. Some investment professionals suggest never letting a stock fall more than 10% below the price you paid. If this sounds like a good idea to you, a trailing stop could work for you.

Costs of different orders

Market orders are the most straightforward orders, so it shouldn't be that surprising that they're also usually the least expensive.

Some brokers charge extra for limit orders, so check the commission fees before you start trading. And some brokers, such as Buyandhold.com, don't offer limit orders.

Tailoring your trades even more

When you enter an order for a stock, you have a few other levers you can pull, including

- **Designating lots:** Many people buy the same stock many times. Each time you buy, that bundle of stock is called a lot. When you sell, your broker will assume you'd like to sell the lot that you've held for the longest time for recordkeeping purposes. This method, called *first in, first out,* or FIFO, is the standard and what the Internal Revenue Service expects. If, for tax reasons, you'd like to sell a specific lot that's not the oldest, you can tell your broker which lot you'd like to sell.

- **Setting time frames:** You can enter an order for a stock that is active only the day you place the trade. If it's not filled — perhaps a limit order for the price you ask for isn't reached — the order expires. That is called *day only.* You can also enter orders and let them stay active until you cancel them. That is called *good till canceled.* Good-till-canceled orders are generally active for up to six months after you enter the order, but that limit varies for each broker.

- **Placing rules:** When you issue an "all or none" restriction on your trade, your broker must completely fill the order or not fill it at all. Say you want to sell 100 shares of stock at a limit price of $45, but the broker can find buyers only for 10 shares at that price. If you stipulated all or none, none of your 100 shares will be sold.

Going off the Beaten Path with Different Trading Techniques

If all you could do was buy and sell investments, traders would get awfully bored. Investors looking for a little more excitement can dabble with some more advanced ways to enter online trades that go beyond everything I have discussed in this chapter so far. The most common ways to get a little fancier with your trades are

- **Selling stock short:** A way to make money even if a stock declines in value.

- **Buying stock on margin:** This method lets you bet big on a stock you think will go up. You borrow money to buy stock, which will magnify your returns if it rises.

- **Trading after hours:** Perfect for night-owl investors who aren't satisfied with the 9:30 a.m. to 4 p.m. EST regular trading hours of the NYSE and NASDAQ.

Cashing in when stocks fall: Selling stock short

Most investors are pretty optimistic folks. When they go to a restaurant, see long lines, and enjoy the food, they rush home to buy stock in the company that owns the restaurant. These types of investors, who hope to profit from a company's good times and rising profits, are called *longs.*

But there's a whole other class of investors, called *shorts,* who do just the opposite. They search the Internet for news stories about diners getting food poisoning at a restaurant, for instance, and look for ways to cash in on the stock falling.

Investors looking to *short a stock* do it through four steps:

1. They borrow the stock they want to bet against.

   Short sellers contact their brokers to find shares of the stock they think will go down and they request to borrow the shares. The broker then locates another investor who owns the shares and borrows them with a promise to return the shares at a prearranged later date. The shares are then given to the short seller.

2. They immediately sell the shares they've borrowed.

   The short sellers then pocket the cash from the sale.

3. They wait for the stock to fall and then buy the shares back at the new, lower price.

4. They return the shares to the brokerage they borrowed them from and pocket the difference.

Here's an example: Shares of ABC are trading for $40 a share, which you think is way too high. You contact your broker, who finds 100 shares from another investor and lets you borrow them. You sell the shares and pocket $4,000. Two weeks later, the company reports its CEO has been stealing money and the stock falls to $25 a share. You buy 100 shares of ABC for $2,500, give the shares back to the brokerage you borrowed them from and pocket a $1,500 profit.

When you short a stock, there are some extra costs to be aware of. Most brokerages, for instance, charge fees or interest to borrow the stock. Also, if the company pays a dividend between the time you borrowed the stock and when you returned it, you must pay the dividend out of your pocket. You're responsible for the dividend payment, even if you already sold the stock and didn't receive it.

Tracking the short sellers

You might be interested to find out how many investors are shorting a stock you own, a statistic known as *short interest*. Some investors even incorporate tracking short interest in their strategies by seeking stocks that are heavily shorted, on the theory if the shorts are wrong the stock might surge higher in a *short squeeze*. A short squeeze is what happens when the short sellers get nervous that a stock they're betting against will rise and they rush out and buy the stock back so they can return it to the brokers they borrow from.

Exchanges release short interest data on stocks on the third Monday of each month. You can easily get the data online. A helpful source I've found is NASDAQ.com, shown in Figure 5-1. You can look up the level of short interest on almost every stock, including those that trade on other exchanges such as the New York Stock Exchange. Here how:

1. **Point your browser to www.nasdaq.com.**

2. **Enter the stock's symbol in one of the blank spaces beneath the Get Up to 10 Quotes heading. Click the silver Info Quotes button underneath the blanks.**

Figure 5-1: NASDAQ.com lets you track how many investors are betting against the company by providing data on short interest.

3. Choose Short Interest from the leftmost drop-down menu.

You see a detailed list showing you the number of shares being shorted, as shown in Figure 5-1. That number in itself doesn't tell you much because different companies have different numbers of shares trading, or *shares outstanding*. So, to put the level of short interest in perspective, you also see the *average daily share volume* — the number of shares that usually trade hands in a given day. Lastly, you see *days to cover,* which is the number of days it would take, on average, for the number of shares that are being shorted to trade. Days to cover is calculated by dividing the number of shares shorted by the average daily share volume. The bottom line? The higher the days to cover, the greater the amount of real short interest in the stock.

Living on borrowed time: Buying stock on margin

The standard brokerage account is called a *cash account.* That's where you deposit cold hard cash with the broker and use that pooled money to buy stocks. But when you set up your account, as described in Chapter 4, you can also request a *margin account.* This is an account type that lets you borrow money you can use to buy stocks.

Buying stock on margin isn't for the faint of heart. Remember, if you borrow money, you must not only pay interest on that cash but also pay back the money you borrowed even if the stock goes down. Buying on margin is generally a good idea *only* if you're a highly risk-tolerant investor. You can determine your taste for risk by reading Chapter 1.

As is the case anytime you borrow to invest, buying stock on margin can boost your profit when you're right and sting badly when you're wrong. When you buy a stock that goes up, using margin, you can boost your returns. But if you bet wrong and buy one that goes down, margin magnifies your loss. To understand why, take a look at the following example:

Imagine buying 100 shares of a stock that goes from $15 a share to $32 a share. Your investment of $1,500 turns into $3,200. Assuming you paid a $5 commission to buy and sell the stock, your rate of return, as explained in Chapter 1, is 112.3%, and your profit is $1,690.

It's calculated like this:

1. **Subtract the commission of $5 from the sale proceeds of $3,200. Write this down.**

2. **Add the commission of $5 to the amount paid of $1,500. Write this down.**

3. **Subtract the answer in Step 2 from the answer in Step 1 and divide that answer by the answer in Step 2. Multiply by 100.**

That's not bad. But if you bought on margin, your return would be even greater. Here's what I mean. Say your broker has a 60% *margin requirement,* meaning you must put up 60 cents of every $1 you invest. In this case, you'd have to put up $900 of your own cash because that's 60% of the $1,500 purchase price. You then borrow the remaining $600 at 10% interest. Your gain, thanks to margin, goes from 112.3% to 180%.

Here's how your rate of return when using margin is calculated, using the facts above as an example:

1. **Subtract the commission of $5 from the sale proceeds of $3,200.**

   Write this down, $3,195.

2. **Add the commission of $5 to the amount paid of $1,500.**

   Write this down, $1,505.

3. **Multiply the amount you borrowed, $600, by 0.10 to calculate the interest you owe.**

   You use 0.1 because that is 10% converted from percentage form. You get $60.

4. **Subtract the answer from Step 2 from the answer from Step 1.**

   Subtract that difference by the answer from step 3. You get $1,630.

5. **Divide the answer from Step 4 by $905, which is the amount of your own money you put up plus the commission you paid to buy the stock.**

   Multiply by 100. The answer is 180.1%

If the preceding is too much math for you, do it online. Most online brokers' sites calculate your margin requirements. If you're interested in buying on margin, be sure to make sure the broker has margin-tracking capabilities. Figure 5-2 shows Fidelity's Margin Calculator.

The call you don't want to get: The margin call

Most online brokers require investors to maintain a certain percentage of ownership of stocks relative to what has been borrowed. This is called the *maintenance margin,* and it's typically 30% at most firms. If a stock rises, this isn't a problem because the value of the loan becomes a smaller slice of the position. But if the stock falls in value, the shareholder's stake shrinks. If it falls below 30%, the broker requires the investor to put up more cash, or the shares will be sold.

Figure 5-2:
Fidelity's
Margin
Calculator
helps you
measure
how much
stock you
can buy
with
borrowed
money and
estimate the
costs.

Imagine that, when you bought the $15-a-share stock above, you borrowed 40% or $6 a share, meaning your ownership stake is $9 a share or 60%. But say the stock falls to $7 a share. Because you borrowed $6 a share, you own only $1 of the $7 a share price. That means you own just 14% of the stock, violating the 30% margin requirement.

If you still have questions about investing on margin, Citi provides an easy to follow description of margin at

```
http://web.da-us.citibank.com/cgi-bin/citifi/scripts/
infrastructure/article.jsp?BV_UseBVCookie=yes&BS_Id=
LBP-12&M=S
```

Some online brokers will crunch down the numbers for you automatically and let you know when margin calls will kick in. And you can be certain online brokers won't waste any time contacting you for a margin call. But if the preceding math seems too complicated to do yourself, you might want to steer clear of using margin.

The nightshift: Trading in the extended hours

One of the great things about stocks and bonds is they're easy to sell. Unlike real estate, which usually requires hiring a realtor who sprinkles air freshener through the house and invites prospective buyers to an open house, you can sell stocks pretty much instantly. The main stock exchanges are open every business day, for *regular trading hours,* from 9:30 a.m. to 4 p.m.

But thanks to ECNs, discussed above, you can trade before 9:30 a.m. in what's called *premarket trading* and after 4 p.m. in *after-hours trading.* Here are several reasons why some investors pay attention to after-hours trading:

- ✔ **A chance to react to late-breaking news:** Some active traders believe they can use after-hours trading as a way to profit from news companies that might report *after the close.* It's common for companies to release important information, either good or bad, after 4 p.m. to give investors time to digest. But investors don't have to wait and can place trades after hours.

- ✔ **An indication of how late-breaking news might affect the stock when regular trading hours begin:** You don't have to be a high-profile online trader to get access to after-hours quotes. Most online financial Web sites discussed in Chapter 2, including Yahoo! Finance (http://finance.yahoo.com) and MSN Money (http://moneycentral.msn.com/investor/home.asp), let you see how stocks and indexes are trading in the after hours. Both of those sites — as well as Google Finance (http://finance.google.com) — also show you the after-hours *volume,* which is the number of shares trading hands. Volume is very important when looking at after-hours trading because the more shares trading hands, the more reliable the price is.

Trading after hours isn't a good idea for most online investors for several reasons:

- ✔ **Lower participation:** Fewer buyers and sellers participate in after-hours trading, so there's a chance you'll get a lower price for a stock you're selling or pay more for a stock you're buying than had you waited for regular trading to begin. After-hours trading attracts very little interest, as Table 5-1 shows. Only about 1% of the trades placed each day on the NYSE are conducted after hours.

- ✔ **Limit orders are required:** Most online brokers accept after-hours trades only if they're entered as limit orders. Limit orders present their own shortcomings, as explained in the "Types of orders" section, earlier in the chapter.

- ✔ **Unpredictable pricing:** Sometimes stock prices set in the after hours aren't necessarily harbingers for how things will open the next day. They can be a poor indicator of the next day's trading if the after-hours volume is low.

Table 5-1	The After-Hours Party Few Showed Up For	
Year	*Volume (Millions)*	*Percentage of Daily Trades*
2003	8.0	0.6%
2004	14.0	1.0%
2005	13.8	0.9%
2006	17.0	0.9%
2007	20.2	1.0%

Source: NYSE Group

Knowing Your Options: Basic Ways to Best Use Options

If you've ever put down a deposit so someone would hold something for you, you know what an option is. For instance, you might pay a landlord a $100 nonrefundable deposit to hold an apartment so that it'll be available for you if you decide to rent it. If you don't rent the apartment, you're out the $100.

Options are the financial version of that idea. If you own an option, you have the right, but not the obligation, to buy or sell an investment, including shares of stock by a certain preset time in the future. Options can be extremely powerful in the right hands, and they can either help you boost your returns or reduce your risk depending on how you use them.

I often describe options as the financial version of dynamite. If used prudently and safely, options can remove perils in the way of your financial goals. But if abused, misunderstood, or used recklessly, options can blow your financial plan to smithereens.

When you own an option, you have the power to make someone follow through on a trade for an *underlying asset,* such as a stock, no matter what happens to the price. Options expire on the third Friday of every month.

Need an example? Say ABC stock is currently trading for $30 a share, and you own an option to buy it for $20 a share on its *expiration date* in one month. That option is worth $10 a share, the difference between $30 and $20, which is its *intrinsic value.* If you own an option like this that lets you buy a stock for less than its current value, it's *in the money.* But if the price you can buy the stock at, known as the *exercise price,* is higher than the current price, the option is *out of the money.*

The different types of options

Option strategies can get pretty complex. If you're serious about trading them, you can find out all the gory details in *Future & Options For Dummies*, by Joe Duarte (Wiley Publishing). But I'm perfectly willing to give you the basics.

Two types of options exist:

- ✔ **Calls** give their owners the right to buy a stock at a certain price (called the *exercise* or *strike price*) at a certain time (called the expiration date) in the future. One call contract gives you the right to buy 100 shares of the underlying stock.

- ✔ **Puts** give their owners the right to sell a stock at a certain price at a certain time in the future. One put contract gives you the right to sell 100 shares of the underlying stock.

Basic options strategies

The real beauty of both call and put options kicks in because you can either buy or sell them to other investors. That gives you four distinct strategies:

- ✔ **Buying a call:** When you buy a call, you have the right to force someone to sell you the stock at the exercise price you agreed upon ahead of time. You make money on a call when the stock price rises above the exercise price. This strategy is for investors that are convinced a stock will rise and want to bet big. Buying a call isn't free. You must pay the seller for the option, in what's called the *premium.*

    Nothing says you must exercise an option. But, not exercising an option that's worth something would be foolish. So foolish, in fact, that most online brokers will automatically exercise options that are worth something, or in the money.

- ✔ **Selling a call:** When you sell a call, you're on the other side of the option strategy of buying a call. You get paid the premium and pocket the money. And it gets better; if the stock falls, you keep that money free and clear. But if the stock rises, you're in trouble because you've agreed to sell the stock for the lower price. If you don't already own the stock, you're what's called *naked.* That means you'll have to go out and buy the stock you've already sold, no matter the price.

    You should never sell a call unless you know what you're doing. If you sell a call and don't own the underlying stock, that's called writing a naked call. If the stock rises, your losses are unlimited because in theory the stock could rise hundreds of points.

If a call sounds like something you'd like to trade, here are places online where you can find out more:

- *The Chicago Board Options Exchange's Options Institute* (`http://cboe.com/LearnCenter/cboeeducation/Course_01_02/mod_02_01.aspx`)

- *Optionetics* (`www.optionetics.com/education/basic/call.asp`)

✔ **Buying a put:** When you buy a put, you have the right to make someone buy a stock from you for a prearranged price. You're betting that the price of the underlying stock will fall. And like buying a call, it lets you make a big gamble with little upfront money. It's another way to bet against a stock, similar to shorting a stock, as described earlier in this chapter.

✔ **Selling a put:** This strategy places you on the other side of the person who is buying the put. When you sell a put, you're usually betting the price of the underlying stock will rise. But you might also sell a put if you're willing to buy the stock at the current price but think it might go lower in the short term. That way, if the stock does fall, you must buy the stock at the higher exercise price but get to keep the premium.

Selling a put can be extremely risky. If the stock falls, you keep losing money until it hits $0. Don't sell a put unless you know exactly what you're doing. Some online resources can help:

- *The Chicago Board Options Exchange's Options Institute* (`http://cboe.com/LearnCenter/cboeeducation/Course_03_01/mod_01_01.aspx`) has a special section dedicated to selling put.

- *Optionetics* (www.optionetics.com/education/basic/put.asp)

Table 5-2 explains the four main options strategies and the basics on how they work.

Table 5-2	The Four Basic Option Strategies	
	Calls	*Puts*
Buy	A bet that the stock will go higher. If you're right, you can make a large profit with little investment.	A bet that the stock will fall. If you're right, you can make a large profit with little investment.
Sell (or *writing*)	A bet that the stock will fall. It's very risky, because your loss is unlimited if you're wrong.	A bet that the stock will rise. It's risky, but your losses are limited because a stock can fall only to $0.

Buying trouble by buying calls

Buying calls is the best way to maximize returns if a stock is about to go up. And that's why they're perfect tools for investors who use *illegal insider information* about stocks for personal gain. Illegal insider information is important information the public doesn't know about yet but will move the stock when the news gets out. It's illegal to trade using important and confidential information you got from working for a company or being connected to people with such secret information. For just a little cash, these investors can post giant gains when the market-moving news — news they already know about — hits the market.

Regulators are aware of this, too, though. Options activity is one of the first things the Securities and Exchange Commission (SEC) looks into following a big move of a stock, especially on news that a company is being acquired. A classic case came in August 2005, when the SEC uncovered a ring of nine investors who allegedly made more than $6 million in illegal profits largely by buying call options ahead of the August 3rd announcement that athletic apparel maker Adidas was buying Reebok. The case included lurid details of the illegal traders meeting with an exotic dancer to exchange tips as well as secret meetings inside Russian spas. A few members of the ring worked for investment banks and knew the deal was coming, giving them time to make the options trades. You can read all about it in one of the SEC's complaints at `http://sec.gov/litigation/complaints/2006/comp19775.pdf`.

How to get option prices online

Most of the leading stock quote sites provide options prices. They're usually called *options chains* because they show data on options for many exercise prices and for different expiration dates. Two helpful places to get options chains are NASDAQ.com (`www.nasdaq.com`) and Yahoo! Finance (`http://finance.yahoo.com`). Options quotes are also provided by most online brokers.

No matter where you look up options chains online, most providers will give you a chart with the same basic information, including

- ✔ **Premiums (or prices) of both call and put options at all price levels:** The bid is how much you will get for selling the option and the ask is how much you'd pay to buy one.

- ✔ **Volume:** This shows you have many contracts are being bought and sold.

- ✔ **In the money and out of the money:** You can see which options are in the money or which are out of the money. Remember, a call option is *in the money* if the stock price is higher than the option's strike price. A call option is *out of the money* if the strike price is higher than the stock's price.

✔ **Prices for different dates:** You can see how much options with different expiration dates are trading for.

✔ **The trading symbol of the option:** Options have five-letter symbols. The first three letters represent the stock. (Sometimes it's the same as the stock ticker symbol, but not always.) The next two letters represent the month the option expires and its exercise price. Nearly all the options sites described in this chapter have a feature that will look up a symbol for you. You can also find out about the symbols from Yahoo! Finance (http://biz.yahoo.com/opt/symbol.html).

How to buy options online

Most of the mainstream online brokers allow you to buy and sell options. Some of the brokers are specialists with options and can help you calculate your gains and losses. Those specialty firms are listed in Chapter 4. You also need to pay a commission to buy or sell options, just as you pay to buy or sell stocks. The fees vary by broker. Table 5-3 lists a few examples.

Table 5-3	Some Online Brokers Options Commissions
Broker	*Commission Per Contract*
Zecco.com	$4.50 plus $.50 per contract
TradeKing	$4.95 plus $0.65 per contract
TD AMERITRADE	$9.99 plus $0.75 per contract
Scottrade	$7 plus $1.25 per contract

Entering an option order is very similar to placing a trade for a stock. You must follow these steps:

1. **Go to the option-trading section of the online broker's site.**

2. **Enter an order to buy or sell a call or put option.**

3. **Enter the number of contracts you want to trade.**

   One options contract controls 100 shares of the stock.

4. **Enter the option contract symbol.**

5. **Select an order type, such as a limit or market order.**

   For more on limit and market orders, see the "Types of orders" section, earlier in the chapter.

Insurance to protect you from losing money investing online

You can buy insurance to cover you in case your house burns down or your car is stolen. But what about your online stock portfolio? Can you buy insurance to protect yourself from losing a catastrophic amount of money from investing online? Yes, you can, but instead of buying a policy from an insurance company, you can buy a put option.

Buying a put is normally a way to bet against a stock. But if you buy a put for a stock you already own, you have what's called a *protective put*. Say you own 100 shares of ABC. The stock is trading for $30 a share, and you're worried about a market meltdown. You can buy a put that would give you the right to sell ABC for $30. Even if the stock crashes and falls to $15 a share, you can still sell it for $30. You've essentially bought catastrophic insurance.

Discovering more about options online

Options aren't complicated, but they can be a little bewildering to novices. You need to make absolutely certain you know what you're doing before trying to play with options. These online resources can help:

- ✔ **Your broker's Web site:** Most brokers have an education section, where options are explained in detail. Brokerages that specialize on options, like TradeKing (www.tradeking.com), have very comprehensive tutorial information.

- ✔ **The Chicago Board Options Exchange (CBOE) Options Institute:** (http://cboe.com/LearnCenter/OptionsInstitute1.aspx) Online tutorials, courses, and educational Webcasts will step you through the options process before you risk inflicting some major damage on your portfolio. You can see how the CBOE explains put options in Figure 5-3.

- ✔ **The International Securities Exchange:** (www.ise.com) This options exchange provides great options tutorials. Just click the Resource Center tab on the left side of the screen. From the Resource Center page, select the Education tab on the left side of the screen, which will give you a list of tutorials. Click the Options Glossary option on the left side of the page to start the options tutorial.

✔ **optionMONSTER:** (`www.optionmonster.com`) This site is a haven for options speculators who are trying to boost their returns. You can also find interesting information about what options activity can tell regular share holders about what the market thinks of stocks.

✔ Other educational sources include **Optionetics** (`www.optionetics.com`) and **The Options Guide** (`www.theoptionsguide.com`).

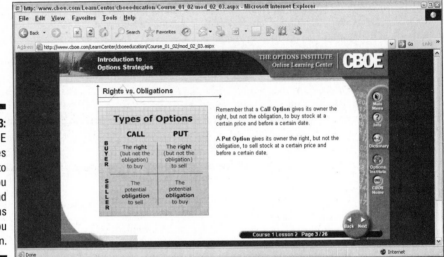

Figure 5-3:
The CBOE provides tutorials to help you understand options before you dive in.

Part II
Using Online Investment Resources

The 5th Wave   By Rich Tennant

"I'm not sure — I like the mutual funds with rotating dollar signs, although the dancing stocks and bonds look good too."

In this part . . .

*O*pening an online brokerage account doesn't suddenly make you an online investing master. To get to the next level and boost your sophistication and success investing online, you need to upgrade your knowledge of the inner workings of online investing and understand how to use the Internet to your advantage.

The chapters in this part help you lift yourself above the click-happy masses of online investors who just buy and sell stocks willy-nilly. You find out what forces drive stock prices and how to track those forces by using online calculators and communities on the Internet. I then introduce you to one of the most important, and most ignored, skills that all online investors need: measuring the risk and return of stocks and your portfolio. You find out how to use the Internet to design an asset allocation, a (boring-sounding) step that determines your success as an online investor. You also get tips on how to research and buy mutual funds and exchange-traded funds online.

Chapter 6

Why Stock Prices Rise and Fall

*I*nvestors often wonder why bad things can happen to shares of "good companies." It's common for a company to report seemingly solid news, like sharply higher profit, and its stock will fall anyway. It doesn't seem right to many investors. This chapter answers the burning question you and many investors might have: "Why do stocks rise and fall?" It's a two-part answer because one set of forces causes stocks to move in the short term, and another set influences stock prices in the long term. I explain what moves stocks and show you online tools that can help you track market-moving events.

How Stocks Get into the Public's Hands

If you've ever seen the screen of a stock trader's computer, on most days, it looks like a Christmas tree. Ticker symbols are flashing red and green, indicating that stock prices are moving up and down during the day. But why are the stocks moving up and down so much? To understand that, it's helpful to see how and why companies decide to sell stock to the public, allowing you to become an online investor. The following sections take a look at how the process works.

Step 1: An idea becomes a company

Clever entrepreneurs with an idea for a product or service form a company. Young companies usually pay for the equipment and materials they need by using private money. Let me clarify: They use *their* money. But, if it's a promising concept that could sell on Wall Street, the entrepreneurs might hit up *venture capital* (VC) investors for cash. VCs are specialized investors who buy stakes in very young companies, most of which will fail, on the hope they hit just one future Microsoft or Google and make a bundle. You can track trends in the VC industry at The National Venture Capital Association (www.nvca.org) and PriceWaterhouseCoopers' MoneyTree Report (www.pwc moneytree.com).

When a company finally sells its shares to the public in an initial public offering, you can see which VC firms were investors in the *prospectus*. The prospectus is a legal document that explains everything about the company selling shares to the public. You can find out how to access an IPO's prospectus in Bonus Chapter 2 on the Web site associated with this book.

Step 2: The company expands and grows

If the entrepreneur's hunch is right and there's a demand for what the company sells, the business takes off. At this point, the company needs more money to grow. The company might remain *private* by finding large institutional investors, like pension funds, insurance companies or companies that invest in private companies. These *private placement investments* aren't typically open to online investors. Private placements are very selective sales of investments to a small and savvy group of money managers, such as pension funds or insurance companies. But if you're interested, you can more find out about them here:

✔ **Drew Field Direct Public Offerings** (www.dfdpo.com) is trying to allow more regular people to invest in private companies. Some private companies choose to raise money through Direct Public Offerings (also known as DPOs) so they can sell their private stock to their customers, who will be more patient than Wall Street.

Although some direct public offerings might work out, they're highly risky and are only for investors willing to lose their entire investment.

✔ **Private Placement Letter** (www.privateplacementletter.com) provides information about private placement investments in case you want to track them. Most of the information concerns bonds that companies sell to private investors. I discuss how to invest in bonds online in detail in Chapter 16.

For an overview of this stage of the process, check out a speech made by Laura Unger, the former acting head of the Securities and Exchange Commission, available on the Web at www.sec.gov/news/speech/spch471.htm. Her speech describes all the ways companies raise money at this stage — as well as the related dangers associated with such schemes for raising cash.

Step 3: The company goes public

To raise money, the company sells a fraction of itself in an *Initial Public Offering* or IPO. The shares are first sold mostly to large institutional investors, such as mutual funds, pension funds, and investment banks at the IPO price. When the large institutions and other initial investors sell their shares, they're available for you to buy online. I cover IPOs in more detail in Bonus Chapter 2 on the Web site associated with this book, but great places to start researching IPOs include

- ✔ **Renaissance Capital's IPOhome** (www.ipohome.com) maintains all sorts of statistics about IPOs, ranging from how many there are to how well they do. You can also find research about upcoming IPOs and read their prospectuses.

- ✔ **Gaskins IPO desktop** (http://gaskinsco.com), which provides detailed information on the types of companies that are coming public as well as links to expert commentary on the deals.

Step 4: The new shares trade

After the IPO shares get into the hands of investors, the investors are free to buy and sell them at will on the exchanges. If you have a broker, as described in Chapter 4, you're free to participate and bid for stocks you want to buy. After you buy, you can sell.

This constant buying and selling of shares creates a dynamic way to determine stock prices. The process of how shares trade hands on the exchanges is described at length in Chapter 5.

Why Stocks Move Up and Down in the Short Term

Shares of large companies generally gain about 10% a year on average, as explained in Chapter 1. But getting there is far from a smooth ride. The ups and downs can be vicious as investors react to different news and corporate developments that trickle out randomly.

Stock prices are volatile in the short term because investors can either worry about or get excited about countless things. Stock prices reflect what investors know and expect from the company. But stock prices change the second there's a bit of unexpected news that changes investors' outlook for the stock. Investors instantly react to any news about the company, including the following:

- ✔ **Movement by the rest of the stock market:** If the entire market goes up or down, most stocks move in the same direction.

- ✔ **Earnings reports:** Such reports are released quarterly by companies to give investors a status report on the business. Investors usually react quickly and intensely to these reports.

- ✔ **Industry developments:** What's happening to the industry as a whole can affect every company in the field. If one company, for instance, creates a new product that makes rivals' offerings obsolete, there can be a swift reaction.

- ✔ **Management changes:** Who gets hired and fired at the top can be critical because such moves might signal a turn in the company's direction or a power struggle in the executive suite.

- ✔ **Raw materials:** Changes in the price of raw materials can significantly affect companies that must buy basic ingredients to make their products. Higher raw material costs must be passed on to the company's consumer, or profit will suffer.

- ✔ **Trading momentum:** When a certain stock gets its mojo going, it might seem as if there's no stopping it. Many times, companies become darlings with investors and can enjoy big rallies as everyone piles in.

- ✔ **Merger chatter:** When the buzz tells you that a corporate wedding is in the offing, that can be market-moving information because companies are usually bought out for a premium to the existing share price.

- ✔ **Bond yields:** The yield on bonds determines how much stocks are worth to investors, so a move in yields has a swift effect on stocks.

- ✔ **Economic reports:** Official pronouncements about the state of the economy, including changes in short-term interest rates by the Fed, help investors decide whether they want to own stocks at the time.

- ✔ **Legal insider buying or selling:** When corporate executives are doing a lot of buying or selling of their company's stock, that's worth watching closely. When the company's chief executive officer (CEO) is buying, for example, investors assume he knows what he's doing and might want to go along for the ride. (Don't confuse legal insider trading with illegal insider selling, discussed in Chapter 5. Illegal insider trading occurs when anyone with special connections to the company, including the management, use important information not known by the public to unfairly make a profit.)

The preceding list just gives you a taste of all the things that can cause a stock that you own to go up or down. In the following sections, I expand on a few of these things and show you places online where you can track them insofar as they pertain to investments in your portfolio.

Tracking the market's every move

Perhaps the biggest factor on the short-term moves of stocks is the direction of the broader market. Investors generally watch stock market indexes — tools that track a basket of stocks — to find out what the market is doing. Popular indexes include the Dow Jones industrial average, Standard & Poor's 500, and the NASDAQ composite index. You can find out how to track these indexes online in Chapter 2. Monitoring the broad market is telling because when market indexes are falling, it's not uncommon for investors to dump all stocks, including those of companies that are doing well. Traders describe this phenomenon with an old cliché: "Investors are throwing the baby out with the bathwater."

Getting in tune with earnings reports

Your stock's ultimate value will be determined by how profitable the company is in the long term. But even the best market forecasters are unable to measure a company's profits 10 years in the future, much less in 20 years. So, investors tend to overcompensate for their lack of long-term vision by focusing on how companies are doing in the short-term. *Earnings reports* tell you how much the company made during the quarter. Earnings reports also contain all the vital financial results for the quarter, including the *net income* (or total profit) as well as earnings per share, which is how much of the company's profit you can lay claim to as a shareholder.

Investors and online databases usually use the shorthand term EPS when referring to earnings per share. If you see the abbreviation, *EPS TTM,* that means earnings per share over the trailing, or past, 12 months.

All public companies that trade on major exchanges, such as the New York Stock Exchange and NASDAQ, are required to tell investors how they did during the quarter. These earnings reports can be incredibly important to investors in the short term. But stocks that trade on other markets, including the Pink Sheets, are often not required to make these important disclosures, adding a great deal of risk if you choose to invest in them. You can read more about the risks of investing in stocks listed on the Pink Sheets in Chapter 2.

Getting the goods

Here are several ways to get your hands on earnings reports the second they're released:

✔ **Financial news Web sites:** Nearly all the financial news sites described in Chapter 2, including Yahoo! Finance (`http://finance.yahoo.com`) and USA TODAY (`http://money.usatoday.com`) provide the earnings reports directly from the companies as soon as they're published.

Earnings releases are easy to find because in the list of news stories they're usually tagged as being from one of two sources: PR Newswire (`http://prnewswire.com`) or Business Wire (`http://home.businesswire.com`). These reports are very formal and written in almost legalese language. They describe how the companies did, in exhaustive detail, and provide the quarterly financial statements. (I cover how to analyze financial statements in more detail in Chapter 12.)

If you don't want to take the time to pick apart the company releases, look for earnings stories written by the wire services, such as Reuters and The Associated Press. These stories are analyzed by reporters trained to look for the important things and put their findings in plain English. Wire stories are also available on most financial news sites.

✔ **Press release distribution services:** Most companies hire one of two companies — either the PR Newswire outfit or the Business Wire outfit, mentioned in the preceding bullet — to electronically distribute their earnings press releases. Both these sites let you search press releases that might have been released by different companies.

✔ **The regulators:** You can get earnings reports, called 10-Qs, directly from the Securities and Exchange Commission (`www.sec.gov`). The 10-Qs are the official reports, so they usually take a few days to be released. Prior to that, the company must file an 8-K report stating that it put out a press release with quarterly earnings information. If you're interested in getting the information this way, I show you how to do that in Chapter 2.

✔ **Earnings calendars:** Earnings calendars like the one maintained by BigCharts (`www.bigcharts.com`) let you see what companies have reported their earnings most recently. In the case of BigCharts, just click the BigReports tab on the site's home page and then click the NYSE, AMEX, or NASDAQ link for the Most Recent Corporate Earnings Releases row, and you can find out who's reporting. (Figure 6-1 shows you what the report for the NYSE looks like.) And if you want to find out what companies are scheduled to report earnings when, go to Yahoo! Finance's earnings calendar at `http://biz.yahoo.com/research/earncal/today.html`.

Figure 6-1:
BigCharts
not only
shows you
which
companies
have
reported
earnings,
but it
summarizes
the results.

BigCharts - BigMarkets - Earnings Announcements (NYSE) - Microsoft Internet Explorer

File Edit View Favorites Tools Help

Back   Search   Favorites

Address http://bigcharts.marketwatch.com/reports/bigmovers.asp?date=20070706&data=1&start=1&report=9&report_country_code=us   Go   Links

BigCharts The best of both worlds now in one place.

Enter Symbol/Keywords: BASIC CHART   ADVANCED CHART   INTERACTIVE CHART
Global Symbol Lookup

Home   Quotes   News   Industries   Markets   Historical Quotes   BigReports   Advanced Tools   Premium Products

The BigReports

Select Date to View   Friday, July 06, 2007

More than a trade. More for the trader.   *Charles* SCHWAB

THE BIGMARKETS REPORTS   NYSE | NASDAQ | AMEX

NYSE
Earnings Announcements
Report published on Friday, July 06, 2007

The following report lists companies who released their most recent quarterly earnings per share (EPS) numbers on Friday, July 06, 2007. The companies are ranked by their percentage growth in earnings this period vs. the earnings for the same period one year ago.

Rank	Company Name	Symbol	Go to:	Recent EPS Release	Percent EPS Change	Annual EPS
1	Laidlaw Intl Inc	LI		0.77	75%	1.54
2	Copa Holdings Sa	CPA		1.13	51%	3.48
3	H B Fuller Company	FUL		0.45	34%	1.57
4	CarMax, Inc	KMX		0.30	11%	0.95
5	Jabil Circuit Inc	JBL		0.03	-90%	0.26
6	Material Sciences Corporation	MSC		(0.02)	-113%	0.25

Done   Internet

Stocks often react immediately to the release of earnings statements by companies. However, you might be surprised at the counterintuitive reactions such news sometimes provokes. This can be one of the greatest riddles on Wall Street, and it reveals just how deeply investors pick apart everything a company says to determine the price of the stock. Oftentimes, a company will release sharply higher earnings, but the stock will fall. Pure perversity? An Alice-in-Wonderland kind of world? Not necessarily. It's just a complicated world, as the next section makes clear. (Hey, if it were easy, everybody would be rich.)

What's so important about earnings reports?

To get into the head of short-term investors and understand how they read quarterly earnings statements, ask yourself the following questions:

✔ **Were the company's results better than expected?** When a company releases its earnings per share, investors instantly compare those results to what Wall Street analysts who follow the stock expected. Even if a company's EPS is just a penny short of expectations, the stock can get punished. But the stock can fall even if earnings per share is up, if it's not up as much as analysts expected. How do you find out how much the analysts thought the company would earn?

• **Financial wire stories:** Most of the wire stories from financial Web sites contain how figures on much analysts were expecting and how the actual results compared with said expectations.

- **NASDAQ's Stock Research – Earnings Per Share:** (`http://quotes.nasdaq.com/asp/MasterDataEntry.asp?page=analystinfo`) Here you can see how much analysts were expecting the company to earn and whether the actual results were a positive surprise or a negative surprise. Yahoo! Finance also has an entire section dedicated to tracking the analysts. Just enter the stock's ticker symbol and click the Get Quotes button to get the company's summary information. Under the Analyst Coverage section on the left side of the page, click the Analyst Opinion and Analyst Estimates links.

When looking up analysts' expectations for earnings, be sure to find out how many analysts cover the stock and how many have provided an earnings estimate. If three or more analysts are on the stock, the estimate is more meaningful than if there's only one.

✔ **What did the company say about the future?** What the company says about the just-completed quarter is practically ancient history. Investors spent all quarter anticipating the results and are usually pretty close. But sometimes a company drops a bomb in its press release regarding what it expects in the future. Usually, though, companies make comments about the future in so-called *investor conference calls* — scheduled teleconferences between Wall Street analysts and other investors with the company's top brass, where management discusses how the quarter went and what it expects to happen in the future.

You're not likely to be on the To Call list for such investor conference calls, but you can still get the highlights from these calls from wire stories or earnings news stories. And, if you're really curious, you can often access such investor conference calls yourself online from a variety of sources, including

- *The company's Web site:* Start here. There's usually an Investor Relations link you can use to access the feed for earnings calls. Most companies let you click a link to hear the calls as they're being made, and many rebroadcast the call for 24 hours after it occurred.

- *Financial news sites:* The major sites provide calendars of upcoming conference calls as well as the audio broadcasts from the calls themselves. Yahoo! Finance (`http://biz.yahoo.com/cc`) provides a calendar of company conference calls and lets you listen to some as they're ongoing and some that are over. Briefing.com (`www.briefing.com/Investor/Private/Calendars/EarningsConferenceCallListingByCompany.htm`) and Earnings.com (`http://earnings.com`) provide similar services.

✔ **Are analysts changing their opinions on the company?** The minute a company releases earnings, Wall Street analysts are already picking the results apart. They're looking for anything that changes their expectations for the company. Analysts publish their opinions on stocks in analyst reports, which I show you how to read and interpret in Chapter 15. But, for quick ways to find out whether analysts are changing their expectations, here are some sources:

- *Zacks Investment Research* (www.zacks.com) closely tracks analysts' opinions of stocks. If analysts change their opinion on a stock, you can find out immediately. Zacks helps you keep tabs on the analysts and closely track *analyst revisions,* which occur when researchers either increase or decrease their expectations for earnings.

    From the Zacks Investment Research home page, just enter the stock's symbol and scroll down to the section called Brokerage Recommendations. The Current ABR number is the average broker recommendation. This number averages all the recommendations made by the Wall Street analysts. A current ABR of 5 means all the analysts covering the stock give it a "strong buy" rating, whereas an ABR of 1 means the analysts give it a "sell." A 3 means "hold." You can also see what the stock's ABR was in the past so you can tell whether analysts are getting more bullish or bearish.

    Zacks also provides a Zacks Rank, which scores stocks from a high of 5 to a low of 1. But unlike the ABR number, which looks only at analyst ratings, the Zacks Ranks considers four factors: How much the analysts agree, how dramatically estimates have been increased or cut, how quickly the average estimate is rising, and how much the recent financials have differed from the estimate.

    You must subscribe to Zacks to get stocks' Zacks Ranks, and it costs $25 a month or $199 a year. However, you can access some of the stocks with top Zacks Rank scores for free.

- *Reuters* (http://today.reuters.com/investing/default US.aspx) has a comprehensive database of analysts' ratings on stocks so you can see how Wall Street is reacting to an earnings release. Just enter the stock symbol into the Enter Symbol text field (you might have to scroll down a bit to find it) of the Reuters Investing home page, choose the Estimates option below the text field, and then click Go. You're greeted by a page that lets you look up what analysts have been expecting and also lets you track whether the company has the tendency to beat estimates in the past and by how much. You can view estimates for both revenue and earnings.

- *Yahoo! Finance's Upgrades Center* (http://finance.yahoo.com/ marketupdate/upgrades) tells you what stocks are getting higher ratings from the analysts that track them.

- *Briefing.com* (http://briefing.com/Investor/Public/ Calendars/UpgradesDowngrades.htm) shows you what stocks were downgraded by which analysts on what day.

In addition to tracking earnings reported by companies, it's valuable to see how earnings from all the companies in the Standard & Poor's 500 index are coming in. S&P 500 earnings are closely watched by pros because it gives them an idea of how healthy companies are. Standard & Poor's (www2. standardandpoors.com/spf/xls/index/SP500EPSEST.XLS) lets you see how much companies in the S&P 500 have earned each quarter for decades and also how much the companies are expected to earn.

Companies and the company they keep in their industries

Sweeping changes in an industry can have a tremendous influence on all the companies in it. A new product coming to the market can affect all the companies in its industry. Apple's iPod music player, for instance, shook up other electronics companies, software companies, and music companies. Other times, good news for one company, such as a change in regulation, can help other players in the industry. If you're interested in keeping up with industry trends, here are several online sources:

- ✔ **Specialized boutique research firms:** These guys closely track an industry or a collection of related industries called a *sector*. These firms usually charge large sums for their research. Sometimes, though, they provide useful industry data on their Web sites for free. You can usually find them by searching for "research" and the name of the industry in most search engines. Table 6-1 lists a few of the more prominent boutique research firms.

- ✔ **Industry associations:** Can you say "lobbyist"? Industry associations are usually groups paid by companies in the industry to represent them on Capital Hill. So, they're certainly biased in favor of the industry. Still, most release helpful information that can tell you about industry trends. Typically, the easiest way to find such groups is by just entering the name of the industry and "association" into a search engine, as described in Chapter 2, and see what that turns up. The online encyclopedia Wikipedia (http://en.wikipedia.org/wiki/Industry_trade_group) keeps a list of many industry groups. Table 6-2 lists a few of the larger industry associations.

- ✔ **Pay services:** Hoovers.com (http://premium.hoovers.com/ subscribe/ind/dir.xhtml) provides full reports on a wide range of industries to subscribers. Standard & Poor's also publishes industry surveys (`www2.standardandpoors.com/portal/site/sp/en/us/page.category/equityresearch/2,5,1,0,0,0,0,0,0,0,0,0,0,0,0,0.html`), but be forewarned, they can cost hundreds of dollars.

✔ **The U.S. Government:** The U.S. Department of Labor's Bureau of Labor Statistics (`http://stats.bls.gov/iag/iaghome.htm`) maintains a set of comprehensive industry data that's free to the public.

✔ **Competitor information:** Sometimes the best way to find out about a company is finding out what its rivals are saying about the industry. You can hear what companies are saying about each other with a two-step process online:

- *Find the competitors.* You can get Yahoo! Finance (`http://finance.yahoo.com`) to display the main rivals of any company. Just enter the stock symbol of the company you're interested in into the Enter Symbol(s) text field on the Yahoo! Finance home page and click the Get Quotes button. Next, click the Competitors option under the Company heading on the left side of the page. Hoovers.com (`www.hoovers.com`) will also list a company's top rivals.

  You might also want to see which companies in the industry are planning an IPO or recently have gone public. Regulatory filings from newly public companies contain great details about the industry. Renaissance Capital (`www.ipohome.com/marketwatch/priced.asp`) provides a detailed list of recent IPOs and what industry they are in.

- *Find the competitors' filings.* Regulatory filings published by rivals can be very revealing. Using the Securities and Exchange Commission's database, you can look up regulatory filings made by competitors. The annual reports, labeled 10-Ks in the SEC database, will usually have a section on the industry. And don't miss the registration filings made by companies planning to go public, called S-1s. There's usually excellent industry information in those. (Chapter 2 tells you how to pull regulatory filings from the SEC's Web site.)

✔ **BusinessWeek's Sectors:** (`www.businessweek.com/investor/list/main_sectors_toc01.htm`) This venerable business magazine publishes data and commentary on market industries and sectors. It features research by Sam Stovall, a Standard & Poor's strategist known for closely watching industry trends.

✔ **ClearStation:** (`http://clearstation.etrade.com`) This online investment community/research hub — owned by E*Trade, the online brokerage firm — has tons of information about how industries or groups of industries (sectors) are doing relative to other industries and the rest of the stock market. From the ClearStation home page, just click the Markets link in the upper left to access the Markets page. From there, just click either the Sectors link or the Industries link to start your research from the screen shown in Figure 6-2.

✔ **Standard & Poor's:** (www2.standardandpoors.com/portal/site/sp/en/us/page.topic/indices_500/2,3,2,2,0,0,0,0,0,5,6,0,0,0,0,0.html) This industry heavyweight provides detailed and free information on corporate profit growth of different industries.

Table 6-1	Boutique Research Firms That Track Select Industries	
Industry	*Research Firm*	*Address*
Cars	Motor Intelligence	www.motorintelligence.com
Consumer goods	NPD Group	www.npd.com
Financial	SNL Financial	www.snl.com
Technology	Forrester	www.forrester.com
Travel	PhoCusWright	www.phocuswright.com

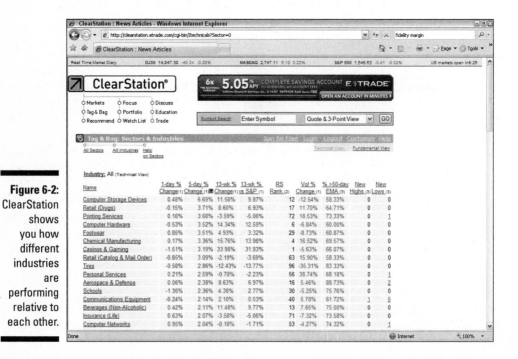

Figure 6-2: ClearStation shows you how different industries are performing relative to each other.

Table 6-2	Large and Influential Industry Associations	
Industry	*Research Firm*	*Address*
Finance	Securities Industry and Financial Markets Association	www.sifma.org
Real estate	National Association of Realtors	www.realtor.org
Retail	National Retail Federation	www.nrf.com
Manufacturing	National Association of Manufacturers	www.nam.org

Monitoring the big cheese

Investors usually have a strong reaction to management changes. Stocks might fall when the chief financial officer (CFO) resigns because it might make folks wonder whether the company's books are okay. But the opposite is also true — stocks might rise if a CEO who has worn out his welcome with investors decides to ride off into the sunset.

You can track management changes with the help of the following:

✔ **Press releases:** Such releases are required by regulators be put out the moment a company announces a significant personnel change. The news sources described in Chapter 2 all have this information.

✔ **CEO Go:** (http://ceogo.com) This Web site provides detailed data on the comings and goings of corporate executives. You can get data on CEO departures and pay, and you can even find out which CEOs have the best reputations.

✔ **The Corporate Library:** (www.thecorporatelibrary.com) This particular Web site closely tracks trends and data on executives. It has a database, for instance, that can tell you which executives hobnob with each other by sitting on corporate boards together. Most of the data, though, must be paid for and the charges can vary.

Where it all begins: Tracking prices of raw materials

Companies can make more money in two main ways: Either sell more products or reduce costs. Most companies must buy certain raw materials including *commodities* like coffee, copper or oil in order to make what they sell. When the prices of these goods rise, that can be bad for their bottom lines. I have much more on how commodities are traded online in Chapter 11, but for just checking price information, you can track the pricing of key commodities at the f ollowing sites:

- ✔ **The Chicago Board of Trade** (www.cbot.com) maintains a list of prices on everything from corn to soybeans, from oats to gold. The front page of the Web site lists all the prices, and you can click them to get historical price changes.

    The CBOT has been acquired by the Chicago Mercantile Exchange, also described in this list, so it'll be interesting to see whether the online tools are merged, too.

- ✔ **The New York Mercantile Exchange** (www.nymex.com) is a great resource for prices on many energy products such as oil, gas, and heating oil. Click the icon of the material you're interested in to view the pricing.

- ✔ **Chicago Mercantile Exchange** (www.cme.com) is home for the trading of many financial instruments, making it a good place to see the prices of different foreign currencies. But it's also home to many agricultural product trading, including pork bellies and live cattle. To see prices, click the View All Delayed Quotes link on the right side of the home page.

Raw materials costs and that morning cuppa joe

Never underestimate how rising raw materials costs can jolt a company. For instance, early in Starbucks' history, in June 1994, skyrocketing coffee costs posed a grave danger to the company as it weighed how to handle the higher costs. A more recent price shock came in September 2004, after coffee and sugar prices spiked more than 35% in a year's time. Starbucks reacted by boosting prices by 3% for all its drinks. It was the first time Starbucks had raised prices since August 2000.

Getting with the mo'

Stocks, in the short term, often get what traders call *momentum*. There's always a handful of darling stocks that short-term speculators jump on due to the fact they might have a hot product or simply because the stock is going up. Some speculators try to jump into these stocks and hope they can enjoy the ride higher and get out before the fall. The following sites highlight these high-octane stocks:

- ✔ **BigCharts.com:** (`http://bigcharts.marketwatch.com`) This site has a BigReports tab that gives you access to all the stocks with the biggest moves or those that are up the most or down the most over the past year. You can also see the stocks with the most short interest. Short interest is the number of shares being sold short by investors and is an indictor of how many investors think the stock will go down. (Stock shorting is described in Chapter 5.)

- ✔ **USATODAY.com:** (`http://markets.usatoday.com/custom/usa today-com/html-mktscreener.asp`) This page of the USATODAY. com site provides lists of stocks that have been actively trading. That gives you an idea which stocks investors are making heavy bets on. It can also show you which stocks you own in your portfolio are up the most that day.

- ✔ **Briefing.com:** (`www.briefing.com/Investor/Private/OurView/IndustryInsight.htm`) This page of the Briefing.com site indicates which industries are investors' current favorites and have the momentum. It also breaks down details on other market-moving events that are being followed by investors who attempt to make money by investing based on stocks' momentum.

Mania over merger chatter

It's common for shares of a company being acquired to rise. That's why investors love trying to predict takeover candidates.

Trying to guess what companies are buyout bait is not a great way to make money. Many of the merger and acquisition deals — M&A deals, for short — investors expect to happen *don't* happen, and in rare cases, companies' shares can fall if investors expected a buyer to offer more.

Most of the leading trackers of merger activity, including Dealogic, Thomson Financial, and FactSet Mergerstat, sell their data only to institutional investors able to pay large sums. But some other places track merger activity, including the following sites:

- ✔ **mergermarket:** (www.mergermarket.com) These folks have comprehensive merger tracking information, ranging from scuttlebutt on what companies are in play and some summary data about merger activity.

- ✔ **FactSet Mergerstat** (www.mergerstat.com) This Web site provides some free data about the merger and acquisition market in its Press Release area under the Press & Media tab on the front page. Its quarterly updates are informative and give you an idea about the market.

- ✔ **Yahoo! Finance:** (http://biz.yahoo.com/topic/m-a) Count on Yahoo! to summarize all its M&A news in one place.

Why bond yields aren't boring

Stocks can be highly sensitive to changes in the yield on debt sold by the U.S. government, called Treasuries. Investors keep a close eye on two types of Treasuries: Treasury Notes that mature in ten years or less and Treasury Bills that mature in less than a year. The yield on Treasuries is very important because it indicates what return investors can expect in exchange for taking no or low risk.

Stocks and Treasuries have an interesting relationship with each other. When Treasury yields rise, stocks often suffer because there's less impetus for investors to risk money on stocks. I discuss the basics about tracking yields online in Chapter 2 and give more advanced tips in Chapter 16. These sites help show the relationship between Treasury yields and stocks:

- ✔ **StockCharts.com:** (http://stockcharts.com/charts/Yield Curve.html) This page of the Web site has a Dynamic Yield Curve function, which shows you, graphically, how the yields for short-term Treasuries, typically called *bills,* compare with yields for long-term Treasuries, called *notes* and *bonds.* This graph is called the *yield curve.* But more importantly, it plots the yield curve against the stock market so you can understand the relationship between bond yields and stocks.

- ✔ **Smart Money's Living Yield Curve:** (www.smartmoney.com/onebond/index.cfm?story=yieldcurve) This site plots the yield curve but also helps you understand it by explaining what it means if short-term rates are higher, lower, or equal to long-term rates.

The heartbeat of the economy: Economic reports

If you can picture a patient at the hospital with probes and sensors on every inch of his body, you get the idea of how closely investors monitor the health of the economy. Investors are looking for any sign the economy is speeding up, slowing down, or going sideways. They rapidly buy or sell stocks if their opinion changes even a little. You can look in countless places for economic indicators, but the key sites are

✔ **Conference Board:** (`www.conference-board.org`) The Big Daddy of economic prognosticators, the Conference Board, shown in Figure 6-3, measures everything from manufacturing activity to unemployment claims, from building permits to consumer confidence. Pay special attention to the *U.S. leading index,* which falls when the measures it monitors predict an economic decline.

TIP

Although the Conference Board's leading index is widely watched, it's not always right. Investment pros like to joke that the leading index has predicted six of the last three recessions. For instance, the indicator fell in 1984 and 1987, but the economy didn't contract either time.

Figure 6-3: The Conference Board makes a variety of important measures of the economy's health available on its Web site.

✔ **U.S. Department of Labor Bureau of Labor Statistics:** (`http://stats.bls.gov`) The U.S. Government is also in the predicting business, tracking a vast majority of the indicators investors focus on, including the following:

- The *Consumer Price Index,* which measures how much prices for the things individuals buy are changing.

- The *Producer Price Index,* which tracks prices paid by companies that create goods. When prices are rising, both bond and stock investors pay attention because that affects the value of their investments. Stock investors typically don't like inflation because it drives up costs and makes their investments worth less.

- *Employee wages.*

- *Unemployment.*

✔ **U.S. Department of Commerce Bureau of Economic Analysis:** (`www.bea.gov`) More government predictors at work. The Bureau of Economic Analysis monitors how fast the economy is growing, generally using a measure called the Gross Domestic Product or GDP. You can also look up how much individuals are spending on average, what personal income levels are like, and how corporate profits are doing.

✔ **The Federal Reserve Board:** (`www.federalreserve.gov`) Investors look long and hard at the Fed for two reasons. First, the Fed sets short-term interest rates, which determines how much money is worth. Short-term rates affect every aspect of the economy, from how fast it grows to how much you have to pay to borrow money, and how you earn from investments and savings. You can track the *intended federal funds* rate here: `www.federalreserve.gov/fomc/fundsrate.htm`.

Don't confuse short-term interest rates and long-term interest rates. The Fed sets the short-term rates in order to steer the economy. When the Fed wants to slow the economy, it tightens by raising short-term rates, making it more expensive for companies and people to borrow and spend. It can loosen credit by cutting short-term rates, which boosts the economy. Long-term interest rates are set by traders who guess the direction of the economy. The difference between short and long-term rates is known as the *spread.*

The Fed publishes the Beige Book eight times a year. The Beige Book indicates the nation's economic health. You can view the results at `www.federalreserve.gov/FOMC/BeigeBook/2007`.

✔ **National Association of Realtors:** (`www.realtor.org`) The fate of the housing market has a major impact on the economy as a whole. The National Association of Realtors' Web site releases closely watched data on both new- and existing-home sales, data investors can use to get a better sense of the health of the economy as a whole.

- ✔ **Yahoo! Finance's Economic Calendar:** (http://biz.yahoo.com/c/e.html) This calendar from Yahoo! is handy when trying to track important economic reports. You can see which reports are coming up each week, what they are, how important they are and what analysts are expecting. It's all in one place, too, saving you the trouble of bouncing between all the sites in this list.

- ✔ **Economics and Statistics Administration:** (www.economicindicators.gov) Yet another U.S. Government entity, the Economics and Statistics Administration offers a handy free calendar of important upcoming economic reports. You can access the calendar under the Calendar tab. The site also has a free service where alerts of upcoming data releases will be e-mailed to you.

What do they know that you don't? Insider buying and selling

Some investors closely watch what the top officers and directors are doing when deciding whether they should buy or sell a stock. This is *legal insider buying* or selling, which is very different from the *illegal insider trading* described in Chapter 5.

Investors assume that when officers of a company are buying the stock, it's a sign the company is doing well. Some investors get bearish on a stock when executives are selling company stock.

When you see executives selling stock, it doesn't necessarily mean they're bailing out. Executives might sell stock to buy a home or to diversify their holdings. Diversification offers great benefits to investors, as I describe in Chapter 9, so it shouldn't come as a big surprise if higher echelon types diversify as well.

Nevertheless, major sell offs or a run on stocks by executives might actually be saying something significant about the stock. If you'd like to track what officers are doing, the following sites can help:

- ✔ **NASDAQ's Real-Time Institutional Holdings/Insider Ownership:** (www.nasdaq.com) You get to this page on the NASDAQ site by accessed by entering a stock symbol in one of the Quotes text boxes, clicking InfoQuotes and then choosing Holdings/Insider Summary from the InfoQuotes drop-down menu on the new page that appears. You'll get a list of what all the big investors, including both officers, directors and mutual funds are doing. The Insider Trades section shows how many officers are buying or selling stock, how much and when. You can view insider-trading data for stocks listed on the major exchanges, including the NASDAQ and New York Stock Exchange.

✔ **USATODAY.com:** (`http://money.usatoday.com`) The USATODAY Money page lets you overlay all the insiders' buy and sell transactions on the stock chart. That's useful because you can see if the officers have an uncanny ability to buy and sell at just the right time. Enter a stock symbol into the Get a Quote text field (you might have to scroll down to find it), click the Go button and then click the Insider Trading link above the chart on the new page that appears for the full report.

✔ **GradientAnalytics:** (`www.gradientanalytics.com`) Gradient-Analytics is a well-regarded research firm that looks at insider trading with great precision. The reports it produces are sold only to large investors and are very expensive. But the firm's cofounder, Carr Bettis, has described some of his techniques in an academic paper, *Insider Trading in Derivative Securities,* available at `http://papers.ssrn.com/sol3/papers.cfm?abstract_id=167189`.

Many market pros who track insider trading don't get too interested if just a few executives are selling. After all, CEOs might want to sell stock for many reasons such as for buying a house, diversifying their portfolios or sending a kid to college. But if you see executives at many companies in an industry dumping shares, you might want to take a closer look.

Knowing how investors are feeling: Tracking market sentiment

The way investors are feeling about stocks at the moment can greatly influence the market's movements in the short term. Typically, during a brutal *bear market,* a period of time when stocks are falling in value, investors sour on stocks and want nothing to do with them.

When investors hate stocks, market sentiment is negative, and that can be a good time to buy them because you'll likely pay less. Investors who buy stocks when they're out of favor are called *contrarians.*

When stocks enter a *bull market* and start rising, more investors pile in and push markets higher. Eventually, sentiment becomes overly positive, and anyone who wanted to buy stock already has. When there's a whiff of bad news, these investors bail out and send stocks lower. That's what happened during the tech-stock boom in the late 1990s. And, as you might remember, when investors were overly bullish in March 2000, that was a bad time to buy stocks.

A number of online tools can help you monitor sentiment:

✔ **Schaeffers Investment Research:** (www.schaeffersresearch.com) This site is a haven for investors who want to know what the crowd is doing, and then do the opposite. The Stock Screen Center (www.schaeffersresearch.com/streetools/stockscreen.aspx) helps you pinpoint stocks the herd likes the most and the ones it hates. The idea is that buying stocks no one else wants can be profitable. The site also shows you the put/call ratio, an indicator of how bullish investors are. The higher the put/call ratio, the more bearish investors are. You can access such put/call ratio data at www.schaeffersresearch.com/streetools/market_tools/cboe_eqpcr.aspx, as shown in Figure 6-4.

✔ **Chicago Board Options Exchange:** (www.cboe.com/micro/vix/introduction.aspx) This Web site maintains the CBOE Market Volatility index, a popular measure of how bullish investors are. (It's referred to fondly as the "VIX.") It's also known as the "fear gauge" by investors because the higher the VIX, the more nervous investors are about the stock market, as defined by the Standard & Poor's 500 index. You can track the VIX much like you'd track any other index or stock, as described in Chapter 1.

Figure 6-4:
Schaeffers
Investment
Research
gives you
quick and
easy access
to the
put/call
ratio.

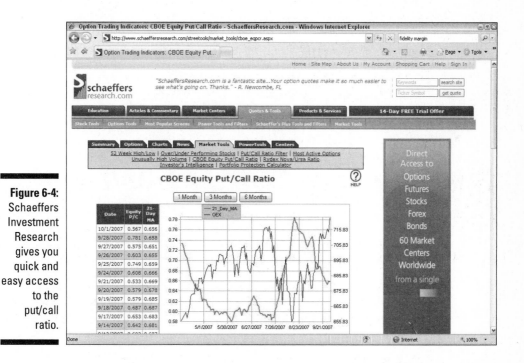

✔ **Investment Company Institute:** (www.ici.org) This site tracks how much money investors are putting into mutual funds.

So what's the big deal about mutual funds? It might seem insulting, but Wall Street pros closely watch *fund flows* as a measure of what the "dumb money" is doing. The idea is that if tons of cash surges into mutual funds, investors are getting overly optimistic, and it might be a good time to sell. You can see fund flows at www.ici.org/stats/mf/index.html; as for how effective mutual funds are at pointing out what *not* to do, check out Table 6-3. Basically, the market doesn't always work out the way the mutual fund investors want.

Table 6-3	Don't Follow the Money	
Mutual Fund Investors . . .	*The Stock Market . . .*	*Interpretation . . .*
Panic and pull out $16.1 billion and $7.7 billion in October 2002.	Rallies. The S&P 500 hit its bear market low on October 9, 2002.	Mutual fund investors pull their money out at just the wrong time and miss out on a powerful market rally.
Pour in a record $53.7 billion in February 2000 and $35.6 billion in March 2000.	Tanks. The S&P 500 hit its then-record market high on March 24, 2000 and began a vicious decline that lasted until 2002.	Mutual fund investors piled into stocks at just the wrong time.

Source: Data from Investment Company Institute

What Moves Stocks in the Long Term?

Almost anything can move stocks in the short term. Investors are so touchy on a minute-by-minute basis that they might even sell stocks if a Wall Street trader sneezes. Long term, though, the market is much more, well, sane. Several key factors stocks' returns over the long term:

✔ **Company fundamentals,** such as how much the company generates in cash and earnings over its lifetime, are the major contributor to how its stock performs. I discuss how to analyze long-term financial performance in Chapters 12 and 13.

✔ **Long-term economic trends** set the table for stocks. If there's a chronic problem with inflation or low economic growth, that will spell trouble for many investments.

What doesn't move stocks: Stock splits

My readers are always asking me to explain stock splits to them. For some reason, individual investors are fascinated by stock splits, perhaps because they think they're getting something for nothing.

A stock split occurs when a company believes its stock price is getting high enough to scare off investors with sticker shock. Companies might consider a split if their shares get to $75 or higher. After a split, investors own more shares, but the stock price is cut. For instance, when a company does a 2-for-1 stock split, investors get twice the number of shares, but the stock price is cut in half. So if you had 100 shares of a $10 stock, worth $1,000, after the split you'd have 200 shares worth $5. There's no change in the size of your stake; you still own $1,000 in stock.

Most financial Web sites show you if a stock has split. MSN Money, for instance, places a box on a historical stock chart to indicate when a split occurred. StockSplits.net (www.stock splits.net) also tracks splits and has a free newsletter for people who are interested.

The value of stock splits is controversial. Some academic research shows stock splits are early signals a company will perform well in the future. The theory is a company's management wouldn't split the stock unless it was fairly certain the stock was headed higher.

Other research, though, finds splits to have negligible value for investors. Zacks Investment Research studied small- and midsize companies going back to 1998 to see how splits of at least 1.5-to-1 affected the shares of companies up to 12 months later. Zacks found no discernable difference in the returns of companies that split their stock versus those that didn't over the following 12 months.

Some suggest splits are out of style with investors. Berkshire Hathaway class B shares, trading for more than $3,578, and Google shares that traded above $500 have both been perceived as somehow being attractive precisely because of their high share prices.

✔ **Valuations are how much you're paying for a piece of a company.** A stock's valuation is a measure of how expensive it is based on how much the company is expected to earn in profit. This is pursued in more detail in Chapter 12.

✔ **Risk** is the price you pay for higher returns. If you own a piece of a risky asset, you should demand a higher return in exchange. Academic research discussed in Chapter 1 shows how shares of companies that have been left for dead, called *value stocks*, have generated higher returns over the long term because they're riskier. Shares of small companies and companies based in emerging markets also tend to generate higher returns because they're riskier. I describe the relationship between a stock's risk and return in Chapter 3.

Going back to school with academic research

If you're curious about what moves stocks in the long-term, spend time reading the research put out by academics. Because they're not pressured to sell investments, academics have the time to sit down, study markets, and search for patterns. Some of the work that has come from academia has revolutionized investing and has greatly enhanced the understanding of why stocks do what they do. I mention several critical sources of academic research in Chapter 1. Other online resources worth checking out include the following:

✔ **Google Scholar:** (`http://scholar.google.com`) This particular arm of Google, shown in Figure 6-5, lets you search through millions of academic papers for those that match your search terms. You can follow the links to get access to view the research.

✔ **Live.com:** (`www.live.com`) This site helps you quickly search academic research and view the summaries from a single page. Enter your search terms and click the Search button. When your Results page appears, click the More link and choose Academic from the drop-down menu to access this feature.

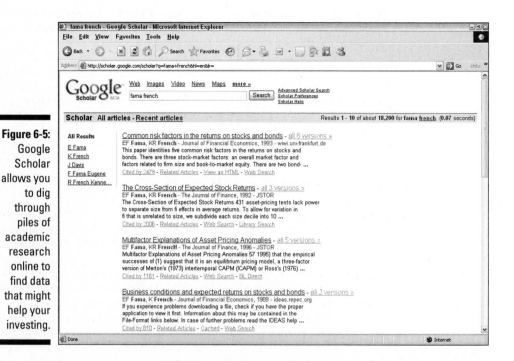

Figure 6-5: Google Scholar allows you to dig through piles of academic research online to find data that might help your investing.

Not all academic reports are boring

I'm not going to mislead you; most academic reports are hardly light reading. Many are packed with scary-looking mathematical formulas and exhaustive research. But don't let this frighten you from taking advantage of these (often-times free) research reports. Most of the time, the summary or abstract page at the front of the report will be enough to give you the gist.

And sometimes, academic reports can be surprisingly fun. For instance, "Deal or No Deal? Decision Making under Risk in a Large-Payoff Game Show" analyzes the behavior of investors by studying how people react in the popular TV game shows, including *Deal or No Deal*. The study finds that investors tend to get more greedy and accept greater risk immediately after a small victory. You can read the study, written by professors Thierry Post, Martijn van den Assem, Guido Baltussen, and Richard Thaler, in its entirety at `http://econ.ucsd.edu/seminars/0607seminars/thaler_paper.pdf`.

✔ **Social Science Research Network:** (`http://papers.ssrn.com`) Here you can find the primary database for published works by academics. The database is fully searchable by keyword and author. You can view some of the research for free, but other parts you have to pay for.

✔ **Jeremy Siegel:** (`www.jeremysiegel.com`) Siegel is a professor at the Wharton School of the University of Pennsylvania, is best known for exhaustive market research. Some of Siegel's data has led to important discoveries, including the concept that stocks become less risky the longer they're held. You can read many of Siegel's work and research at this site, but there's a charge to access most of it. Siegel has also cofounded a company, WisdomTree (`www.wisdomtree.com`), which sells investment products that take advantage of his research. I discuss Siegel's work in greater detail in Chapter 11, where I explain exchange-traded funds.

Learning from the wise men

Some investors have so much experience with markets that they're very worthwhile listening to. No, they're not always right, but you can learn from their mistakes. A few examples, in addition to those listed in Chapter 1, include

✔ **Warren Buffett:** (`www.berkshirehathaway.com`) He's perhaps the best-known and most successful investor ever, so it's worth your while to listen to him. Each year Buffett, CEO of a holding company called Berkshire Hathaway, releases the company's annual report in addition to various letters to shareholders. Even if you're not a Berkshire Hathaway shareholder, Buffett's letters are some of the best reads in finance. Not only are they cleverly written and full of turns of phrase, but they contain market insight you can't find elsewhere. Berkshire Hathaway's financial reports are available for free on the company's Web site, shown in Figure 6-6.

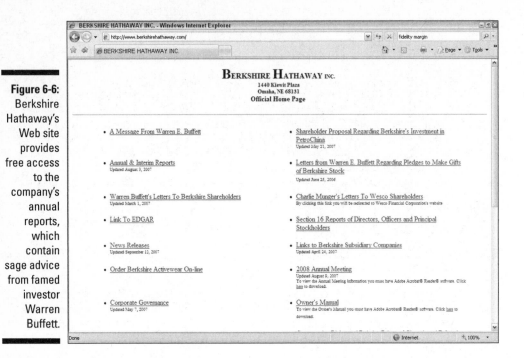

✓ **Ronald Muhlenkamp:** (www.muhlenkamp.com) As president of investment firm Muhlenkamp, Ronald Muhlenkamp does an excellent job explaining the rationale behind his investments in plain English. You can discover a lot about the economy, including how to research companies and make investment decisions, by closely reading his quarterly letters to shareholders.

✓ **Robert Rodriguez:** (www.fpafunds.com/newincomefund.asp) A portfolio manager of the FPA Capital Fund and the FPA New Income Fund, Robert Rodriguez is somewhat unusual in that he manages both a stock portfolio and bond fund. His letters to shareholders contain many reflections on what the bond and stock markets tell you about the future.

✓ **Bill Gross:** (www.pimco.com) As Chief Investment Officer at the bond fund management firm Pimco, Bill Gross shares his insights on the economy and investments.

Chapter 7

Connecting with Other Investors Online

*I*f there's one area of investing online that's evolved most since the last edition of this book, it's the ways in which investors can connect with each other. Online investors used to rely on *stock message boards,* often called *chat boards,* to trade stock tips, gossip, and hunches with each other. Stock message boards are still a way for investors to connect, but they're gradually being supplanted by new types of networking sites, which have distinct advantages. In the first part of this chapter, I show you how to get online with stock message boards, including how to contribute to them and what to watch out for. Later, I explore the dangers of penny stocks, which are some of the favorites on stock message boards and other online forums. And lastly, I explore the emerging area of social investing sites.

Finding Kindred Investment Spirits Online

Whenever you're about to try something risky, or at least something you've never done before, it's comforting to talk to people with experience. That's why many investors attempt to connect with each other. You have several ways to do this: through stock message boards, investment clubs, or social investing sites.

These are a few reasons why you might consider adding a social aspect to your investment strategy:

- ✔ **Moral support:** Many beginning online investors are bewildered by the things they need to remember. By connecting with other investors online who have already done what you're thinking about doing, you can gain first-hand knowledge of the risks and rewards.

- ✔ **A new perspective:** You might think you know the best way to manage your money. But why not run your strategy by others and make sure you're not overlooking anything?

- ✔ **New ideas for investments:** Members of online communities come from different professions and from all over the world. You can use this diversity to your advantage and might even find out about investments you'd never heard of.

Getting the Message with Stock Message Boards

When you think of connecting with other investors, you probably instantly think of stock message boards — and for good reason. These informal, anonymous forums were an early way for investors to chat with each other online. They give you an instant way to brag about your returns, promote a stock you own, or *flame* a stock you've sold for a loss.

Stock message boards aren't for everyone

Some investors, especially passive investors described in Chapter 1, might not care what other investors think about their stocks. They've formed their asset allocation — as described in Chapter 9 — and they're going to stick with that no matter what.

But if you're an active investor and see online investing as a hobby, you might be very interested in the chatter surrounding stocks you're considering. Stock message boards are suited for you if you

✔ **View investing as a form of entertainment:** Some investors buy and sell stocks not so much to accumulate a nest egg, but for speculation. It's almost like a trip to Las Vegas.

✔ **Don't want to hassle with signup procedures:** You can be up and running with most stock message boards in just minutes and usually don't even have to identify yourself.

✔ **Know the rules:** Investors who understand that many of the things said on stock message boards are exaggerations, manipulations, or just plain wrong have a better chance finding any worthwhile nuggets of information.

Blindly following what other investors are doing, generally speaking, isn't a good strategy and can be dangerous. If you're looking for stock message boards for stock recommendations, you'll likely be disappointed with your results.

Understanding the types of stock message boards

Although stock message boards have been around essentially since the start of online investing, they've morphed quite a bit through the past bull and bear markets. But currently, they're available on a number of different platforms. The following sections explore the various corners of the Internet where investors congregate to swap info.

Using online stock message boards as the key to your investment strategy isn't a good idea. Listening to so many other opinions might cause you to second-guess yourself and prompt you to buy and sell stocks too often. But more importantly, you don't know who you're chatting with, and such boards are havens for scammers. Consider Anthony Elgindy, an infamous stock picker who developed a strong following for some of his picks on Silicon Investor as "AnthonyPacific," in addition to promoting stocks on his own Web site. Elgindy was convicted in 2005 in federal court on multiple counts of securities fraud and extortion. Remember, always consider the source when using stock message boards to pick stocks.

The investing areas of general Internet portals

Each of the main general Internet search engines and portals contain message boards. But they aren't created equally, and some get much higher levels of participation than others. The big players here are

✔ **Yahoo! Finance:** (http://finance.yahoo.com) Yahoo! Finance has become a top destination for the casual stock message board participant. Just enter a stock symbol of a company you'd like to hear about into the Enter Symbol(s) text field, click the Get Quotes button, then click the Message Board link in the News & Info section of the new page that appears. You can scroll down through the messages and read them, but if you want to reply to messages, you'll need a Yahoo! sign-on ID and password.

✔ **MSN Investor's:** (http://moneycentral.msn.com/community/ message/default.aspx) This section of the MSN Money site works a little differently than Yahoo! Finance. You can start by checking out the Message Board Summary page, which shows broad investing topics that are being actively discussed. If you're looking for a message board about a particular stock, select the Topics and Tickers link under the Message Board section on the left-hand side of the page. Scroll down and you'll see a list of the letters of the alphabet. Click on the letter the company name starts with and you'll see which stocks are being discussed.

✔ **Google Finance:** (http://finance.google.com) Google Finance provides stock message boards if you enter the company's symbol, click the Search Finance button, and then click the Discuss *Your Stock* link on the new page that appears, where *Your Stock* is the stock whose symbol you just entered.

Specialized stock message boards

These boards are often the most popular sites with individual investors who see themselves as being more advanced than those using the general Internet portals' boards. Examples include

✔ **Raging Bull:** (http://ragingbull.quote.com) One of the favorite spots for day traders and active speculators, you can find a board on just about anything, ranging from individual stocks to specific industries — you can even trade investing jokes!

✔ **Silicon Investor:** (www.siliconinvestor.com) This site tends to attract investors primarily interested in large and mid-sized publicly traded companies.

✔ **Investors Hub:** (www.investorshub.com) Discussions here tend to focus on who's hot (and who's not) among smaller companies.

✔ **ADVFN:** (www.advfn.com) Advanced Financial Network (ADVFN) is the parent company of both Silicon Investor and Investors Hub. ADVFN is a popular source for European investors to discuss investments that are important across the pond.

✔ **ClearStation:** (`http://clearstation.etrade.com`) This site attempts to organize the random chaos of thousands of messages by letting you sort them based on the reputation of the author. You can even receive an alert when a certain ClearStation member you trust posts information.

Stock message board aggregators

You can waste a great deal of time hopping between all the different stock message boards. Some sites, called aggregators, try to solve this problem by pulling in the messages into one place. They include

✔ **BoardCentral:** (`www.boardcentral.com`) Board Central offers a single place to get messages from Yahoo! Finance, RagingBull, ClearStation, Google, Silicon Investor, and others. It also ranks the stocks that are being talked about the most as well as those stocks that investors are most often searching for.

✔ **InstantBull:** (`www.instantbull.com`) This site also compiles messages from multiple stock message boards. InstantBull's biggest advantage is that you can quickly read the messages by just moving your mouse over the subject line. You can see how the site is structured in Figure 7-1.

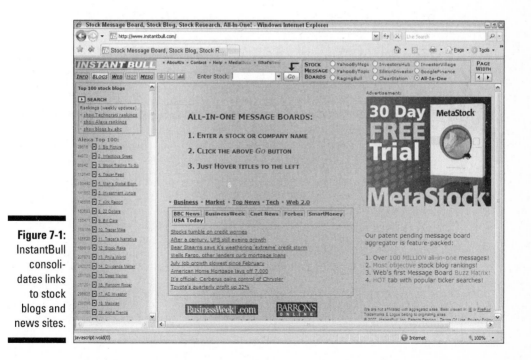

Figure 7-1:
InstantBull consolidates links to stock blogs and news sites.

Stock message boards and the Enron debacle

Despite the many problems with stock message boards, sometimes they can contain very valuable pieces of information. You should carefully monitor the boards for comments that appear to be from informed employees. The stock message boards, in fact, were one of the only places where investors were warned about the coming collapse of Enron in 2001, one of the largest bankruptcies in U.S. history.

Between 1997 and 2001, ahead of Enron's fall, there were more than 129 detailed posts on Enron's stock message board on Yahoo!, according to James Felton and Jongchai Kim in their article "Warnings from the Enron Message Board." These posts, many that appear to be from employees, indicated serious problems at the company, even while most Wall Street analysts rated the stock "buy" or "strong buy." In April 2001, for instance, an anonymous post read, "It will soon be revealed that Enron is nothing more than a house of cards that will implode before anyone realizes what happened. Enron has been cooking the books with smoke and mirrors. Enron executives have been operating an elaborate scheme that has fooled even the most sophisticated analyst."

That post appeared online four months before Enron employee Sherron Watkins wrote the famous warning letter to Enron CEO Ken Lay. You can read the article at `http://papers.ssrn.com/sol3/papers.cfm?abstract_id=918519#PaperDownload`.

Knowing the ulterior motives of some online stock message board members

Although many of the people who use online stock message boards might be upstanding individuals just looking to help their fellow man, great caution is warranted. People can abuse online stock message boards for personal gain in several ways, including the following:

- **Hyping stocks they own:** Some members might exaggerate or even make up good news regarding a stock they own, hoping to fool others into buying the stock. This is commonly called a *pump-and-dump scheme* or *ramping*.

- **Disparaging stocks they're shorting:** Investors can profit from a falling stock by shorting shares, as described in Chapter 5. Some investors might spread false rumors about a company with hopes that such rumors will cause a panic and get others to sell.

- **Promoting companies that pay them:** Questionable companies can hire legions of stock promoters to stoke enthusiasm for their shares. These promoters might float a stream of positive press releases online, trying to create the appearance the company has lots going on.

Determining what exchange or market a stock trades on

If you're going to be using stock message boards, you need to know the difference between unlisted stocks and stocks listed on an exchange. Some of the most popular stocks discussed on stock message boards aren't listed on an exchange like the NYSE or NASDAQ. Instead, they trade on informal and lightly regulated electronic markets such as the Pink Sheets or OTC Bulletin Board.

It's important for you to know whether a stock trades on the Pink Sheets or OTC Bulletin Board, because if it's trading there, it doesn't have to meet the same listing standards that any stock on the exchanges needs to meet. That means the stocks have less oversight. For instance, stocks on the Pink Sheets aren't required to file audited financial statements. And many stocks on these exchanges are abandoned shell companies that can be used by fraudsters to create a pump-and-dump scheme. (These dangers are covered in greater detail in the "A penny saved: Beware of penny stocks" section, later in this chapter.) But for now, you want to know how to find out where your stock trades. The following step list shows you how to find out the primary market for a specific stock :

1. **Point your browser to NASDAQ.com (www.nasdaq.com)**

2. **Click the Symbol Lookup button.**

   The Symbol Lookup screen appears, as shown in Figure 7-2.

   You can find the Symbol Lookup button toward the middle of the screen, just below the Get Up To 10 Quotes section — the one for entering ticker symbols as part of a stock quote search. Since we're looking for a stock's exchange, leave the radio button on its default Stocks setting.

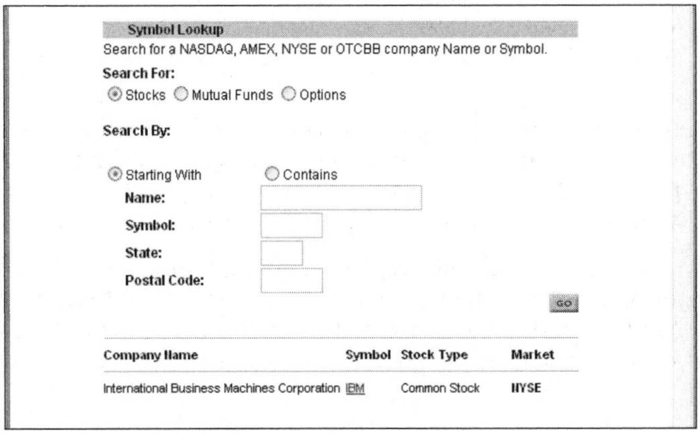

Figure 7-2: The screen as NASDAQ. com makes it easy to see what exchange or market stocks trade on.

Symbol Lookup
Search for a NASDAQ, AMEX, NYSE or OTCBB company Name or Symbol.
Search For:
◉ Stocks ○ Mutual Funds ○ Options

Search By:

◉ Starting With   ○ Contains
   Name:
   Symbol:
   State:
   Postal Code:

GO

Company Name	Symbol	Stock Type	Market
International Business Machines Corporation	IBM	Common Stock	NYSE

3. **Enter either the company's name or ticker symbol**

   If you know the company's name, enter it into the first blank, next to where it says Name. If you only know the symbol, enter that into the second blank, next to where is says Symbol.

4. **Click the Go button at the bottom of the screen.**

   A new page appears, listing the results of your search

5. **View the company name and look at the market.**

   The entry under the Market heading — the heading at the far right of the screen — tells you the stock's primary market. (Table 7-1 tells you what all the abbreviations mean.)

Table 7-1	Guide to Different Stock Markets Using NASDAQ.com
Market Code	*Market or Exchange*
NASDAQ	NASDAQ (National Association of Securities Dealers Automated Quotations)
NYSE	New York Stock Exchange
AMEX	American Stock Exchange
OTCBB	OTC Bulletin Board (OTC stands for Over the Counter)
Other OTC	Pink Sheets

A penny saved: Beware of penny stocks

If you spend much time looking at online stock message boards, you might notice that many of the messages are posted about stocks that trade for less than $1 — so-called "penny" stocks. That's partly because penny stocks, due to their tiny share prices, allow investors to buy large numbers of shares. Owning large chunks of stock is appealing to the same speculator-types that flock to stock message boards to begin with.

But penny stocks can also be popular on stock message boards because they're easily manipulated. Unlike giant stocks like General Electric or Cisco, which are so valuable that you'd need billions of dollars to budge the stock, penny stocks can be nudged with just a few hundred bucks. Just a small amount of hype or negativity can have a large effect on a penny stock's share price. A stock has to move only from one penny to two pennies to double a fraudster's money.

Many penny stocks also trade on the generally unregulated Pink Sheets and OTC Bulletin Board markets, considered to be the Wild Wild West of online investing. It's best to avoid investing in penny stocks, but if you can't resist be sure you have

✔ **Read the warnings from regulators:** The Securities and Exchange Commission (SEC) has released multiple warnings to investors about investing in penny stocks, including this must-read guide: `http://sec.gov/investor/pubs/microcapstock.htm`. You should also search for the company's name and officers using the tools at the SEC's main site (`www.sec.gov`) to see whether there have been prior problems. The SEC outlines the unique risks of investing in Pink Sheet stocks at `http://sec.gov/answers/pink.htm`.

✔ **Checked the company's level of disclosure:** Pink Sheets (`www.pinksheets.com`) rates companies with one of four icons, shown in Figure 7-3, indicating how much information they provide to investors. The highest-quality rating is Current Information, followed by Limited Information, No Information, and then Caveat Emptor. Just enter the stock's symbol, and you can view the rating.

The OTC Bulletin Board (`www.otcbb.com`) offers similar information on its stocks. The site, for instance, has a Delinquency/Eligibility list showing companies that haven't met its standards. (`www.otcbb.com/DailyListContent/delistings/OTCBBDelOpenReport.pdf`). And you can find additional cautionary information at `www.otcbb.com/faqs/otcbb_faq.stm`.

Figure 7-3: Pink Sheets assigns one of four easy-to-understand icons to stocks to let you know how much information is available about it.

Don't be fooled: Starbucks wasn't a penny stock

Some penny-stock investors claim many successful stocks like Starbucks and Microsoft started out as penny stocks. They look at long-term charts online, as described in Chapter 6, and say those stocks started trading at less than $2 a share. That is simply not true, and it's worthwhile to understand why.

Consider Starbucks. Some investors look at a long-term chart and claim the coffeehouse chain's shares closed on their first day of trading on June 26, 1992 at $0.672 apiece. And if you look at a chart, that appears to be true. But it's an illusion caused by stock splits. When a stock splits, as described in Chapter 6, the company cuts its share price and increases the number of shares. A stock split has no effect on the value of the stock or company, but changes historical prices because most charting services split-adjust historical stock prices. Starbucks' shares have had five 2-for-1 splits since they debuted on NASDAQ.

To find out what the actual closing price of Starbucks' stock was on June 26, 1992, you must undo the effect of the five splits that occurred after that date. You do that by multiplying the split-adjusted stock price in 1992, or $0.672, by each split amount. For Starbucks, that's $0.672 \times 2 \times 2 \times 2 \times 2 \times 2 = \$21.50$. That means Starbucks' actual price at the end of its first day of trading was $21.50, not 67 cents.

✔ **Done your due-diligence:** You should, at the very least, see whether the company has released any financial statements. (Chapter 2 has more on how to check for financial statements.) And if financial information is available, you should carefully analyze it using the guide in Chapter 12. StockPatrol (www.stockpatrol.com) also features in-depth investigative reports of companies, including many penny stocks. StockPatrol's search feature will show you whether a stock you're interested in has been written about. Just reading the stories, meanwhile, will give you an idea on how to investigate penny stock companies.

✔ **Double-checked that you can't do better:** With thousands of stocks listed on the NYSE and NASDAQ, you should be able to find a listed stock you'd like to invest in.

Tapping into Online Newsgroups

Newsgroups are similar to stock message boards in that they're giant online bulletin boards where members can post largely anonymous comments. But unlike stock message boards, which run on Web sites, most newsgroups live on a pretty ancient network, called Usenet. Usenet is a corridor of the Internet that's roped off for discussion groups.

Usenet hosts newsgroups pertaining to just about any topic you can imagine, and some you can't. You can find forums where members talk about grooming their pets, tuning their cars, and, oh yeah, investing online.

How to locate specific online newsgroups

Because there are thousands of forums on Usenet, they're all carefully categorized by topic. Usenet uses a very precise naming convention so you can zero in on a topic quickly and find the appropriate forums. Usenet forums are given a three-part address, much like a street address. First, there's the broad category, or *section,* which is equivalent to the state on your home address. Beneath these main sections are the secondary sections. Using my address metaphor, the secondary section is like your city. Lastly, the groups are broken into very specific topic areas, much like your street address.

A typical newsgroup address would look like this: `section.second` `section.topic`. For instance, a newsgroup dedicated to mutual funds is `misc.invest.mutual-funds`, where `misc` is the section, `invest` is the secondary section, and `mutual-funds` is the topic.

In case you haven't noticed yet, the whole newsgroup address naming convention is bit of a hassle. That's why you'll probably access newsgroups using Google Groups, as described in the following section. Google Groups handles the whole Usenet address nightmare for you.

Some sample investing newsgroups you might consider include the ones in Table 7-2.

Table 7-2	Select Investing Newsgroups
Newsgroup Address	*Topic*
`misc.invest.financial-plan`	Creating a financial game plan
`misc.invest.mutual-funds`	Choosing and investing in mutual funds
`misc.invest.stocks`	Analyzing and picking stocks
`misc.invest.options`	Understanding complex options trading strategies
`alt.invest.real-estate`	Buying and investing in real estate

How to participate in online newsgroups

So, you understand how Usenet addresses work and the kinds of topics that are available. But how do you access these newsgroups? Because newsgroups are essentially in the public domain, you can access them in many ways, including the following:

✔ **Google Groups:** (http://groups.google.com) Probably the best way to access Usenet newsgroups, Google Groups (see Figure 7-4) lets you search all available newsgroups by entering the group name or topic in the search field — all without installing any special reader software often required by browsers. Try terms like "investing," "investing online," and "money." There's no need to remember or look up the complicated Usenet addresses. Google Groups also organizes newsgroups by topic area. Just sign up for the service or log in using your Google Gmail account information — although some newsgroups may require additional registration.

If you know the Usenet newsgroup address, such as misc.invest. stocks, Google Groups can still help. Just enter the Usenet address in the search field and you can access the newsgroup.

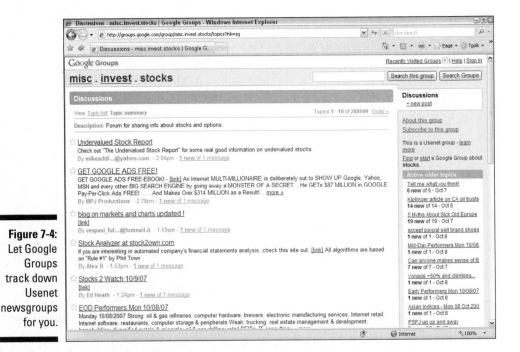

Figure 7-4: Let Google Groups track down Usenet newsgroups for you.

✔ **Yahoo! Groups:** (`http://finance.dir.groups.yahoo.com/dir/Business___Finance/Investments`) Yahoo! Groups doesn't actually connect to Usenet; rather, it links you with groups created within Yahoo!. In this particular corner of Yahoo! Groups, you can find newsgroups that discuss everything from mutual funds to day trading.

Although newsgroups can be okay sources of investment chatter, social investing sites are typically better bets because they make their users more accountable. (I discuss social investing sites later in the chapter.) Generally, I find that newsgroups are best suited for getting technical help when you're having computer problems — when you're having questions about personal finance software, for example. Just post a question to a group listed in Table 7-3, and the experts will help you out. You might also use newsgroups to hear what people are saying about a company's products to give you the inside track.

Table 7-3	Select Useful Technology Newsgroups
Newsgroup Address	**Topic**
`microsoft.public.money`	Guidance for using Microsoft Money software
`alt.comp.software.financial.quicken`	Help with using Intuit's Quicken
`microsoft.public.windows.vista.general`	Discussion about Microsoft's operating system
`comp.sys.mac.system`	Forum regarding Apple Macintosh computers

Connecting with an Investment Club

If online stock message boards seem too wild and scary but you'd still like to connect with other investors, you might consider an investment club. Investment clubs are typically gatherings of investors in a certain geographic area who meet at a local restaurant or a member's house to shoot the breeze. Members pitch stocks they think the group should buy or sell. Investment clubs also have a bit of a party feeling to them, because they're usually designed to be fun, educational, and, oh yeah, profitable. If your city doesn't have an investment club, or if meeting with people in person doesn't fit your schedule, there are a few online investment clubs cropping up. Whether the club you're interested in joining is held in the local Moose club or online, you may be required to buy in by adding money to a pool of cash.

How to find an investment club that suits you

If you're interested in an investment club, here are several (online) ways to get started:

- ✔ **National Association of Investors Corporation,** also known as Better-Investing (www.betterinvesting.org) is one of the top associations of investment clubs. BetterInvesting's Web site lets you find investment clubs in your area. There are also online classes you can take to work on improving your investing success. And if there's no investment club near you, you can find out how to start a club of your own or join an online investment club.

- ✔ **The Motley Fool** (http://boards.fool.com/Boards.asp?fid=10002) maintains a discussion board where investors in different states can find investment clubs. Just enter the discussion group for your state and say you're interested in joining.

- ✔ **Bivio** (www.bivio.com) is perfect if you'd like the friendly and personal nature of an investment club but don't have time to attend monthly meetings. Bivio is a collection of online investment clubs. You can search through the club home pages and choose a club to join or even start your own.

- ✔ **Value Investors Club** (http://valueinvestorsclub.com) is a selective group of just 250 members who pick stocks. You must apply to be accepted, and if you get chosen, you must submit two stock picks a year.

Understanding the drawbacks of investment clubs

Before you rush out and join an investment club, be aware of the potential drawbacks:

- ✔ **Bad decisions by others will cost you.** If the loudmouthed guy in the club talks the group into buying a stinker, you're going to take a bath, too.

- ✔ **They give an incentive to tinker.** Many investment clubs consider themselves to be *long-term investors,* or shareholders who hang onto a stock for at least a year and usually much longer. But an investment club wouldn't be much fun if the members never actually bought or sold anything. That means there's somewhat of an incentive to be constantly buying or selling investments.

  ✔ **Compromise can hurt.** Although nothing is wrong with agreement, having several people steering a portfolio sometimes means there's no single and coherent strategy.

  ✔ **Members' investing skill levels can vary.** Some investment club members are only there for the fun, food, and friends. That can leave much of the grunt work for the few members with the skill or desire to make money in the club.

The Brave New World: Social Networking Meets Online Investing

As the Internet grows up, it's becoming more clear the Internet is all about connecting people who might never have crossed paths in real life. Myspace.com has become the digital version of a high-school lunchroom and is the place for people to talk about what's in and what's not. YouTube lets anyone with a video camera film just about anything and share it with the world. And the online video game Second Life has morphed into a fully developed world where real estate has actual value and companies spend real money marketing to the online community.

Online social networking is now trickling into the investment world, and early signs seem promising. Social investing sites answer some of the shortcomings of stock message boards and investment clubs.

Social investing sites as a higher form of stock message boards?

Social networking stands to be a major advance in how investors interface with each other. Unlike stock message boards, which cloak their users in anonymity, social networking is based on posting actual trades and often even investors' real names. And unlike simulations, discussed in Chapter 2, social investing sites are based on real trades with investors' real money. The main advantages of this exciting new area of investing online are

  ✔ **Showing what's possible in the real world:** Anyone can get lucky picking winning stocks with funny money. Social investing sites take away the fantasy aspect of simulations by encouraging users to disclose actual stocks they own and when they bought and sold them. You can use that information to determine who's credible versus investors who talk a big game and those who might have ulterior motives.

✔ **Separating the good from the bad:** Social investing sites often let you know how often different members are right about their picks.

✔ **Providing some safeguards:** Brokers operating social investing sites are overseen by securities regulators. Fraudsters know this and might avoid certain social investing sites because they could be easily tracked and monitored. It's similar to how a bank robber might not target a bank that's across the street from the police station.

Plugging into social investing sites

I discuss several popular social investing sites below, but they all, at their core, work roughly the same. Follow these six steps to get involved in social investing:

1. **Pick a site.**

   Social investing sites are essentially gated communities of investors. You want to choose the site that fits you best and has a pool of investors you can identify with. I'll help you choose in the later section, "Choosing a social investing site."

2. **Register.**

   Most social investing sites require you to give more details about yourself than some stock message boards do. That might be a slight burden at first, but it's also one of the ways these sites eliminate users that insist on being cloaked in privacy.

3. **Create a profile.**

   Here you describe yourself, only giving details you're comfortable sharing with the rest of the social investing site. Typically, you might say how long you've been investing, what kind of investor you are, and what types of stocks you prefer.

4. **Enter your transactions.**

   The biggest thing that separates social investing sites from stock message boards is that other users can see your real trades if you give permission. That means you'll need to import your trades or give the site permission to share them. Trades may be imported several ways, either manually by you or automatically when you enter an order to buy or sell shares with your online broker.

5. **Set your permissions.**

   Permissions are rules telling the social investing site how much personal information you're comfortable with sharing. You can choose to use a fake name, or *handle,* or reveal your real name. You can decide whether you'll let other users look at your trades or send messages to you. This is an important step. The more information you reveal about yourself, the more credibility you'll have on the site with other users.

Be careful about listening to stock tips and recommendations by social investing users who reveal very little personal information about themselves. These users might be cloaking themselves for the same reasons some investors are attracted to the anonymous world of stock message boards.

6. **Look around.**

   After you're set up with a profile, you can peruse the community to find people you might want to be "friends" with. These are investors you think are worthwhile listening to. You can also read other investors' *blogs* (Web logs), which are their personal narratives on how to invest.

Starting to get social: Trying social investing sites

Two types of social investing sites exist: standalone sites and broker-operated sites. You need to decide which is better for you. The standalone sites might appeal to you if you want to

- ✔ Keep your social investing and brokerage accounts apart from each other.

- ✔ Try out social investing with test trades before linking your real account.

- ✔ Maintain your online accounts with traditional or discount online brokerages that don't offer social investing.

- ✔ Use multiple online brokerage accounts and be able pull in all your holdings and trades to one social investing site.

You might think about signing up with your online broker's social investing service if you want to

- ✔ Have your trades automatically shared with other users, after granting your permission.

- ✔ Don't want to bother getting another username and password and trying to remember them.

- ✔ Feel that the other members of the brokerage firm have similar investing goals and styles as you.

Choosing a social investing site

After you've chosen whether you want to join a standalone or broker-sponsored social investing site, it's time to pick one. This is an emerging area, and new players will certainly be showing up, so be sure to search for new social investing sites that have started since this book was published.

Most online brokers don't offer social investing capabilities, yet. If your broker hasn't jumped on the social investing bandwagon yet, and you want to try it out, you might consider some of the dedicated social investing sites. Here's a few to try:

- ✔ **Covestor:** (www.covestor.com) A standalone social investing site that lets regular online investors emerge as experts, Covestor, with your permission, pulls in your real trades from more than 100 online and traditional brokerage firms. Other investors can see what kinds of stocks you're buying and see how well they're performing. All the investors are ranked so visitors can choose who's worth listening to.

- ✔ **Collective2:** (www.collective2.com) This site is like most other social investing sites in that it tracks and shares your real trades. But unlike Covestor, which downloads your trades from your online brokers, Collective2 works in reverse. You enter your real trades in Collective2, which then sends your orders to actual brokers. The system directly connects with a handful of brokers. Alternatively, you can download TradeBullet software (www.tradebullet.com), which routes your orders from Collective2 to additional brokerages.

Two online brokerage firms, TradeKing and Zecco, have been the innovators in the area of social networking. Both offerings are very pioneering and it will be interesting to see if other online brokerage follow suit and add social networking to their sites, too. Here are the details:

- ✔ **TradeKing:** (www.tradeking.com) TradeKing is an online brokerage that offers social investing. The online brokerage, discussed more fully in Chapter 4, lets its investors interact with each other. You can decide how much information, if any, you choose to share with other members. Often times, you might just begin with a profile page and, after you get more comfortable, begin sharing more — including your trades. TradeKing makes it easy to find the honest investors by giving them Certified status. These are investors that are most forthright and open with their real-life investing activity.

You don't have to have a brokerage account to take advantage of the community site. But if you don't, remember that other TradeKing users probably won't take you all that seriously because they can't see your real-life trades. You can read more about how TradeKing ranks as an online broker in Chapter 4.

✔ **Zecco Share:** (www.zecco.com) Zecco Share, as with TradeKing, is interesting because it lets investors share their real-life trades. Zecco Share makes it easy to find others with similar goals by allowing you to search for investors with the same approach, experience, or research style. After you find other investors you trust, you can communicate with them, watch their trades, and even receive an e-mail if they buy or sell anything.

Finding Information for Investors Like You

Online investors typically fall in one of two categories: active or passive. But investors can classify themselves in many other ways, be it by age, experience level, or gender. Plenty of Web sites are dedicated to serving specific demographics if that's what you're looking for.

Sites for kids

There's nothing better than encouraging young people to start investing. Several sites are dedicated to young investors:

✔ **Young Investor** (www.younginvestor.com) is filled with fun quizzes and games to help your kids understand the value of money and investing.

✔ **Investing for Kids** (http://library.thinkquest.org/3096) offers different stock games for kids and educational materials.

✔ **Kids' Money** (www.kidsmoney.org) provides all sorts of money management tips for children.

✔ **Young Investors Network** (www.smithbarney.com/yin) is a site offered from Smith Barney to make investing approachable and fun.

✔ **Moneyopolis** (www.moneyopolis.com) brings a video-game like approach to teaching kids about money.

✔ **Planet Orange** (www.orangekids.com) lets kids climb mountains and avoid alligators in the quest to learn more about managing their money.

Some parents have told me they get their kids interested in investing by splitting their allowance in two parts. One part is paid in cash and the other is automatically deposited into a savings account that the child chooses. It's a good way to show children how money saved can snowball.

Sites for women

To be honest, there really isn't that much of a difference between how a man or woman would invest. But some sites are tailored to females and provide various money-management suggestions:

- ✔ **Wi$eUp** (http://wiseupwomen.tamu.edu) contains calculators and tutorials for young women.
- ✔ **Women's Institute for Financial Education** (www.wife.org) describes and answers many money questions that women have.
- ✔ **iVillage** (http://home.ivillage.com/homeoffice/saveinvest/topics/0,,4tn5,00.html) contains quizzes and information for women hoping to take control of their money.

Sites for seniors

The financial goals and objectives of senior citizens are completely different than those of a 20-something just entering the workforce. These sites address the unique situation of older investors:

- ✔ **AARP:** (www.aarp.org/research/financial) The American Association of Retired People (AARP) lists information critical to older investors, helping with investing and retirement planning.
- ✔ **MSN Money:** (http://moneycentral.msn.com/retire/home.asp) This section of the MSN Money site contains information older investors need to make sure their nest eggs last.
- ✔ **ElderNet:** (www.eldernet.com/money.htm) This section of the ElderNet site pinpoints links to tutorials, calculators, and other online tools to help individuals become financially independent.

Seniors are constant targets for unscrupulous money managers, so they need to be extra cautious. A group of retirees, many living in the Leisure World retirement community in Orange County, California, learned this the hard way and lost their life savings as a result. The retirees invested $12 million with Christopher Peter Cook and his CD Services, Inc., between 1995 and

1998. Cook promised the retirees interest rates higher than banks were offering, but he said money could be withdrawn anytime. It turns out, though, that Cook and associates were funneling the money into inappropriate investments and took 52% of investors' money as "commissions," according to the Department of Justice (http://losangeles.fbi.gov/dojpressrel/pressrel07/la062507usa.htm). If investors asked for their money, they were told there was a 50% early withdrawal fee. The Cooks ended up taking $4.8 million from the investors. Cook was convicted of mail fraud and money laundering and sentenced to nearly eight years in prison.

Before you give your money to anyone to manage, you should run the person's name through FINRA's Broker Check system (www.finra.org/Investor Information/InvestorProtection/ChecktheBackgroundofYour InvestmentProfessional/index.htm). Make sure the person has the proper licenses to give financial advice and hasn't been disciplined in the past.

Chapter 8

Measuring Your Performance

· ·

In This Chapter

▶ Seeing the importance of tracking your performance

▶ Figuring out the best way to calculate investment performance

▶ Using online tools that can measure your risk and returns

▶ Choosing the right benchmark

· ·

*I*t's surprising how many investors keep buying and selling stocks online even when they have no idea whether they're beating the market or not. They'll brag at cocktail parties about the winning stocks they've bought. But if you ask them what their rate of return is, they'll look at you blankly. Most online brokers don't help either, because many don't have tools that accurately measure your returns.

To me, investing online without knowing how you're doing is like driving with your eyes closed. As an online investor, it's pretty much up to you to calculate your own returns. To help you get back in control, this chapter first shows you how to manually calculate your returns and how much risk you've taken to get those returns. In case you want more handholding, I then discuss online sites and software that do all the calculations for you. Either way you choose, you'll be miles ahead of other investors who keep investing without knowing whether they're successful or not.

The Importance of Tracking Your Performance

You learn from an early age to monitor your progress with most things. As babies, your height and weight were plotted on charts to illustrate how quickly you were growing and how your size ranked with other infants. In school, your progress was constantly monitored using letter grades and tests. And at work, annual reviews and pay often reflect the job you're doing and show what's working and what's not.

That's why it's so strange that many people don't monitor their investment performance. Investors often look through their portfolios, see a few stocks that are up since they bought them, and assume they're beating the stock market.

Psychology plays a big part in investing. Many online investors tend to get overly confident if they've recently picked a few lucky stocks. That prompts them to take more uncalculated risks in the future, which might cost them dearly. Investors also tend to wipe out painful losses from their memories. They remember only the winners. And other investors beat themselves up for losing money on a stock, blaming something that had nothing to do with the loss. By measuring your performance, you can try to remove some of the emotion from investing. (Morningstar, the independent investment research outfit, has a great little lesson on how human nature can affect your success investing online; check out `http://news.morningstar.com/classroom2/printlesson.asp?docId=145104&CN=com`.)

I suspect most folks don't bother monitoring their investment performance because it requires some math and a few scary-looking formulas that most investors don't understand. This chapter, though, demystifies how to track your portfolio's risk and return. I start by showing you how to do the calculations yourself.

It's important for you to understand how all the calculations are done so you don't blindly rely on Web sites to do it for you, but I also know that not everyone has the time or the willingness to crunch down performance stats themselves. And that's why I've included online tools that do the math for you. If you get confused at any point in this section about calculating performance manually, don't dismay. Just skip ahead to the section "Using Online Tools to Calculate Performance for You."

Why it's worth the trouble measuring your returns

Studies have shown that people who regularly weigh themselves tend to have more success reaching their fitness goals. It's similar with investing online. If you take the time to measure your results, you'll likely be a better investor. After all, even if your investments aren't doing well, if you track your performance, you might be able to adjust your strategy. Some investors, for instance, might find that constantly buying and selling stocks isn't working for them.

These investors can adjust accordingly and might find more success being passive investors. (You can review the difference between active and passive investors in Chapter 1.)

If you take the time to measure your performance, you'll be able to figure out whether you're going to do the following

- ✔ **Reach your financial goals.** When you invest, you typically estimate the rate of return you need to reach your goal, such as funding retirement or paying for college. By tracking your returns, you can see whether you're on the right path or not. And if you're not, you can consider ways to improve your results, including changing your *asset allocation.* I discuss how to design the right asset allocation for you in Chapter 9.

  One of the first things you should do before you start investing is decide how much risk you can tolerate and what rate of return you need to meet your goal. You can find out how to do this in Chapter 1.

- ✔ **Hurt yourself more than help.** If you're an active investor who's constantly buying and selling stocks, you might be wasting your time and hurting your portfolio. If you find that your returns are lower than what you could get by just buying an index mutual fund, you might be better served following a more passive approach.

- ✔ **Find your mistakes.** You might have a good investment plan that's working, except for a few investments or stocks that are killing your performance. By tracking your results, you can find what's hurting you and make adjustments if needed.

  Curious what the top mistakes investors make might be? Check out `www.cfainstitute.org/aboutus/investors/articles/ 12investormistakes.html`, where the CFA Institute has posted a Not to Do list compiled by prominent professional money managers. You'll also find my own take on the top 10 mistakes made by investors in Chapter 17.

Why you want to measure your risk, too

I can't tell you how many investors ask me for "ten stocks to buy now." Investors get so obsessed with the potential return for winning stocks that they forget the other side of the picture: the risk. After all, you can get a great return by putting all your chips on black at the roulette table. But are you willing to risk it all? By measuring how much risk you're taking on with your investment, you'll know whether you are

✔ **Getting adequate returns:** When you invest in a savings account, you're not taking any risk, so you shouldn't expect a giant return. But if you invest in a risky stock, you should demand to be compensated with a bigger return. If you're not, you're being shortchanged.

✔ **Invested properly:** Some investors aren't matched up with their investments very well. If you're risk-adverse and can't stomach it when your portfolio falls just 5% in value in a year, you shouldn't be invested in risky stocks that go up and down wildly. You might consider changing what types of investment you own so you can smooth the bumps. This is done by creating your *asset allocation.* (You find out how to use online tools to create a portfolio that fits your personality in Chapter 9.)

✔ **Prepared for volatility:** If you know how risky your investments are ahead of time, you won't be surprised when the value of your account swings up and down. That foresight will help stop you from doing something in haste you'll regret, such as selling all your stocks in panic.

To get higher returns, you must accept more risk. Return and risk are tied at the hip. However, investing in a risky asset doesn't always mean you'll get a higher return. As you find out in Chapter 9, there are many risky assets that have generated poor returns over the years. You'll want to avoid these investments because they're bum deals.

Calculating Your Performance Yourself

If Web sites and software programs can calculate your portfolio's risk and return for you, why bother learning to do it yourself? I've found that many of the automated ways of calculating performance use slightly different methods, so you're not always clear what's going on. And with something this important, you don't want to rely solely on a Web site that might or might not be accurate. If you know how performance is measured and can approximate your performance yourself, you'll know if you're getting the right information from the automated tools.

If you don't care to know how portfolio returns are measured and just want to do it online, go to MoneyChimp's Portfolio Performance Calculator (www. moneychimp.com/features/portfolio_performance_calculator. htm). It automatically calculates your portfolio's return if you enter your portfolio's beginning and ending balance and indicate whether you deposited or withdrew money.

The easiest way to calculate returns

If you haven't deposited money into or taken any money out of your broker-age account, it's relatively easy to measure your rate of return for the year. Just follow these steps:

1. **Get your account balance at the end of the year and write it down.**

   You can get your year-end balance from your online broker's Web site or from a printed statement.

2. **Get your account balance at the end of the previous year and write it down.**

   Again, this information is available from your broker's Web site or from a printed statement.

3. **Subtract the answer from Step 2 from the answer in step 1. Divide that difference by the answer from step 2 and then multiply by 100.**

   Say your portfolio was worth $10,000 on December 31, 2006, and it was worth $12,000 on December 31, 2007. You would subtract $10,000 from $12,000 and get $2,000. Divide $2,000 by $10,000, multiply by 100, and the answer is 20%. You earned a 20% rate of return in that year.

Don't worry about dividends and splits when using this approach. And don't concern yourself if you've bought or sold stocks. As long as your dividends and sale proceeds go into the brokerage account, this way of calculating your return reflects all these things.

An easy way to calculate returns if you've deposited or taken out money

You're probably already asking the logical question: What if you deposited money into or withdrew money from your brokerage account? It complicates things a bit, but it's still not hard. There's an easy way to calculate your return when there are deposits to or withdrawals from your account.

Say your portfolio was worth $10,000 on December 31, 2006, and it was worth $12,000 on December 31, 2007. But you made the following withdrawals and deposits to you account, as shown in Table 8-1.

Table 8-1	Changes in a Sample Portfolio	
Date	*Action*	*Amount*
Dec. 31, 2006	Account balance	$10,000
March 20, 2007	Deposit	$1,000
June 25, 2007	Withdrawal	$500
Oct. 1, 2007	Deposit	$1,000
Dec. 31, 2007	Account balance	$12,000

Okay, time to start crunching some numbers:

1. **Get your account balance at the end of the previous year.**

   Using my example, you'd write down $10,000, which was your balance on December 31, 2006.

2. **Get your account balance at the end of the current year.**

   You'd write down $12,000, which was your supposed balance at the end of 2007.

3. **Add all the money you've added to your account during the year.**

   In my example, you'd write down $2,000 ($1,000 from March 20 plus $1,000 from October 1).

   Only include fresh money you've deposited into your account. Don't include dividends that were paid.

4. **Add up all the money you've withdrawn from your account during the year.**

   In my example, you'd write down $500. That's the only withdrawal you supposedly made.

   Include just withdrawals from the account or checks you have written on the account. Do not include stocks you've sold if you left the proceeds in your account.

5. **Subtract the answer from Step 4 from the answer from Step 3. Divide the result by 2 and write down the answer.**

   In my example, you'd write down $750. You'd get that by subtracting the $500 in supposed withdrawals from the $2,000 in supposed deposits. Divide the answer, $1,500, by 2.

6. **Add the answer from Step 5 to the number from Step 1.**

   You'd write down $10,750. You'd get that by adding $750 to the number from Step 1.

7. **Subtract the answer from Step 5 to the number from Step 2.**

   You'd write down $11,250. That's $12,000 minus $750.

8. **Subtract the answer from step 6 from the answer in step 7.**

   You'd write down $500. That's $11,250 minus $10,750.

9. **Divide the answer from Step 8 by the answer in Step 7 and multiply by 100.**

   You'd get your 4.7% rate of return by dividing $500 by $10,750 and multiplying by 100.

You might want to calculate how your portfolio is doing before the end of the year. For instance, in June, you might want to get your mid-year performance. That's no problem. Just use the value of your portfolio at any date in the year in Step 2. All the formulas remain the same.

The hardest way to calculate returns

The methods of calculating your returns described in the preceding sections can get you accurate measures of your rate of return. But, as you can imagine, there's always a way to measure returns even more precisely. Some mutual funds, for instance, use a complicated calculation called the *dollar-weighted return* or *internal rate of return.* This requires advanced computing that's beyond the scope of this book. I show you some Web sites in this chapter, though, that have computerized performance tracking tools that can measure your internal rate of return for you.

You can find out more about different methods of calculating portfolio returns at the following sites:

✔ **Investment Performance Analysis** (www.andreassteiner.net/performanceanalysis/index.php) provides numerous free spreadsheets and tools that can help you precisely measure how your portfolio is doing. Be forewarned, though, these tools are very advanced.

✔ **dailyVest** (www.dailyvest.com) provides performance calculation services for large investment companies. But dailyVest's Web site contains an in-depth description of the different ways returns are measured.

✔ **USATODAY.com's Ask Matt** (www.usatoday.com/money/perfi/columnist/krantz/2006-06-27-tota-return_x.htm) explains in all the gory details how to calculate your returns using either the easy way or the hard way. Why would you trust someone who calls himself Ask Matt? I can vouch for this character because it's moi. Ask Matt is a running feature at USATODAY.com, and this particular column deals with the issue of measuring performance.

- ✔ **Microsoft Excel's help page** (http://office.microsoft.com/en-us/excel/HP052093411033.aspx) provides instructions on how to use the spreadsheet software to perform sophisticated performance tracking.

- ✔ **Gummy Stuff** (www.gummy-stuff.org/Dietz.htm) provides a free spreadsheet that can measure your returns by using advanced techniques.

Calculating How Risky Your Portfolio Is

The returns you get from investing online are only half of what you need to know. Just as important, if not more so, is how much risk you took on to get those returns. Measuring risk is a little more controversial. There are many ways to do it, and investors generally disagree on the best way.

Most investment professionals, though, acknowledge the value of measuring risk by studying its *standard deviation*. Yikes, that's a scary term and one that might conjure up memories of statistics class. But by using readily available online tools, you can use standard deviation as a way to get a handle on how much risk you're accepting in investing. Standard deviation is a mathematical way to determine how much your portfolio swings in value from its average return.

Just know this: When your portfolio's standard deviation is a large number, there's a good chance you'll see some big ups and downs in your portfolio's value. And when the standard deviation is low, you have a good idea your portfolio will pretty much give you your average return every year.

Statistics tell us that 68% of the time, your portfolio should not rise by more than its average return (plus the standard deviation) or fall more than its average return (minus the standard deviation). And 95% of the time, your portfolio shouldn't rise by more than its average return plus two times its standard deviation or fall by more than its average return minus two times its standard deviation.

For example, if you put your money in a five-year certificate of deposit that pays 5% interest, the standard deviation of your return would be 0. In other words, you will get 5% a year no matter what. But if you invest in a risky stock that returns 15% a year on average, your standard deviation might be closer to 40. That means 68% of the time you can expect your portfolio to be up 55% (the 15% average return plus the standard deviation) or down 25% (the 15% average return minus the standard deviation).

A simple way of calculating your average return

Before you can measure how risky your portfolio is, you must first calculate its average yearly return. Earlier in the chapter you found out how to calculate your portfolio's annual returns. Next, you need to use those annual returns to measure your portfolio's average annual return. You can do this easily by taking all your annual returns, calculated using the directions in the earlier sections, and analyzing them.

After you calculate your portfolio's annual returns for each year, you'll want to write them down or put them in a spreadsheet. I'll use the returns listed in Table 8-2 as an example.

Table 8-2	Returns in a Sample Portfolio
Year	**Return**
2006	15.8%
2005	4.9%
2004	10.9%
2003	28.7%
2002	−22.1%

Source: Global Financial Data

If the returns above look familiar, they should. Those are the annual returns of the Standard & Poor's 500 index, which tracks large company stocks, over the past five years.

How do you measure your average return? You can't just take a simple average by adding up all the returns and dividing by five. Doing that will give you the wrong answer. Instead, you must calculate the *geometric mean*. The geometric mean is the way to correctly measure stock return, trust me. I could explain the technical difference between simple averages and geometric means, but we'll both get headaches for no good reason. If you're truly curious, Deborah Rumsey does a nice job explaining it in her *Statistics For Dummies* (Wiley).

If you don't want to go to the trouble to measure geometric mean as described shortly, the Average Return Calculator at Hugh's Mortgage and Financial Calculators (www.hughchou.org/calc/areturn.php) can do it for you. Just enter your returns for each year, and the site calculates the geometric mean or what it calls the "true average return." Easy Calculation (www.easycalculation.com/statistics/geometric-mean.php) can also calculate the geometric mean.

You can calculate geometric means using a financial calculator or a spreadsheet. But this is *Investing Online For Dummies,* right? So, I show you how to do it online by using the Horton's Geometric Mean Calculator you see in Figure 8-1 (available at www.graftacs.com/geomean.php3).

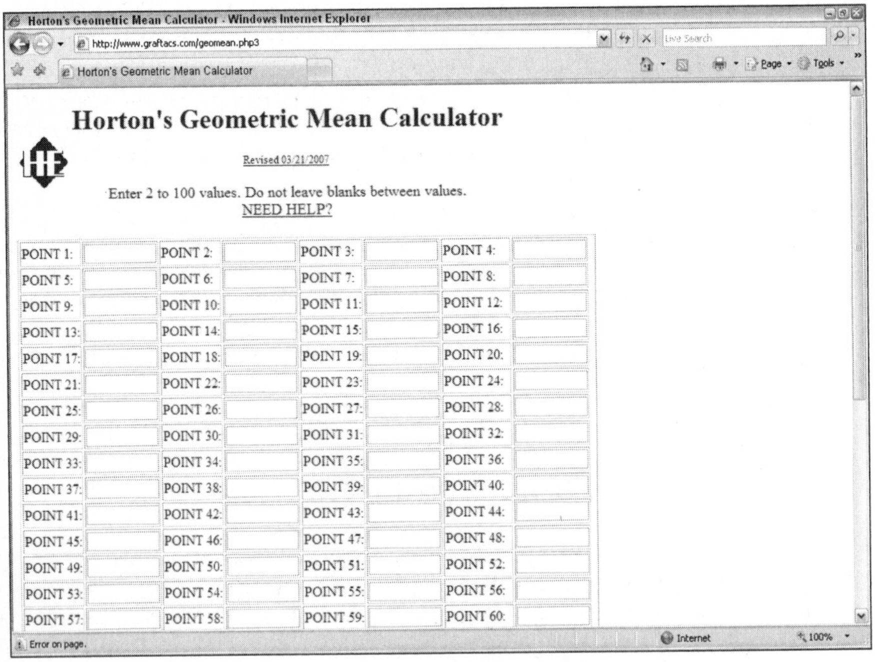

Figure 8-1: Horton's Geometric Mean Calculator can do much of the work for you.

Before you rush and type in the returns from Table 8-2 into Horton's Geometric Mean Calculator, you need to follow an additional step. Horton's Geometric Mean Calculator can't handle negative numbers. I know you don't think you'll ever have a negative return, but just in case, I show you what to do. Just add 100 to each of the returns, giving you what you see in Table 8-3.

Table 8-3	Returns Converted to Get Geometric Mean
Year	*Plus 100 (Adjusted Return)*
2006	115.8
2005	104.9
2004	110.9
2003	128.7
2002	77.9

Enter those returns into the blanks in Horton's Geometric Mean Calculator labeled Point 1 and Point 2 and so forth. After you have entered the returns, scroll to the bottom of the page and click the Submit button. At the top of the page, you see the geometric mean, from which you subtract 100. In this example, the geometric mean is 106.20. You just subtract 100 from 106.20, and you find out your portfolio has a geometric mean return of 6.2%.

If you'd rather measure your portfolio's geometric return in a spreadsheet, Microsoft Excel has a GEOMEAN function that will do it for you. And if you don't have Microsoft Excel, you can download a fairly capable spreadsheet program for free. It's called OpenOffice (www.openoffice.org). And although it's not as slick as Excel, it's hard to argue with the price. (Open-Office's Calc spreadsheet program calls its function the GEOMEAN function as well.)

Calculating your risk

If you used Horton's Geometric Mean Calculator to measure your portfolio's average return, you've also measured your risk. At the top of the page, right below the geometric mean, is the risk, or standard deviation. In this example, the standard deviation of the portfolio is 18.8 percentage points, as shown in Figure 8-2.

Microsoft Excel has a function that measures risk. The STDEV function can measure the standard deviation of returns that you enter.

Standard deviation works best as a measure of risk if you have many years of data to study. If you've been investing for only a few months or years, you can convert your quarterly results into a yearly or *annualized* number. Investopedia (www.investopedia.com/articles/04/021804.asp) shows you how to do this. If all this seems like too much effort, just use the online risk-measurement tools described a little later in this chapter.

Figure 8-2:
Horton's
Geometric
Mean
Calculator
crunches
down your
portfolio's
risk
(standard
deviation)
as well as
the return
(geometric
mean).

Geometric Mean Calculator Results				
Number of points	5	Arithmetic mean	107.64	
Geometric mean	106.20	Maximum value	128.70	Graphs are currently not available.
Standard deviation	18.79	Sum of points	538.20	
Minimum value	77.90	Equation is	y=-5.20 x + 123.24	

What does it all mean? Sizing up your portfolio

You did it. You measured your portfolio's average return and risk. Now what? You can start by shopping for a new pocket protector. But then, you'll need to compare your portfolio's risk and return with another investment so you can put it into perspective. You can see how your performance stacks up by comparing it with a benchmark called an *index.* An index is a basket of stocks used to measure your success. If your portfolio's risk is higher than the index' risk, you want to make sure you're also getting a higher return.

Chapter 2 describes most of the popular market indexes. The Standard & Poor's 500, due to its general acceptance and the fact it closely tracks the stock market, is the most common index used to size up investors' returns. If you want to compare your portfolio's risk and return to the S&P 500 for the same time period, you can download the S&P's annual returns from Standard & Poor's by first going to this page — www2.standardandpoors.com/portal/ site/sp/en/us/page.topic/indices_500/2,3,2,2,0,0,0,0,0,0,5,12, 0,0,0,0,0.html — and then clicking on the S&P 500 Historical Returns link at the bottom of the page. The site opens a spreadsheet. Click the annual total returns tab and enter those returns into Horton's Geometric Mean Calculator. The result you get is the S&P 500's risk and return for the same years.

If you want an easier way to compare returns, you can see how your portfolio fared relative to the long-term returns of major types of investments, such as the ones in Table 8-4.

Table 8-4 Long-Term Risk and Returns of Different Investments		
Investment	_Return_	_Risk (Standard Deviation)_
Standard & Poor's 500	10.3%	20.1
Corporate bonds	6.8%	7.1
Treasury notes (loans to the U.S. government that come due in 10 years or less)	5.2%	8.4
Treasury bills (loans to the U.S. government that come due in a year or less.)	3.8%	3.1

Source: Global Financial Data using data since 1926

Are your returns lower than the long-term returns on the S&P 500? If so, you want to make sure your risk is lower too. You can read the definitions of corporate bonds, and different types of Treasuries called Treasury bonds, Treasury notes and Treasury bills in Chapter 16.

Finding other things to compare your returns to

You don't have to compare your stock portfolio to the S&P 500. Investors commonly choose different indexes to compare their performance to. It's important to rank yourself against the right index in order to get a good understanding of how you're truly performing. For instance, if you want to know how fast your sports car is, you'd compare it with another sports car, not an economy car. You can benchmark your returns against

✔ **More specific indexes:** If you're investing mainly in small company stocks, you'll want to compare your results against an index that tracks small company stocks. iShares' Index Returns Chart (www.ishares.com/tools /index_tracker.jhtml) is a colorful and easy-to-use way to find out how specific areas of the market have performed. You can track stocks of different sizes, sectors, industries, regions, countries, and commodities. You can also measure different time frames, such as five days or five years.

Russell's Index Returns Calculator (www.russell.com/Indexes/ performance/calculator/calculator.asp) can also help you do this. You can download a series of annual returns from many types of stocks, including large company stocks (measured by the Russell 1000) and small company stocks (measured by the Russell 2000) going back 13 years. You can then enter those returns into Horton's Geometric Mean calculator and see how your portfolio stacks up.

Some investors choose to slice the market even more finely when selecting a benchmark. For instance, if you invest mainly in large, undervalued stocks, you would want to compare your performance to a large *value* index that owns similar stocks.

✓ **Broader indexes:** The Capital Markets Index (www.cpmkts.com) gives you an idea of how a diversified basket of stocks, bonds, and money market investors have performed. You can use this index to measure your portfolio's returns.

✓ **A basket of index mutual funds:** Index Funds Advisor (www.ifa.com/portfolios) has created a number of portfolios of index mutual funds that can be used as benchmarks. The IFA portfolios are excellent benchmarks because they are passive index funds designed to deliver the optimum return for the risk taken. You can see where your portfolio would fit on the risk and reward chart. There's also a risk and return calculator (www.ifa.com/portfolios/PortReturnCalc/index.aspx) that you can use to see what the IFA portfolios have done between specific time periods. If you're getting lower returns for higher risk, you might consider switching to a more passive investment strategy. Table 8-5 shows a sample of some of the returns over the past 20 years.

Table 8-5	Index Funds Advisor Portfolios	
IFA Portfolio	*Annual Return between Jan. 1, 1987 and Dec. 31, 2006*	*Risk (Standard Deviation) between Jan. 1, 1987 and Dec. 31, 2006*
100 (riskiest)	13.8%	14.6
85 (moderate)	12.8%	12.9
5 (low)	6.4%	2.7

Source: IFA.com

Using Online Tools to Calculate Your Performance

If you understand the inherent value of tracking your portfolio's performance but maybe the math involved is just too onerous, you've come to the right section of this chapter. Here I show you automated tools that will crunch your performance numbers for you. There are three main advantages to letting your computer do the heavy lifting in measuring performance:

✔ **Ease:** All you have to do is enter your trades, and the computer does the rest. There's no need to look up formulas. You also don't risk making a mistake in the calculations.

✔ **Speed:** The calculations are already programmed in, so after the data is entered, the system can spit out your performance. There's no need to fire up a calculator.

✔ **Customizable:** You can tinker and have the system calculate what your performance would have been, for instance, if you didn't have that one stinker in your portfolio.

Completely relying on online tools to tell you something as important as your portfolio's risk and return isn't ideal. Different sites might use different methodologies and it might be difficult to find out what precisely is being measured. With that said, it's better to rely on online tools than not measure your portfolio's risk and return at all.

Looking at online performance measurement tools

Because many new investors are just now getting interested in tracking their performance, there's been a flurry of new tools promising to do the job. They generally fall into these four categories:

✔ **Financial software:** This is software you install on your computer that crunches the math. It includes personal finance software (discussed in Chapter 1), which contains performance-tracking abilities. There's also specialized software designed just to track returns.

✔ **Online stock simulations and social investing sites:** Most of the stock simulation sites (discussed in Chapter 2) and social investing sites (discussed in Chapter 7) have adequate performance measurement capabilities. I single out a few in this chapter.

✔ **Portfolio-tracking sites:** These services allow you to enter your stock holdings and help measure your returns. Portfolio-tracking sites are kind of like Swiss Army knives: they perform a variety of portfolio tracking tools in addition to measuring your portfolio's returns. Many portfolio-tracking sites, for instance, alert you if a stock is about to pay a dividend or provide links to online news stories about stocks you own.

✔ **Performance-tracking Web sites:** These Web sites are designed with the express purpose of tracking portfolio performance. Because performance-tracking sites focus on performance tracking, they tend to give a great deal of information on your portfolio's risk and return and are very precise and exacting.

Using personal finance and performance-tracking software

If you choose to go the software route, it stands to reason that you're going to be buying and/or downloading software and installing it on your PC. This software runs on your computer and crunches down your returns and sometimes your risk, too. Examples include the following:

- **Microsoft's Money:** (www.microsoft.com/money) This Microsoft product features a portfolio-tracking feature, called Portfolio Manager, that measures your returns on all the stocks you buy and sell. It's convenient if you've already been using Microsoft Money because you've already downloaded or entered your trades. The software also downloads stock quotes automatically, helping you to routinely track your performance. Portfolio Manager lets you sort all your investments in dozens of ways, so you can separate your winners from your dogs.

- **Intuit's Quicken:** (www.quicken.com) A major player in the financial software field, Quicken has an advanced Investing Center that monitors all your returns. What makes Quicken unique is that it measures the expected risk, or standard deviation, of your portfolio in addition to returns. Quicken compares your portfolio's risk with the risk of different benchmarks, including small and large stocks. You can access this feature within Quicken by choosing the Portfolio Analyzer feature on the Investing tab. See Chapter 1 for more information on Quicken and Money.

- **BetterInvesting's Portfolio Manager:** (www.biportfoliomanager.com/index_bipm.php) BetterInvesting's entrant in the financial software market is an advanced software program designed to meticulously track your portfolio's returns. You enter your transactions, and the software does the rest with a great level of precision. The software costs $169 if you're not a member of the Better Investing organization.

- **Analyze Now!:** (www.analyzenow.com) Technically, Analyze Now! doesn't offer a software program; rather, it provides you with a collection of free spreadsheets that will help you calculate everything you need. The Investment Manager spreadsheet not only calculates your annual returns, but also helps you optimize your tax strategy and pick the right type of brokerage account. The Free Return Calculator calculates your portfolio returns even if you moved money in and out of your account. Select Free Programs on the left-hand side of the Web site to download the spreadsheets.

✔ **Spreadsheet plug-ins:** If you're already a spreadsheet jockey and want to track your performance that way, you need a way to pull current stock quotes into your spreadsheet. Microsoft provides a free plug-in that downloads the day's stock quotes into Excel at `www.microsoft.com/downloads/details.aspx?FamilyID=485FCCD8-9305-4535-B939-3BF0A740A9B1&displaylang=EN`.

The QMatix XLQ plug-in (`www.qmatix.com/XLQ.htm`) goes a step further by pulling both current and historical stock quotes into Excel. But QMatix software will cost you $74, and other data access charges might apply.

Using stock simulation and social investing sites

Most stock simulation and social investing sites offer performance-tracking tools. I describe stock simulations in Chapter 2 as a way to get your feet wet by choosing stocks and investing online. And I cover social investing sites in Chapter 7 as a way to connect with other investors. The performance-tracking capabilities of these sites are noteworthy, including the following

✔ **TradeKing:** (`www.tradeking.com`) This site's Certified Trades (accessible from the Community menu on the home page) section tracks your performance. You can share your performance with other TradeKing members so they can see how talented you are. It'll also help you determine which members of TradeKing's social investing site are worth listening to.

✔ **Marketocracy:** (`www.marketocracy.com`) This social investing site deserves special mention. It uses a performance measurement technique that isolates your performance and determines whether it's the result of skill or luck.

✔ **Covestor:** (`www.covestor.com`) In addition to being a leading social investing site, Covestor also has an impressive performance tracking tool. It's one of the few social investing sites that measures both risk and return. And it uses the complex Global Investment Performance Standards, used by professional money management firms, giving you accurate results.

Online brokers are so competitive they often look at what others are doing and match it. Be sure to check with all the online brokers to see whether they have added any portfolio performance tracking tools.

Using portfolio-tracking Web sites

Just about all the sites that track market information, described in Chapter 2, contain portfolio trackers. These sites allow you to enter your holdings or transactions and then sit back, waiting for them to tell you how much your stocks are up or down for the day and year and several, including Yahoo! Finance, let you download your portfolio into a spreadsheet. Portfolio-tracking sites do many things in addition to measuring performance. Still, some of these portfolio-tracking sites can have also advanced capabilities, including the following:

✔ **Morningstar.com:** (www.morningstar.com) Morningstar has a standout portfolio tracker because it tells you more than just whether your stocks went up or down for the day or year. If you click the Performance tab for your portfolio, you can see how its value has changed over the past 12 months. Morningstar will also e-mail you each day, telling you how your portfolio did, or send you alerts when a stock moves up or down 10% in a day or a mutual fund you own got a new manager. The Portfolio X-Ray feature applies advanced statistics techniques to see whether your portfolio fits your needs. Morningstar will import an existing portfolio you might have saved at MSN Money, Yahoo! Finance or using personal finance software. The Portfolio X-Ray feature, though, is available only to subscribers to Morningstar's premium service, which costs $145 a year.

✔ **StockSelector.com:** (www.stockselector.com) A portfolio service for the more active trader, StockSelector.com provides ample links to all sorts of company news and other data designed to help you buy and sell stocks. Stock Selector routinely spotlights specific stocks its members are paying attention to, such as the Latest Member Pick available near the bottom of its main Web page.

✔ **USATODAY.com:** (http://portfolio.usatoday.com/custom/usatoday-com/login/splash.asp) The Portfolio section of the USATODAY site features a tracking system that's pretty similar to those available on other sites. What makes this portfolio tracker unique though, is that it looks at all the portfolios of all the site's users and finds which 50 stocks are the most popular. Those popular stocks, called the USA TODAY Readers' Choice 50, are compiled and made available for everyone to view both in the print edition of USA TODAY and online at www.usatoday.com/money/markets/readerschoice.htm. You'll need to create a free username and password the first time you visit.

Most portfolio-tracking sites make it easy to download your stocks to a spreadsheet. Using Yahoo! Finance, for instance, you'd scroll to the bottom of your portfolio, click the Download Spreadsheet link, and then click Save.

Using performance-tracking Web sites

Performance-tracking Web sites focus on measuring how your portfolio is doing. These sites provide much more detail about your portfolio's risk and return than general portfolio-tracking Web sites. They take the mathematics seriously and explain exactly how they're getting the numbers they are getting. But best of all, their computers do the work so you don't have to. Sites to check out include the following:

- ✔ **RiskGrades:** (www.riskgrades.com) As the name suggests, this Web site is completely focused on risk, which many investors ignore. The site uses an advanced risk-measurement system to assign either individual stocks or your portfolio as a whole a RiskGrade. The lower the RiskGrade, the less risky your portfolio or stock is. A RiskGrade of 0 means the asset has no volatility. A RiskGrade of 1000 means the asset is ten times more volatile than one with a RiskGrade of 100. You can also see how RiskGrades change over time as the factors that affect stocks in the short term come to bear. (I detail the factors affecting stocks in the short term in Chapter 6.)

- ✔ **Profitspi:** (www.profitspi.com) This site lets you enter your trades and quickly calculates your returns. You can sort your stocks to see which ones are performing the best and instantly compare your results to the Dow Jones Industrial Average, NASDAQ and Standard & Poor's 500. You can also download the results to a spreadsheet.

- ✔ **Icarra:** (www.icarra.com) Icarra is primarily a sophisticated performance-tracking site that has social investing aspects. It's one of the few sites that can calculate your returns similarly to how mutual funds track their performance — by using the advanced internal rate-of-return method described earlier in this chapter. Icarra.com also lets you benchmark your performance against several major market indexes. You can share your performance with other users if you choose.

- ✔ **Stockalicious:** (http://stockalicious.com) This site with the trendy name allows you to enter your trades and see how your performance matches up against the market and other users. It's designed to be slightly easier to use than some portfolio-tracking sites. You can also easily share your trades with your friends.

By measuring your portfolio's risk and return, you're already miles ahead of many other online investors. You have the know-how to tweak and refine your investments to make sure you get the optimal return for the risk you're taking.

Chapter 9

Choosing an Asset Allocation

● ●

In This Chapter

▶ Seeing what an asset allocation is and how it can improve your success

▶ Deciding what kind of asset allocation is right for you

▶ Using online tools to pick the right asset allocation

▶ Creating a custom index to track your asset allocation's success

● ●

*Y*ou wouldn't sail a ship without a map or bake a cake without a recipe, but so many online investors do the equivalent when they buy and sell stocks and other assets without understanding how they fit into a broader plan. That plan, in investment language, is called an *asset allocation.* Your asset allocation determines how much of your portfolio is placed into different types of *asset classes,* or types of investments — typically stocks, bonds, and cash. By following this plan, you can make sure you get the maximum return for the amount of risk you're taking. One controversial study even claims more than 90% of a portfolio's swings, on average, is due to the asset allocation.

In this chapter, I show you how an asset allocation plan can improve your success investing online. You also find out how to build your ideal asset allocation using online tools to help you find an allocation that's right for you.

The Recipe for Your Online Investing: Asset Allocation

Many investors make the mistake of chasing random stocks they hear about, buying them and throwing them into their portfolios. They pick up stock tips from TV and neighbors and blindly invest. Some of these investors wind up owning so many stocks they have an unmanageable portfolio, which generates disappointing returns. Others try to be more selective and invest in just a few stocks they think are promising, but they later find out their portfolios are too risky for their taste.

The answer is simple: Approach investing like a chef with a recipe in hand. Rather than tossing all sorts of ingredients into your portfolio pot and guessing what it will taste like, it's best to know what needs to go into the pot to get what you want. In investing, this plan is called an *asset allocation.*

An asset allocation might be general and tell you what percentage of holdings to put in stocks, how much in bonds, and how much in cash. But it can also get more detailed and exotic, calling for a dash of large U.S. company stocks, a pinch of international stocks, and just a touch of bonds.

Asset allocations are designed to let all the investments in your portfolio blend together into a stew that will be most likely to generate the highest possible return for the lowest amount of risk.

The advantages of creating and sticking with an asset allocation include

- ✓ **Diversification:** Hands down, diversification is the biggest advantage of having an asset allocation. An asset allocation will call for certain percentages of your portfolio to be in certain investments. For instance, you might put 70% in stocks and 30% in bonds. You want your investments to be spread into different investments that tend to move up and down at different times. That will hold the value of your total portfolio steady — and reduce risk — over time.

- ✓ **Rebalancing:** A great way to boost your returns without taking on additional risk, rebalancing pretty much does what the term implies. Periodically, one group of investments in your asset allocation will fall in value. Stocks might fall and bonds rally, for instance. When that happens, the percentage of your portfolio in stocks will fall below your plan, and the percentage in bonds will rise. To stick to your allocation and maintain the percentages, you need to buy more of the investments that have fallen in value and sell those that have gained. And when you do that, you will be buying investments when they're cheaper and selling them when they get pricier, which isn't a bad strategy.

- ✓ **Discipline:** Staying in control is priceless with online investing. Because trading online is so inexpensive and easy, it's tempting to chase after popular stocks that are in the news or new investments other investors are talking about. Many of those investments end up disappointing investors, though, because they're overvalued. I explain how to measure a stock's valuation in Chapter 13, but if you stick with your asset allocation, you can avoid this pain.

What's so great about diversification?

If you were to design the perfect portfolio, you'd certainly want the maximum returns for the least amount of risk. The way you do this is by *diversifying,* or spreading your risk over a wide swath of investments. This certainly can reduce risk, which I define in Chapter 8 as standard deviation.

A high standard deviation means the portfolio is riskier, and a low standard deviation means it's less risky.

The first aspect of diversification is the idea of safety in numbers. As you add more stocks to your portfolio, you reduce the odds that a vicious decline in any one stock will depth-charge your portfolio.

Before you rush out and buy thousands of stocks, though, you need to be aware of two things. First, your portfolio's risk falls by smaller amounts as you add stocks. For instance, the reduction of risk when you go from 30 stocks to 40 is less impressive than when you go from one stock to two.

Also, before you start buying every stock you can get your hands on, remember that there are better ways to buy hundreds of stocks at a time: You can buy *index funds* and *exchange-traded funds*. These single investments are baskets that own hundreds of stocks. So with just one trade, you get the same benefit of an investor who spends hundreds of dollars in commissions building a massive portfolio of stocks. That's why for many investors, buying an index fund or exchange-traded fund is the optimum strategy. (I talk about index funds in Chapter 10 and exchange-traded funds in Chapter 11.)

Zig-zag: The second element of diversification

Diversification isn't just the result of owning many stocks. You can reduce your risk further by combining different types of assets that zig when the others zag. Stocks that move differently than each other are said to have little *correlation* with each other. Investors build asset allocations by piecing together investments from popular asset classes such as the following:

- ✔ **Cash** is typically parked in funds that buy short-term IOUs, such as money market funds. Money market funds are discussed in Chapter 10.

- ✔ **Bonds** are generally longer-term IOUs issued by governments and companies.

- ✔ **U.S. stocks** are the shares of the thousands of companies that trade on U.S. stock markets.

- ✔ **Foreign stocks** are shares in companies that trade on exchanges in other countries. Foreign investing is covered at more length in a bonus chapter on international and emerging markets at the companion Web site for this book.

- ✔ **Emerging market stocks** own pieces of companies in up-and-coming economies. The risk is very high, but the returns can be high, too.

✔ **Real-estate investment trusts (REITs)** own commercial property such as strip malls, apartment buildings or offices. They tend to have low correlation with other asset classes, making them attractive in many asset allocations. Invest in REITs, a Web site dedicated to REITs, provides a page that explains the benefits to REITs (www.investinreits.com/reasons/diversification.cfm). The page, called Diversification Benefits of REITs, provides a study from market research firm Ibbotson Associates that explains how REITs can benefit your portfolio.

TIAA-CREF (www.tiaa-cref.org/support/basics/getting_started/asset_classes.html), a large investment manager that specializes on retirement planning for people in the education and medical fields, provides a helpful primer on the different asset classes.

Smart asset allocations put the asset classes together in optimal ways. For instance, foreign stocks and U.S. stocks don't move in lockstep with each other, so they work together well in a portfolio. Bonds and stocks also move differently. Blending the right doses of these different investments together helps give you the perfect portfolio and is the very purpose of diversification.

The degree to which investments move together is called the correlation. It's a complicated mathematical problem that is discussed at more length in *Statistics For Dummies,* by Deborah Rumsey (Wiley Publishing), and online at www.investopedia.com/terms/c/correlation.asp.

Just know this: When an investment moves identically to the market, it has a correlation of 1 with the market. When an investment moves exactly opposite to the market, it has a low correlation, or –1. If you can find investments with a low correlation and add them to your portfolio, you might be able to reduce your portfolio's risk.

The secret to creating a portfolio is a balancing act between three factors: expected returns, risk, and correlation. Sure you want to pick asset classes with high returns and low risk, but you also want those asset classes, which tend to move differently than each other. That way you get the best return and lowest risk possible. Designing a perfect asset allocation can require more higher math than a college physics final exam. To make things easy, later in this chapter, I show you Web sites that can do the number crunching for you.

But for now, just know that most asset allocations will recommend you own a certain percentage of stocks, bonds and cash. Some asset allocations, though, dissect some asset classes, especially U.S. stocks, with even more precision. U.S. stocks are generally sliced into the categories described in Table 9-1.

Table 9-1	Popular Ways to Categorize Stocks	
Large value	Large blend (contains value and growth)	Large growth
Mid-sized value	Mid-sized blend	Mid-sized growth
Small value	Small blend	Small growth

Source: © 2008 Morningstar, Inc. All Rights Reserved. Reprinted by permission of Morningstar.

Let me explain the boxes in Table 9-1. Each box contains a *size,* such as large or small, and a *style,* such as value or growth.

Bigger isn't always better: Understanding size

You'll often see references to *large-cap, mid-cap, small-cap,* and *micro-cap* companies when you're researching asset allocations. Those terms are critical to asset allocations and are the basis on how online asset allocation sites work.

When you hear reference to large-cap companies, for instance, it's a way to describe the company's total market value or *market capitalization.* The market cap is the total price tag the stock market places on a company and is calculated by multiplying the stock price by the number of shares the company has outstanding. Market cap is a valuable way for investors to look at stocks because studies show that companies with similar market values have similar returns, risk, and correlations. For instance, small companies tend to have higher returns than large companies, but they're also riskier.

That begs the question: What's a small company and what's a large company? That changes over time as the stock market rises and falls. But, Table 9-2 gives you a general idea of where the lines are drawn.

Table 9-2	What's Big and What's Small?
Asset Class	*Market Value Is . . .*
Large	Greater than $10.2 billion
Medium	Greater than $1.1 billion but less than $10.2
Small	Greater than $159 million but less than $1.1 billion
Micro cap	Less than $159 million

Source: Standard & Poor's based on year end 2006

The definitions of large, medium, and small companies are constantly changing as the stock market rises and falls. You can look up current definitions from Russell, a big name in index tracking (www.russell.com/Indexes/membership/US/Reconstitution/cap_ranges.asp).

Want to know whether a stock you own is a large or small company? Nearly all the quote services described in Chapter 2 can give you the market value. You can even type a stock's symbol into Google (www.google.com), click the Google Search button and the market value will appear below the stock price. Just take that market value figure and see where it ranks in Table 9-2.

Picking investments with the right styles

Companies' market values aren't the only thing that matter when it comes to asset allocations. Some investors also pay attention to stocks' *styles,* such as *value* and *growth*. The definition of what makes a value or growth stock isn't as cut and dried as market value. You'll learn ways to decide if a stock is considered to be a value stock or growth stock in Chapter 13, but for now, just know that value stocks are those that are generally bargain-priced. Value stocks tend to be cheaper relative to the earnings and dividends they are generating. Value stocks, though, are cheaper for a reason: They're perceived as being risky because they are in trouble or in a mature industry. Growth stocks, on the other hand, generally command lofty prices relative to their assets and earnings because investors expect them to grow rapidly in the future.

When you put market value, style, and correlation together, you have everything you need to construct a perfect portfolio. These are the building blocks that help you get the highest return for the amount of risk you're taking on. Table 9-3 shows the long-term returns, correlation, and risk of some of the types of investments suggested by asset allocation sites.

Table 9-3	Stocks That Zig When the Market Zags		
Asset Class	*Long-Term Return Risk*	*Correlation with Large Stocks (S&P 500)*	*(Standard Deviation)*
Large company stocks	10.3%	1	19.2
Large value-priced stocks	11.5%	0.81	25.7
Micro-cap stocks	12.8%	0.62	33.0
Small value-priced stocks	29.6%	0.68	29.6
International value-priced stocks	11.4%	0.61	25.9
Emerging markets stocks	15.2%	0.56	28.7

Source: IFA.com

TIP

You can read more about how asset allocations balance the three factors at the following sites:

- ✔ **Investopedia:** (www.investopedia.com/articles/pf/05/061505. asp) This site provides a comprehensive explanation of how an asset allocation plan is created.

- ✔ **Path to Investing:** (www.pathtoinvesting.com/portfolioman/ assetalloc/assetallocdiv_index.htm) The folks at Path to Investing summarize the asset allocation process and describe how it's done. (See Figure 9-1.)

- ✔ **Gummy Stuff:** (www.gummy-stuff.org) Here's a dream site for investors interested in figuring out how to do all the math needed to design an asset allocation plan themselves. The site contains all sorts of calculators and tutorials to help you do it.

- ✔ **Investor Home:** (www.investorhome.com/asset.htm) Yet another description of how asset allocation has become so important in investing today.

- ✔ **Securities and Exchange Commission:** (www.sec.gov/investor/ pubs/assetallocation.htm) This section of the SEC site runs through all the benefits of having an asset allocation.

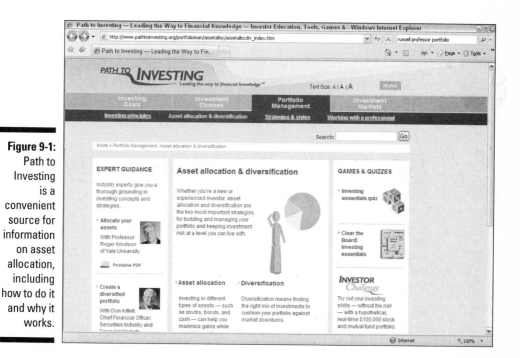

Figure 9-1: Path to Investing is a convenient source for information on asset allocation, including how to do it and why it works.

> ✔ **IndexInvestor.com:** (`www.assetallocation.org`) Here you can find in-depth explanations of why asset allocation is so important as well as guidelines for creating your own asset allocation plan.

Investors commonly make the mistake of thinking their portfolios are diversified if they own shares of companies in many different industries, such as energy, financial, and technology. But if you own only shares of a large energy company, large financial company, and large technology company, you might not be truly diversified.

How rebalancing steadies your portfolio

When you have an asset allocation, you're given a recipe that you stick with. And doing this forces you to be a smart investor by buying more of certain asset classes when they're down. It may seem counterintuitive to buy investments when they're down. And, to be clear, buying individual stocks when they're plunging can be hazardous. Individual stocks are a different animal, and are explained more fully in Chapter 12 and Chapter 13. But if you invest in index mutual funds or exchange-traded funds that own large baskets of hundreds of stocks, buying when shares go on sale can be smart because you lower your cost. This approach, called the *rebalancing bonus* by respected financial historian William Bernstein, is described fully here: `www.efficient frontier.com/ef/996/rebal.htm`.

Rebalancing is only advised when you're buying diversified baskets of assets, such as mutual funds or exchange-traded funds, which track sections of the market. Buying individual stocks is a completely different animal. Buying when a stock is nose-diving is called "catching a falling knife" and can be hazardous to your financial health.

How discipline will save your portfolio from getting spanked

When you have an asset plan, it gives you something to stick to if the markets get choppy. Sometimes that saves you from yourself and helps you resist the temptation to chase after the hot stock or an index your neighbors are talking about. And that's a good thing because investing in last year's winner is a good way to find this year's loser.

For instance, large growth stocks were the rage between 1995 and 1998 and were the top-performers in each of those years with gains of between 24% and 42% a year, according to Callan Associates. But jumping into the hot asset class was a bad idea. Between 2000 and 2006, large growth stocks underperformed other stocks badly. The Callan Periodic Table of Investment Returns (www.callan.com/resource/periodic_table/PertblDark.pdf) uses a color-coded chart that shows how asset classes rarely stay on top.

Using and Finding Your Perfect Asset Allocation

There are three main ways to design your asset allocation

- ✔ **Follow guidelines.** These simple rules, available on Web sites I point out, are great if you just want to keep things simple.

- ✔ **Take a risk-based approach.** Calculate how much risk you can tolerate and select a blend of investments to give you the highest return for that risk.

- ✔ **Take a return-based approach.** You can work backwards and measure how much return you need to meet your goal and design a portfolio that will get you there.

In this chapter, I help you choose an asset allocation, which gives you a roadmap of the types of investments you should buy to get the returns you're looking for. But an asset allocation doesn't do you any good if you don't act on it. In Chapter 10, I show you how to buy the investments your asset allocation calls for by picking the right mutual funds. Chapter 11 gives you the low-down on exchange-traded funds, and in Chapter 13, I show you how to find individual stocks that match your asset allocation.

Determining your current asset allocation

If you own any investments now, you already have an asset allocation. It just might not be what you think it is, and it might not be designed to give you the returns and risk you want. It's important to understand what types of investments you own currently and what your current asset allocation is. You can do this by using the following:

- ✔ **Personal finance software:** The big players here are Microsoft's Money and Intuit's Quicken. Both can classify all the stocks, bonds, and mutual funds in your portfolio and tell you what percentage of your holdings are in each. You can read more about both in Chapter 1.

✔ **Morningstar's Instant X-Ray:** (www.morningstar.com) This handy tool is free and accessible on the Tools tab on the Morningstar home page. (You might need to scroll done the Tools page to find the link for Instant X-Ray.) Just enter the ticker symbols of all your current holdings and the dollar value of each holding. Click Show Instant X-Ray, and your holdings are broken down in the major categories such as cash, U.S. stocks, foreign stocks, bonds, and other. You also see how much of your stocks are in value-priced or growth stocks and also whether they're large, mid-sized, or small companies. There's also a breakdown of what industries your holdings fall in. (You can see a sample in Figure 9-2.)

✔ **David Grabiner's home page:** (http://remarque.org/~grabiner/assetalloc.html) Coming from a mathematics background, David Grabiner came up with an advanced spreadsheet, which analyzes your current portfolio and tells you how it's currently allocated. What makes this spreadsheet unique is that it considers the effect of taxes on your portfolio. And it's a free download!

Figure 9-2:
Morning-
star's Instant
X-Ray
dissects your
portfolio by
looking for
patterns in
the types of
stocks,
industries,
and regions
you're
invested in.

Source: © 2008 Morningstar, Inc. All Rights Reserved. Reprinted by permission of Morningstar.

Using guidelines

If you're the kind of investor who wants to have an asset allocation but doesn't want to delve into all the complications, this method is for you. The resources covered in the next sections make asset allocation easy, either by suggesting a general purpose asset allocation that will work for most people or letting you choose from simple but effective allocations.

Intuit's Quicken financial software

Quicken has a helpful Asset Allocation Guide that lets you choose from several off-the-shelf asset allocations. You can look them over and decide which one gives you the level or return you're interested in at the amount of risk you can tolerate, such as conservative, moderate, or aggressive.

EasyAllocator.com

The EasyAllocator site (`http://easyallocator.com`), shown in Figure 9-3, is true to its name. After signing in or creating a new account (free, by the way) just click the Allocator tab and enter the balances of your taxable and retirement accounts. When you're done, click the GO button. EasyAllocator doesn't help you decide how much risk you can tolerate. It leaves that up to you and asks you to decide by marking Very High, Very Low, or something in-between in the Risk Tolerance question. EasyAllocator does let you tailor your asset allocation a bit by deciding what types of stocks you want included or excluded. You can leave out micro-cap or real-estate stocks, for instance. The site then breaks down your asset allocation for you and tells you what your risk exposure will be if you use that allocation. Even better, it recommends specific low-cost index mutual funds and exchange-traded funds you should buy, and gives you the ticker symbols.

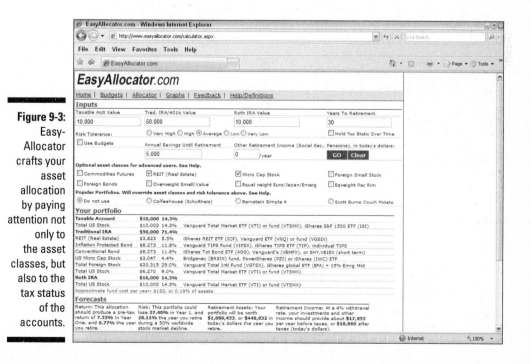

Figure 9-3: Easy-Allocator crafts your asset allocation by paying attention not only to the asset classes, but also to the tax status of the accounts.

EasyAllocator is one of the few systems that looks at all your accounts, including your taxable and retirement accounts, as a whole. This is a smart approach. Not only does EasyAllocator create an allocation, but it shows you the types of investments to hold in which types of accounts to save yourself taxes. The tax advantages of certain accounts are explained in Chapter 3. But EasyAllocator does much of the work for you.

For instance, if you're going to own bonds, you could own them in a retirement account. That way, when the bonds pay interest, you don't have to pay the tax until you withdraw the money, which could be in 30 years. Meanwhile, your taxable accounts are good places for your holdings in stock index funds that don't generate large dividends. Lastly, if you own risky investments with large expected returns, such as emerging market stocks, you should put them in your Roth IRA. That way, you'll never have to pay tax on the large gains you're likely to obtain.

Efficient Frontier

Efficient Frontier (www.efficientfrontier.com/ef/996/cowards.htm) is a site managed by well-known and well-respected market scholar and advisor William Bernstein. He suggests a Coward's Portfolio, which he says is designed to be an easy way for investors to build a solid portfolio with international exposure. He also suggests which mutual funds to buy to match the portfolio.

Scott Burns' Couch Potato portfolio

Scott Burns has put together a site (www.dallasnews.com/shared content/dws/bus/scottburns/columns/2007/vitindex.html) that appeals to anyone who appreciates the simple. In his role as financial columnist for Dallas Morning News, Burns recommends the easiest-to-follow allocation you can find: 50% stocks and 50% bonds. Put half your money in an index fund that tracks the Standard & Poor's 500, which I discuss in Chapter 10, and half in one that tracks the bond market and you're done. That's it. Burns describes his system in an online log of all the personal finance questions he has answered. Scroll through the questions to find the ones dealing with asset allocation.

AOL Money & Finance

This corner of the AOL Web empire (http://money.aol.com/investing/fct1/_a/asset-allocationinitial-allocation/20050225133309990005) suggests a few general asset allocations for aggressive, moderate, and conservative investors.

Money Chimp

Okay, Money Chimp isn't as big as AOL, but the folks there know investing. The Asset Allocation page (www.moneychimp.com/articles/risk/

portfolio.htm) gives you a general breakdown of what types of assets you should own with a simple calculator.

Iowa Public Employees' Retirement System

Manifesting some good Midwestern common sense, the folks at the Iowa Public Employees' Retirement System have set up a free and easy-to-use online tool that gives you an idea of what your dream allocation would be (www.ipers.org/calcs/AssetAllocator.html). You tell the system how old you are, how much you have, how much you save, your tax rate, and your risk tolerance by moving a series of sliders back and forth. It then spits out your asset allocation.

SmartMoney.com Asset Allocator

Part of the Dow Jones publishing empire, SmartMoney's Web site has come up with its own asset allocator (www.smartmoney.com/oneasset). The tool lets you move various sliders to indicate your personal preferences for risk and return, just like the one from Iowa. If you enter your current portfolio, the Asset Allocator tells you the dollar amount you must sell or buy of each investment type to achieve your ideal asset allocation.

AARP Asset Allocation Planner

It should come as no surprise that the American Association of Retired People has its own asset allocator (www.aarp.org/bulletin/yourmoney/asset_allocation_calculator.html). The tool asks a number of basic questions to help you understand how much you should invest in cash, stocks, and bonds.

Gummy Stuff

Coming straight from the Great White North, the Gummy Stuff site is chock-full of tutorials, spreadsheets, and financial tools, including an asset allocator (www.gummy-stuff.org/allocations.htm). It lets you play with different asset allocations and see how you would have done.

Picking an asset allocation based on your risk tolerance

Some investors may decide they want to tailor their asset allocation with a bit more precision for their individual taste. And if you're like most investors, the disappointment you feel when your portfolio falls more than you'd like is definitely greater than any happiness you might feel at eking out a slightly better-than-expected return. That's why online tools that assess your appetite for risk, and then design a portfolio, make sense for many investors. A few to try include the following:

✔ **IFA.com:** (`www.ifa.com/SurveyNET/index.aspx`) The folks at Index Fund Advisors offer a Risk Capacity Survey — mentioned in Chapter 1 — as a way to determine what kind of investor you are. The survey asks you a battery of questions to assess how much risk you can take, which is the way it recommends a portfolio to you. The Quick Risk Capacity survey has just five questions, and a longer survey has 25 questions. After you answer the questions, the Web site suggests one of several portfolios. The most risk-tolerant investors are pointed to Portfolio 100, and risk-adverse investors to Portfolio 5.

IFA's asset allocations are much more detailed than some of the sites that provide guidelines. For instance, rather than suggesting owning large-cap stocks, IFA.com distinguishes between large-cap stocks and large-cap value-priced stocks. The portfolios also recommend specific index funds sold by asset management firm Dimensional Fund Advisors, which you can buy through a financial advisor licensed to sell them.

✔ **Vanguard's Investor Questionnaire:** (`https://flagship.vanguard.com/VGApp/hnw/FundsInvQuestionnaire`) This section of the Vanguard site, shown in Figure 9-4, asks you ten questions in an attempt to try and figure out how much risk you can stomach. At the end, the site recommends that you own certain mixes of short-term reserves, stocks and cash. You can view all the recommended portfolios at `https://flagship.vanguard.com/VGApp/hnw/planningeducation/general/PEdGPCreateTheRightMixContent.jsp`.

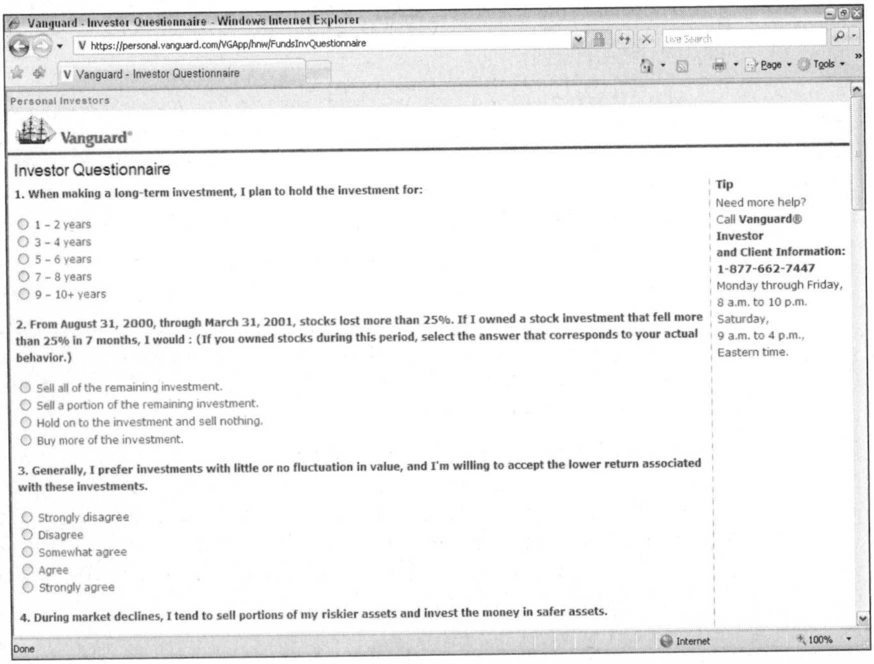

Figure 9-4:
Vanguard's Investor Questionnaire will help you decide how to construct a portfolio that fits your needs.

✔ **CNNMoney:** (http://cgi.money.cnn.com/tools/assetalloc wizard/assetallocwizard.html) CNNMoney steps you through four questions designed to figure out what kind of risk taker you are. It then generates a fairly basic asset allocation mix.

✔ **Asset-Analysis:** (www.asset-analysis.com/assetalloc/aaquest. html) With a name like Analysis of Asset Allocation, you can't go wrong, right? This section of the site steps you through five questions that measure your appetite for risk. When you're done, the site determines how much risk you can take and tells you how much of your portfolio should be invested in cash, bonds, emerging markets, domestic stocks, real estate, and international stocks.

Picking an asset allocation based on your goals

The other way to figure out how to allocate your portfolio is to first determine what kind of rate of return you need to reach your goal and then pick an asset allocation that will get you there. Several of the asset allocation sites take this approach:

✔ **MSN Money's Asset Allocator** (http://moneycentral.msn.com/ investor/calcs/assetall/main.asp), which starts by asking you the rate of return you desire. You can choose a rate of return between 4.5% and 11.5%, and then the site crunches down the right mix of investments.

Want to calculate the rate of return you need to reach a goal? Try Money Chimp's Return Rate Calculator (www.moneychimp.com/calculator/ discount_rate_calculator.htm). Just enter how much money you have now, how much you need to have, and when you need to have it, and the calculator tells you the rate of return you need.

✔ **TIAA CREF's Asset Allocation Evaluator** (https://ais2.tiaa-cref. org/cgi-bin/WebObjects.exe/DTAssetAlcEval), which designs your allocation based on what your goal is, as shown in Figure 9-5. The first question it asks is what you're saving for, such as retirement, education, or a first home. The site then asks you additional questions that are relevant to that specific goal.

✔ **Forbes' Asset Allocation Calculator** (www.forbes.com/tools/ calculator/asset_alloc.jhtml), which asks you to enter the current mix of investments in your portfolio. The site then estimates how much you'll earn based on 50-year historical returns of cash, stocks, and bonds. You can then tweak the allocation to see whether you can get the rate of return that you need.

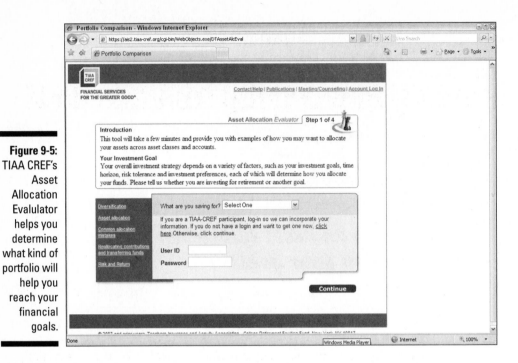

Figure 9-5: TIAA CREF's Asset Allocation Evalulator helps you determine what kind of portfolio will help you reach your financial goals.

✔ **Fidelity.com's Portfolio Review** (`http://personal.fidelity.com/products/funds/content/DesignYourPortfolio/build_portfolio.shtml.cvsr?refpr=mfrt14`), which helps you plan for a wide array of goals, ranging from retirement and education to more specific things like a vacation, wedding, or wealth accumulation. The Portfolio Review also studies how much risk you can stomach. The site can analyze your current portfolio and make suggestions on ways to improve and suggest an asset allocation. You don't have to be a Fidelity account holder to use the system; you can sign up for a free membership instead.

✔ **AmericanCentury Investment Plan** (`www.americancentury.com/OnlineFGS/OnlineFinancialPlannerRegistrationServlet`), which starts by asking you what you're saving for and then goes further to make suggestions. You'll need to enter your personal information to use the site, but you are not required to register with the site.

Some brokers and mutual fund companies provide asset allocation tools to their customers. Mutual fund company T. Rowe Price, for instance, offers tools that analyze your portfolio and generate asset allocations to customers.

Chapter 10

Finding and Buying Mutual Funds

. . . .

In This Chapter

▶ Seeing the advantages — and disadvantages — of mutual funds

▶ Finding mutual funds online that fit your needs

▶ Finding out where to buy and sell mutual funds online

▶ Understanding funds' risk and return

▶ Determining the best ways to buy mutual funds

. . . .

*O*nline investing isn't just for individual stock pickers. The Internet can also be used to pick, track, and monitor investments in *mutual funds* — funds that pool money from many investors so that it can then be invested in stocks, bonds or other assets. By pooling money, mutual funds give small investors some of the benefits enjoyed by larger investors, especially the ability to spread money over many investments, or diversify. Mutual funds are the way most people invest. More than 96 million individual investors, and half the nation's households, own a piece of mutual funds. U.S. mutual funds hold more than $10.4 trillion in investor assets, which they pool together and use to buy stakes in investments.

In this chapter, I explain how online tools can maximize your success investing in mutual funds. I also show you how to use online tools to pick the right investments for you and walk you through the process of setting up an account to buy or sell the funds.

The Feeling Is Mutual: Understanding Mutual Funds

If all the work it takes to pick individual stocks, described in Chapters 12 and 13, sounds exhausting, mutual funds might be for you. By their design, mutual funds give investors what they're looking for with minimal work. Most mutual funds own large baskets of stocks, giving investors the benefit of diversification (as described in Chapter 9) right off the bat. And mutual funds come in many flavors, allowing investors to buy exactly what they want, such as specific types of stocks or industries. Want to own small value-priced stocks? No problem, there's a mutual fund you can buy that takes care of it. Passive investors can also buy *index mutual funds,* which match market indexes and charge low fees. Active investors can choose from *actively managed mutual funds* that rely on human stock pickers who try to beat the market (although very few do).

There's just one problem. The sheer number of mutual funds is so enormous that it's hard to know where to start. There were 8,120 mutual funds at the end of 2006. That's greater than the 5,906 stocks trading on the New York Stock Exchange and NASDAQ. Meanwhile, the amount of money invested in funds, called *net assets,* also continues to swell.

Considering the pros of mutual funds

Just because mutual funds are so popular, though, that doesn't mean they're right for you. You might decide that buying individual stocks is more your speed. Even so, it's worth first considering what you gain and lose by investing in mutual funds. First, what you gain:

- **Instant diversification:** If you buy just one mutual fund, you own a piece of dozens, if not hundreds, of stocks. Buying a share of a fund is more cost effective than buying and managing hundreds of stocks yourself.

- **Easy asset allocation:** As I explain in Chapter 9, it's important to have an asset allocation that helps guide you in what kinds of stocks you should buy to get more return for the amount of risk you're taking on. Some of these asset allocations get pretty specific, calling for a certain percentage of your portfolio to be in small value-priced stocks or large stocks. You can easily pick up the right exposure by buying mutual funds dedicated to these *sizes* and *styles.* Buying just five or more mutual funds can give you an easy-to-manage and completely diversified portfolio.

- **Low fees:** By pooling your money with many other investors', you gain significant cost savings. Large mutual fund companies can save money on commissions, research, and other fees, which means they pay less than what you'd have to pay if you were doing all this on your own. Mutual funds must also disclose their fees, so you can quickly find those that are the most efficient. The Securities and Exchange Commission (www.sec.gov/investor/tools/mfcc/mfcc-int.htm) describes how fees can eat into your returns.

If you're interested in keeping your costs down, index mutual funds have extremely low fees, sometimes less than 0.1% a year. If a fund charges 0.1%, that means if you have $1,000 invested, you pay just a $1 fee that year.

Drawbacks of mutual funds worth considering

Despite mutual funds' advantages, they have some significant drawbacks that might be deal killers for you:

- **Lack of control:** When you buy a mutual fund, you're putting your investment in the hands of an investment company. If you invest with an actively managed fund, which hires a professional portfolio manager to select stocks for the fund to buy, you don't have much say in investment decisions. If the manager sells a stock — one you think is a good long-term hold, for instance — there's nothing you can do about it. This is the case with index mutual funds, too. If a stock is added to the S&P 500, for instance, your S&P 500 index fund will buy the stock, too.

- **Tax inefficiencies:** When mutual funds buy and sell stocks during the year, their actions often create result in tax bills you weren't expecting. The most unfortunate type occurs when a fund sells a stock for a gain.

Yes, you have to pay tax when you sell an individual stock for a gain. But *you* can decide when to sell that stock. Mutual funds may sell stocks for gains anytime, including a time that's not good for you. That gain is then distributed to you, the mutual fund owner, and you must pay tax on it. *Capital-gain distributions* often come with no warning and can spoil a well-thought out tax plan. This tends to be much less of an issue with index mutual funds because the turnover, or number of stocks bought and sold, tends to be lower than with actively managed funds.

Capital-gain distribution nightmare

Capital-gain distributions are one of the biggest drawbacks of actively managed mutual funds. These distributions can be very large and unexpected, two things you don't want when it comes to managing your taxes. Consider the whopper of a capital-gain distribution paid by Fidelity's Magellan mutual fund in 2006. After the fund changed portfolio managers, the new manager cleaned house and sold off giant chunks of stocks owned by the fund under the previous manager. That resulted in 19% of the fund's assets, or more than $22 a share, to be distributed to shareholders. Making things worse, if a portfolio manager sells stocks owned for a year or less for a gain, shareholders who own the funds in a taxable account can get hit with high short-term capital gains taxes. Capital gains taxes are explained in detail in Chapter 3.

✔ **Index shadowing:** The most sinister actively managed funds are those that pretend to be adding value by picking winning stocks but are actually just tracking or shadowing the market. It's unfortunate when this happens because investors are paying for the expertise of a fund manager but not getting anything in return. These investors could get the same results, and save money on fees, by investing in low-cost index funds.

Types of Investment Companies

Investment-fund companies are usually structured in one of two ways. The structure dictates how the value of the fund is determined and how you buy and sell your shares. The main types of structures are the following:

✔ **Open-end investment companies:** These folks are all mutual funds, all the time. Open-end investment companies — also known as *fund companies* — buy baskets of stocks and then sell pieces of the portfolios they've assembled to outside investors. The price of a share of a mutual fund is set at the end of each day when the fund company adds up the value of the shares it owns and divides by the number of shares outstanding. The result, called the *net asset value* (NAV), is what one share of the mutual fund is worth. The NAV is how much the mutual fund company would pay you if you redeemed, or sold, your shares. You can redeem or purchase shares through most of the online brokers discussed in Chapter 4 or directly from the fund companies.

How do you find a mutual fund's NAV? Nearly all the sites that provide stock quotes, described in Chapter 2, provide the mutual fund's NAV if you enter the fund's symbol. Some sites provide additional information about the fund. For instance, Morningstar also tells you

• **Performance** of the fund compared to other similar funds and the closest benchmark.

• **Long-term returns** going back three and five years.

• **Total assets invested with the fund.** This is a tally of how much investor money is invested in the fund.

• **Portfolio managers' names.**

• **Dividend yield,** if any.

• **Expense ratio,** which is an important area that's discussed more fully later, in the section "Deciphering the morass of mutual fund fees."

• **Purchase information.** There is a link to the fund company to help you find out how to invest.

✔ **Closed-end investment companies** are part mutual fund, part stock. Like open-end investment companies, closed-end funds buy portfolios of stocks. But closed-end funds don't redeem shares held by investors directly. Instead, shares of closed-end funds trade on the stock market just like a regular stock. That means the price is set very differently than with mutual funds. Investors study the value of the stocks in the closed-end portfolios and decide how much the basket is worth. The price of the fund moves during the day as buyers and sellers agree on a price. The fact investors set the price on closed-end funds often creates an interesting situation where the price of the closed-end fund is less than the value of the stocks owned by the fund. When that happens, that means the closed-end fund is trading at a *discount*.

You can find all the closed-end investment companies that are trading for a discount by logging into Morningstar's closed-end fund center (`http://news.morningstar.com/CELists/CEReturns.html?fsection=CELists`) and clicking the Premiums/Discounts column twice to sort by funds trading for a discount.

You can also find out more about closed-end funds in general at the Investment Company Institute (`www.ici.org/statements/inv/bro_g2_ce.html`) as well as at the Closed-End Fund Association (`www.closed-endfunds.com`).

Categorizing Mutual Funds

Because there are more mutual funds than stocks, it's probably not too surprising that there are also many types of mutual funds. Mutual funds at their most basic level come in four basic flavors: those that invest in stock funds, bond funds, money market funds, and hybrid funds. But if you drill down, you find even more categories. The following sections give you a sense of how categories and subcategories branch off from each other.

Stock funds

Stock funds invest in shares of publicly traded companies. These funds typically go for large gains by pursuing one of a number of strategies:

✔ **Growth funds** are filled with shares of companies investors generally expect to expand their earnings the fastest. Portfolio managers of actively managed growth funds are typically willing to pay higher valuations for *growth* stocks because they think the companies are worth it.

Growth index funds buy shares of companies that have the highest valuations, often measured by the price-to-book ratio, a concept I explain in more detail in Chapter 13.

If you're young and retirement is still years off, many experts advise to invest in growth funds. The trouble, though, is that academic studies have shown growth funds, including growth index funds, tend to own the most overvalued stocks. That means they tend to have lower future returns and higher risk than value funds that own less glamorous stocks.

✔ **Value funds** own companies that are generally out of fashion or considered to be ho-hum and mature by Wall Street. Actively managed value funds are constructed by portfolio managers trained to look for *undervalued* stocks, or stocks that sell for less than what they're truly worth. Value index funds generally own stocks that have the lowest valuations.

✔ **Income stock** funds seek to invest in companies that pay fat dividends, such as utilities and real-estate investment trusts (REITs). Income stock funds aren't looking for stock price appreciation.

✔ **International funds** invest 80% or more of their money in companies located outside the U.S. Some international funds concentrate on specific areas of the world, such as Europe or Japan. Yet others, called emerging markets funds, focus on up-and-coming parts of the world.

✔ **Global funds** invest in companies in any part of the world, including the U.S.

✔ **Sector funds** pick specific industries investors often like to invest in, such as technology, energy, and utilities.

Bond funds

Bond funds own diverse baskets of bonds, which usually have similar characteristics. Bond funds are generally seen as a way to reduce risk because they collect income from a variety of borrowers. If one borrower defaults on the loan, you own many other bonds and aren't wiped out. There are many types of bond funds, which I will discuss in more detail in Chapter 16. The main ones to know about are the following:

✔ **Government bond funds** tend to invest in debt issued by the U.S. government. These funds usually invest in Treasuries that mature in the short-term, intermediate term, or long-term, or a blend of each.

✔ **High-yield bond funds,** nicknamed *junk bond funds,* generate higher returns by investing in debt issued by companies with shakier finances. The overall risk is reduced by spreading the investment over many companies' debt.

- ✔ **Corporate bond funds** own bonds issued by large companies. Their yields are generally higher than those paid by government bonds but less than high-yield bonds.

- ✔ **Municipal bond funds** invest in debt issued by state and local governments. These bonds can be attractive because they're usually not taxed by the federal government.

Money market funds

Money market funds are a great place to park cash you might need at short notice. They invest in very low risk short-term Treasuries issued by the federal government or IOUs from banks. Money market funds can be great places to get a decent return on cash you've set aside for emergencies. The SEC (www.sec.gov/answers/mfmmkt.htm) provides more information about money market funds.

Hybrid funds

Hybrid funds blend aspects of all the types of funds in the preceding sections into a unique package that suits some investors. Some examples include the following:

- ✔ **Balanced funds** split their portfolios into a preset mix of bonds and stocks. Investors who want to diversify their holdings between stocks and bonds can in theory just buy one of these and leave it up to the portfolio manager.

- ✔ **Target date funds** are an increasingly popular type of investment where you tell the mutual fund company how old you are and it determines the right mix of investments for you. It will split your money into a preset blend of stocks and bonds. As you age, and your appetite for risk declines, the funds automatically shift your portfolio to be more weighted toward bonds and away from stocks. TargetDatePortfolio (www.targetdate portfolio.com) provides additional information about these types of funds and can help you find some that might fit your needs.

- ✔ **Fund of funds** are mutual funds that buy other mutual funds. The idea is that these funds can assemble a collection of mutual funds so you don't have to.

What to Look for in a Mutual Fund

When you're shopping for a fund, you want to have a checklist of all the things that are important. Pay attention to the following things:

- ✔ **The fund's style:** If your asset allocation calls for investing in large value-priced stocks, you want to go with a fund that invests in large value-priced stocks. Sounds easy, right? Watch out, though, because the name of a mutual fund might make it sound like one thing, when in reality it's something else.

    How could this "what's in a name" business affect you? Say you're debating between two mutual funds that claim to invest in small stocks. Both have the words "small stock" in their names, but the funds might define small stock differently.

    Finding out which one owns smaller stocks is easy. Log in to the site of mutual fund tracker Morningstar (www.morningstar.com), enter the first mutual fund's ticker symbol, press Enter, and then click the Portfolio link on the left of the new page that appears. You see the fund's average market value, which measures how much the average stock held by the fund is worth. Do the same for the other fund and compare the results. If you want a small-cap fund, make sure the average market value falls in the small range in the chart in Chapter 9. Figure 10-1 shows you what happens when you check the Vanguard 500 Index's portfolio.

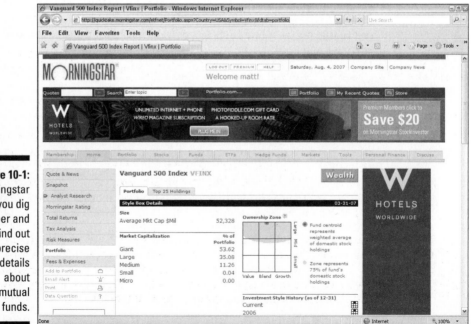

Figure 10-1: Morningstar lets you dig deeper and find out precise details about mutual funds.

✔ **Long-term performance:** It's tempting to chase after mutual funds that did the best last year or in the last decade. But studies have shown explosive mutual funds are rarely able to maintain their streaks. You should concentrate on a fund's five- or ten-year track record, at the least. If you can get performance data going back further, that's even better. And always compare a mutual fund's performance to the comparable index. If you're looking to buy a mutual fund that invests in large value-priced stocks, you should compare its performance to a large value index.

✔ **Turnover:** The amount of buying and selling a fund does is called its *turnover*. It's important to keep turnover low because when your fund sells stocks, you can face serious tax consequences if it causes capital-gain distributions.

✔ **Ratings:** Mutual fund trackers Morningstar (www.morningstar.com) and Lipper (www.lipperweb.com) rank mutual funds based on many dimensions of their performance. Although you can't rely solely on these rankings, they're worth paying attention to. Plus they're easy to understand.

✔ **Size:** There's a dilemma when shopping for actively managed mutual funds. When they get too large and have huge chunks of money to invest, performance usually suffers as they struggle to find enough investments to plow the money into. A general guideline on this is if you own a fund that invests in large companies, it might be getting too big when it has $50 billion in assets. You can find out how much money is invested in a fund by logging in to Morningstar.com, entering the fund's symbol, typing enter, and checking out the default Snapshot page.

Popular funds attempt to stop themselves from getting too bloated by *closing* to new investors. When this happens, if you were already an investor in the fund, you can add money, but you can't buy the fund if you're not already an investor.

Being too small can be a problem, too. If a fund doesn't attract enough assets, it might be shut down.

✔ **Fees:** The fees are how much the fund charges you every year to invest your money. The fees charged by your fund are typically taken annually no matter what. That means even if the fund falls in value, you pay fees. That's why fees are one of the most important things to pay attention to. They're so important that the next section is dedicated to understanding them.

Actively managed mutual funds tempt investors with the promise that their portfolio managers are so smart they can beat the market. The reality, though, is very few beat the market consistently, and they wind up charging investors fees for a promise that's never realized. A look at history shows how the odds are stacked against active mutual fund managers. Of the funds that existed in 1970, only 37% were still around by 2005, according to John Bogle (`www.vanguard.com/bogle_site/sp20060515.htm`), founder of Vanguard, which pioneered the low-cost index mutual fund. The other 63% of mutual funds were shut down due to poor performance. Even if you picked one of the survivors, you didn't necessarily score. Of the funds that lasted, 45% lagged the stock market, and 36% turned in performance that nearly matched the market. That means just 7% of the funds that existed in 1970 beat the stock market by more than one percentage point a year. That's why investing in a low-cost index fund, for many investors, is often the best option.

Deciphering the morass of mutual fund fees

Mutual fund performance swings up and down, along with the stocks and bonds the fund is invested in. But one thing that's for sure, the mutual fund company will make sure to collect its cut.

If you're not careful, mutual funds can sting you with all sorts of fees. The good thing, though, is that all fees must be disclosed ahead of time so you can avoid expensive funds if you know what to look for. The short list of things to be on the lookout for includes the following:

- **Front-end loads** are charged to investors immediately when they buy a fund. These fees are the most sinister because a bite is taken out of your portfolio even before you get started. Investor outcry has helped to drive these fees down to 1.3% in 2006 from 5.6% in 1980. Regulators don't allow funds to charge more than 8.5%. You can read more about how the regulators oversee fees from the Securities and Exchange Commission (`www.sec.gov/answers/mffees.htm`). You can usually spot a fund charging a front-end load because it sells what're called Class A shares.

- **Back-end loads** are essentially commissions charged when you redeem shares. They're also called *contingent deferred sales* and will sometimes be waived if you own the mutual fund shares long enough. For instance, you'll be socked with a 5% fee if you redeem shares in a year or less, 4% if you redeem in two years, and the fee keeps falling until it vanishes after you own the fund for five years. Back-end loads include so-called 12b-1 fees that the fund company charges shareholders to promote its fund. These fees cannot exceed 0.75% of the fund net assets per year to pay for marketing costs. Funds that charge back-end loads are designated as Class B shares.

✔ **Redemption fees** are charged when shareholders redeem, or sell, their shares. Redemption fees are technically different from back-end loads because the fees go to paying the costs that arise from your redemption. But they sting just the same. Regulators prohibit redemption fees from exceeding 2% of the amount sold.

✔ **Purchase fees** are charged when shareholders buy shares of a fund. This fee might not be called a front-load fee, but it is still a fee you must pay upfront and costs you money.

✔ **Management fees** are the ongoing fees the mutual fund charges you to run your money.

✔ **Other fees** include exchange fees if you shift money into a different fund owned by the same mutual fund company, or an account fee if you, for instance, don't meet a minimum account balance.

Although it might seem like the number of charges levied by mutual funds are limitless, mutual fund fees have been falling. The average fees and expenses collected by stock mutual funds were 1.1% in 2006, down from 2.3% in 1980. And the fees of bond funds have fallen to 0.8% from 2.1% during the same time period.

No-load mutual funds don't charge front or back-end load fees. But that doesn't mean they're free. Even no-load funds can charge redemption, purchase, exchange, and management fees.

You can easily find out online how much a fund charges in fees. Enter the symbol at Morningstar.com and click the Fees & Expenses link on the left in the new page that appears. The site shows you both the initial (front-end load) and deferred fees (back-end load) plus all other fees, including 12b-1 and management fees on a screen like the one in Figure 10-2. Morningstar also shows you how much the fees will eat from your portfolio over the next three, five, and ten years.

Before paying a load, be absolutely certain there isn't a less expensive mutual fund/index mutual fund that will accomplish the same thing for you. The Securities and Exchange Commission (www.sec.gov/investor/tools/mfcc/mfcc-intsec.htm) provides a fee calculator that shows just how costly fees can be. Personal Fund (http://personalfund.com) can also analyze mutual funds' fees and calculate how much they will cost you.

Figure 10-2:
Morningstar.
com helps
you find out
which funds
charge high
fees, such
as this one
that was
charging
an 18.4%
expense
ratio.

Finding mutual funds that work for you

With so many mutual funds to choose from, you need your computer's help to find the ones best suited to you. You can use computerized *screening tools,* which scour a database of all mutual funds, looking for criteria you select. A number of Web sites provide such screening tools, including the following:

✔ **Morningstar:** (www.morningstar.com) That Morningstar is on the list shouldn't come as a surprise. To pinpoint the types of funds you're look-ing for, just click the Funds tab on the Morningstar home page, scroll down a bit and then click the Fund Screener link under the Find a Fund header on the left side of the page. You can screen mutual funds based on everything from the type of fund, such as large-value, to funds with expense ratios below certain levels, low turnover, average market values of specific amounts and ten-year returns that you choose. You can even exclude funds that charge loads or only view funds that have received Morningstar's highest ratings. When you're done entering all your crite-ria, click the Show Results tab, and you get a list of all the funds that meet your standards.

It's generally a good idea to stick with mutual funds that charge total fees of well below 1.5%.

✔ **Lipper:** (www.lipperweb.com) The other big-name mutual fund tracker, Lipper, lets you begin a search by clicking the Fund Screener link on the right side of its home page. You can narrow your search by type of fund (such as stock or bond) or classification (size and fund family, for instance). You can also limit your search to funds that receive Lipper's top rating in five categories, including total return, consistent return, preservation, tax efficiency, and expense.

✔ **MSN Money Mutual Fund Screener:** (http://moneycentral.msn.com/investor/finder/customfunds.asp) This corner of the MSN Money site offers an easy-to-use system that lets you search for very specific funds that meet your needs. You can also save your search criteria in case you want to try again later.

Many of the discount online brokers provide free access to mutual fund screening tools, most of which are based on either Morningstar or Lipper data.

How to buy mutual funds with an online broker

You have two main ways to buy mutual funds: directly from the mutual fund company or through a broker.

Nearly all the online brokers discussed in Chapter 4 let you buy mutual funds. Buying this way is convenient because your mutual fund holdings will be listed on your account statements next to your stock investments.

To buy a mutual fund this way, just log in to your account and enter the mutual fund's stock symbol and proceed to buy it just as you'd buy a stock. The online broker's site then gives you the NAV (net asset value) from the previous day. (After the stock market closes, the mutual fund determines the NAV for the day. That NAV, measured after the market closes, determines the price you pay for the shares.)

Some online brokers charge exorbitant commissions for buying and selling mutual funds. Table 10-1 shows you some sample commissions from a few top online brokers.

Table 10-1	Mutual Fund Commissions
Broker	*Regular Online Commission*
Charles Schwab	$49.95
E*Trade	$19.99
Fidelity Brokerage	$75
TD Ameritrade	$49.95 for no-load funds, $0 for load funds
TradeKing	$14.95 for no-load funds, $0 to buy load funds and $14.95 to sell
Zecco	$10

Online brokers often offer a number of transaction-free mutual funds that you can buy and sell for no commission. Just be careful, though, because these online brokers also usually hit you with a *short-term redemption fee,* even on a transaction-free mutual fund, if you sell the fund too quickly after buying it. These fees are usually around $50.

How to buy mutual funds without a broker

You might not want to fuss with getting a broker, or perhaps you hate being limited to the transaction-free mutual funds. You might be a candidate for buying shares directly from the mutual fund companies. This might save you money because mutual fund companies typically don't charge commissions.

If you're interested in buying a fund that isn't one of the transaction-free choices with a broker, it's best to buy directly from the fund company to avoid paying commissions. It's especially a good idea if you plan to periodically make small investments, which could ring up hefty fees if you use a broker.

To buy mutual funds from a mutual fund company, you need to set up an account, which you can do pretty quickly online. After you decide which fund you'd like to buy, just log in to the fund company's site and click a link that's usually labeled Open an Account. You have to answer the same questions needed to open an online brokerage account, described in Chapter 4, including your address and type of account (individual or joint). You also need to tell the mutual fund company whether you want dividends deposited to your account or used to buy additional shares of the fund. You can fill out the application online in about 20 minutes or print it and mail it in.

Most mutual fund companies offer Automatic Monthly Investment programs (AMI). If you sign up for an AMI, the fund company automatically takes money from your bank savings or checking account each month. It's a good way to make sure you're regularly saving money. Some funds will even let you start with a smaller initial investment if you sign up for the AMI.

Table 10-2 is a directory of some of the larger mutual fund companies.

Table 10-2	A Few Leading Mutual Fund Companies	
Mutual Fund Company for Regular Account	*Web Site*	*Minimum Deposit*
American Century	www.american century.com	$10,000 to avoid a $25 annual fee. You can also avoid the fee if you manage your account online only.
Artisan	www.artisanfunds. com	$1,000 per fund.
Dodge & Cox	www.dodgeandcox. com	$2,500 per fund.
Fidelity	www.fidelity.com	$2,500.
Janus	www.janus.com	$2,500 per fund.
Oakmark	www.oakmark.com	$1,000 per fund.
Royce	www.roycefunds.com	$2,000.
T. Rowe Price	www.troweprice.com	$2,500.
Vanguard	www.vanguard.com	$10,000 to avoid $20 annual fee. You can also avoid the fee if you manage your account online only. Be sure to sign up for a mutual fund account, not a brokerage account.

Some mutual funds can't be bought directly by individual investors. A few mutual fund companies, including leading index fund provider Dimensional Fund Advisors, sell their funds only through certified financial planners.

Comparing Mutual Funds to Each Other

When you're choosing a mutual fund, it's always a good idea to compare several similar funds to each other to make sure you're getting the best one for your needs. You want to consider both the fund's characteristics and risk.

Putting funds' characteristics side by side

MSN Money (http://moneycentral.msn.com/investor/home.asp) offers a useful tool that lets you compare mutual funds. For instance, it shows you the average price-to-earnings ratios of all the stocks the funds hold. The price-to-earnings ratio, discussed at more length in Chapter 13, is one way to see how pricey stocks are. Just visit the site and click the Research Wizard link on the menu on the left-hand side of the page — right under the Funds heading. Enter the first mutual fund's symbol and hit the Go button. This takes you to the fund's snapshot page. Click the Comparison link under the Guided Research heading on the left-hand side of the page. In the Enter a Symbol to Compare blank, enter the symbol of a mutual fund or two you'd like to size up based on all the key factors and click the Compare button.

Analyzing a mutual funds' risk

Understanding the potential returns you might enjoy from a fund is just half of the equation. It's equally — if not even more — important to know how much risk you're taking on to get the return. Many of the same online tools used to measure your portfolio's risk, explained in Chapter 9, can be used to gauge your mutual fund's risk, too.

Online mutual fund investors, though, can get additional information about risk from Morningstar. Enter the mutual fund's ticker symbol at Morningstar. com in the Quotes blank at the top left-hand side of the page and press Enter. Next, click the Risk Measures link on the left side of the new page that appears. You see all the vital measures of the fund's risk, including

✔ **Standard deviation:** As explained in Chapter 8, standard deviation is a way to measure an investment's risk. All you really need to know is that the higher the standard deviation, the higher the fund's risk.

✔ **Sharpe Ratio:** This measure gives you, at a glance, an idea of how much bang you're getting from the mutual fund for the risk you're taking. The higher the Sharpe Ratio — named after Nobel Laureate William Sharpe — the more return you're getting for the risk.

✔ **R-Squared:** This measure helps you figure out how much of a fund's movement is due to the judgment of the portfolio manager and how much is due to the movements of the stock market. The closer R-Squared is to 100, the more the fund mirrors what's going on the stock market. An index fund tracking the S&P 500, for instance, would have an R-Squared of very close to 100.

Don't pay a mutual fund manager high fees for just investing in an index. You could pay much less and just buy an index fund. To know whether your manager is shadowing the market, look at R-Squared. If an actively managed fund you own has an R-Squared close to 100, consider dumping it and buying an index fund.

✔ **Beta:** Measures how sensitive your fund is to movements by the rest of the stock market. A fund with a beta of 1 moves up and down by the same order of magnitude as the stock market. A beta of 0.75 shows the fund tends to underperform by 25% when the market gains but declines 25% less when the market falls. If you want less wild swings in your financial life and can accept lower returns as a result, look for a fund with a low beta.

✔ **Alpha:** Definitely one of the best statistics out there for measuring mutual funds. This single number tells you whether the portfolio manager is adding value or destroying value. When a fund has a negative alpha, that means it performs worse than it should, based on the amount of risk that's being assumed. When the alpha is positive, it means the manager is adding value by getting a better return than would be expected for the risk being taken. Always look for mutual funds with positive alphas. In measuring alpha, Morningstar compares all funds not only to the market (S&P 500), but also to the index that most closely matches a fund's investment objective.

Getting the Full Story: Reading a Mutual Fund's Prospectus

Mutual fund companies are required by regulators to clearly explain to investors, in writing, everything an investor would need to know. This information is contained in a regulatory filing called the *prospectus*. These documents are very detailed and worth reading before you invest in a fund.

Nearly all the most vital data contained in mutual fund prospectuses are captured by mutual fund Web sites described in the preceding sections. There's no need to dig through a prospectus to get things like fees or investment objectives. But a section of the prospectus that's often left out of the Web sites is the risks section, which outlines all the things that could go wrong.

That's worth checking out. Also, the SEC provides guidelines on what to look for in the prospectus at `www.sec.gov/answers/mfinfo.htm`.

You have several ways to get the prospectus online, including the following:

- **The Mutual fund provider's Web site:** The mutual fund company's Web site almost always has a link to the prospectus.

- **Sources for regulatory filings:** Mutual fund prospectuses are regulatory filings, so you can retrieve them from many of the same places you can get companies' filings, described in Chapter 2. The Securities and Exchange Commission's Web site (`www.sec.gov`) provides the information for free. (Figure 10-3 shows the SEC's Search page for Mutual Funds Prospectuses.)

Figure 10-3:
The SEC's Web site makes mutual fund prospectuses readily available to online investors who know where to look.

Getting more information about funds

The funny thing about mutual funds is that they can be extremely hands-off or an addiction. On the one hand, you can buy a target date mutual fund, set up an AMI and never think about your mutual fund again. But, you can also read about the ins and outs of mutual funds and keep up on all the new developments. If you're interested in studying funds, there are some sites to check out, including the following:

- **MAXfunds.com:** (www.maxfunds.com) Maxfunds features a blog that constantly presents news developments regarding the mutual fund world.

- **Brill's Mutual Funds Interactive:** (www.brill.com) Brill's digs deeply into timely mutual fund topics such as whether target-date funds would make sense for you or how to pick mutual funds that hold up well during economic downturns.

- **John Bogle's Web site at Vanguard:** (www.vanguard.com/bogle_site/bogle_speeches.html) A collection of Vanguard founder John Bogle's speeches, this page is an invaluable source for investing insights not just for mutual fund investors, but for everyone.

- **USATODAY.com:** (www.usatoday.com/money/perfi/columnist/waggon) Home for the Mutual funds guy at USATODAY, John Waggoner, this page features regular columns in which Waggoner discusses mutual fund developments as well as strategies to improve your success.

- **TheStreet.com:** (http://find.thestreet.com/cgi-bin/texis/tscsection/?k=Mutual%20Funds&sec=Mutual%20Funds&submenu=personalfinancemenu&ref=tscnav) It's a long URL, but it's worth all the typing. The Mutual Funds section of TheStreet.com provides a good selection of stories written about mutual funds.

- **The Mutual Fund Education Alliance's Mutual Fund Investor's Center:** (www.mfea.com) This site has helpful information on everything from how to get started with mutual funds to help with asset allocation and retirement saving.

- **SmartMoney:** (www.smartmoney.com/funds) SmartMoney has its own Mutual Funds corner, which offers a complete section for mutual fund investors. You can find stories about — and rankings of — mutual funds.

Chapter 11

Finding and Buying Exchange-Traded Funds

In This Chapter

▶ Finding out how exchange-traded funds differ from mutual funds

▶ Locating ETFs that that fit your needs using online tools

▶ Understanding how ETFs are bought and sold online

▶ Uncovering ways to research exchange-traded funds

A relatively new type of fund called an *exchange-traded fund,* or ETF, is exploding with popularity. Like index ETF mutual funds, ETFs invest in baskets of stocks tied to a stock market index. But ETFs differ from mutual funds in that they trade during the day just like an individual stock. This important difference gives ETFs an edge over mutual funds for some investors.

ETFs have lured $422.5 billion of investors' cash since they started to catch on in the early 1990s. In this chapter, I explain how online tools can maximize your success investing in mutual funds and ETFs. I help you use online tools to pick the right investments for you and show you how to set up an account to buy or sell the funds.

Getting to Know the Newcomers: ETFs

Exchange-traded funds have been one of the biggest developments in the world of finance since banks started giving away free toasters to customers.

ETFs are baskets of stocks, much like mutual funds, that trade like stocks. You can buy and sell them using your online broker just like you would with other stocks. All ETFs have trading symbols and qualify for the low commission rates from online brokers. You can even get price quotes by using your favorite stock-tracking Web sites, including those listed in Chapter 2.

You can buy and sell ETFs by using the online broker you've already signed up with. Just enter the ETF's trading symbol, and you can buy and sell just like you would shares of a company's stock.

Investors like ETFs because they're easy to buy without the hassle of signing up for accounts with mutual fund companies or checking to see whether they're transaction-free. Unlike mutual funds, which update their price once a day after the market closes, ETF prices are constantly updated during the trading day. That means investors can just buy ETFs and sell them whenever they want during the day. This explains why the number of ETFs has taken off, as shown in Table 11-1.

Table 11-1	ETFs Everywhere
Year	*Number of ETFs*
2002	113
2003	119
2004	152
2005	204
2006	357

Source: Investment Company Institute (www.icifactbook.org/fb_sec3.html)

ETFs have the same advantages of mutual funds, as described in Chapter 10. That includes diversification and access to specific corners of the stock market, including certain sizes of stocks or industries. ETFs, though, offer several advantages over mutual funds including the following:

✔ **Intraday trading:** Mutual funds price once a day, meaning you don't know how your portfolio has done until the markets close and the fund companies get around to publishing the net asset value (NAV) for the day. The prices of ETFs constantly update during the day just like stocks.

✔ **Access to tougher areas of the market:** Investors interested in buying commodities, bonds, and currencies can buy them easily, just like buying a stock, thanks to ETFs. And because ETFs are priced during the day, speculators can get in and out of risky positions anytime they want. ETFs are a great way to add foreign exposure to your portfolio, as I explain in the "Broadening Your Horizons: International Stocks" bonus chapter on the Web site associated with this book.

✔ **Low fees:** If you thought the fees on index mutual funds were low, ETFs in many cases are even lower. It's not unusual for ETFs to charge lower maintenance fees than mutual funds that mirror the same stock index by owning all the stocks in the index. The average expense ratio of ETFs is roughly 0.5%, well below the 1.1% charged by mutual funds.

✔ **Tax advantages:** Due to their structure, ETFs rarely stick investors with capital-gain distributions. That helps investors plan tax strategies. Keep in mind, though, many ETFs still pay dividends, which are usually taxable.

✔ **Offer advanced trading options:** Most ETFs offer *options,* specific trading vehicles I discuss in Chapter 5. That's attractive to investors who want to do more than just buy or sell the investments. ETFs can also be *shorted,* a technique used to bet an investment will decline in value that I also explain in Chapter 5.

Invest in Popular Indexes with ETFs

So far, most ETFs track a stock market index much like an index mutual fund. That's not a bad thing because indexes often outperform actively managed mutual funds and have lower fees.

Most of the oldest and largest ETFs, not surprisingly, track the most popular stock and bond market indexes. Some of the largest ETFs that track widely followed indexes include those listed in Table 11-2.

Table 11-2		Popular ETFs	
ETF Proper Name	*ETF Nickname*	*ETF Symbol*	*Index Tracked*
SPDR S&P 500 ETF	Spider	SPY	Standard & Poor's 500 (large companies).
Diamonds Trust	Diamonds	DIA	Dow Jones industrial average (large companies).
PowerShares QQQQ	Cubes	QQQQ	NASDAQ 100 (100 largest, nonfinancial stocks that trade on the NASDAQ).

(continued)

Table 11-2 *(continued)*

ETF Proper Name	ETF Nickname	ETF Symbol	Index Tracked
iShares MSCI EAFE Index	N/A	EFA	MSCI EAFE index (stocks from Europe, Australia, and the Far East).
iShares Russell 2000 Index	N/A	IWM	Russell 2000 (small companies).
SPDR DJ Wilshire Total Market ETF	N/A	TMW	DJ Wilshire 5000 (all companies).
iShares Lehman	N/A	AGG	Lehman Aggregate Aggregate Bond Bond index, a broad measure of the value of bonds. It tracks government and highly rated corporate bonds.

How to Find the Right ETF for the Job

As with mutual funds, one of the toughest things about ETFs is just finding them amid the hundreds of choices out there. But as with mutual funds, online screeners can help you scour through the universe of ETFs and find the ones that fit your needs. The following list gives you a representative sampling:

- **ETFConnect:** (www.etfconnect.com) This particular site allows you to search for an ETF by using a keyword or by selecting a type of ETF, such as those that track bonds and stocks. Searching by keyword is especially handy if you're looking to invest in a somewhat offbeat type of stock, commodity, or part of the world. Want to invest in an ETF that invests in natural resources stocks, for instance? Just type the words **natural resources** in the search field, click the Go button, and you get a list.

- **ETFZone:** (www.etfzone.com/data/funds.php) ETFZone provides an advanced ETF screener that lets you find ETFs based on their size and style (such as large cap, value, or growth) and also by short-term and long-term returns.

✔ **Morningstar:** (`http://screen.morningstar.com/ETFScreener/Selector.html`) Yes, Morningstar does ETFs, too. This section of the site provides a complete screening tool, with detailed search capabilities that help you quickly find the ETF that passes all your criteria.

Some investors seek ETFs that track specific industries. Morningstar makes it easy to find them. From the screener, select the industry you hope to invest in from the Morningstar Category drop-down list. You can also search for the industry's name by using ETFConnect.

✔ **Online brokers:** The big players often provide tools that help you find the right ETFs for you. For instance, TD Ameritrade (`https://wwws.ameritrade.com/cgi-bin/apps/Horizon`) offers a site that studies your investment objectives and suggests ETFs that might help get you there.

✔ **ETF providers' Web sites:** The largest ETF providers, Barclays Global (`www.ishares.com`), Vanguard (`https://flagship.vanguard.com/VGApp/hnw/funds/etf`), and State Street (`www.ssgafunds.com`) provide very detailed information about their families of funds.

Don't assume these are just worthless promotional sites. They're well organized and make it easy to find what you're looking for. You can find some interesting features on these sites, including State Street's Correlation Tracker (`www.ssgafunds.com/resources/correlation_tracker.html`), which can tell you which ETFs have a low correlation with any stock you enter. (Investments are said to have low correlations with each other when they don't move in lockstep with one another.) Buying ETFs with low correlations, as I explain in Chapter 9, is attractive because it can lower your portfolio's total risk.

Curious which stocks an ETF owns? All the online resources I mention here provide ETFs' *top holdings*. These are the stocks that have the largest positions in an ETF.

Tracking ETFs' every move

Because ETFs are priced during the day just like stocks, they can be useful tools to tell you what types of stocks and industries are moving each day. NASDAQ's ETF center (`http://quotes.nasdaq.com/asp/investmentproducts.asp`) provides in-depth analysis of the ETFs that went up and down the most in value each trading session. It also shows you the most popular ETFs, ranked by trading activity, or volume. (*Volume* is a measure of how many times shares of a stock trade hands.) The ETF Dynamic Heatmap (`http://screening.nasdaq.com/heatmaps/heatmap_ETF.asp`) uses a color-coded grid to show which ETFs are moving the most.

Don't assume the most popular ETFs are the best

When you buy an ETF, you're most frequently buying a basket of stocks mirroring a stock index. And when shopping for index funds, you typically want to find the ones that either best track the type of stocks you're interested in or have the lowest fees.

Ask yourself the same questions you consider when buying an index mutual fund:

✔ **How large is the ETF?** In the case of an ETF, the more assets under management, the better. You don't want to invest in a small ETF that doesn't attract enough investors and ends up being shut down. This is becoming more of an issue as more ETFs are rushed to the market.

To find out how large an ETF is, go to the Morningstar site (www.morningstar.com), enter the ticker symbol of the ETF in the Quotes field, and then press Enter. On the new page that appears, click the Snapshot link on the left side of the page and you'll find the fund's total assets.

✔ **What index does the ETF track?** Some small-cap indexes, for instance, track the Russell 2000, and others track the Standard & Poor's 600. Both track small stocks, but there are differences between the indexes themselves. Make sure that you're tracking the index you prefer.

Imagine, if you will, that you want to buy an ETF that invests in small companies. It's a good idea to check the Web site of the ETF company and check the average market value of the stocks held by the ETF and compare it with the competition.

✔ **What are the expenses?** If everything else is equal, there's nothing wrong with looking at the price tag and going with the ETF that's cheapest. Vanguard, a low-cost leader in mutual funds, has emerged as a low-cost leader in ETFs as well. Vanguard almost always deserves serious consideration for that reason. The rampant competition in the ETF business has dramatically driven down fees. That's why it's worthwhile to use one of the screening tools mentioned in this chapter to see what fee the fund charges and compare it to other options.

ETF fees can vary

Using screening sites like the ones in the preceding section, you can easily find and compare the fees charged by ETFs. Here's how you do it using ETFConnect, for example:

1. **Point your browser to www.etfconnect.com.**

2. **Enter the symbol or name of the ETF you're interested in checking fees for into the Search field in the upper-right corner of the page and then click the Go button.**

3. **Look over the screen.**

The screen shows all the vitals about the ETF, including its price, the fund company that sponsors it, when it was created, what it invests in, and what its top holdings are. You also see the breakdown of industries it owns and what countries the stocks are based in.

4. Scroll down until you see the ETF Facts box.

You need to scroll down quite a ways — the box is on the right side. The ETF Facts box shows you several things, including the ETF's expense ratio.

The _expense ratio_ is a very important number that tells you the annual fee the ETF provider will charge you for owning the ETF. If you invest $1,000 in an ETF with an expense ratio of 0.5%, that means you'll pay an annual fee of $5. You want to compare this ratio with other ETFs you might be considering. You can see a sample in Figure 11-1.

Finding out how pricey an ETF is

Stock investors commonly look at the _price-to-earnings ratio,_ or P-E, of an individual stock to find out how expensive it is. The higher the P-E, the more richly valued the stock is, as I explain in detail in Chapter 13. But ETF investors can also use P-E ratios to find how cheap or expensive the stocks held by the ETF are.

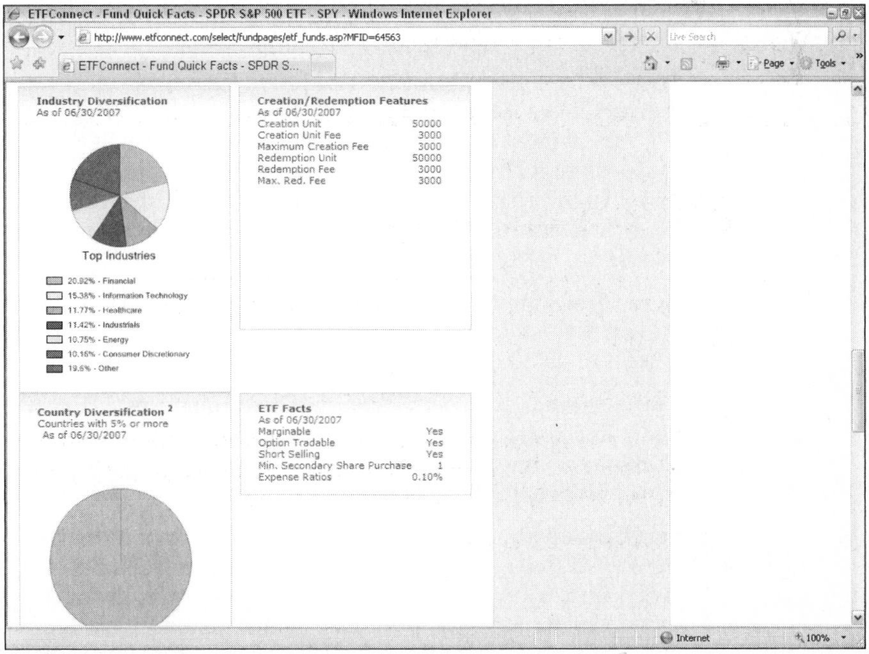

Figure 11-1: You can find all sorts of particulars about ETFs at ETFConnect, including the all-important expense ratio.

Several Web sites provide P-E ratios for ETFs. Using Yahoo! Finance (`finance.yahoo.com`), enter the ETF's symbol into the search field at the upper left area of the page. Click the Get Quotes button. You see the ETF's P-E listed on the right-hand side of the quote box, next to the label P/E (ttm), which stands for price-to-earnings ratio for the trailing (or last) 12 months.

Yahoo! Finance also provides risk and performance measures for ETFs. The risk measures, such as standard deviation, help you determine how much the ETF will give you indigestion by swinging up and down in value. (These risk measures are explained in detail in Chapter 1.) The performance measures tell you how well the ETF has done. After entering an ETF's symbol, just click the Performance and Risk links on the left side with the blue background.

To get the P-E ratio of an ETF from Morningstar (`www.morningstar.com`), enter the symbol of the ETF you're interested in and click the Go button. In the new page that appears, click the Portfolio link on the left side. There you can find the ETF's P-E ratio and how it compares with the Standard & Poor's 500 index. You can also find lots of other details on the Portfolio page, such as other valuation ratios and which industry sectors the ETF's holdings fall into.

ETFs That Go off the Beaten Path

Most ETFs are pretty typical and closely track their designated indexes. But ETFs are so new and relatively easy to create that some companies, including the following, have experimented with some interesting concepts:

- ✔ **WisdomTree** (`www.wisdomtree.com`) lets investors bet on academic research from Wharton Professor Jeremy Siegel. Rather than following the lead of most ETFs and index mutual funds, which hold bigger chunks of stocks that have the greatest market values, Siegel suggests that it's better to own bigger chunks of companies that pay large dividends. There's an entire set of WisdomTree funds, enough to satisfy any asset allocation, based on this theory.

- ✔ **Rydex Investments** (`www.rydexfunds.com`) offers some offbeat ETFs, including the Rydex S&P Equal Weight (symbol RSP) which holds equal chunks of all 500 stocks in the S&P 500 index.

- ✔ **PowerShares** (`www.powershares.com`) provides ETFs that track just about any industry you can imagine, ranging from biotech to companies working on nanotechnology as well as specialized portfolios that include companies that pay large dividends or buy back their stock.

- ✔ **ProShares** (`www.proshares.com`) is attempting to make advanced trading strategies more accessible. For instance, its Short QQQ ETF (PSQ) goes up when the NASDAQ 100 goes down, giving investors a way to bet against technology stocks. Similar funds let investors bet against other indexes like the Russell 2000 and Dow Jones industrial average.

ETFs Have Issues, Too

ETFs are great for many investors looking for ways to keep their costs down and simplify their lives. After all, you can buy all your stock and ETF investments from the same brokerage account. But ETFs have drawbacks, too, as the following list makes clear:

- **Commissions:** Unlike mutual funds, which can often be bought with no commissions through online brokers or directly from fund companies, ETFs are treated like stocks. That means your online broker's standard stock commission applies. That can be a deal-killer if you make frequent and small investments. Unless you use an online broker with free trades, such as those discussed in Chapter 4, you might be better off with an index mutual fund.

- **Temptation:** The ability to trade in and out of ETFs is too irresistible for some investors — the kind who can't keep their fingers off their mouse buttons. If the constant pricing of ETFs encourages you to trade too much and veer off your asset allocation course, you might be better off with mutual funds.

- **Invisible cost: the spread:** ETFs come with an invisible, but costly fee. Just as with stocks, ETFs have a *bid* and an *ask* price. The bid is the price other investors are willing to pay for the ETF, and the ask is the price the seller will take. The difference, called the *spread,* costs investors money.

  For example, say you bought 100 shares of an ETF at the ask price of $100. Most likely, you'd only be able to sell it for $99.90 or less, costing you in effect 10 cents a share. The less popular an ETF, the wider the spread becomes, and the greater this cost becomes. Are you curious about what an ETF's bid and ask prices are? They're available from the same places you get stock quotes.

- **Premiums and discounts:** ETFs are priced based on what buyers and sellers are willing to pay for the basket of stocks they own. That means it's possible the price of an ETF might be greater or less than the value of the stocks it owns. When the ETF price is greater than the value of the stocks it owns, that situation is a *premium,* and when the opposite is true and the ETF is worth less than the value of its stocks, the ETF is said to be trading at a *discount.* You can look up the size of the premium or discount for an ETF at www.etfconnect.com.

  Don't get overly concerned with the premium or discount. Most ETFs' premium or discount is rather small. And for popular ETFs, it's practically nonexistent.

A Few Final Things to Consider About ETFs

One of the reasons ETFs have been so popular is that they make it easy to invest in assets that were difficult to invest in before. By buying a single ETF just as you'd buy a stock, you can instantly invest in a basket of companies working on alternative energy or in financial commodities like gold. Since ETFs have made it much easier to invest in a wide array of investments, it's more important than ever for investors to know how to find out exactly what they're buying when they purchase an ETF by reading the prospectus. This section will show you how.

Using ETFs as a way to invest in themes

Investors might periodically want to get a stake on a trend they feel will be important in the future. Some investors, for instance, feel global warming is a serious issue and want to invest in stocks that are finding new sources of energy that generate less pollution. Other investors can't bear to invest in companies they feel contribute to social ills, so they focus on socially responsible ETFs. ETFs are perfect for this kind of thing because you can invest in an index that tracks a basket of stocks involved in the theme you're interested in. You can invest in the trend by just buying one investment and spread your risk over several companies.

ETFs that invest in specialty areas of interest generally charge higher expense ratios and may not generate large returns to warrant the costs. Before investing in an investing theme, make sure you're not getting caught up in a fad. Also, make sure you're not spending money on management fees that could have been better spent just donating directly to charity.

A few examples of specialty ETFs include those listed in Table 11-3.

Table 11-3	Green Investing Options	
Investment Name	*Symbol*	*Invests in Companies That Are . . .*
PowerShares WilderHill Clean Energy Portfolio	PBW	Researching clean sources of energy
PowerShares WilderHill Progressive Energy	PUW	Finding ways to clean up traditional energy sources

Investment Name	Symbol	Invests in Companies That Are . . .
PowerShares Water Resources Portfolio	PHO	Positioned to benefit from the demand for clean water
iShares KLD Select Social Index	KLD	Dedicated to maintaining respect for humans and the environment

Investors who buy an ETF that tracks a theme might feel they've reduced their risk by owning many companies, not just one. There's a bit of truth to that because you're spreading your risk over many different companies. But don't make the mistake of thinking that owning an ETF alone saves you from risk. You're still at risk if the trend falls apart.

Betting on commodities and currencies with ETFs

Buying commodities like oil, gold, and steel, even today, isn't as convenient as you'd think. You usually need to establish a special account with a broker that specializes in commodity trading if you want to invest in commodities directly. Buying and selling currencies can be a hassle, too. That's why ETFs are a boon for stock investors who would like to add some commodities and currencies to their portfolios.

Most of the major commodities and many currencies can be invested in through ETFs. Table 11-4 shows examples for many of the major commodities.

Table 11-4		Ways to Play Commodities with ETFs
Investment Name	**Symbol**	**Commodity the ETF Tracks**
iShares COMEX Gold Trust	IAU	Gold
iShares Silver Trust	SLV	Silver
iShares S&P GSCI Commodity-Indexed Trust	GSG	A basket of many types of commodities, measured by the Goldman Sachs Commodity-Index Total Return Index
PowerShares DB Energy Fund	DBE	Energy commodities ranging from oil to gasoline, heating oil, and natural gas

(continued)

Table 11-4 *(continued)*

Investment Name	Symbol	Commodity the ETF Tracks
PowerShares DB Precious Metals Fund	DBP	Gold and silver
PowerShares DB U.S. Dollar Bearish Fund	UDN	Gains in value when the U.S. dollar loses value
PowerShares DB U.S. Dollar Bullish Fund	UUP	Gains in value when the U.S. dollar gains value
PowerShares DB Commodity Index Tracking Fund	DBC	Crude oil, heating oil, gold, aluminum, corn, and wheat
iPath S&P GSCI Crude Oil Total Return Index ETN	OIL	Oil
Market Vectors Steel Index ETF	SLX	Steel

Just because you *can* invest in commodities doesn't mean you *should.* Gold, for instance, has been a poor long-term performer that has generated subpar returns and greater risk. Be sure you understand the risks of commodities before jumping in.

Reading the fine print: The prospectus

Like mutual funds, ETFs must be fully described to investors in a *prospectus.* These documents describe ETFs' structures, investing objective, fees, and all other details to investors — and are filled with legal jumble. But they're worth taking a look at if you're going to invest in an ETF.

There are several main ways to get the prospectus online, including from the following sources:

✔ **The ETF provider's Web site:** If you log in to the Web site of the company that provides the investment, you can almost always find a link to the prospectus. This is typically the easiest way to find a prospectus.

For example, say you're interested in investing in the SPDR S&P 500 ETF. Log in to State Street's Web site (www.ssgafunds.com), enter the ticker symbol of **SPY** into the Enter Ticker field, and click the Go button. On the new page that appears, you see a View Prospectus link on the right side. Click it to check out the prospectus.

✓ **Sources for regulatory filings:** ETF prospectuses are regulatory filings, so you can retrieve them from many of the same places you'd use to get companies' filings, as described in Chapter 2. Due to the structure of ETFs, though, it's easier to download prospectuses directly from the ETF provider. Many ETF families, such as iShares, make it easy to click a link and download the prospectus. Figure 11-2 shows the Prospectus link at iShares.com. (You see the link on the left side.)

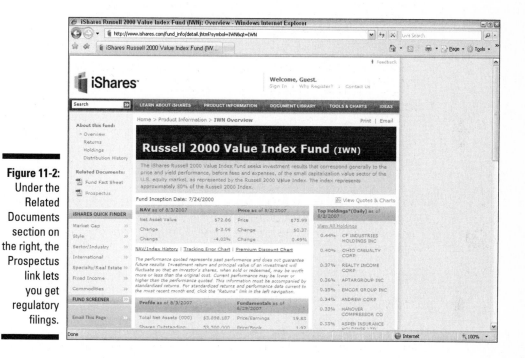

Figure 11-2: Under the Related Documents section on the right, the Prospectus link lets you get regulatory filings.

Part III
Maximizing Investment Knowledge

The 5th Wave   By Rich Tennant

"Oh, that's Jack's area for his paper crafts. He's made some wonderful US Treasury Bonds, Certificates of Deposit, $20's, $50's, $100's that sort of thing."

In this part . . .

If you're the kind of person who can't stop after just mastering the basics, you'll find yourself at home in this part. Here I dig in deeper and take on more advanced topics that savvy investors rely on when choosing investments and constructing their portfolio. I show you how to use online tools to closely examine companies' earnings, cash flow, and financial statements to get a clearer picture about whether a stock is for you. You get exposure to advanced online techniques used by the pros to measure stocks' prospects, including evaluating their risk, potential cash flow, and valuation. You find tutorials on how to make your computer do much of the hard work for you by building online screens that unearth stocks and investments from thousands of candidates. I show you how to find out whether certain experts and analysts are worth listening to by using online tools that evaluate their performance. And for investors looking for more stability, this part tackles the topic of bonds and other fixed-income investments.

Chapter 12

Putting Companies Under the Microscope

*I*f you're the kind of online investor looking to buy the next Google, this chapter offers tips that might help you. I show you how to use online tools to unearth details about companies that aren't picked up by general investing Web sites explained in Chapters 2 and 6. I explain how you can glean insights about companies by picking apart *financial statements,* and I show you how to compare companies with their peers.

Just be careful. Consistently picking winning stocks and buying and selling them at the right times is infamously difficult and time consuming. If you don't know what you're doing, you might make less money picking individual stocks over the long term than you would if you just bought a mutual fund or exchange-traded fund that keeps up with the market.

Understanding Financial Statements

Most investors focus on companies' quarterly earnings reports. It's understandable. Stocks rapidly respond to whether a company topped, matched, or missed earnings expectations for the quarter. Online tools, described in Chapter 6, also make it easy to instantly see how a company did during the quarter and decide whether that changes your opinion on a stock. When companies report earnings, though, they provide only the most basic and top-level information in a press release.

Short-term performance can cause stocks to swing momentarily, but *long-term investors* know a company's true value is based on how it performs over the years, not just the most recent quarter. Examining a company's long-term performance requires a bit more effort and calls for digging into a company's financial statements. Investors that study a company's financial statements are said to analyze the *fundamentals*.

Financial statements are detailed documents that show you all the important numbers from a company, ranging from how profitable it is to how financially secure it is. Most of the detailed financial statements are available online a few weeks after the company puts out its earnings press release. The financial statements must be contained in documents required by regulators, including

- ✔ **The 10-Q:** The official quarterly report that must be filed with the Securities and Exchange Commission (SEC), the main regulator for stocks. It gives an update for the just-completed three-month period. The report is due 40 days after the end of the quarter for companies that have market values of $700 million or more.

- ✔ **The 10-K:** The official version of a company's annual report required by the SEC. After the end of a company's fiscal year, the company must provide an annual report called a 10-K. The 10-K, for most companies, is due 75 days after the end of the fiscal year according to the SEC (www.sec. gov/answers/form10q.htm).

The 10-Q and 10-K statements are vital because they contain these three key financial statements:

- ✔ **The income statement** measures the company's bottom line. It tells you how much the company earned during the quarter or year based on Generally Accepted Accounting Principles, or GAAP. (GAAP provides the rules all companies and their accountants must follow so investors know how to read the numbers.) This statement is also provided in the earnings press release, but with less detail.

- ✔ **The balance sheet** tabulates the company's net worth. The statement shows you what a company owns and owes at the end of the period. Do you want to know how much cash the company has in the bank or how much debt it has? Both numbers are in the balance sheet. The balance sheet might also be provided with the earnings press release, but with less detail.

✔ **The cash flow statement** tells you how much cash came into and went out of the company during the period. The report, often called the *cash flow statement,* is considered one of the most important documents provided by companies. The cash flow statement is typically not included in a company's earnings press release, but it's worth waiting for in the 10-Q and 10-K. A company's cash flow is more difficult to manipulate using accounting tricks because it's based on the amount of cold hard cash that comes into the company.

You can spend a great deal of time mastering the complexities of reading companies' regulatory filings and financial statements. If that interests you, Merrill Lynch (www.merrilllynch.com/media/14069.pdf) offers an excellent primer for financial statements, which you can download and print. It goes into great detail and is good resource for investors who want to know more. The SEC (www.sec.gov/investor/pubs/begfinstmtguide.htm) has a helpful article on financial statements. And IBM (www.ibm.com/investor/tools/resourcesPrint.phtml) provides a list of books and other resources that you can read to become more of an expert. I've also written an interactive online guide (www.usatoday.com/money/perfi/basics/2003-08-22-10q-intro_x.htm) that steps you through how to read a company's 10-Q, including the financial statements.

Downloading financial statements

Investors can get their hands on financial statements almost instantly. Numerous sites, listed in Chapter 2, let you download regulatory filings for free. The SEC (http://sec.gov/investor/pubs/edgarguide.htm) also provides a users manual online to show you how to download regulatory filings. When you download a regulatory filing, you might be shocked at how it looks. They're typically seas of text and no pictures — they certainly aren't the colorful magazine-like document you recall when you think of an annual report.

The *annual report* is a different document. The annual report contains all the required financial statements and information contained in the 10-Ks, but they're contained in a colorful format. If you've read the 10-K, you probably don't need the annual report. But, annual reports might provide additional, mostly promotional information about the company, such as photos of new products or happy customers, and they can be fun to look at depending on what the company does. You can order these paper documents from the investor relations section of most companies' Web sites or download an electronic copy. Many of these annual reports are also available from services like AnnualReports.com (www.annualreports.com), Annual Report

Resource Center (www.irin.com), and The Public Register's Annual Report Service (www.prars.com). Keep in mind, though, that annual reports from these services are often provided in Adobe's Acrobat format. The Acrobat format preserves the photos of the annual reports but is harder to download into a spreadsheet to analyze.

The SEC's Interactive Financial Report Viewer (http://216.241.101.197/viewer) represents one of the newest and best ways to download financial statements. This free viewer, shown in Figure 12-1, allows you to download and easily analyze statements from the hundreds of companies that are filing their financial results using the increasingly popular eXtensible Business Reporting Language, or XBRL. Using the viewer you can easily download many companies' financial information into a spreadsheet. The SEC (www.sec.gov/spotlight/xbrl.htm) is encouraging other companies to file using XBRL.

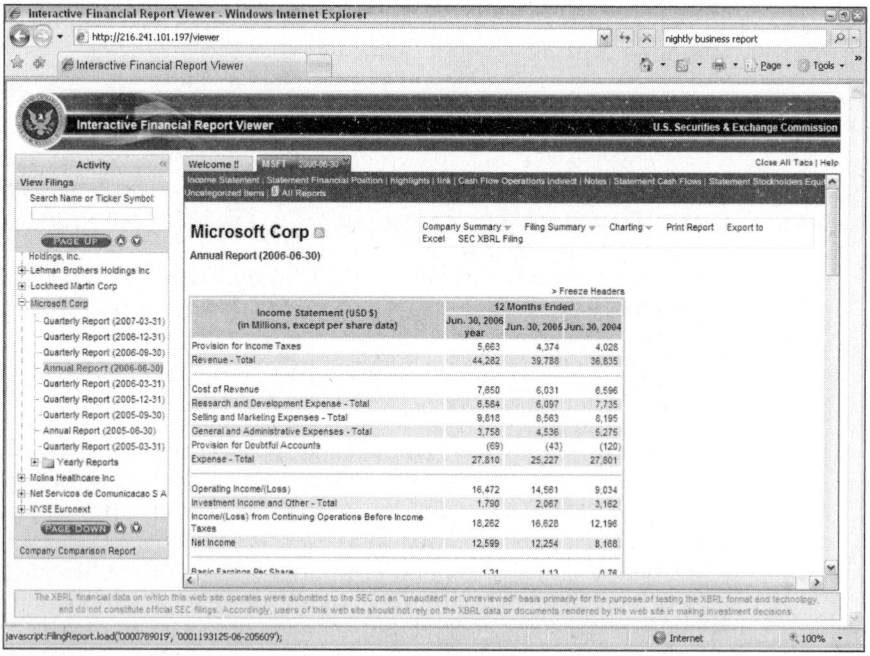

Figure 12-1:
The Interactive Financial Report Viewer lets you access and download financial statements from participating companies, including Microsoft.

How to read the income statement

How much money did the company make? That common question is answered, in detail, by the income statement. The income statement begins with revenue, which is a measurement of the value of the goods and services sold by the company. The company's expenses are then subtracted from revenue to arrive at the company's profit. Making things a bit more complicated, though, is that profit can mean one of several things:

- **Operating profit,** which measures how much the company makes after paying day-to-day costs, such as buying raw materials that go into the product as well as paying salaries. Operating profit is closely watched by Wall Street analysts because it shows how much the company earns from its business and excludes distortion from one-time charges and gains.

- **Net income,** also known as "the bottom line." It shows you how much the company made after subtracting all its costs. If the company lost money, it's said to have a net loss.

- **Diluted earnings per share,** which is what most investors should pay attention to. Diluted earnings per share converts a company's net income or net loss into a number that's more relevant to them: The investor's share of the profit. Diluted EPS is the earnings number most professional investors watch. Diluted EPS is measured by dividing adjusted net income by the number of shares *outstanding* — that's to say the number of shares currently in shareholders' hands added to the number that could be in shareholders' hands if stock options were exercised.

- **Basic earnings per share,** arrived at by simply dividing a company's net income by shares outstanding. It doesn't factor in the cost of dilution.

- **Proforma earnings per share,** a controversial way to measure earnings that was originally designed to help investors. Proforma earnings allow companies to leave out certain expenses to help investors understand how the company did excluding the effect of a big event, like a merger. Some companies, though, abused proforma earnings. These companies twisted proforma earnings in a way to leave out costs that made their results look better than they actually were. Proforma earnings drew such ire from regulators that companies are now required to detail step-by-step in their earnings press release what charges were left out of the proforma earnings calculation.

The first company accused by regulators for abusing proforma earnings was Trump Hotels (`http://sec.gov/news/headlines/trump hotels.htm`). You can read more about this accounting trick, and others that companies play, in a summary I wrote back in 2002 (`www.usatoday.com/money/energy/enron/2002-02-11-tricks-trade.htm`).

The stock buyback blues

You'll want to monitor a company's number of shares outstanding after it says it's buying back stock. Sometimes companies use excess cash to buy their own shares. Investors often applaud stock buybacks because they can, in theory, reduce the number of shares outstanding. And that means each shareholder's slice of the pie gets bigger.

Sounds like a great idea, right? But stock buybacks aren't always what they're cracked up to be. Keep the following in mind when you hear that a company has announced a stock buyback:

✔ **Stock buybacks can distort earnings per share.** If you see a company's earnings per share rise, don't assume that's because the company is more profitable. If a company buys back stock, earnings per share can rise even if net income is flat.

✔ **There's no rule that says the company must follow-through.** Just because a company announces it's buying back stock, that doesn't mean it will. In fact, some academic research has found many companies that announced stock buybacks actually increased their shares outstanding as they issued additional shares to give to employees and executives. You can find out more about buybacks at The Buyback Letter (www.buybackletter.com).

Basics about the balance sheet

The balance sheet tells you what a company owns and what it owes. The company separates what it owns, called its *assets,* from what it owes, its *liabilities.* The difference between assets and liabilities is what portion of the company shareholders' own, called *shareholders' equity.* The following list breaks it all down for you piece by piece:

✔ **Assets** are objects of value the company owns, including property, equipment, and machinery. Assets you can't see or touch like patents and trademarks, called *intangible assets,* are also included. Assets are further classified as

  • *Current assets:* Stuff that will be turned into cold hard cash within a year.

  • *Non-current assets:* Stuff like trucks and physical equipment that isn't expected to be turned into cash within a year.

✔ **Liabilities** are the company's obligations. Liabilities include such things as bank loans, IOUs given to suppliers, taxes owed, or promises to deliver products to customers in the future.

- *Current liabilities:* Bills and other obligations due within a year. The current portion of long-term debt, for instance, is the chunk the company must pay off within a year.

- *Non-current liabilities:* Long-term obligations the company doesn't have to pay back within a year.

✔ **Shareholders' equity** measures the value of the investors' ownership of the company. It's kind of the corporate version of your net worth. Your *net worth* is the value of your assets minus your debt. Shareholders' equity is the same: It's equal to a company's assets minus its liabilities.

One of the best things to pay attention to in the balance sheet is the company's *number of shares outstanding*, which is the number of shares that are in the hands of investors. A company's number of shares outstanding is very important because it measures how many pieces the company's profits is sliced into and how big a piece each shareholder gets.

What you need to know about the cash flow statement

Don't make the mistake of ignoring the cash flow statement. This statement cuts through all the smoke and mirrors of accounting to show you how much cold hard cash came into or went out of a company. The statement is divided into the following three parts:

✔ **Cash from operating activities** tells you how much cash the company used or generated from its normal course of business. This portion of the cash flow statement adjusts net income by adding back expenses that didn't cost the company cash, most importantly an expense called *depreciation* that accounts for the cost of wear and tear on equipment.

✔ **Cash from investing activities** shows how much cash a company uses to invest in new property and equipment, also known as *capital expenditures* or *Cap Ex*. The section also shows how much cash the company generates selling assets.

✔ **Cash from financing activities** illustrates how much cash a company brings onto its balance sheet, mostly by selling bonds.

Putting it all together

Some of the real power of financial statements occurs when you take elements of one statement and compare it with numbers on other statements.

The first thing many investment professionals do when they get an annual report, for instance, is compare the cash flow statement with the income statement. If a company is reporting banner profits on the income statement but not bringing in as much cash, that's a potential red flag. Low cash flow can be a sign the company has *low quality of earnings*. A company has low quality of earnings when it shows large profits on its financial statements due to accounting gimmicks, not because it's selling lots of goods and services to actual customers.

Here's an easy way for you to analyze a company's cash flow: Just compare a company's free cash flow with its net income.

You can get the data by doing the following:

- **Analyzing the financial statements yourself:** A company's free cash flow measures how much cash it brings in the door after paying expenses to keep itself going. Free cash flow (FCF) is a cousin to cash from operating activities. FCF, however, is stricter than cash from operating activities in that it accounts for the fact companies use cash to buy new equipment and facilities. To calculate free cash flow, enter the stock's ticker symbol into one of the Get Up to Ten Quotes text fields on NASDAQ's home page (www.nasdaq.com) and the click the Info Quotes button. In the new page that appears, choose Company Financials from the InfoQuotes drop-down list at the top of the page. (The Company Financials option is about halfway down the menu.) In the new page that appears, click the Statements of Cash Flow link at the top of the page, which brings you to a page similar to what you see in Figure 12-2. To get the company's free cash flow, subtract the number in the Capital Expenditures row from number the Net Cash Flow-Operating row. Compare that difference with the number in the Net Income row.

- **Getting the data from a Web site:** Several sites, including Forbes (www.forbes.com), provide free cash flow data. On the Forbes site, scroll down to find the Quotes/Research box on the right side with a text field for entering a stock symbol. Enter the stock's symbol (GE, for instance) in the Quotes/Research box and click the Go button. On the new page that appears, scroll down quite a ways and then click the More GE Ratios & Returns link that appears right beneath a Ratios & Returns table. You can find the company's Free Cash Flow per Share listed in the new page that appears, under the Latest 12 Months Data Item section.

  Multiply the company's Free Cash Flow per Share figure you get from Forbes by the company's number of shares outstanding to get the company's total free cash flow. You can get a company's number of shares outstanding from almost any financial Web site discussed in Chapter 2. You can get shares outstanding from Forbes.com by clicking on the At A Glance link on the left side of the page under Quotes & Chart.

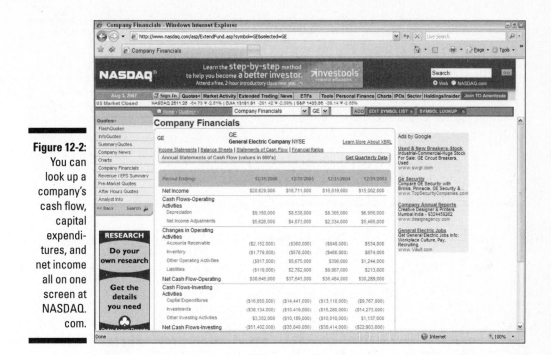

You have a company's free cash flow and net income. Now what? Table 12-1 tells you how to interpret what you've found. It's the same thing many professional investors do.

Table 12-1	Measuring a Company's Quality of Earnings
If Free Cash Flow Is . . .	**It Means the Company . . .**
Greater than net income	Brings in more cash than it reports as profit. That is a good sign and can be an indication of high quality earnings.
Less than net income	Brings in less cash than it reports as profit. That can be a red flag and means you want to analyze the company more closely.

Forbes.com provides other online tools to help you make sure you're not investing in the next Enron. After entering a stock's symbol at www.forbes. com as described in the preceding list, click the Accounting Risk link on the left side of the new page that appears. (It's under the Financials heading.) You get a free online report that studies the company's books and highlights potential red flags you should be aware of.

How free cash flow saved investors from Enron

Investors who compared Enron's free cash flow with net income were glad they did. Enron's quarterly statement from the first quarter of 2001 before its collapse (http://sec.gov/Archives/edgar/data/1024401/000102440101500014/ene10-q.txt) is very telling. During the quarter, Enron wowed investors with net income of $425 million. But investors who took the time to study the quarterly report saw the company burned $464 million in cash from operations and another $382 million in capital expenditures. That means Enron effectively burned up $846 million in cash, even while telling investors how profitable the company was.

You can read more about free cash flow at Investopedia (www.investopedia.com/articles/fundamental/03/091703.asp) and Morningstar (http://news.morningstar.com/classroom2/course.asp?docId=2937&CN=COM&page=1&_QSBPA=Y&t1=1184108876).

How to spot trends in financial statements

When you're studying the financial statements, you should either look for patterns or look for things that don't fit the company's usual trend. The following sections highlight a few of the things you'll want to pay attention to.

A company's growth rate

When you get a raise from your boss, what's the first thing you want to know? How much of a percentage increase it is from your previous year's salary. The same goes for every item on a company's income statement and balance sheet. You could go through every item on the financial statements and calculate the change from last year by hand, but Reuters, shown in Figure 12-3, will do it for you. Here's how:

1. **Point your browser to www.reuters.com/investing?WTmodLOC=L2-LeftNav-3-Investing.**

   The Reuters Investing home page appears.

2. **Scroll down to the Stocks & Mutual Funds section of the page and enter the stock's ticker symbol into the Enter Symbol field.**

3. **Select the Ratios radio button option below the Enter Symbol field and then click Go.**

   You see the Ratios page for the company whose ticker symbol you entered.

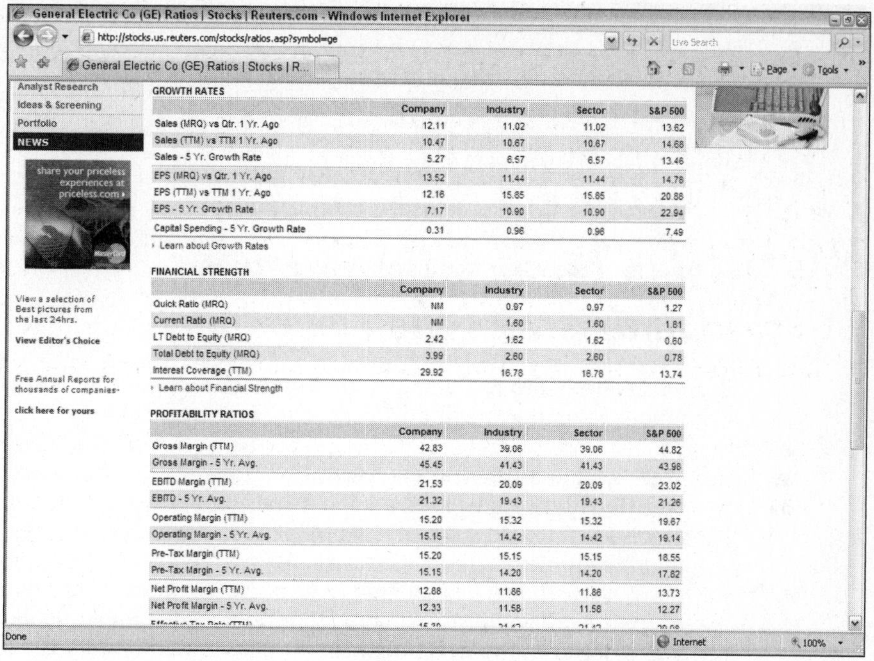

Figure 12-3:
Comparing a company's sales and earnings growth rates with the industry, sector, and stock market rates as a whole.

4. On the Ratios page, scroll down to the Growth Rates section.

Here you can find the growth rates of sales and earnings per share (EPS) in the most recent quarter, called MRQ. Reuters also shows you the company's earnings growth rate in the trailing 12 months, called TTM. Lastly, you can view longer-term growth rates in earnings and capital expenditures over the past five years.

If you'd like to see a breakdown of quarterly growth, MSN Money (http://moneycentral.msn.com/investor) provides an easy summary screen. First, enter the stock's ticker symbol into the Symbols field and click Go. On the new page that appears, click the Financial Results link from the list on the left. In the Financial: Highlights page that appears, scroll down and find the quarter-by-quarter breakdown of the company's growth.

A company's financial composition

Many professional investors compare each item on the income statement with revenue and each item on the balance sheet with total assets. This lets you find interesting trends, such as whether the company is increasing its spending on research and development or the company's debt is rising. You just need to divide each item on the income statement by revenue and each item on the balance sheet by total assets to perform this analysis, called *common sizing.* Investopedia teaches you how to common size a balance sheet (www.investopedia.com/terms/c/commonsizebalancesheet.asp) and an income statement (www.investopedia.com/terms/c/commonsizeincomestatement.asp). NetMBA (www.netmba.com/finance/statements/common-size) also explains why common sizing financial statements is a good idea.

Using financial statements to understand the company

Financial statements can help you understand the structure and objective of a company. Consider the following aspects of the company:

- ✔ **Value:** Some investors try to figure out how much a company is worth by using its financial statements. If the company is worth more than the stock price would suggest, that tells these *value investors* the stock might be undervalued. One way investors determine how much a company is worth is by examining *book value.* Book value is a complex accounting principle. Just know that book value generally measures the value of the company's tangible assets recorded in the financial statements minus liabilities. If the company's market value is less than the book value, some investors see it as being undervalued. The market value, the stock price times the number of shares outstanding, tells you how much the company is worth in investors' eyes. I show you how to use the price-to-book ratio to determine whether a stock is undervalued or overvalued in Chapter 12.

- ✔ **Growth prospects:** Some investors look for companies posting gigantic earnings or revenue growth, hoping to dig up the next market leaders. *Growth companies* generally don't pay large dividends and prefer to keep any extra cash to invest in new products. Rapidly rising revenue and earnings are signs that a company has morphed into a growth company.

- ✔ **Link to broader economic cycles:** Some companies' earnings and revenue rise and fall along with swings in the broader economy. These companies are called *cyclical* companies because they follow economic cycles. Typically industrial companies like steelmakers belong to this category.

- ✔ **Protection from economic cycles:** Companies that don't follow the economy's ups and down are often called *defensive* companies. These include companies, such as utilities and grocery stores, that tend to sell the same amount of goods no matter what the economy is doing.

- ✔ **Stability and sustainability:** Some companies generate steadily increasing revenue and earnings because they rely on several products with stable demand. Many large companies belong to this category. But companies involved in finding breakthroughs, such as biotech companies researching cures and oil companies looking for untapped reserves, have big ups and downs in their earnings based on their luck. Companies with volatile earnings are called *speculative* companies.

✓ **Debt load:** The balance sheet shows you how much money the company is borrowing. You can compare a company's debt load with its shareholders' equity to see how heavy the debt load is. I show you how to use computer screening tools to find companies with low debt levels in Chapter 13.

Unearthing Details About the Company from Regulatory Filings

Many of the things you need to know about companies, contained in quarterly and annual reports, are pulled out for you by the financial Web sites I describe in Chapters 2 and 6. Nearly all the vital company information you need is easily obtained that way, including the following:

✓ Company descriptions, or *profiles,* telling you what the company does

✓ Major owners of the stock, including large mutual funds and pension funds

✓ Names of the officers and directors, their ages, and their experience

✓ Dividends paid by the company

✓ Number of employees

But as helpful as the financial Web sites are, they're missing a great deal of textual information contained in companies' annual reports. That means it's up to you to read the company's regulatory filings to get the full picture. You can glean some interesting details about the company if you take the time.

Finding the nitty-gritty description of the company

Most 10-K filings contain a company overview section. This overview goes into exhaustive detail about the company's business, well beyond the quick snapshot descriptions offered on financial Web sites. For instance, a company will outline what countries it has facilities and employees located in. The company might also break out what parts of its business is largest.

If you're investing in a large diversified company like General Electric, which is involved in many businesses, you can get a grasp of the company's entire empire from the company overview in the 10-K. The company overview might also show you what parts of its business are the largest and most profitable.

Getting the details on company announcements

When a company has an important event — referred to by investment pros as a *material event* — the company is required to tell shareholders about it. Companies might inform shareholders by issuing a press release, which you can find out how to access online in Chapter 2. But it must also provide details of the announcement to regulators in the form of a Form 8-K. The SEC (`http://sec.gov/answers/form8k.htm`) explains all the corporate events that require companies to file 8-Ks.

Finding out whether the company is being sued

When companies put out glowing press releases about their new products or services, they rarely bring up news about the lawsuits they might be facing. Although most lawsuits end up amounting to nothing, they're something you want to be aware of. Nearly all companies' 10-Ks contain a Legal Proceedings section that lists pending lawsuits and says how serious the company thinks they are.

My one Julia Roberts reference

Remember the movie *Erin Brockovich*? It was based on the famous lawsuit brought by Brockovich over alleged injuries that resulted from chromium exposure near Pacific Gas & Electric's Hinkley Compressor Station in San Bernardino County. The allegations were described in detail in the company's 1994 10-K (`http://sec.gov/Archives/edgar/` `data/75488/0000950149-94-000070.` `txt`). In the filing, the company also disclosed various environmental protection measures that would cost it $55 million over five years. (And, yes, Julia Roberts won the Best Actress Academy Award for 2001 for her role as Erin Brockovich.)

Regulatory filings are typically giant seas of text. When perusing a filing online, you can quickly skip to different areas by holding down the Ctrl key and pressing the F key. You can then enter a search term, such as "legal proceedings," and jump right to that section in the filing.

You can also check online whether a company is being sued as part of a securities class action lawsuit, where investors alleged they were defrauded. The Stanford Law School Securities Class Action Clearinghouse (http://securities.stanford.edu) is an excellent resource to see whether a company you're invested in is a party of one of these suits.

Getting the truth from management

CEOs and top management must include in their company 10-Ks a section called Management's Discussion and Analysis, or MD&A. This is where the company must tell regulators how the year went and give their honest assessment of how the business is performing.

Many professional investors read the MD&A section from the prior year before reading the one from the just-completed year and compare the two. It's telling to see what forecasts management made in the previous year and then find out whether they came true.

BusinessWeek (www.businessweek.com) makes it easy to compare last year's 10-K with this year's. Just enter the company's ticker symbol in the Stock Quotes field in the center of the page and then click Go. On the new page that appears, click the Financials tab and then click the tab's SEC Filings link. The site provides links to all the company's quarterly and annual filings for the past four years.

Seeing whether the company has gotten into a tiff with its auditors

Companies must hire accounting firms to look over, or *audit,* their annual financial statements. Typically, the accounting firms study the company's results and sign off with a Good Housekeeping seal of approval. But periodically, the auditors find a problem, and that's something you want to know about as an investor.

You can find out about accounting problems by opening a company's annual report and searching for the word *restatement.* A restatement usually outlines any problems the company or its auditor has found with the accounting. Restatements can be a real shock to investors because they mean companies might not have earned as much money as they previously said they did.

When a company finds problems with its financial statements, it's given a warning by the stock market exchange to fix the problems. During the time the company tries to fix its accounting, it's said to be *delinquent* in its filings. This can be a dangerous time to invest in a company's stock because it's unknown what the company's actual results will end up being. The easiest way to find out whether a company is delinquent is by going to Yahoo! Finance (`http://finance.yahoo.com`), entering the stock symbol into the ticker symbol field, and clicking Get Quotes. If the company is delinquent, you can see a warning on the top of the quote page stating that fact.

Weighing the risk of failure

One of the biggest reasons to bother with reading financial statements is to look for red flags or warnings of trouble at the company. One of the easiest signs of trouble you might find, albeit late, is when auditors warn that they question whether the company can continue as a "going concern." If you see these words in a company filing, take notice.

Seeing what the company is worried about

Companies must include a Risks section in their annual reports. These sections are stuffed with blanket statements about all the bad things that could happen. Sometimes the company will point out a risk it faces that you might not have thought of. Just search for the word *risks.*

Assessing how much the company's management is getting paid

When you're searching through the company filings, don't overlook the boring sounding DEF 14A. These reports, more commonly called *proxy statements,* are about the juiciest reading you can get about a company. These statements are among the most frank documents released by a company because they disclose how much the company executives get paid. You can download them by using the same steps used to download other regulatory filings, but the SEC (`http://sec.gov/answers/proxyhtf.htm`) explains specifically how to download company proxy statements.

Search the proxy for the compensation table. Typically, you see each top executive's pay broken down into the following categories:

- ✔ Salary
- ✔ Bonus
- ✔ Stock awards
- ✔ Stock option awards
- ✔ Pension value
- ✔ All other compensation
- ✔ Total compensation

The proxy statement also contains details about what other perks executives receive, such as paid-for apartments and personal use of the corporate jet. How do you know whether the company executives are being overpaid? A few Web sites help you analyze executives' pay packages, including the following:

- ✔ **AFL-CIO:** (`www.aflcio.org/corporatewatch/paywatch`) Big Labor has a stake in what Fat Cat executives make, so it shouldn't come as a surprise if the AFL-CIO provides a free Executive Paywatch, which shows you how much executives were paid and how they rank. Just enter the stock symbol into the Ticker Symbol field and click Go.

- ✔ **Salary.com:** (`http://swz.salary.com/execcomp/layoutscripts/excl_companysearch.asp`) This site offers a free salary wizard that breaks down how much all the top dogs at publicly traded companies earn.

- ✔ **CompanyPay:** (`www.companypay.com`) This site ranks the pay packages of all the largest companies.

- ✔ **BusinessWeek:** (`www.businessweek.com`) The online version of the weekly magazine provides executive pay data for industries. Just enter the company's ticker symbol into the Stock Quotes field and then click the People tab on the new page that appears. When the People tab displays, scroll down a bit to see how the company's executive pay ranks on the right side of the screen (compared with the industry as whole).

Determining how independent the company's leadership is

A company's board of directors is supposed to be the shareholders' champion in the board room. All pay packages and strategic decisions must be approved by the board, so you want to make sure the board represents the best interests of the shareholders.

The proxy statement is an excellent source of information about the company's officers and board members. There's almost always a Related Party Transactions section where the company must disclose any insider dealings between the company's officers, directors, and the company itself. For instance, if a board member's firm has a business relationship with the company, you'd want to know because it could skew the board member's judgment. With the proxy statement loaded on your screen, just search for the terms "related party transactions."

You might also want to know how cozy members of the executive team are with other executives. BusinessWeek makes that a snap to figure out. Just enter the company's ticker symbol into the Stock Quotes text field and then click the People tab on the new page that appears. You can see whether the officers and directors have professional relationships with other company executives, either by sitting on other company boards or being part of the same organizations.

Chapter 13

Evaluating Stocks' Prospects

In This Chapter

▶ Measuring the potential risk and return of a stock

▶ Valuing a stock using a discounted cash flow analysis

▶ Determining the valuation of a stock, including price-to-earnings ratios

▶ Using online stock selection tools to study investments

▶ Comparing a company to its peers and industry

*W*hen investors say they bought a stock because "it's a good company," you should automatically become skeptical. As you find out in this chapter, one of the biggest mistakes investors make is confusing a company and its stock. They're not the same thing.

A company's success is measured by its revenue and earnings growth, things that are discussed in Chapter 11. But a stock is a different animal. Stock prices are determined by how much investors are willing to pay. If too many people think a company is good, they might pay top dollar for the stock and drive up its *valuation*. And when a valuation rises, your potential return decreases. Valuations are the root of one of the most perverse realities in investing: Good companies can be bad stocks. If you overpay for a stock, even if the company delivers great earnings growth, you can still lose money. Savvy investors know the price they pay for a stock is one of the biggest factors that determines how much they'll profit.

This chapter shows you how to find good stocks with reasonable valuations. Although measuring valuations can get math heavy, I spare your calculator by showing you online tools that will do much of the work for you. You also discover the ins and outs of the price-to-earnings ratio, one of the most commonly used — and misunderstood — ways to measure a stock's valuation. I show you stock tools that step you through the process of picking stocks and ways to compare a company's valuation with its peers.

Finding Out How to Not Overpay for Stocks

Even if you find a great company with a top-notch management team and popular products, it doesn't mean you should buy the stock. Why not? The sad truth is you're probably not the first or only person to know about the company's bright future. And if other investors bought the stock already, they likely have pushed the stock price higher. When a stock price has already risen in anticipation of good news, the good news has been *priced in.* That could mean that, even if the good news you're expecting pans out, the stock price might not budge because it already had nosed up previously in anticipation of the good news.

The difficulty of evaluating a stock's valuation is one reason why investing in individual stocks is more complex than buying and holding index mutual funds and exchange-traded funds. Before I show you how to measure a stock's valuation, I run through the things you should ask yourself before you decide to buy a stock:

✔ **Does the stock fit into your asset allocation?** If your portfolio is already stuffed with small companies, you might not want to add another small company. Instead, you'll want to invest in different types of companies that better fit your asset allocation plan. (I talk about asset allocation plans in Chapter 9.)

Morningstar (www.morningstar.com) provides an easy way to find out where a stock would fit in your asset allocation plan. Just type the stock symbol in the Quotes box, press Enter, and then click the Data Interpreter link on the left side of the new page that appears. After the Data Interpreter page loads, check out the Morningstar Style Box on the right, which uses a nine-by-nine grid (see Figure 13-1) to show you if the stock is large, mid-sized or small. (The grid also tells you whether the stock is value priced or a growth stock.)

✔ **Does the stock have solid fundamentals?** When you pick apart a company's financial statements as described in Chapter 11, you're doing what's known as *fundamental analysis.* Essentially, you determine how fast the company's revenue and earnings are growing and examine the management. (Pretty much all you need to know about fundamental analysis can be found in Chapter 11.)

✔ **Does the stock stack up favorably against the competition?** Companies that have a defendable edge against rivals — typically thanks to a strong brand name — can remain more profitable. (I show you how to find a company's competitors in Chapter 6.)

Figure 13-1: Morningstar shows you whether a stock is large, mid-sized, small and value-priced, growth, or somewhere in between.

✔ **Is the price for the stock reasonable?** You'll want to study how much other investors are paying for the stock before you jump in. Overpaying for a good company is just as bad as overpaying for a bad one. You might lose money in both cases. You see how to measure a stock's valuation in the "Quick ways to determine how pricey a stock is" section, later in this chapter.

A stock's price alone doesn't tell you how expensive or cheap a stock is. Just because one company's stock price is $100 and another company's stock is trading for $1 doesn't mean the $1-a-share company is cheaper. The stock's share price must be compared with something else, such as earnings or revenue, to determine its value.

Quick ways to determine how pricey a stock is

Determining whether a stock is cheap or overvalued is an arduous process that can be a full-time job even for investment pros. Luckily, there's one quick way you can get an idea of how pricey a stock is: *valuation ratios*. Valuation ratios give you a rough idea of a stock's value by comparing the stock price with a measure from the company's financial statements.

In search of low returns

Investors figure if they buy the stocks of "good companies," they'll get great returns. But research has shown that's not true. Companies that are growing and have popular products, but are so trendy with investors that their shares have lofty valuations, tend to be poor investments.

It's not just theory. In Tom Peters' 1982 book called *In Search of Excellence,* Peters, a management expert, extolled companies he determined to be the best. Had you bought $100 worth of stock in these excellent companies in 1981, your investment would have grown 82% to $182 through 1985, according to research by market strategist Michelle Clayman. But here's

the funny part: Clayman created a portfolio of "unexcellent" companies missing all the things that made the excellent companies great. The same $100 invested in these unexcellent companies outperformed the excellent ones by a wide margin. The same $100 invested in the unexcellent companies jumped 198% and turned into $298. The counterintuitive idea that the best companies are often not the best stocks is described at length at Damodaran Online (http://pages.stern.nyu.edu/~adamodar/pdfiles/invfables/ch6 new.pdf), a site dedicated to stock valuations maintained by Aswath Damodaran, Professor of Finance at New York University.

Most financial Web sites that provide stock quotes, including the ones discussed in Chapter 2, provide several valuation ratios. Reuters (www.investor.reuters.com), for instance, provides you with nearly all the important valuation measures on one screen. Just enter the stock symbol in the Enter Symbol text field (you have to scroll down to find it), select the Ratios radio button, and then click Go. The Ratios page for the stock you chose appears, displaying more ratios than you can shake a stick at.

Table 13-1 lists a few valuation ratios you should pay the most attention to.

Table 13-1	Guide to Valuation Ratios That Matter
Valuation Ratio	*It Tells You How Much Investors . . .*
Price to earnings (P-E)	Are willing to pay for each dollar in earnings the company generates. P-E is measured by dividing stock price by the company's annual earnings. A high P-E tells some investors the stock is overvalued, and a low P-E shows it's undervalued.
Price to sales	Are paying for each dollar the company brings in as revenue. It's the company's stock price divided by its annual revenue. This ratio is typically used to value *early-stage* companies, like biotech firms, that lose money so they don't have a P-E ratio.

Valuation Ratio	It Tells You How Much Investors . . .
Price to book value	Are paying for each dollar of the company's assets, minus money owed to others. The price-to-book ratio is the stock's price divided by the company's book value per share. A company's book value measures the value of what it owns (assets) minus what it owes (liabilities). The price-to-book ratio is very important and is a key measure used to determine whether a stock is a value-priced stock or a growth stock. A low price-to-book ratio, typically 1 or lower, might signal an undervalued stock.
Price to tangible book value	Are paying for each dollar of physical assets owned by the company. It's the stock price divided by the company's book value per share, excluding assets you can't touch or feel.
Price-earnings to growth	Are willing to pay for the company's earnings growth. The price-earnings to growth (or PEG) ratio compares a company's P-E ratio to its expected growth rate. The PEG is calculated by dividing the stock's P-E by its expected growth rate. A PEG of two or higher tells investors that the stock is either expected to grow very rapidly or the stock is overvalued. Reuters doesn't give you the PEG, but it gives you the P-E and the growth rate, so you can easily figure it out.
Price to free cash flow	Value each dollar of cash that flows into the company as part of its doing business. It's the stock price divided by free cash flow.
Dividend yield	Receive in dividends relative to the stock price. The dividend yield is the company's annual dividend payment divided by the stock price. If a $30 stock has a dividend yield of 5%, that means it is paying $1.50 per share every year in dividends ($30 × 5% = $1.50). Stocks with high dividend yields are seen as potentially being undervalued.

The P-E ratio is the rock star of valuation ratios and gets most of the attention. The P-E is popular because it's easy to understand. Imagine a stock price is $30 a share, and the company earned $1.50 a share. That means investors are paying a price that's 20 times higher than the company's earnings. If the price of earnings, or P-E, is high, it means the earnings are very valuable to other people, usually because they expect the company to grow rapidly.

Still confused about what a P-E means? Imagine that a company put all the money it earned per share during the year in a box, promised to add more money if it was profitable in the future, and auctioned it off. Say the company earned $1 a share, so there was $1 in the box. If investors paid $1 for the box, the stock would have a P-E of 1. But if a bidding war ensued and someone paid $20 for the box containing a dollar of earnings, the stock would have a P-E of 20.

P-Es can get more complicated because different people measure earnings differently. A *trailing* P-E divides the stock price by the company's earnings over the past four quarters. A *forward* P-E divides the stock price by what the company is expected to earn over the next four quarters. Both ways to measure P-E are correct; just know which one you're talking about. Google Finance (http://finance.google.com) gives both the trailing P-E and the forward P-E. Just enter the stock's symbol into the search field, click the Search Finance button, and look for the P/E item (trailing) and F P/E item (forward) on the new page that appears.

Ways to interpret valuations

If you took a look at Chapter 1 and figured out from my discussion there that you're a passive (as opposed to an active) investor, you're probably pretty sure that the stock price actually measures what one share of a stock is worth, or its *fair value.* If the market is willing to pay $20 for a stock, the stock is worth $20. Passive investors believe markets are *efficient* over the long term and set stock prices that reflect all available public information. But *active investors* (including bargain hunters known as *value investors*) believe the stock market is *inefficient* and tends to over or underpay for stocks from time to time. These investors try to find out whether a stock is too expensive or cheap by studying its valuation ratios and comparing them with

✔ **The rest of the market:** Some investors compare valuation ratios, such as the price-to-book and dividend yield, with the Standard & Poor's 500 to get an idea of whether the company might be undervalued. If the valuation ratios are lower than the S&P 500's, that tells some investors the stock might be undervalued.

S&P provides data on its index's valuation at www.spglobal.com. Concentrate on finding out the following:

• *Dividend yield:* Click the United States link under the Equity Indices heading of the S&P Global Indices page — the www.spglobal.com address. In the new page that appears, click the S&P 500 link under the Major Indices heading. When the page refreshes, click the Data tab at the top of the page and then click the Earnings link in the Index Table box. On the new page that appears, click the Click Here link in the middle of the page. A spreadsheet pops up on your screen. At the top of the spreadsheet you see the S&P 500's dividend yield over the last 12 months. It's a little tricky to find, but Figure 13-2 should help you.

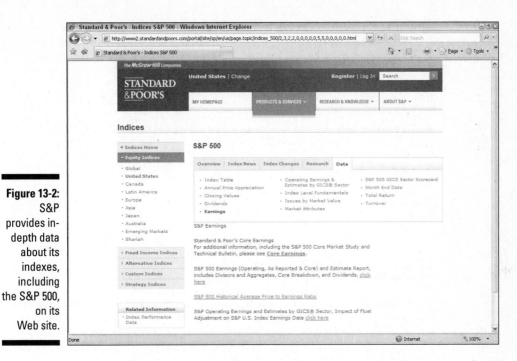

Figure 13-2:
S&P provides in-depth data about its indexes, including the S&P 500, on its Web site.

- *P-E ratio:* The same spreadsheet you downloaded in the preceding bullet gives you the S&P 500's P-E over several years. Notice the As Reported Earns P/E column, which lists the S&P's P-E at the end of each quarter. Notice as well that the P-E ratio rises and falls as investors get bullish and bearish about stocks and the economy.

✔ **The industry:** It's also a good idea to compare a stock's valuation ratios with other stocks in the industry. Some industries tend to grow more slowly and almost always have a lower valuation than the stock market. That means the only way to know whether a stock's valuation is truly lower than average is to compare it with the ratios of similar companies.

Reuters' Ratios pages, described in the previous section, give you valuation ratios for individual stocks in addition to the industry and stock market. Enter the stock's symbol into the Enter Symbol text field, click the Ratios radio button and click Go. You'll see how the ratios compare with the company's industry, sector, and the S&P 500. If you'd like to dig a bit deeper, Damodaran Online (`http://pages.stern.nyu.edu/~adamodar/New_Home_Page/datafile/pbvdata.html`) provides price-to-book ratios for many industries.

Some investors completely ignore P-E ratios. These investors figure that good companies are worth paying more for and deserve higher P-Es. In these investors' minds, a high P-E is justified just as a Monet deserves a bigger price tag than a velvet Elvis painting sold at a flea market. These investors tend to pay more attention to how fast a company is growing and patterns in its price movements.)I discuss such investors in greater detail in the "Taking It Further: Technical Analysis and Initial Public Offerings" bonus chapter on the book's companion Web site.

✔ **Guidelines:** Investors typically have a general idea of what they think makes a cheap or expensive stock. Some investors, for instance, think a stock is reasonably priced if the PEG is less than 2. You can calculate a stock's PEG yourself by dividing the P-E by the growth rate, or you can get it from Yahoo! Finance (`http://finance.yahoo.com`) by entering the stock symbol into the search field, clicking Get Quotes, and scrolling down the new page that appears. You see the PEG ratio on the right side, in the Analyst table. MoneyChimp (`www.moneychimp.com/articles/valuation/peg.htm`) provides more information about the PEG ratio. Investor Home (`www.investorhome.com/anomfun.htm`) provides a few guidelines for you to follow regarding other valuation ratios.

✔ **Index membership:** Most of the major providers of stock market indexes categorize stocks as being value or growth. The index providers have sophisticated screens that rank stocks based on a number of valuation metrics. If you're not sure whether a company you're considering is a growth or value stock, you can see which index it fits in. For instance, if you want a list of the largest value-priced stocks, go to S&P's Web site (`www.spglobal.com`) and click the United States link under the Equity Indices heading. In the new page that appears, scroll down and then click the S&P 500/Citigroup Pure Growth and Pure Value link. (It's under the Style Indices heading.) If you then click the Constituent List link near the top of the new page that appears and then the S&P/Citigroup Pure Style Constituents link, you can download a list of all the largest stocks in the Standard & Poor's 500 index and see whether the company you're considering is ranked as value or growth.

Studying stocks using automated tools

Is your head spinning with all this talk of P-Es, book value, and ratios? Don't worry. There are several online tools that will hold your hand through the process of analyzing a stock's valuation. The following list highlights sites that are excellent places to start to get you thinking about what goes into evaluating a company's stock price and whether it might fit in your portfolio:

✔ **MSN Money's Stock Research Wizard:** (`http://moneycentral.msn.com/investor`) This corner of MSN Money steps you through the process of evaluating a stock from beginning to end. Just enter the stock's ticker symbol into the Symbol(s) field, click Get Quote, and then click the Research Wizard link on the left side of the new page that appears. The wizard first steps you through the company's fundamentals, going over many of the things I tell you to look for in Chapter 11.

You then see how the company's P-E compares with other companies' P-Es in its industry.

✔ **Quicken's Stock Evaluator:** (www.quicken.com/investments/seceval) This site is the online presence of the popular financial software program. You need a member ID and password to access this corner of the Quicken site, but once you do, the Stock Evaluator tool takes you step by step through a five-part analysis of any stock you enter into the Enter Symbol(s) field. Stock Evaluator analyzes stocks' growth trends, financial health, management performance, valuation and intrinsic value. You can register for the site for free, but you must own a copy of Quicken that's three years old or newer.

✔ **Value Point Analysis Model:** (www.eduvest.com/vpaff2.html) Developed by the folks at the Value Point Analysis Financial Forum, the Value Point Analysis Model asks you to enter basic company information about a stock, including many of the things I tell you to look out for in Chapter 11. A few of the things you must enter include the company's number of shares outstanding, long-term debt, current dividend, projected earnings, and current stock price. After you get all that stuff entered, click the Execute button, and the Web site tells you what it thinks the stock is worth — what the site calls its Value Point.

✔ **BetterInvesting:** (www.betterinvesting.org) BetterInvesting provides a Stock Selection Guide to its members that helps evaluate a company's valuation to determine whether the stock is a Buy, Hold, or Sell. The Stock Selection Guide compares the company's expected P-E with its P-E ratios in the past. The Stock Selection Guide is available as a paper form you must meticulously fill out, but also in different software programs you can buy from BetterInvesting, which pull down company data automatically.

✔ **InvestorGuide:** (www.investorguide.com) Enter a stock symbol in the Enter Ticker or Company Name field, click Go, and then click the Analysis tab on the new page that appears. You end up on a page that offers a detailed commentary on your chosen stock, including readings of the stock's valuation, recent announcements made by the company, and other industry trends. InvestorGuide offers commentary on stocks if you click on the Analysis tab after entering the stock symbol at the top left corner.

✔ **SmartMoney's Price Check Calculator:** (www.smartmoney.com/pricecheck/index.cfm?story=worksheet) SmartMoney gives it to you short and sweet. Enter a stock symbol into the Ticker field and click Enter, and the Web site crunches the numbers and gives its opinion on what the stock is worth.

Shortcomings of studying stocks' valuation ratios

I don't want to leave you with a misconception many investors have: Just find "cheap" stock with a low valuation, buy it, hold on to it forever, and you'll make money. Unfortunately, investing isn't that easy. There are several problems with using valuation ratios alone to pick stocks, including the following:

✔ **Cheap stocks might be cheap for a reason:** Sometimes a stock has a low valuation because the company is poorly run, it's in a slow or no-growth industry, or other companies or technologies are stealing away customers.

✔ **You get what you pay for:** Sometimes a company might appear to be overvalued and have a high P-E. But if the company's profits grow by a huge amount, the P-E will fall and the stock price may skyrocket.

If a company reports strong earnings, a stock's P-E can suddenly go from looking high to looking low. The P-E is the stock price divided by earnings. That means if earnings, the denominator of the fraction, rise rapidly, the P-E plunges. Imagine a company trading for $40 a share that has posted earnings over the past four quarters of $1 a share. That gives the stock a pricey-looking P-E of 40. But if the company's quarterly profit surges and pushes earnings to $2, the P-E falls to a more reasonable 20.

✔ **Dividends aren't a contract:** Some investors target companies with high dividend yields. They figure these stock's prices are temporarily depressed. And, as a bonus, even if the stock doesn't go up, they get paid their dividend.

Watch out, though. Dividend payments aren't written in blood. Companies can cut or stop their dividend payments at any time.

The Armchair Investor's Way to Not Overpay

If you want to buy cheap stocks, but studying P-E ratios and price-to-book ratios make your head swim, there's an easy shortcut: Buy an index mutual fund or an exchange-traded fund that owns value-priced stocks. That way, you own stocks that are in value indexes. Generally, the companies that create indexes use many measures to determine whether a stock is value or growth. S&P (www2.standardandpoors.com/spf/pdf/index/SP_US_Style_Indices_Methodology_Web.pdf) ranks companies by book value, cash flow, sales, and dividend yield to see whether a stock is a value stock. If you're interested in finding index mutual funds that mirror value stock indexes, check out Chapter 10. For exchange traded funds that do the same thing, check out the "Finding and Buying Exchange-Traded Funds" bonus chapter on the Web site associated with this book.

The Four (headless) Horsemen of the Internet

Despite the problems with valuation ratios — problems described elsewhere in this section — they're still a good way to get a quick idea of how highly valued a stock is. When you start seeing stocks' P-E ratios going above 60, though, you should get suspicious. Few stocks are able to maintain such lofty valuations before getting their comeuppance, as investors realize they've been too bullish. Even if the company can boost its earnings by 100% for a year or two, eventually the industry or the company will stumble and bring its stock back to earth.

Internet stocks were a classic example of how valuations were inflated as investors got caught up in the dot-com mania. Many investors rightly viewed the Internet as a huge phenomenon for society and business. But, unfortunately, these investors overpaid for Internet stocks in March 2000 and doomed themselves to lackluster returns. Many Internet stocks vanished completely, and those that didn't have been very poor investments for anyone who invested at the peak.

The valuations of Cisco, EMC, Oracle and Sun, the leaders of the Internet nicknamed the Four Horsemen of the Internet, soared in March 2000. Their stock prices have since plunged, though, erasing tremendous amounts of shareholder wealth on the way.

Evaluating Stocks' Potential Return and Risk

If you're taking a gamble on a stock, you'd better get an ample return to make it worth your while. I tell you how to measure your portfolio's risk and return in Chapter 8. It turns out that you can apply the same techniques to individual stocks. I show you how.

Measuring a stock's total return

Past performance is no guarantee of future results, but studying how stocks have done in the past can help you get a very crude handle on what to expect. To find how stocks have done previously, you need their *total return* in previous years. A stock's total return is the amount its price has gone up — its *price appreciation* — plus its dividend. You can get a stock's total return by the following methods:

✔ **Checking the company's Web site:** Some companies include total return calculators in the Investor Relations section of their Web sites.

✔ **Calculating it by using online stock price downloading services:** You can download a stock's annual stock price for different years using services described in Chapter 2. Add the company's stock price at the end of the year to the amount per share it paid in dividends during the year. Divide that sum by the stock's price at the end of previous year and multiply by 100 and you'll have the total return for the year.

✔ **Using Morningstar:** The investment tracker (www.morningstar.com) provides stock's total returns going back for three years. Just enter the stock's symbol into the Quotes field, click the Go button, and then click the Data Interpreter link on the left side of the new page that appears. Ideally, you'd want more years of data than Morningstar gives you, but it's a start.

After you get the stock's total returns for many years, enter them into Horton's Geometric Mean Calculator at www.graftacs.com/geomean.php3. (If you're not sure how to do that, refer to Chapter 8.) After doing that, Horton's Geometric Mean Calculator shows you how much you would have gained in the stock each year on average and also how risky it is. You can then compare the stock's returns and risk with popular indexes, just as you do with your portfolio in Chapter 8. If the stock's returns are lower than the stock market's and the risk is higher, it might not be a good fit for your portfolio.

Before you decide that a stock is too risky or the returns are too low, you should compare its movements to the rest of your portfolio. If a stock rises when your portfolio goes down, it might actually reduce your portfolio's total risk by offering diversification. Some online tools can show you whether a stock will diversify your portfolio. The Thomson South-West Simple Linear Regression calculator (www.swlearning.com/finance/investment_calculator/m02/LinearRegression.html) makes it easy. Enter the stock's total returns in the X column and your portfolio's returns in the Y column. The R blank shows you, on a scale from -1 to 1, how closely the stock tracks your portfolio.

Don't get bogged down with all the scary math terms. Just know this: If the R is closer to –1, that means the stock and your portfolio are mirror images of one another. That's a good thing because it means if your portfolio sinks, this stock might rise and decrease your overall risk. If the R is close to 1, the stock and your portfolio move in lockstep, so there's no diversification benefit. Microsoft (http://office.microsoft.com/en-us/excel/HP052090231033.aspx?pid=CH062528311033) provides instructions on how to calculate correlations using Excel.

Many online stock quote services let you compare several stocks by graphing them on the same chart. An easy way to see which stock has done best than looking at a colorful chart. Go to MSN Investor (http://moneycentral.msn.com/investor), enter the symbol of the stock you're interested in into the Symbol(s) field, make sure Get Quote is selected from the drop-down list, and click the Go button. In the new page that appears, click the Historical link. (You can find it under the Charts option on the left side.) You can then type additional symbols in the Compare With field and click the Add button to plot more stocks on the charts. Don't just compare the stock with other stocks, though; you should also compare it with market indexes like the S&P 500 and exchange-traded funds that track narrow slices of the market.

Finding out more about risk and return online

If you're interested in learning more about how stock's risk and return are linked, you can consult several sites dedicated to the topic. The sites listed here are a good start:

- ✔ **Path to Investing:** (`www.pathtoinvesting.org/invchoices/stock/risk_return/ic_risk_return_011.htm`) This part of the Path to Investing site describes why it's so important for investors to understand the correlation between the returns they're getting from stocks and the risk they're accepting.

- ✔ **Index Funds Advisors:** (`www.ifa.com`) The IFA site helps you understand how individual stocks are often riskier than baskets of stocks in index mutual funds.

Digging Even Deeper: Advanced Valuation Techniques

Valuation ratios are often the most popular ways to measure how pricey stocks are. But even proponents of valuation ratios acknowledge that such ratios *do* have problems. For instance, it's not unheard of for a stock with a seemingly high P-E, of 50 or more, to go even higher.

Investors use valuation ratios as general rules, but there are other more involved ways to try to figure out whether a stock is a good buy. Some investors try to use advanced mathematics to figure out what a company is truly worth, or what's sometimes called its *intrinsic value*.

Using the dividend discount model to see whether a stock is on sale

Sometimes investors get so wrapped up in the drama of online stock investing that they lose sight of what they're buying. As a stock investor, you're letting a company use your money to sell goods and services for a profit. If the company makes money, it will ultimately give back your fair share of the profits over time. Typically, that's done by paying a dividend. Even young companies that don't pay a dividend now eventually start to as their profits exceed their needs for cash.

And that's the basis of the *dividend discount model* approach to valuing stocks. The idea is that most companies pay a dividend, and those that don't will. The size of the dividend a company pays, and how quickly it grows, can help you figure out how much a company is worth. There's an ugly formula for a dividend discount model, but I'll spare you the agony. If you can't resist finding out how the calculation is done, Motley Fool (www.fool.com/research/2000/features000406.htm) provides a helpful description.

Because this is *Investing Online For Dummies*, I just list a few handy places on the Internet where you can enter a couple variables and have your computer do the rest:

- ✔ **DividendDiscountModel.com:** (www.dividenddiscountmodel.com): This aptly named site does most of the work for you and doesn't bog you down with knowing what goes into the sausage. Just enter a stock symbol into the Symbol field and click the Start button, and the rest is done. The site's database goes out and gets all the important data for you, ranging from the dividend and dividend yield to dividend growth and earnings growth. DividendDiscountModel then tells you what the stock's expected return is.

- ✔ **Thomson South-Western:** (www.swlearning.com/finance/investment_calculator/m04/consGrowth.html) This page offers a free calculator that may appeal to you if you'd like more control of the assumptions being used in the model. The site can tell you how much a stock is worth if you enter just three variables:

  - *The most recent dividends:* The value of the dividends paid by the company in the most recent four quarters.

  - *The required rate of return:* This is the return you're expecting from the stock. If it's a risky stock, your required rate of return might be 15% or much higher. And if it's a conservative stock, you might have a required rate of return of less than 10%.

> • *Expected growth rate:* This specifies how rapidly you expect the company to boost its dividend. You can either use the rate the company has increased dividends in the past or use its expected earnings or dividend growth rate.
>
> The calculator spits out how much it thinks the stock is worth based on the data you entered.

The dividend discount model is pretty clever and is used by many serious investment professionals. But the model has some big problems. The model is extremely sensitive to your assumptions, especially the required rate of return or discount rate that you enter. The discount rate is the return you demand in return for investing your money in the company. If you enter a discount rate of 10%, you get a wildly different answer than if you enter 12% or 8%. And good luck determining what a company's growth rate will be. Still, it's a useful tool to get a general understanding about a fair value for a stock.

The value hunter's favorite weapon: The discounted cash flow analysis

Ask someone who the best investor ever is, and you'll probably hear the name Warren Buffett. Buffett doesn't publish a playbook that tells the world how he picks companies. He offers some pretty good clues, though, through his Berkshire Hathaway's annual reports. In a nutshell, Buffett tries to measure a company's intrinsic value and buy shares of the company only when it's trading for less than the intrinsic value.

Many speculate that Buffett and investors like him use what's called the discounted cash flow (DCF) analysis. The DCF method works on the assumption that successful companies generate cash flow every year and will hopefully generate more each year. The DCF model attempts to estimate how much cash the company will generate over its entire lifetime and tells you how much that cash would be worth if you got it today. If the company's intrinsic value is greater than the stock price, the company is a good deal.

Time for a concrete example. Imagine that you were a lucky lottery player and had just won a million dollars. Say the state said you could either have the million now or wait 30 years for it. You wouldn't even have to think about it: You'd take the money now. You didn't realize it, but you just did a discounted flow analysis in your head. Because money received today is more valuable than the same amount received later, you know that a million dollars paid 30 years from now is worth less than a million paid today.

The discounted cash flow analysis can get somewhat complicated. You must first estimate a company's free cash flow, as described in Chapter 11. Next, you have to determine how rapidly the company's free cash flow will grow over the years and how much it would be worth if paid to shareholders right now. If you're interested in the nitty-gritty of this analysis, Incademy Investor Education (www.incademy.com/courses/Ten-great-investors/-Warren-Buffett/1/1040/10002) offers a helpful and in-depth description of how the discounted cash flow model is crunched.

Luckily, you can use online resources and get the benefits of the DCF model without actually doing any math. Check out the following helpful sites:

✔ **Money Chimp:** (www.moneychimp.com/articles/valuation/dcf.htm) Definitely one of the easier discounted cash flow model sites to use. You need to enter only five pieces of information and the Web site will generate the stock's value. You must enter the following data:

  • *Earnings per share over the past 12 months.* You can also use the company's cash flow per share, which is probably more accurate.

  • *Initial expected annual growth rate.*

  • *Number of years earnings will grow at that pace.*

  • *What the growth rate will fall to after the initial growth period.*

  • *The return you can get on a similar investment.* If the stock is a large company stock, you would enter the 10.3% average return of the S&P 500 here.

  Money Chimp does all the math for you and tells you how much the stock is worth. If you're interested in the approach Buffett uses, Money Chimp also provides a slightly different discounted cash flow model believed to be more similar to Buffett's approach at www.moneychimp.com/articles/valuation/buffett_calc.htm.

✔ **Valuation Technologies:** (www.valtechs.com/r2.shtml) This site offers several different online worksheets that use discounted cash flow and dividend discount model techniques. The first worksheet lets you enter future cash flows and find out what they'd be worth if received today. The second one estimates a stock's value based on its dividend track record. And the last one measures the value of a company that slows down as it ages. It's an interesting site because it provides text that explains how the calculations are performed.

✔ **Numeraire DCF Valuator:** (numeraire.com/value_wizard) A page from the Global Value Investing site offering all sorts of free valuation calculators. Read the Intro text and then click the Portal link to find the model that fits your needs.

- **Expectations Investing:** (www.expectationsinvesting.com) This site takes the discounted cash flow analysis and turns it on its head. The site owners, Alfred Rappaport, a professor emeritus at Northwestern University, and Legg Mason Capital money manager Michael Mauboussin say investors should examine a stock's price first and then work backwards. By dissecting the stock price, you can figure out what the majority of other investors expect the company's cash flow and growth to be. Then you can decide whether the market is expecting too much or too little. You can read about the approach in the tutorials section and also download all the spreadsheets you need to do the analysis yourself.

- **Damodaran Online:** (http://pages.stern.nyu.edu/~adamodar) NYU Finance professor Aswath Damodaran offers dozens of advanced valuation models that use variations of both the dividend discount model and the discount cash flow model. The site even has a "right model" spreadsheet that tells you which valuation model to use.

- **NewConstructs:** (www.newconstructs.com) This site uses a sophisticated discounted cash flow model that does everything for you. It enters all the data from its database, adjusts the company's financial statements to the appropriate format, and crunches all the math. That's the good part. The bad part is that access to the system is expensive. NewConstructs, however, provides reports on some individual stocks through Yahoo! Finance (finance.yahoo.com) that cost less than access to NewContructs' site. Just go to the Yahoo! Finance site, enter the symbol of the stock you're interested in into the search field, and click Get Quotes. On the new page that appears, click the Research Reports link, found under the Analyst Coverage heading in the listing on the left. Scroll through the research reports to see whether New-Constructs covers the stock you're interested in.

Chapter 14

Finding Investment Ideas with Online Stock Screens

. . . .

In This Chapter

▶ Getting to know stock screens

▶ Discovering how stock screens can pinpoint stocks that meet your standards

▶ Locating and using online stock-screening tools

▶ Deciding which criteria to base your screens on

▶ Finding out what kinds of screening tools online brokers offer

▶ Using screens to compare a company with its peers and industry

. . . .

*O*ne of the most popular questions investors ask is "What stock should I buy?" These investors figure that, amid the pile of thousands of publicly traded stocks, there's a handful of stocks that will be the big winners for the year. They're right. There will be stocks that are big winners and big losers each year. The problem, though, is that no one knows ahead of time which ones.

No online tool can tell you what stocks will be next year's winners. But, some online resources and databases can help you find stocks with traits you believe make them likely candidates.

This chapter shows you how online *screening tools* are your best friend when you're trying to sort through thousands of stocks for those you might want to own. Online screening tools scour Wall Street for stocks that meet criteria you set. I show you a few of the top online stock screening tools and give you some pointers on how to use them. You also find out about many ways you can filter stocks and how to pick criteria for your screen. I also cover methods to compare companies with their peers or other companies.

Getting Familiar with Stock Screens

No one person can do in-depth analysis of all the publicly traded stocks out there. There's just not enough time. Even large Wall Street investment companies, with giant teams of researchers, can only study so many stocks. But that doesn't mean you want to miss out on stocks that might belong in your portfolio.

Stock screening tools are the answer. Screening tools are systems that let you describe what kind of stock you're looking for, and then the screening tool returns a list of results to you. The screening tool searches through thousands of stocks in a database and find the ones that match your parameters.

Stock screening tools aren't all that different from online dating services. Say you're looking for a mate with dark brown hair and brown eyes who likes to run and follow the stock market. You can enter those traits into an online dating service and get a list of people who match. Similarly, stock screens are excellent tools to help you come up with a list of stocks that might be attractive. You enter a list of traits for the stock such as the industry, growth rate, and valuation. After you get a list of the companies that fit your criteria, you have a smaller and more manageable list of stocks you can study more closely.

Investors who use online stock screening tools benefit in a number of ways:

- ✓ **Less time wasted:** Screening tools keep you from wasting time studying companies that aren't appropriate. You can design your stock screen to throw out companies that are undesirable to you for certain reasons, such as having too much debt or too little profit.

- ✓ **No stone unturned:** Screening tools can highlight stocks you might have overlooked. One of the best things about stock screens is that they're dispassionate and robotic. Screens don't get caught up in marketing hype — they look only at the numbers. That means screens might find stocks you've overlooked because you weren't familiar with the companies' products.

- ✓ **Great head-to-head comparisons:** Screening tools are great when it comes to comparing stocks. Stock screens are built using specific financial metrics and ratios, which are calculated for all stocks. Online screening tools allow you to rank companies against each other based on these objective measures.

The biggest gripe about stock screens is that they do only what they're told. If you filter stocks using meaningless variables, your results are only as good as the elements you're searching for.

How you can create an online screen

There are many stock screening sites and they all work slightly differently. But the general procedure of getting into the screening game is essentially the same:

1. Choose a screening site.

   I discuss several of the Web sites that provide free or low-cost screening tools later in this chapter.

2. Decide what kind of stock you're looking for.

   Perhaps you're trying to find a stock that fits your asset allocation. Are you looking for a company that's being ignored by other investors and should therefore be considered value-priced? Are you trying to find a fast-growing company that will blow away earnings forecasts? Are you looking for a stable stock that pays a large dividend? You can find all these types of stocks by using screens.

3. Pick measurable traits shared by stocks and companies you're looking for.

   I show you general traits that you can include in your search, as well as premade screens where professionals have already created the search criteria so you don't have to spend your time doing it.

4. Refine your screen.

   Screening for stocks is a bit of a trial-and-error process. At first, the list of companies that meet your standards might be too large. You can make the criteria more stringent or add additional criteria to help narrow down the list even more.

Now that you understand how the screening process works, the fun part begins. The best screens are carefully designed to pinpoint stocks that have the traits you're looking for. When building screens, it's best to be as specific as possible so you find stocks that are the perfect matches for your portfolio.

General characteristics you can use to screen stocks

The number of characteristics you can use to screen stocks is virtually unlimited. If you can measure it, you can screen stocks for it. Even so, most investors use the following primary measures in screens:

✔ **Company information:** I'm talking basic elements of companies' location, size, or industry here. Common criteria you might use would include the number of employees, the stock market exchange the stock trades on, the industry the company is in, and what stock market index the company is part of. How much money the company brings in — its *revenue,* in other words — is also important.

If you're looking for a job and want to find companies in your area, stock screens can be useful. Many stock screening sites let you search for companies in certain states, and some let you search for companies in cities. Hoovers (www.hoovers.com), although technically not a stock screening site, is particularly good at finding companies headquartered in specific cities.

✔ **Trading characteristics:** This category deals with how the stock has been moving. You can search for stocks that tend to swing more or less than the general stock market, stocks that are close to their highs or lows, and stock that trade hands between investors more often or less often. You can also find companies that investors are betting against by *shorting* the stock. (For more on shorting stock, see Chapter 5.)

✔ **Market value:** This measures how much the company is worth. Market value is used to determine whether a company is small, mid-sized, or large.

✔ **Profitability:** The level of earnings and cash flow a company generates is of utmost importance to investors. Not surprisingly, you can search on both earnings and cash flow. You can drill down even further by looking for specific things about profits, including how quickly profit has grown over the most recent quarter, year, or over the longer term.

✔ **Analyst ratings:** Analysts often evaluate stocks and rate them as a Buy, Hold, or Sell. You can set up your screen so that it finds stocks with a certain rating. Analysts ratings are covered in more detail in Chapter 14.

✔ **Valuation ratios:** Investors pay close attention to how much they're paying for companies, or what's called a stock *valuation.* Valuations are covered at length in Chapter 12.

✔ **Dividends:** These periodic cash payments made by companies to shareholders are important because they account for about a third of many large companies' total return. Dividends are also widely watched because they're an indication of a stock's valuation.

Many stock screens use the cryptic terms TTM and MRQ to describe the time frame in which you'd like to base your search. TTM means *trailing 12 months,* which means the most recent 12 months. MRQ is the *most recent quarter.*

Choosing an online screening site

Before you can start screening, you need to pick an online screening site. Most investors are more than satisfied with the many free screening sites that are available, and I focus mostly on those sites. The vast majority of these sites provide pre-made screens that you can call up immediately, without programming in specific criteria. If using pre-made screens seems like your speed, I'll provide more details on how to do that with some of the screening sites in the "Getting started with pre-made 'canned' screens" section in this chapter. You might decide, though, that you want to go off the beaten path a bit and build a screen exactly to your taste. I show you how to design a screen from scratch using a few of the sites as examples in the "Designing your own custom screens" section at the end of this chapter. No matter if you decide to go with canned or custom screens, the screening sites you might consider are (in no particular order):

- ✔ **MSN Money's Deluxe Screener:** (http://moneycentral.msn.com/ investor/finder/customstocks.asp) MSN Money's take on the stock screener lets you design stock screens by using drop-down lists, which you're probably already familiar with from Word and other software programs. With very little instruction, you can build elaborate screens to quickly find companies with specific valuations, market values, and growth rates, and you can compare companies to industry averages.

- ✔ **MSN Money's Stock Matcher:** (http://moneycentral.msn.com/ investor/finder/matcher.asp) The Stock Matcher is a slightly different take on stock screening. Rather than asking you to enter characteristics of stocks you're looking for, you instead enter a stock that you like. Stock Matcher then looks at its database for other stocks that are similar with respect to market value, trading volume, valuation, and stock-price changes.

- ✔ **Zacks Investment Research's Screening tool:** (http://www.zacks. com/research/screening/custom/index.php) The Zacks tool lets you filter stocks using the standard criteria, but adds some unique things too. For instance, you can filter stocks based on estimate uncertainty, which finds stocks where analysts strongly disagree over how much the company will earn in the next quarter. You can also find companies that have surprised Wall Street the most with earnings over the past quarters.

- ✔ **Yahoo! Finance:** (http://screen.yahoo.com/stocks.html) This particular tool focuses on the basics. You can filter stocks based on industry, stock price, volatility, valuations, and analyst estimates. The screener is simple and easy to use.

✔ **SharpScreen:** (`http://nasdaq.sharpscreen.com`) This NASDAQ product, shown in Figure 14-1, provides users with an easy-to-use interface that lets you build a screen in seconds. You can pinpoint stocks based on their stock prices, earnings growth, revenue growth, industry sector, and several other factors.

✔ **USA TODAY's Stock Screener:** (`http://markets.usatoday.com/custom/usatoday-com/screener/screener.asp`) Not one to be left in the dust, USA TODAY has come up with its own stock screening tool, one that lets you find stocks based on the industry they're in, stock price, market value, and P-E ratio.

✔ **Morningstar's Stock Screener:** (`http://screen.morningstar.com/StockSelector.html`) The Morningstar offering in the Stock Screener sweepstakes is designed to make it easier for beginning investors to design sophisticated screens. Rather than requiring you to pick through dozens of criteria you might not understand, you can just pick a Growth Grade, Profit Grade, or Financial Health Grade, based on a scale from A to F. After you're done, click the Show Results tab, and you see all the stocks that made the cut.

Figure 14-1:
Sharp-
Screen
simplifies
the process
of designing
a stock
screen
with its
easy-to-use
interface
that lets you
quickly
select
different
criteria.

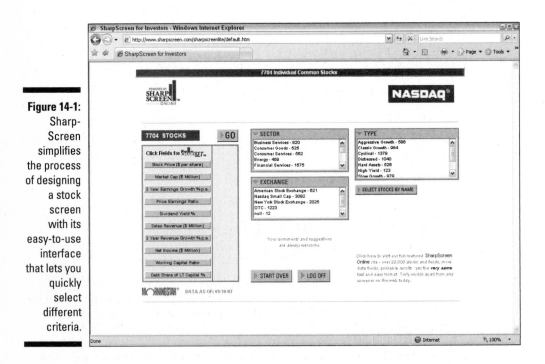

✔ **Portfolio123:** (www.portfolio123.com): This site provides a number of pre-made screens that will help you find stocks with improving earnings or that are industry leaders. You can access the site's basic screener if you register, which is free.

✔ **Brokerage Web sites:** Many of the leading online brokers, especially those I refer to as *discounters* back in Chapter 4, offer stock screening tools on their Web sites. Charles Schwab's stock screener, described here (https://promo.schwab.com/AD046/AD046Home.asp?campaign=tour&mp=res) lets you screen for many standard criteria, but it makes things a little easier by letting you click preset ranges. It also lets you find stocks that rank high or low with the Schwab Equity Ratings, discussed more fully in Chapter 14. TD Ameritrade, E*Trade, and several others provide screening tools as well. The screener is available to you if you have a Schwab account.

If you're interested in stock screening, most online brokers sites offer a tour or tutorial of the tools they can provide. If screens are important to you, you might consider checking out the tools on various online brokers' sites to see whether they're good enough for you to open an account.

Knowing What You're Looking For: Popular Screening Variables

Investors can search for countless criteria by using screens, but I've noticed that certain variables routinely show up in stock screens because they're so useful. If you know what these variables are and why they matter, you can build some very helpful screens.

The basics: 'Cause you have to start somewhere

When you're first figuring out how to build screens, you want to start with some of the more basic variables. That way you can get comfortable with the idea of building screens first and then add more advanced variables as you narrow your search. In this Basics category I'd include the following:

✔ **Valuation ratios:** These ratios include the price-to-earnings (P-E) ratio and price-to-book ratio. Valuation ratios are ways to compare a stock price with the company's value. If you're looking for potentially undervalued stocks, for instance, search for stocks with low P-E and price-to-book ratios.

The P-E ratio and other valuation ratios are discussed at length in Chapter 12.

✔ **Shares outstanding:** A company's shares outstanding measures the total number of shares in the hands of investors. It's related to a company's *float*, which is the number of shares that are available to be bought and sold by the public. When companies buy back their stock, shares are removed from the shares outstanding and float, and they sit on the sidelines. Those sidelined shares are called *treasury stock* and aren't included in shares outstanding.

✔ **Market value:** This is a measure of the price tag the stock market puts on the whole company. The market value — usually called the market capitalization or market cap — is measured by multiplying the stock price by its number of shares outstanding. This measure determines whether a stock is large, mid-sized, or small.

✔ **Earnings per share (EPS):** Earnings per share is the bottom line. It measures what portion of the company net income holders of each share of stock are entitled to. Investors generally use diluted EPS in screens. (The diluted EPS figure is a way to measure a company's bottom line that factors in the effect of companies issuing large amounts of stock options to employees.)

✔ **Current ratio:** Measures how prepared a company is to pay bills that are due in a year's time. You can calculate the current ratio by dividing current assets (assets that can be turned into cash in a year or faster) by current liabilities (bills due in a year or less). If the company's current ratio is 1, the company has enough assets to cover bills coming due in a year. The higher the ratio, the more solid the company's financial condition is.

✔ **Revenue per employee:** Shows you how efficiently the company uses its workforce. The ratio is the company's revenue divided by its number of employees. The higher the number, the more revenue the company derives from each employee.

Getting more particular: More advanced variables to screen for

Just using the basic screening variables is somewhat limiting. If you want to carve the list of stock candidates down further, you can use some more advanced variables. Good choices here include

✔ **Gross margin:** One of many ways to measure a company's profitability, gross profit is how much of revenue a company keeps after paying for things directly involved in the production of the good or service sold. A lemonade stand's gross profit is the dollar value of the lemonade sold minus the cost of things used in the lemonade such as sugar and lemons. This gross profit, divided by the company's revenue, gives you gross margin. Gross margin tells you how much of every dollar in sales the company keeps after paying costs directly tied to making the good or service. The higher the gross margin, the more profitable the company is.

✔ **Operating margin:** This method of measuring a company's profit includes more costs than gross margin. Operating profit is gross profit minus indirect costs, such as overhead. Overhead might include the cost of hiring a company to promote the business. Operating margin is the company's operating profit divided by revenue. The higher the operating margin, the more profitable the company.

✔ **Net profit margin:** This particular margin compares the company's bottom line with its revenue. Net profit is measured by dividing a company's net income, which counts all company costs, by its revenue. It tells you how much of each dollar in revenue the company keeps as profit after paying all costs. The higher the net profit margin, the more profitable the company.

✔ **Return on equity:** A great way to see how efficiently the company's management is using the money invested in the company, return on equity (ROE) is measured by dividing net income by shareholder's equity. Shareholder's equity measures how much money shareholders have invested in the company. So, ROE shows you how much profit the company generates per dollar invested in the company.

✔ **Return on assets:** Shows you how much profit the company is able to squeeze out of its assets. The higher the number, the better the company is at making money from things it owns.

✔ **Dividend payout ratio:** Tells you what portion of profit a company is paying out as dividends. You calculate this ratio by dividing a company's dividends by net income.

If a company's dividend payout ratio gets high — paying 85% or more of its profit out as earnings, for example — it might be paying more than it can afford depending on what industry it is in.

✔ **Dividend yield:** Tells you what kind of return you're getting as a dividend from the money you've invested in a stock. The dividend yield is a company's annual dividend paid per share divided by the stock price. A $10 stock that pays $2 a year in dividends has a 2% dividend yield.

- ✔ **Institutional ownership:** This measure tries to show you whether the "smart money" is buying a stock. The ratio shows you what percentage of shares are in the hands of large mutual funds and pension funds, which presumably have large research units. Some investors look for stocks with low institutional ownership, figuring the stock will rise rapidly as these big investors discover the stock and buy shares.

- ✔ **Debt to equity ratio:** Shows you how deeply in debt a company is. The ratio divides a company's liabilities by its shareholder equity. The higher the ratio, the more *leveraged,* or in debt, the company is. Remember, though, that different levels of debt are acceptable in various industries.

- ✔ **Beta:** Most online screening tools use a measure called *beta* to gauge volatility. The higher beta is, the more volatile the stock is compared to the rest of the stock market. If a stock has a beta greater than 1, that means it's more volatile than the Standard & Poor's 500. If a stock's beta is less than 1, it's less volatile than the S&P 500. And it a stock's beta is equal to 1, it's equally as volatile as the S&P 500.

If you can't stomach stocks that swing as wildly as the stock market, you want to add a beta filter to your screens. Just look for stocks that have betas of less than 1.

- ✔ **Short interest:** Short interest measures how many investors are betting a stock will fall. The measure is calculated by dividing the number of shares being *shorted* — or being sold in a complex maneuver by investors betting the stock price will fall — by the number of shares that normally trade each day, or the *average daily volume.* (For more on shorting stock, see Chapter 5.)

Finding stocks using trading-pattern variables

Some investors are interested more in a company's stock than the company. These investors, generally known as technical analysts, believe stocks follow certain patterns. And if you detect the pattern fast enough, you can figure out where the stock is going and make money. Some screening variables are designed to find *technical stock patterns* including

- ✔ **Average daily volume:** Some investors think if there's heavy trading in a stock when it rises or falls, that means more than if there's light trading volume. If a stock goes up, these investors look at trading volume to find out how many investors are buying. If the stock is rising and trading activity is strong, that tells these investors there's great demand for the stock and the uptrend might continue.

✔ **Proximity to moving averages:** This indicator tells you whether the current stock price is higher or lower than where it has been in the past. The 200-day moving average, for instance, tells you what the stock's average price has been over the past trading year. If the stock falls below the 200-day moving average, some see that as a bad sign because it means everyone who bought the stock in the past year, on average, is losing money and might be eager to sell.

✔ **Proximity to stock's price highs and lows:** You can use screens to find out whether a stock's price is close to its high price over the past year, called the *52-week high,* or its low price, the *52-week low.*

✔ **Stock performance:** This is a simple measure that shows you how much the stock has risen or fallen in a set period of time.

Getting Started with Premade "Canned" Screens

If you've never built a stock screen before, you might want to first try out some of the premade screens available on various Web sites. The Web sites have done most of the work for you and entered in all the variables, saving you the hassle. The following list highlights some of the better-known "canned" stock screens:

✔ **Quicken's One-Click Scorecard:** (www.quicken.com/investments) This Quicken tool takes a novel approach toward screening. It screens stocks for those that meet the criteria described by money manager Robert Hagstrom (www.robertghagstrom.com), author of *The Warren Buffett Way.* The One-Click Scorecard seeks stocks with traits that Hagstrom says Buffett looks for, including a high return on equity, high net profit margin, and most importantly, a stock price that's lower than the company's *intrinsic value* — its true worth based on how much it's expected to earn in the future.

You must own a copy of Quicken that's three years old or less to access Quicken's Web site. Just click the One-Click Scorecard link at the top of the page to access the system.

Just because a stock scores high in the Robert Hagstrom screen in the One-Click Scorecard doesn't mean Buffett bought the stock or wants to buy it. The screen merely tells you what stocks have traits that match what Buffett looks for.

Want to find out what stocks Buffett owns?

The One-Click Scorecard helps you screen for stocks with some of the traits Buffett (Warren, not Jimmy) looks for in winning investments. But what if you want to find out what Buffett's Berkshire Hathaway actually owns?

You can find out using online tools. You can download Berkshire Hathaway's annual reports (`http://berkshirehathaway.com/`

`reports.html`), which list the company's stock investments. You can view Berkshire's investments at the end of 2006 in the 2006 annual report (`http://berkshirehathaway.com/2006ar/2006ar.pdf`). (Hmmm . . . Looks like he had a thing for American Express, Coca-Cola, Proctor & Gamble, and Wells Fargo.)

✔ **NASDAQ's Guru Analysis:** (`www.nasdaq.com`) This particular NASDAQ canned stock screen uses preset criteria to help you determine whether one of several famous investors would buy a stock that you're interested in. From the NASDAQ home page, enter the ticker symbol of the stock you're considering into one of the Get Up to Ten Quotes text fields and then click the Info Quotes button. On the new page that appears, choose Guru Analysis from the InfoQuotes drop-down list to access your Guru Analysis results. The tool tells you whether famous former Fidelity portfolio manager Peter Lynch, value investor Benjamin Graham, contrarian investor David Dreman, or growth investor Martin Zweig would be interested in the stock. The GuruAnalysis is free — but you do have to register to get access.

✔ **Zacks' Predefined Screener:** (`www.zacks.com/research/screening/predefined/index.php`) Zacks' entry in the predefined screener market offers screens that focus on the key factors you'd expect, such as value, earnings growth, and dividend payments. But Zacks' premade screen also offers several criteria that highlight stocks on the move and those enjoying the most positive or negative changes in analysts' recommendations. You can narrow down all the screens to include small, mid-sized, or large stocks.

✔ **Morningstar's Stock Screener:** (`www.morningstar.com`) Actually, stock screeners, because Morningstar offers a number of helpful screeners with catchy and self-explanatory titles. A few of the screeners include Low-Priced Growth Stocks, Profitable but Unloved, Bargain in Small Caps, Aggressive Growth, Blue Chips, and Classic Companies. You can access all these screeners by clicking the Stocks tab at Morningstar's home page and scrolling down the new page that appears to the Stock Screener box on the right side.

✔ **MSN Money:** (http://moneycentral.msn.com/investor/home. asp) MSN Money divides its premade screens into two categories: Technical screens and fundamental screens. The technical screens look for stocks that have posted a certain type of stock price performance, such as a new high, a low, or when the stock moves above or below its moving average. The fundamental screens look for stocks where the companies meet specific earnings or valuation criteria. You can access the premade screens from the MSN Money Investing page by clicking the Stocks tab and then clicking the Stock Power Searches link from the list on the left side of the page. (The link is under the Find Stocks heading.) Just click the link for the screen you're interested in, and the corresponding stocks are displayed on a new page.

Most of the online screening tools in this section let you customize canned screens. Tweaking an existing screen can be a good way to get started because you don't have to start from scratch. Instead, you can modify the variables to your tastes.

Designing Your Own Custom Screens

After you start dabbling with stock screens, you'll probably start enjoying it. You can get a rush sifting through thousands of stocks for precise variables and get a list of candidates in a matter of seconds. Many investors, when they realize what stock screening is and how easy it is to do, can get kind of addicted to building screens.

The premade screens described in the preceding section cover most of the main searches investors would want to do. But sometimes, a canned screen isn't good enough. Many of the same sites that offer canned screens also let you create a screen from scratch. You might consider building a screen from the ground up if you encounter the following issues with a premade screen:

✔ **The screen is too lenient.** A premade screen might not be as restrictive as you'd like. That's especially true when searching for value-priced stocks because investors' opinions on what makes a cheap stock varies. A canned screen might consider a P-E of 10 to be cheap, but you might want to limit the list to stocks with P-E of less than 8 or even 5.

✔ **The screen is not aggressive enough.** If you're looking for a company that's expanding very rapidly, you might want to ratchet up what it takes to get into your screen. Many screens consider 20% annual earnings growth to be rapid, but you might want 30% or more.

✔ **The screen is not to your taste.** Some investors go after stocks that defy characterization. You might want to find stocks with high P-E ratios and low price-to-book ratios, which are unusual things to look for at the same time. You need to build these personalized screens yourself.

Finding different industries' best companies using MSN Money

If you're trying to figure out which companies in an industry are performing the best or worst, MSN Money's screening tool makes it easy:

1. **Point your browser to MSN Money's screening tool at** `http://money central.msn.com/investor/finder/customstocks.asp`.

2. **Choose Company Basics⇨Industry Name from the first row's Field Name drop-down list.**

   An equal sign (=) should appear in the Operator text field. If not, click the text field and choose the equal sign from the drop-down list that appears.

3. **From the Value drop-down list, choose the industry you're interested in.**

4. **Use the second row's Field Name drop-down list to define what you mean by a "best company."**

   The definition of a "best company" is in the eyes of the beholder. You might, for instance, want companies with return on equity that's higher than the industry's. To find companies with an industry-beating return on equity, you'd choose Investment Return⇨Return on Equity from the menu, choose >= from the Operator menu, and then choose Investment Return⇨Industry Average Return on Equity from the Value drop-down list. Your screen should look something like Figure 14-2.

5. **Add more variables.**

   Filling in the second row automatically added a new blank row. That means you can keep working your way down, adding different criteria if you choose. You can add criteria that will find stocks that miss, match, or exceed industry averages on a variety of things, including price-to-book, price-to-earnings, revenue per employee, and many other items.

6. **Click the Run Search button.**

   Your Search results appear on a new page, displaying the leading companies that beat the industry.

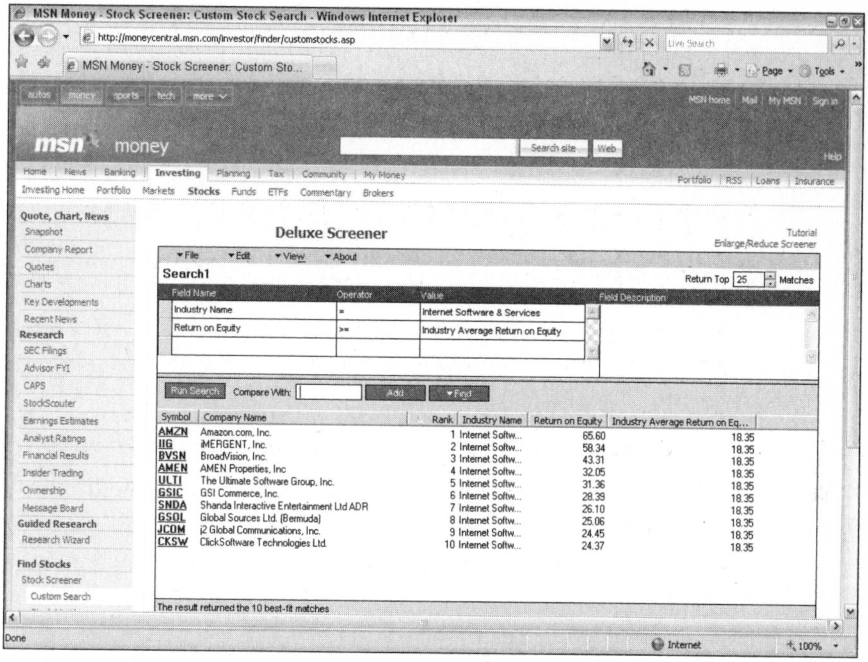

Figure 14-2:
MSN
Money's
screening
tool allows
you to
see how
companies
and their
stocks
compare
with
industry
peers.

Finding value or growth companies using Morningstar's Stock Screener

You could go to the trouble of designing a convoluted set of criteria to find value and growth stocks. But why go to the trouble when Morningstar's Stock Screener has done the work for you? Morningstar's Stock Screener helps you design a custom screen, but with some helpful handholding. Here's how:

1. **Point your browser to Morningstar's screening tool at http://screen. morningstar.com/StockSelector.html?ssection=StockScreener.**

   The Stock Screener page appears in all its glory.

2. **Choose the Growth or Value criteria you want from the Morningstar Equity Style Box drop-down list — the third drop-down list from the top.**

   You could go for Large Value, for example.

3. **Limit your search further if you want.**

   You can narrow your search further, based on growth or profitability grades and other items.

4. **When you're done, click the Show/Score Results tab at the top of the screener.**

   You get a lovely list of results.

Chapter 15

Analyzing the Analysts and Stock Pickers

· ·

In This Chapter

▶ Accessing analysts' reports online

▶ Evaluating analysts to determine which ones are worth listening to

▶ Deciding whether stock-picking newsletters and Web sites are worth the money

▶ Understanding the "whisper number"

▶ Getting stock ratings from other investors online

· ·

*W*hen you're looking to make a big purchase, such as a car, house, or big-screen TV, you probably ask other people questions before making your decision. You might ask a friend or family member for their recommendation or consult with a magazine or Web site that ranks products.

Recommendations play an important role for some investors when picking stocks, too. Traditional brokers have long made it their business to recommend stocks for their clients to buy. And even before the hot dogs hit the grill, many family barbeques start sounding like an investment club meeting as everyone brags about their winners (and somehow fail to mention stocks they've lost money on). Many financial TV shows feature guests who can fire off stock tips.

Stock recommendations are impossible to avoid, and that makes them important to think about. There are smart ways, though, to handle recommendations. In this chapter, I show you various online resources for stock recommendations as well as how to interpret them. You get a chance to read about different stock-picking newsletters and sites and how to evaluate them. And I show you some new online sites that reveal how other individual investors rate stocks.

Picking Apart Professional Analyst Reports

Nearly all the major Wall Street brokerage firms have teams of research *sell-side* analysts. It's the sell-side analyst's job to study companies and tell investors who are clients of the brokerage firm which stocks are attractive. You can also find *independent* research firms — research groups not connected with a brokerage firm that analyze stocks and sell their research.

Blindly following "buy" or "sell" recommendations is generally a bad idea. Smart investors know how to scan through research reports to pick out important insights on the company or industry. Later in this chapter, I show you how to quickly pull the most important information out of analyst reports.

How to access analyst reports online

Before you can analyze research reports, you have to get your hands on them. There are several techniques to do this online — some that will cost you money, but many that won't. The following list highlights a few resources of both the free and not-so-free types:

- ✔ **Online brokers:** You don't have to be a client of the full-service brokerage firms like Credit Suisse or Goldman Sachs to get their analysts' research reports. Online brokers can sometimes get the goods for you. Charles Schwab, for instance, allows you to download reports from Goldman Sachs and E*Trade offers access to Credit Suisse reports. Most online brokers also offer access to independent research, including reports from Standard & Poor's, Argus, and Morningstar. Getting research from your online broker is generally the best route because there's usually no charge.

- ✔ **Research providers:** Some independent research providers sell their reports directly to investors. Standard & Poor's, for instance, sells reports on more than 5,000 companies. (See http://sandp.ecnext.com/coms2/page_industry2 for a listing.) The reports include a forecast of what the stock's future price could be, called a *target price,* in addition to an analysis of the company's earnings. The reports often cost around $35.

S&P reports also use an easy-to-understand rating system. S&P rates thousands of stocks using a star rating system where the most attractive stocks are given five stars and the least attractive stocks get one star. If your broker offers S&P reports, you can get the S&P ratings from the top of the reports. Also, S&P provides a few of its ratings for free in its The Outlook site (www.outlook.standardandpoors.com). Scroll down and on the left side in the light blue area you see a link that says High Yield stars. Click that link to get a list of the highest-rated stocks that pay large dividends.

TIP

Don't assume that just because stock research comes from an independent research firm, it's more accurate or better. Sometimes research from Wall Street brokerage firms is very good. The quality of research varies greatly and largely depends on the strength of the specific analyst covering the stock. I show you how to track down the best analysts on various stocks in the "Determining which Wall Street analysts are worth listening to" section, later in this chapter.

✔ **Research resellers:** Yahoo! Finance allows you to search for research reports on specific companies or by specific firms with the help of its Report Screener tool (http://screen.yahoo.com/reports.html). Some of the reports are free, but you must pay for most of them. Prices range from just $15 to more than $100. You can also buy research reports from Reuters (www.reuters.com/investing) by entering the stock's symbol into the Enter Symbol field, selecting the Analyst Research radio button and clicking the Go button.

✔ **Summary sites:** If you want just the bottom line recommendations from analysts, several sites summarize the data. Nearly all the Web sites that provide stock quotes also compile analyst recommendations. Some examples include

- *Yahoo! Finance* (http://finance.yahoo.com) has a comprehensive database of analyst recommendations. Enter a stock symbol into the search field at the top of Yahoo! Finance, for instance, click the Get Quotes button and then click the Analyst Opinion link on the left side of the new page that appears. You see how analysts, on average, are rating the stock and also the stock's *average price target* — what most of the analysts, on average, expect the stock's price to be in a year or less. You can find out from Yahoo! Finance whether analysts raised their opinion on a stock, called *upgrading,* or cut their opinion, called *downgrading.*

- *Reuters* (www.reuters.com/investing) provides analyst recommendations if you enter a stock symbol and click the Recommendations radio button before you click Go.

- *Zacks Investment Research* (www.zacks.com) provides brokerage recommendations at the bottom of the stock quote page. Just enter a stock's symbol into the Quote text field, click Go, and scroll down the new page that appears. Pay close attention to the average brokerage recommendation (ABR), a number that will fall somewhere between 1 and 5. If the ABR is 1 that means analysts, on average, rank the stock a strong buy. If the ABR is 5, analysts, on average, rank the stock a strong sell. Zacks also ranks stock ratings by industry.

When "hold" really means "sell"

Research reports issued by Wall Street investment banks got a bad rap in 2002. That's when the former New York attorney general Eliot Spitzer began investigating a number of internal e-mails sent within several large Wall Street brokerage firms. The e-mails allegedly indicated that sell-side analysts routinely issued glowing "strong buy" and "buy" ratings on stocks they had serious reservations about. During the Internet boom, for instance, for every stock with a sell rating, there were 100 stocks with a buy rating, according to the University of Pennsylvania (www.upenn.edu/researchatpenn/article.php?76&bus). Those ratings proved to be overly optimistic in many cases, and some investors who followed the research suffered large losses as a result. The regulators alleged analysts promoted stocks of companies the brokerage firms hoped to sell lucrative investment banking services to. The analysts, in turn, would receive bonuses resulting from the business that came from the companies they wrote positively about. The investigations resulted in dramatic reforms in the way investment banks handled stock research.

In 2003, ten investment banking firms agreed to a settlement with regulators in which they would pay roughly $1.4 billion in various penalties and fees in connection to issuing allegedly misleading research reports. (See the SEC page at www.sec.gov/news/press/2003-54.htm for more about the case.)

The settlement resulted in several changes to research that affect online investors. One of the significant outcomes of the settlement included the requirement that Wall Street investment firms make their analysts' ratings and price targets available to the public. By giving investors access to analysts' track records, investors gained the ability, thanks to several Web sites, to see which analysts might be worth listening to and which ones to ignore. Following the reforms, perhaps due to the greater accountability, analyst ratings improved in accuracy.

- *NASDAQ.com* (www.nasdaq.com) offers a handy guide to upgrades and downgrades for all stocks, not just those that trade on the NASDAQ. Scroll down to find the Analyst Changes section, where you can see how many stocks were upgraded or downgraded that day. Click the number for upgrades, for instance, and you can get stocks' names.

Most summary sites convert stock ratings into numbers on a one-to-five scale, where 1 is a "strong buy" or "outperform" and 5 is a "strong sell" or "underperform."

Determining which Wall Street analysts are worth listening to

Don't just assume research from an independent analyst is better than research from a sell-side analyst. What really matters is performance. If an analyst is always wrong, independent or not, you probably don't want to listen to his or her advice.

But how do you find out which analysts are the best? These two online tools can help you find the best analysts:

✔ **Investars:** (www.investars.com) This site offers a free version of its analyst tracking service, called Investars Light, to individual investors. You can search the Investars database to find out which research firms and individual analysts are the most accurate and look up ratings based on sectors and individual stocks.

To get started, just click the green Enter button under the Investars Light box on the front page to call up the screen displayed in Figure 15-1. From there, you can get started searching the analyst-tracking database.

Most often, you'll probably want to get the ratings and performance of analysts who cover a particular individual stock. To do this, click the Find the Best Analysts by Ticker link. On the new page that appears, enter the stock's symbol in the Select Stock text field and specify the time period you want to analyze using the Time Period drop-down list. (Leave the other drop-down list choices as they are.) Click the Update Settings button, and Investars then shows you each research firm's *overall daily return* — how much money you would have made, or lost, per day had you followed the analyst's advice.

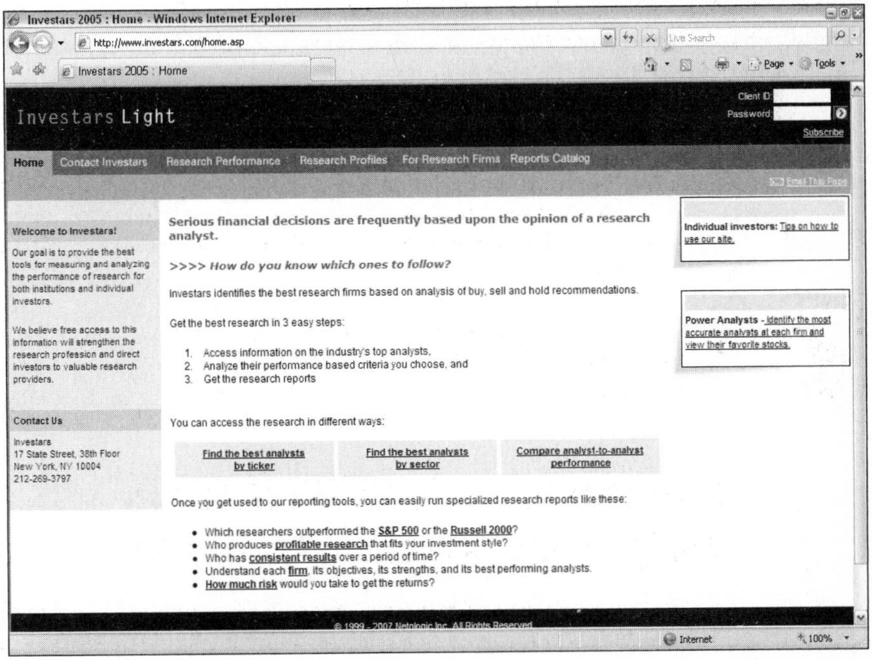

Figure 15-1: Investars Light lets you track the quality of stock picks based on individual stocks, analysts, and research firms.

✔ **StarMine:** (www.starmine.com): StarMine lets investors view lists that rank the top analysts. You can find the best overall analysts and firms and also find the ones that are the most accurate in specific industry sectors, such as financial, industrials, and utilities.

StarMine's own Web site is geared for professional money managers and Wall Street firms. If you're not part of that crowd, the easiest way to get StarMine data is through Yahoo! Finance (http://finance.yahoo.com). Enter the stock's symbol in the search field at the top of the page, click the Get Quotes button, and then click the Star Analysts link on the left side of the new page that appears. (The link is under Analyst Coverage heading.) On the new page that appears, you see a list of the top-ranked analysts on the stock for the last two years. The page also has an EPS Accuracy link you can click to find out which analysts have been the best at predicting the company's earnings per share (EPS), as well as an Industry Excess Return link you can click to see which analysts' recommendations have outperformed the industry group by the widest margin.

What to look for in an analyst report

Many investors who read Wall Street analyst reports tend to concentrate on the analyst's rating. These investors want to know instantly whether the stock is rated a Buy, Hold, or Sell.

Savvy investors often skip past the analyst's rating on a stock. Much of the worthwhile information in an analyst report isn't in the rating, but in the insights about the company, management, and industry. Investopedia (www.investopedia.com/articles/01/013101.asp) provides a useful guide in how to read analysts' research reports.

Pay the most attention to these portions of the report:

✔ **Industry comparisons:** Many Wall Street analysts are assigned to cover companies in a specific industry. As a result, these analysts spend time going to industry conferences; meeting with employees, customers, and suppliers to build deep knowledge of industry trends. Industry information is one of the top things you should look for. Pay special attention to any signs that one company is taking market share from other competitors.

✔ **Channel checks:** The better industry analysts take the time to see how much of the product that companies are shipping is actually making it into the hands of customers. The process of tracking the flow of goods from the company to warehouses to resellers and retailers and ultimately to consumers is called a *channel check*. If you get the feeling the company is shipping product that's just stacking up on retailers' shelves, that's a bad sign. A pileup of product might indicate the company is trying to boost its earnings in the short term and might suffer later as the glut of products is sold off.

✔ **Price-target justification:** Analysts often use a variety of stock valuation techniques (explained in more detail in Chapter 13) to put a *price target* on a stock. A price target is the analyst's best guess at how much the stock might be worth in the future, usually one year from now. The most interesting part of the price target is often analysts' explanation of how they arrived at the number.

Pssst . . . understanding the "whisper number"

Many analysts put their MBAs to good use and pick apart the financial statements of companies to determine how much the stocks are truly worth. But, some analysts take the lazy way out by blindly following the forecast given to them by the company. This presents a problem for online investors because companies can steer some analysts to lower their expectations for growth. And if the company is successful in lowering the earnings bar, it's easier for the company to beat the results. The opposite can happen, too. A company might convince analysts to go along with an overly optimistic view of the future, setting investors up for a disappointment.

That's where the earnings *whisper number* comes in. The whisper number, in theory, is the unofficial earnings number most investors honestly expect the company to report.

Whisper numbers gain even more prominence during strong bull markets when investors' expectations begin to soar. For instance, in April 2000, Yahoo!'s stock fell 9% in the two trading days after reporting a profit of 10 cents a share, which topped official earnings estimates, but missed the whisper by 2 cents a share.

You can get whisper numbers for free online. WhisperNumber.com (www. whispernumber.com) is an easy way to see what the whisper number might be. Just enter the symbol of the stock you're interested in, click the Get It! button, and you can view the whisper number for the current quarter. (See Figure 15-2.)You can also look up the whisper number for the previous quarter and see how close it was to the actual number reported by the company. Lastly, you can see how the stock reacted in 1, 5, 10, and 30 days following the company's last earnings announcement. The site is free, but you must register.

Figure 15-2:
Whisper
Number.
com lets
you in on
the secret
of how
much
investors
really think
a company
will earn.

Accessing and understanding credit ratings

Research analysts who study companies and their stocks get the most attention from many investors. But there's a second type of company analysts out there — debt-rating analysts or bond analysts. Debt-rating analysts study companies to determine how creditworthy they are. *Debt-rating analysts* are important because if they determine a company is stable and trustworthy, the company can borrow money at lower interest rates. Debt-rating analysts give companies letter grades to measure their financial strength, with A being high and either C or D being the lowest grade possible.

Credit and Finance Risk Analysis (www.credfinrisk.com/ratings.html) provides a handy definition of the ratings and what they mean.

There are three major debt-rating firms, Moody's, Standard & Poor's and Fitch. The ratings used by Moody's vary slightly from the ratings used by the other two firms. The debt-rating firms employ armies of analysts trained to pick apart company's financial statements looking for trouble. While they miss problems from time to time, they're still a helpful source of information for investors.

Even if you're buying a company's stock, not its debt, credit agencies' ratings are very important because they give you an idea of how solid the company's financials are. There are three leading credit agencies, but only the following two agencies make their ratings available for free online:

- ✔ **Moody's Investors Service:** (www.moodys.com) Moody's provides easy online access to its credit ratings. Just enter the company's symbol or name in the Search For field and click Go. (See Figure 15-3.) Scroll down until you see the company's name and put your cursor over the gold icon, and Moody's ratings for the company pop up. You might see several ratings for each company, but the rating of most importance to investors is the one called Senior Unsecured. Moody's site is free, but you must register to get any information from it.

- ✔ **Standard & Poor's:** (www.standardandpoors.com) S&P lets you view its credit ratings for the thousands of stocks it covers. Click the Ratings link near the center of its home page and then click the Credit Ratings Search link on the left side of the new page that appears. After the page refreshes, enter the company's name in the Keyword field and scroll down until you see the company's name. After you click the company's name, you see S&P's credit rating for the company. The site is free, but you have to register to use it.

Figure 15-3:
Moody's Investors Service lets you see its debt-rating analysts' ratings which measure how secure they think a company's financial standing is.

Connecting with Online Stock Ratings

Wall Street analysts aren't the only sources for ratings on stocks. There's a handful of online stock rating services that either let a computer or other investors rate a stock. Some of these rating services are based on computer models, sometimes called *quantitative* (or *quant*) *models,* which analyze companies' financial statements and key ratios to decide whether the stock is a good buy. Other stock rating services allow investors to share their ratings on stocks, with the idea that as a whole the average of the crowd's opinions will be close to accurate. I cover both types of stock rating services in the following sections.

Putting quant stock models to work for you

Research reports issued by Wall Street analysts and debt-rating analysts can be helpful, but they're not perfect. These analysts are human, too, and often fail to sound the bell before financial catastrophes occur — think the collapse of dot-com stocks as well as the implosion of Enron and companies in the sub-prime mortgage industry. These missteps by human analysts have led some investors to think that it would be great if you could get ratings and recommendations on stocks yet somehow eliminate the potential of human error or lapses in judgment. That's where quant models come in. These models are programmed by market experts to analyze stocks by using a series of criteria and to rate them. Most of these systems are untouched by human hands after they're designed. Instead, they follow very strict preset guidelines. A few online quant models include the following:

- **Schwab Equity Ratings:** (www.schwab.wallst.com/ser/perfMonitor/public/?period=52wk) Schwab ranks thousands of stocks (using an A through F scale) based on company's valuations plus the risk, valuation, and momentum of their stocks. Even if you're not a Schwab customer, you can get limited access to the Schwab Equity Ratings.

  For instance, say you'd like to get a list of all the stocks that have been rated an A. Start out by making sure the Performance Over Recent 26-51 Weeks tab is selected, as shown in Figure 15-4, and then choose the most recent period from the Select Performance Time Period drop-down list. You see a table underneath a few charts. In this table, you can click the time period, listed under the Performance for the Period header, and get a list of all the stocks that were rated A, and also B through F, 26 weeks ago.

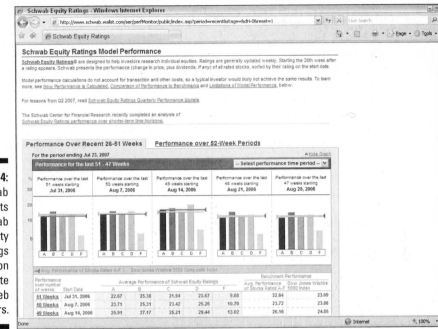

Figure 15-4:
Schwab
makes its
Schwab
Equity
Ratings
available on
its Web site
for all Web
surfers.

You need to be a Schwab customer to get access to current Schwab Equity Ratings for all stocks.

✔ **MSN Money's StockScouter:** (`http://moneycentral.msn.com/investor/StockRating/srsmain.asp`) Yet another online tool from MSN Money, the StockScouter first evaluates a stock's potential risk and return and then assigns a rating between one, as unattractive, to 10, which means attractive. The rating is based on dozens of variables, ranging from the stock's P-E to analysts' opinions on the stock. Just enter the stock's symbol into the Name or Symbol(s) field and click Go, and MSN Money spits out the rating.

✔ **USATODAY.com's Stock Meter:** (`http://money.usatoday.com`) The Stock Meter ranks stocks on a scale of one to five, with one being the most conservative to five being the more aggressive, based on an analysis of many of the important things highlighted in Chapter 13 including return on equity, liquidity, debt load, dividend record, and volatility. You can get ratings on stocks by entering their symbol in the Get a Quote blank on the left side of the page and clicking the Go button (you may have to scroll down a bit to see the Get a quote blank). A new page will come up showing the stock's Stock Meter score on the right side.

Sharing stock ratings with other investors online

In his book *The Wisdom of Crowds*, journalist James Surowiecki argues that a crowd of regular people making decisions, on average, will get closer to the right answer as a whole than just a few experts. Collectively, a group of diverse and independent-thinking people will, on average, come up with an accurate guess.

Several online sites are trying to harness this wisdom of crowds and turn the masses' guess into information you can use to boost your returns. Some good sources for this collective intelligence are listed here:

✔ **The Motley Fool CAPS:** (`caps.fool.com`) This particular corner of the Motley Fool Web site allows members to enter their ratings on thousands of stocks. The ratings are then compiled into a single average rating that's available to all users of the Web site. Just enter a stock's symbol into the search field and click Go, and you see how other CAPS users rate the stock, based on a star rating. A stock with five stars is a strong buy, and a stock with a one-star rating is a strong sell.

But CAPS gets more interesting the more you dive into the menus. For instance, you can read why certain CAPS members rated a stock the way they did. And even these blurbs are rated by members, so you can read the most highly rated comments on a stock. And if you click the CAPS Rating tab in the Stock Trends chart, you can see how the CAPS rating has changed over the past few months. Anyone can view most CAPS ratings and information. but to rate stocks yourself, you'll need to register with the site, which is free.

And what does CAPS stand for? You're going to be sorry you asked. CAPS doesn't appear to stand for anything, but rather seems to be a play on the word cap, since the Motley Fool's founders are known for wearing jester hats. Participants in the CAPS system are assigned a color-coded hat, or cap, icon to signal how good they have been at picking stocks.

✔ **Stockpickr:** (`www.stockpickr.com`) This site allows you to enter your portfolio and the system looks for other investors with similar portfolios. Stockpickr then recommends stocks that commonly appear in these similar portfolios. The Stockpickr system figures that you might want to check out the stocks similar investors own. You must register for a free username and password to use the site.

✔ **Consensus View:** (`www.consensusview.com`) At Consensus View, you get to rate just about every stock, foreign market, or investment you can think of as bullish or bearish. All the users' predictions are compiled and averaged, and you can see what other members think and how their opinions have changed over the months. You must sign up for a free membership to use the site.

✔ **SocialPicks:** (www.socialpicks.com) This site tracks stocks that are getting the most ratings from members of the site and features them on the front page so you can quickly see what the site's members are talking about online. The site also tracks and ranks investment pros and stock-picking bloggers by giving them a SocialPicks Rank. The SocialPicks Rank quickly shows you whose stock recommendations are most valued. You can use the site to find out which users are the best overall experts and see their ratings on various stocks. You must sign up for a free registration to use the site.

✔ **PredictWallStreet:** (www.predictwallstreet.com) PredictWallStreet lets you start sharing recommendations with others pretty quickly and easily. From the front page, just enter a stock symbol into the search field and click the Up button if you recommend the stock and the Down button if you think the stock will fall. You can see the average recommendations of other users for other popular stock market indexes or popular stocks. One of the nice things about this site is that you can use it without registering.

Following the crowd when it comes to investing can often be a bad idea. During periods of market manias, when investors become overly bullish about particular types of stocks, they often bid stock prices up too high and set themselves up for disappointments. Some investors, who call themselves *contrarians,* instead figure out what the crowd is doing and then do the opposite. If the crowd is bullish about a stock, a contrarian would assume the group is wrong and be bearish about the stock. (For more info on the Contrary Market View, check out iTulip.com at www.itulip.com.)

Evaluating Stock and Mutual Fund Picking Newsletters and Web Sites

Whenever a crowd is trying to make quick money, there's no shortage of people happy to offer their expertise and skill . . . for a fee. Stock investing is no different. You can find dozens of stock and mutual fund picking newsletters, Web sites, books, and seminars. They all make great pitches for why you need to pay to subscribe to their wonderful services.

By and large, many of the pitches you see for stock-picking newsletters aren't worth much, and you should be very skeptical before paying money for "systems" and "programs" that claim to be able to beat the market. A 1998 study by Jeffrey Jaffe and James Mahoney — available at http://papers. ssrn.com/sol3/papers.cfm?abstract_id=937407 — found that stocks recommended by newsletters don't outperform the market. The study also found that newsletters tend to pile onto yesterday's winning stocks by recommending stocks that had done well in the recent past.

Before you sign up for a stock picking service . . .

Before you pay a dime for any stock-picking newsletter or Web site, take the time to educate yourself about the specific service you're considering.

Your first stop should be a column written by Mark Hulbert (`www.marketwatch.com/news/newsletters`). Hulbert is a well-known tracker of newsletter performance. Hulbert uses advanced performance-tracking methods to measure not only how well stock-picking newsletters perform, but also how much risk they've taken to get those returns. After all, a 30% annual return isn't that impressive if your portfolio swings up and down 80% a year.

Hulbert writes a number of financial columns at MarketWatch that are worth reading because he tells you about trends among stock pickers. If you want to look up how a specific newsletter scores in Hulbert's ratings, you need to sign up for his Hulbert Interactive service, which ranks more than 180 newsletters. (You can sign up at `www3.marketwatch.com/Store/products/hulbert_interactive.aspx?`.)The service costs $150 a year, but you can buy a one-day pass for $9.

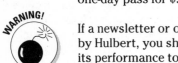

If a newsletter or online stock-picking service you're considering isn't tracked by Hulbert, you should be skeptical. It might mean the service doesn't want its performance to be tracked — perhaps for shady reasons.

You can also view some of Hulbert's research by clicking the Free Sample Issue button at the bottom of any of his columns at MarketWatch. The sample issue is a few months old, but it still contains information about newsletter rankings. Hulbert's data show how few newsletters actually beat the market on a risk-adjusted basis. For instance, during the 25 year period ending in February 2007, only two newsletters tracked by Hulbert beat the market. And you can be sure the other 23 still collected the subscription fees.

Using newsletters to your advantage

You might be wondering whether stock-picking newsletters are often so wrong, how can they help you? Again, the contrarian approach might make sense, and it's a strategy used by many professional money managers.

The simplest way to see what newsletters are saying about stocks and doing the opposite is by determining how many newsletter writers are bullish and how many are bearish. When newsletter writers are nervous about the market and selling stocks, that's a signal to contrarian investors that now is a good time to buy stocks. And when newsletter writers are bullish and buying stocks, these contrarian investors start to take money off the table by selling stocks.

Don't let reading newsletters bring on a junk-mail deluge

One potential peril of signing up for stock-picking services and newsletters is that some sell your name and address to other companies for profit. This might fill your mailbox with ads you don't want, including pitches for shady penny stock shams.

Here are two strategies to prevent you from getting slammed from junk mail:

- Use a slightly different name when you sign up for the stock-picking service. Instead of signing up as Joe Smith, use JoeD Smith or something like that. If junk mail starts showing up to that unique name, you'll know it's the stock-picking service that's selling your information. You can call the service up and tell them to stop.

- Sign up for the Direct Marketing Association's Mail Preference Service (www.dma consumers.org/consumerassis tance.html). This service helps you take your name off of many lists used by companies to send out advertising and promotion material. You can fill out the form online at www.dmaconsumers.org/online form.php. There's a $1 fee to register with the service.

Schaeffer's Investment Research (www.schaeffersresearch.com) provides some of the information you need to be a contrarian. Click the Market Tools link on the Quotes & Tools tab and then click the Investor's Intelligence link on the new page that appears. Doing so brings up the Investor's Intelligence's newsletter indicator in both tabular and chart form, which tells you what percentage of newsletters are bullish and what percentage are bearish.

Chapter 16

Researching and Buying Bonds Online

In This Chapter

▶ Figuring out whether bonds are for you

▶ Finding out how bonds differ from other investments

▶ Locating information about bond prices and performance

▶ Determining the best way for you to buy bonds online

*B*onds don't make very good cocktail party chatter. Just try to brag about your 5%-a-year bond return at a party. The only heads you'll turn will be the ones running away from you yawning. Bonds just aren't as exciting or glamorous as stocks, which can often gain more value in an hour than you'll collect from bonds all year.

But don't let the fact bonds are, well, often boring discourage you from owning them. Bonds, often called *fixed-income securities,* are essentially IOUs issued by companies, cities, governments, and government agencies. These IOUs come with a promise to repay the lender by a specific time at a specific interest rate. These stable streams of cash flow can be very valuable if you choose bonds wisely. Bonds can help smooth out the ups and downs in your portfolio and help you reach your financial goals.

In this chapter, I explain what a bond is and how it differs from other investments, including stocks. I also show you ways to find out more about bonds and get up with the terms and lingo. You get a chance to discover Web sites that let you research bonds to find the ones that might fit your portfolio the best. And I show you ways to buy bonds online as well as a few alternatives to bonds you might consider.

Getting Acquainted with Bonds

If you've ever lent money to someone and set up a repayment program, you already know what a bond is. A bond is an IOU that entitles you to a stream of payments from the borrower. Companies, governments, cities, and government agencies often sell bonds so they can raise money to build facilities, build bridges, or finance their operations. The money that was borrowed must be repaid at a predetermined *interest rate* and by a set period of time in the future (called the *maturity date*) along with the money borrowed (called the *principal*).

Bonds by their nature offer investors several benefits:

- **Generally stable and predictable cash payments:** Investors who aren't looking for any big surprises tend to appreciate bonds' preset rate of return. When you buy a bond and hold it until maturity, you know ahead of time what your return will be. This can be useful for reaching financial obligations.

- **Repayment of principal:** When you buy a bond, you'll receive interest payments in addition to the money you loaned back, as long as the borrower can afford the payments and doesn't *default*. Investors who want to preserve their initial investment like bonds for this very reason.

- **Liquidity:** You might be familiar with bank certificates of deposit (CDs), which also pay interests and return the original investments. But unlike most CDs, which you must hold for a set period of time or pay a penalty, you can sell your bonds to other investors, in most cases, at any time just like you'd sell a stock. This characteristic of bonds means you can raise cash if you need to.

You have two ways to make money from a bond. You can hold it until it comes due, or *matures*. That way, you collect the interest as it's paid. Your other option is to sell the bond to someone else before it matures. Just remember, though, when you sell a bond you might not get back what you paid. The bond's price might fall if the bond because less desirable for reasons discussed later in the chapter.

- **Diversification:** Bond prices tend to move up and down in a different pattern than stocks price. By owning stocks and bonds, you can smooth out the bumps in your portfolio. Table 16-1 shows you how bonds might not go up as much as stocks, but they don't usually fall as much either.

Table 16-1	Biggest Gains and Losses for Stocks and Bonds	
Investment	*Biggest Gain*	*Biggest Loss*
Stocks (Standard & Poor's 500)	52.8% (1933)	–43.9% (1931)
Corporate bonds	34.9% (1982)	–5.0% (1980)

Investment	Biggest Gain	Biggest Loss
Treasury bills	14.6% (1981)	0% (1940)
5-year Treasuries	33.0% (1982)	–4.3% (1994)
10-year Treasuries	44.3% (1982)	–7.5% (1999)

Source: Global Financial Data, using data from 1926

Typically, investors who need a more stable portfolio place most of their investments in bonds. But even if you're terrified of the thought of losing money, it's usually not a good idea to put your entire portfolio in bonds. Mixing some stocks in your portfolio can reduce your risk and increase your returns because bonds and stocks usually don't rise and fall at the same time by the same degree.

Knowing who issues debt

Before you can buy or sell bonds, you must understand there are several types of bonds, based on who sold them. Each type of bond has unique traits and can be bought or sold online differently. The following is a quick rundown of the major issuers of bonds:

- ✔ **U.S. government:** Debt instruments sold by the U.S. government are popular because they're backed by the full faith and credit of the U.S., which stands behind these loans and promises that they'll be repaid. That greatly reduces, if not eliminates, the risk you won't get paid. These fixed-income securities are often called *Treasuries*, and come in three main varieties: Treasury bills mature in one year or less, treasury notes mature in more than a year up to 10 years and treasury bonds mature in more than 10 years. TreasuryDirect (www.treasurydirect.gov) provides in-depth information about Treasuries.

  Even if you're not interested in buying bonds, the yield on Treasuries is a very important figure to keep in mind. Treasury yields tell you how much return you can get for taking little to no risk. If a risk-free Treasury pays 5%, you probably wouldn't be willing to buy a risky stock unless it would return considerably more than 5%.

  Treasuries are often called risk-free investments, but that's not really true. Even Treasuries face *interest-rate risk*. Say you buy a Treasury that pays 5% interest. If inflation rises, and interest rates rise to 6% as a result, your 5% interest rate isn't looking so hot anymore. If you sell the bond, you'll get less for it than you paid. And if you hold onto the bond, your 5% interest rate is lackluster.

- ✔ **Government agencies and government-sponsored enterprises:** Individual government agencies can also borrow money. Debt issued by agencies is still considered safe, while perhaps not as safe as Treasuries. That means agency bonds may pay slightly higher interest rates than Treasuries. Some examples of agency bonds include those sold by the Government National Mortgage Association, or Ginnie Mae (www. ginniemae.gov), to provide financing to low and moderate-income families to buy homes. Ginnie Mae loans are backed by several government agencies. Similarly, there are lenders called government-sponsored enterprises (GSEs) that, although closely tied to the government and often created by Congress, are private companies and are therefore not technically agencies.

The Federal National Mortgage Association, or Fannie Mae (www. fanniemae.com), is a GSE that buys and sells mortgage-backed securities that pass interest and principal payments made by homeowners to investors who own the securities.

Fannie Mae, as a private company sponsored by the Federal government, has stock listed on the New York Stock Exchange. The Federal government has determined that Fannie Mae must help provide money to the mortgage industry and provides it with help and supervision. But the government doesn't legally stand behind Fannie Mae's bonds. Most investors, though, believe the government would step in and intervene before a GSE like Fannie Mae was unable to pay its debts.

✔ **Companies:** Bonds issued by companies, sometimes called *corporates,* allow them to pay for equipment and services they need in order to expand or grow. Companies pay higher interest rates than the government because there's a larger chance they will default, or hit hard times and have trouble paying the money they borrowed back. Bonds sold by rock-solid companies are called *investment grade.* Small companies or companies with shaky finances issue what's called high-yield or junk-bond debt. Investment grade bonds pay lower interest rates than junk bonds because investors are more certain they'll get their money back.

✔ **Cities and municipalities:** Cities may borrow money by selling bonds, called *municipal* bonds or just *munis.* The biggest attraction of munis to investors is the fact that their interest often isn't taxable by the federal government. And if you buy a muni bond issued by a government in the state or city you live in, the interest might also not be subject to state or city tax. Munis are often called tax-exempt bonds for this reason. There's a price of this tax benefit, though. Munis might pay lower interest rates than bonds with similar risk. InvestorGuide.com (www.investorguide.com/igu-article-575-bonds-municipal-bonds.html) provides more information about munis.

Don't just look at the seemingly low interest rate offered by a tax-exempt muni bond when deciding if you want to buy it. The actual interest rate is higher after you factor in the fact that the interest payments often aren't taxable. For example, if an investor in the 28% tax bracket buys a muni bond paying 5% interest, that's equivalent to a 6.94% interest rate from a taxable bond. And that's a good thing. One other thing to remember: Not all muni bonds qualify for the tax breaks so be sure to check before you buy one.

Investing in "Bowie" bonds

Bonds are usually sold by governments and companies, but some interesting exceptions have cropped up. One of the more famous and unorthodox sellers of bonds was rock star David Bowie. Bowie generated $55 million for himself in 1997 by selling "Bowie Bonds." Investors who bought the bonds were entitled to the cash stream generated by sales of Bowie's albums for a decade. Similar music-based bonds followed, allowing investors to buy the cash streams from James Brown and the Isley Brothers. Individual investors were unable to invest in Bowie Bonds. The Bowie Bond was the innovation of the Pullman Group (www.pullmanco.com). The future of music-based bonds is uncertain as more consumers buy individual music tracks from online music stores, rather than full-length albums from music retailers.

Want to compare the interest rate on a tax-exempt muni bond with a taxable bond? The Investing in Bonds Web site provides a table that converts tax-exempt interest rates to taxable rates for different tax brackets at (www.investinginbonds.com/learnmore.asp?catid=5&subcatid=24&id=206). And Smith Barney (www.smithbarney.com/cgi-bin/bonds/teymey.cgi) offers a free calculator that tells you what a taxable bond's interest rate would need to be to match the interest rate paid on a muni bond.

Online resources to find out more about bonds

One of the toughest things about bonds is just figuring out the vocabulary. Investors who focus on buying and selling stocks often struggle with the different terms when they enter the brave new world of bonds. It's critical, though, for you to understand the lexicon of bonds before jumping in. Several Web sites, though, step you through the bond world and can get you up to speed in no time. Here's the (relatively) short list:

✔ **Investopedia's Bond Basics:** (www.investopedia.com/university/bonds) This corner of Investopedia runs through everything you need to know to get started with bonds. The site covers the terminology and shows you how to calculate how much bonds are worth.

✔ **SmartMoney Economy & Bonds:** (www.smartmoney.com/bonds) SmartMoney's Bonds section contains useful tools and information for bond investors. You can find news stories that update investors with developments in the bond markets as well as the Bonds Toolbox, which offers several useful calculators, including one that measures how much it would cost you to sell one bond to buy another.

✔ **BondsOnline:** (www.bonds-online.com) This site conveniently pulls together all sorts of fixed-income securities information, ranging from articles about bonds to charts showing the interest rates paid by different types of bonds.

✔ **Investing in Bonds:** (www.investinginbonds.com) The name says it all. Check out the site, shown in Figure 16-1, for several well-written checklists and guides for beginning bond investors and be sure to look on the right side of the page for the Learn More column. There you can find articles that cover bond basics and things you should know.

✔ **The Investment FAQ:** (http//invest-faq.com) This general purpose investment site has dedicated a section to beginning bond information. Click the Bonds link from the site's directory of categories and you'll find information on bond basics as well as more advanced information.

✔ **Yahoo! Finance:** (http//finance.yahoo.com/bonds) This corner of Yahoo! Finance provides all sorts of education on bonds, including a bonds primer and glossary.

✔ **The Bond Buyer:** (http://bondbuyer.com) This site tracks new developments in the bond world. You can follow trends in bonds and find out about new offerings.

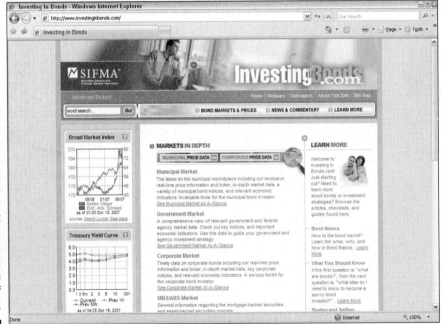

Figure 16-1:
Investing in Bonds answers most questions you might have when considering investing money in bonds of any type.

✔ **Briefing.com:** (`http://briefing.com/Investor/Public/MarketSnapshot/BondMarketUpdate.htm`) You'd expect Briefing.com to have a Bonds section, and you'd be right. It provide updates during the day on the direction of the bond market and also summarizes news that is affecting bond prices.

Common traits of bonds

Bond investors have their own language — and InvestinginBonds.com (`www.investinginbonds.com/learnmore.asp?catid=46&id=7`) provides a comprehensive glossary of terms. But before you get overwhelmed by all the terms, the following list offers a quick description of the most important ones you need to know. Nearly all bonds have the following characteristics:

✔ **Face (or par) value:** The face value is the amount of money you'll get back when the bond matures. For many bonds, the face value is the principal, or amount that you've lent. The face value is also sometimes called the *principal.*

✔ **Interest rate:** The interest rate measures how much you'll receive as a payment in exchange for lending the money. Generally, the interest rate is a percentage of the money lent, known as the face value of the bond. Interest, often called the *coupon rate,* is often paid twice a year.

Example: If you bought a $1,000 bond that pays 5% interest, you would be paid $50 a year in interest or $25 twice a year. You would get your $1,000 back when the bond matured.

Interest rates can be *fixed,* meaning the same rate of interest is paid to the investor for the life of the bond. Interest rates can also be *floating* and move up or down based on the direction of interest rates paid by Treasuries. Some bonds don't pay interest until the bond matures. These bonds, called *zero-coupon bonds,* are bought for less than their face value. Instead of receiving an interest payment twice a year as with many bonds, a zero-coupon bond pays nothing until it matures. When the zero-coupon bond matures, the investor receives the face value, which includes the interest.

Another example: Imagine an investor who pays $600 for a zero-coupon bond that matures in ten years, when it will pay $1,000. At the end of the ten years, the investor gets his $600 principal back plus $400. That $400 is the interest, which in this case amounts to an interest rate of more than 5% a year.

✔ **Maturity:** A bond's maturity is the date by which it must be paid off. Debt maturities can range from days to 20 or more years. A fixed-income security's maturity is very important and determines what it's called. Table 16-2 shows you what different fixed-income securities (excluding Treasuries, which have their own naming convention, as explained above) are called based on their maturities.

Table 16-2	Maturities Determine What a Fixed-Income Security Is Called
Fixed-Income Securities' Name	**Maturity**
Short-term note	Five years or less
Intermediate notes/bonds	More than five years but less than 12 years
Long-term bonds	12 years or longer

Source: Securities Industry and Financial Markets Association

- ✔ **Special provisions:** Bonds can be customized by the borrowers and contain unique privileges for either the seller or the buyer of the bonds. A Call provision is especially important if you're interested in buying bonds. If a bond can be called, that means the borrower can repay the loan before the maturity date. You can expect a bond to be called if current interest rates fall below the interest rate on the bond. If you're collecting a fat 7% interest rate on a bond, and interest rates fail to 5% for similar bonds, the issuer will likely call the bond and end your gravy train. Similarly, some bonds have Put provisions, which allow the bond buyers to force the bond seller to buy the bond back before the maturity date.

- ✔ **Price:** You can buy bonds directly from the issuers, and when you do, you often pay the face value. But, you can also buy bonds from previous owners in the secondary market, and when you do, you'll pay the current price. A bond's price is determined by many variables, such as the current interest rates on similar bonds.

Understanding the yield curve

Anytime you read about or investigate bonds, you'll inevitably hear someone mention the yield curve. The yield curve is a chart that shows you how yields on short-term fixed-income securities (with maturities of three months or less) compare with long-term bonds (with maturities of 30 years or so). The Investing in Bonds site (http://investinginbonds.com/learnmore.asp?catid=46&id=8) describes the yield curve. But I step you through the basics here. Generally, yield curves come in four shapes:

- ✔ **Normal:** Most of the time, investors demand higher interest rates on long-term bonds than they do on short-term notes. That's natural. If you let someone borrow money for 30 years, you'll want more interest because there's a greater chance you'll never see your money again. That's why yields (most of the time) will be at their lowest point for the short-term fixed income securities and gradually move higher.

- ✔ **Steep:** Most of the time, investors demand two or more percentage points in extra yield when lending money for 30 years compared with loaning money for a short time. If the interest rate on a three-month note is 4%, investors will demand 6% or higher on a comparable long-term bond in normal times. But, if the difference between the short-term and long-term rates gets even wider, that creates a steep yield curve. A steep yield curve often indicates investors expect economic growth to speed up.

✔ **Inverted:** When investors are willing to lend money for the long term and accept lower interest rates than they'd take for a short-term loan, the yield curve is inverted. Inverted yield curves can indicate that investors are worried the economy is about to slow down for a prolonged period of time. If the economy slows down, interest rates in the future might also fall. That means investors want to lock in current interest rates for the long term before they decline.

✔ **Flat:** When the interest rates on short-term loans equal long-term rates, you have a flat yield curve. A flat yield curve indicates investors aren't all too sure about where the economy is headed.

SmartMoney's Living Yield Curve feature helps explain this critical element of bond investing. The Living Yield Curve lets you see how the yields on bonds of different maturities compare to each other and how they've changed over time. The Living Yield Curve graphically shows you how the yields compare and lets you watch them change by watching a movie. To see how it looks, go to www.smartmoney.com/bonds and click the Living Yield Curve link in the Bonds Toolbox section. In the new page that appears, just click on the Play button under the Charting the Curve box (see the following figure) and you can see the yield curve change.

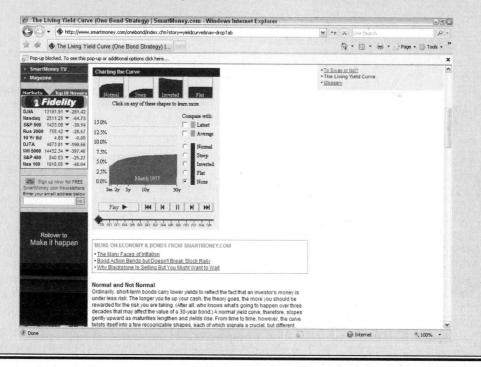

When a bond's price is less than its face value, it's said to trade at a discount. Bonds trade at a discount when interest rates rise (say, to 6%), making the bond's interest rate (say, just 5%) less attractive. When a bond's price is greater than its face value, it's said to trade at a premium. This happens when interest rates fall (perhaps to 4%), making this bond's interest rate (still at 5%) look more attractive and the bond worth more.

✔ **Credit ratings:** When you buy a bond from a company, one of the biggest dangers you face is the chance the company won't be able to pay you back, or default. *Debt-rating agencies* study companies' financial statements and rate them based on their ability to pay. The shakier the company, the more it will need to pay in interest to attract investors. Debt ratings are discussed more fully in Chapter 14, including instruction on how to access them. The three main debt-rating agencies, Moody's Investors Service (www.moodys.com), Standard & Poor's (www.sandp.com), and Fitch Ratings (www.fitchratings.com) provide more details about their ratings online.

✔ **Current yield:** The current yield tells you how much interest you'll receive from the bond based on the bond's price. You can calculate a bond's current yield by dividing the annual interest payment by the purchase price.

Example: You paid $900 for a bond with a $1,000 face value that pays 5%, or $50 a year, in interest. The current yield is 5.6%, which is calculated by dividing $50 by $900 and multiplying by 100 to convert the answer into a percentage.

✔ **Yield to maturity:** Tells you how much interest you'll gain as a percentage of the price you paid for the bond if you hold the bond until it matures. Yield to maturity is one of the best ways to measure the true return of a bond.

Money Chimp's online Bond Yield calculator (www.moneychimp.com/calculator/popup/calculator.htm?mode=calc_bondytm) can calculate a bond's current yield and yield to maturity for you. You need to enter the bond's current price, face value, coupon rate, and years to maturity.

Remember that bond prices fall when yields rise, almost like a teeter totter. Many beginning investors get hung up on this concept. Just think of it this way: If you own bond that yields 5%, but yields on similar bonds rise to 6%, your 5% looks pretty paltry. If you tried to sell your bond, you'd have to cut the price to find a buyer. If someone tells you bonds are down, make sure you know if they're talking about bond yields or bond prices.

✔ **Duration:** A bond's duration measures the time it takes, on average, for the bond buyer to get their money back. Duration differs from maturity in that it counts the interest payments made before the bond comes due. Duration is very handy because it can help you compare different bonds and determine which ones are more volatile. The larger the duration, the longer it takes for investors to get their money back, which makes them more volatile. Investopedia's Bond Duration calculator (`www.investopedia.com/calculator/BondDurCDate.aspx`) will tell you a bond's duration if you enter the bond's details, including face value, yield to maturity, interest rate, current maturity, and the schedule for payments.

How to Find and Buy Bonds Online

Just as with stocks, there's no one way to buy bonds. You can buy individual bonds using a mainstream online broker, you can buy directly from the borrowers, or you can deal directly with brokers that specialize in bonds. But you can also buy bonds through a mutual fund or exchange-traded fund. In the following sections, I show you how to buy bonds using these major methods.

Finding individual bonds online

Finding and buying an individual bond is very similar to finding and buying an individual stock. It's up to you to find the bonds that have what you're looking for in terms of risk and reward.

Online tools can help you find bonds that fit your needs. You can use various bond *screening tools,* which let you define characteristics of a bond you'd like to find. The bond screener then cross-checks what you're looking for in a bond against its database of available bonds. A few bond screeners that can help you quickly find bonds you're interested in include the following:

✔ **Yahoo! Finance's Bond Screener:** (`http://screen.yahoo.com/bonds.html`) Yahoo!'s bond screener first asks you whether you're interested in buying a Treasury, a zero-coupon Treasury, a corporate security, or a municipal security. (If you're looking for a muni bond, you can also indicate what state you're interested in.) You can narrow your search by other factors, ranging from the bond's price, coupon, yield to maturity, and credit rating. After you enter what you're looking for, click the Find Bonds button to get a list of all the bonds that meet your standards. Click a bond and write down the name of the issuer, coupon, and maturity date. You need this information to buy the bond.

✔ **Zions Direct's Bond Center:** (`www.zionsbank.com/zd_bonds_about-guest.jsp`) The Zions Direct site provides a full-fledged screener that lets you be even more specific about what you're looking for in a bond. You can filter not only on muni bonds and Treasuries, but also on high-yield, investment-grade, and agency bonds. Just click the button for the type of bond you're interested in, wait for a page similar to what you see in Figure 16-2 to appear, and then enter all your search criteria into the appropriate text fields. When you're done, click the Search button, and you see the list of bonds that make your cut. Write down the name of the issuer, coupon, and maturity date.

✔ **Online brokers' sites:** Most of the large online brokers mentioned in Chapter 4 — including Charles Schwab, TD Ameritrade, and E*Trade — all provide bond screening tools on their sites. Check with your online broker to see whether it has a feature that lets you screen for fixed-income securities.

Bond screeners tell you what the all-important yield to maturity of a bond is. This is a great tip because it saves you and your calculator the hassle of measuring the yield to maturity yourself.

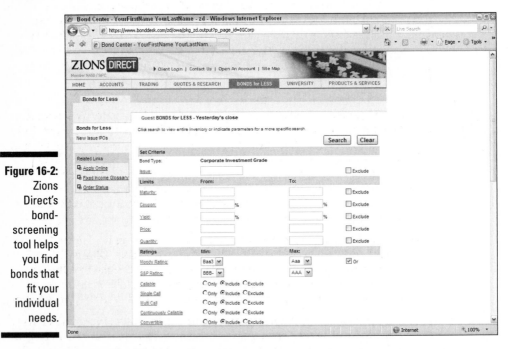

Figure 16-2: Zions Direct's bond-screening tool helps you find bonds that fit your individual needs.

Sealing the deal: Buying individual bonds online

After you've found the perfect individual bond for you, you need to know how to buy it. You can buy bonds in several ways:

✔ **Buying straight from the government:** If you're interested in buying Treasuries, you can cut out the middleman and buy directly from the U.S. Treasury at TreasuryDirect (www.treasurydirect.gov). TreasuryDirect lets you buy

- *Treasury bills, notes, and bonds.*

- *Treasury Inflation-Protected Securities (or TIPs):* TIPs are unique securities that pay you more interest and principal if interest rates rise.

- *Savings bonds:* These bonds, designed for individuals, don't pay very high interest rates and aren't appropriate for investors looking for the best returns. But savings bonds might have some tax advantages, are backed by the government, and pay predictable interest. TreasuryDirect's Tax Advantage Calculator (www.treasury direct.gov/BC/SBCTax) can help you measure whether you can get a tax benefit from owning savings bonds. The Savings Bond Calculator (www.treasurydirect.gov/indiv/tools/tools_ savingsbondcalc.htm) can help you decide whether savings bonds are right for you.

Buying Treasuries from the government is a good option because there's no fee for most investors. You also don't have to invest much. The minimum investment is just $1,000 for Treasuries and TIPs and $25 for savings bonds. Not sure how to use TreasuryDirect? TreasuryDirect's Guided Tour (www.treasurydirect.gov/indiv/TDTour/default. htm) steps you through the specific process of buying bonds through the site. The Federal Reserve Bank (www.federalreserve.gov/ generalinfo/faq/faqts.htm), the U.S.'s central bank, also provides instructions on how to buy Treasuries.

✔ **Buying from a mainstream online broker:** Several of the bigger online brokerage firms, (including Charles Schwab, E*Trade, TD Ameritrade, and Scottrade) also let you buy and sell bonds. But remember that the stock-trading commissions don't apply, and the bond commission can vary wildly depending on the broker and what kind of bond you're buying.

Schwab has one of the more straightforward fee structures for bonds. You can buy Treasuries online for no commission and most other types of bonds — including agencies and corporate bonds — for $1 per bond.

Some brokers charge so-called *mark-up* fees for bonds. Mark-up fees are added to the price of the bond. For instance, you might buy a bond for $1,000 but later see that you actually paid $1,045, where $1,000 is the price of the bond and $45 is the mark-up. There's nothing illegal about mark-up fees, and they've been a common way for brokers to charge commissions for buying bonds. You just want to find out ahead of time how much the mark-up fee will be and confirm you weren't overcharged by reviewing the confirmation of your order.

Some brokers charge commissions when you buy Treasuries. E*Trade, for instance, charges $40. You should think long and hard before paying any commissions or fees to buy Treasuries because you can buy them for free and online from TreasuryDirect.

✔ **Buying with the help of a bond broker:** Some brokers specialize in just bond trading. Zions Direct and JW Korth (`www.shop4bonds.com`) are two examples. FMSbonds.com (`www.fmsbonds.com`) specializes in munis, whereas Tradebonds.com (`http://tradebonds.com`) is geared mainly for large investors, but anyone who registers can use the site to get prices for bonds.

✔ **Buying via a bond mutual fund:** Buying individual bonds can be somewhat complex. You need to understand yields, prices, duration, and other cryptic measures of value. And that doesn't even scratch some advanced bond techniques, such as *laddering*.

Laddering is a technique used to lower your risk when investing in bonds. When you ladder, you buy bonds that expire at different times, say at one year, two years, and ten years. That way, if you buy bonds and interest rates rise, when your one-year bonds mature, you can reinvest the proceeds at the higher interest rate. Fidelity (`http://personal.fidelity.com/products/fixedincome/ladders.shtml`) provides a helpful description of what laddering is and how it can help you.

You can ladder and diversify your own bond portfolio. But for many investors, it's easier to just buy a bond mutual fund that does it for you. With a bond mutual fund, the laddering and diversification is taken care of for you. Just as with stock mutual funds, you can buy actively managed bond funds run by portfolio managers who try to beat the market or passive index bond funds.

You can find bond funds with the mutual fund–screening tools discussed in Chapter 10, but a good bet here would be the Vanguard Total Bond Market index. The fund owns a smattering of government, corporate, agency, and other bonds and charges a reasonable 0.2% annual expense ratio. If you're looking for an easy way to add bonds to your portfolio, this might be a good choice.

Think twice before buying a long-term government bond mutual fund. You'll pay an annual fee for the mutual fund, sometimes 1% a year. That's probably not a good idea considering you can buy Treasuries for free from TreasuryDirect.

✔ **Bond exchange-traded funds (ETFs):** Another option for buying bonds is through exchange-traded funds. ETFs, explained in depth in Chapter 11, are baskets of investments that trade like stocks. A bond ETF is ideal for investors who primarily buy stocks but want to easily add bonds to their portfolio and keep fees down. These ETFs track bond indexes, such as the Lehman Aggregate Bond index, which tracks a broad basket of bonds. Buying a bond ETF is the bond version of investing in a stock index like the Standard & Poor's 500.

It's easy to get started. Just pick the bond ETF you want and buy it through your online broker just as you'd buy a stock. You can read how to buy and sell stocks in Chapter 5. Note as well that you can find bond ETFs using the ETF-screening tools discussed in Chapter 11. (3 ETFs you may want to check out are iShares Lehman Aggregate Bond [AGG], SPDR Lehman Aggregate Bond [LAG], and Vanguard Total Bond Market [BND]. All three are diversified and have low fees.)

Considering Bond Alternatives

The relative safety of bonds as well as their lower volatility make them well suited for many investors' portfolios. But don't make the mistake of thinking bonds are without risks. The Investing in Bonds site (www.investingin bonds.com/learnmore.asp?catid=3&id=383) describes the risks of bonds in detail. But these are the risks you should be most aware:

- ✔ **Default risk:** Unless you're buying Treasuries, you're taking a chance the borrower won't pay you back.

- ✔ **Market risk:** If bonds go out of favor because investors are seeking higher returns, the price of your bonds might decline.

- ✔ **Liquidity risk:** From time to time, investors get nervous about the economy or about bonds, and they simply refuse to buy bonds. This is generally more of a problem with unusual or rare bonds, and it isn't a worry with Treasuries or investment grade bonds.

- ✔ **Interest rate risk:** The threat of higher interest rates is one of the biggest risks you face when you buy a bond. If rates rise, the interest rate you locked in suddenly isn't so lucrative, which decreases the value of your bond.

Some investors have an aversion to bonds for these reasons and others. These investors don't like the fact that bond values can fall, because bonds are supposed to be safer investments. If you're a bond hater, keep reading. The rest of this section explores a few bond alternatives.

Money market funds and certificates of deposit

If you're looking for safe investments but want to get more interest than you're getting in a bank savings account, you might consider money market funds or certificates of deposit.

✔ **Money market funds** are a great place to park money you need in case of emergency. They invest in very safe fixed-income securities, such as highly rated investments that come due in 90 days or less. Money markets generally invest in short-term Treasuries and *commercial paper.* Commercial paper obligations are loans generally given to creditworthy companies to fund short-term needs, such as buying goods to be sold in a few months. Money markets, however, aren't insured by the Federal Deposit Insurance Corporation. (You can find out what is, and isn't, insured by the FDIC at www.fdic.gov/consumers/consumer/information/fdiciorn.html.)

Bankrate.com (www.bankrate.com) is a useful site to find the best money market fund for you. The site's CD & Investments tab has a great money marker account screener that you can use to pick a money market account that best suits your needs.

✔ **Certificates of deposit (CDs):** If you want an even safer investment than a money market — and are willing to take a lower return — you might want to consider a certificate of deposit. CDs are typically issued by banks, and their interest rates can vary quite a bit. CDs are also usually insured by the FDIC.

If you buy a CD, your money is locked up, and you'll usually get hit with a penalty if you need the money earlier. If you need access to your money, a money market might be a better choice.

If you're looking for the highest CD rates, these sites might help:

- *Bankrate.com:* (www.bankrate.com) Bankrate.com can help you track down a money market fund, but it can also help you pinpoint the highest yielding CDs. Just click the CDs & Investments tab to bring up a page with various CD tables, CD calculators, and CD search tools.

- *Money-Rates.com:* (http://money-rates.com) This site lists national averages for CDs, money markets, and Treasuries.

- *iMoneyNet:* (www.imoneynet.com) And you thought iMoney was the green stuff you set aside to buy a new iPhone. iMoney is in fact a great source of info for all things money funds related. It explains the different types of money funds and provides average rates. You can also use the site to find large and highly regarded money market funds. iMoneyNet's Money Fund Basics (http://imoneynet.com/mfBasics.htm) explains the details about these investments.

You might be able to buy some money market funds through your online broker, but sometimes you need to contact the money market provider directly through its Web site. With CDs, you need to sign up over the bank's Web site.

Wall Street's lost child: Preferred stock

There are advantages and disadvantages to bonds and stock, which is probably why there's room for both in most portfolios. But there's a unique security that's kind of like the Dr. Jekyll and Mr. Hyde of Wall Street: preferred stock.

Preferred stock, commonly called preferreds, tries to give investors the best of both worlds. Preferred stock is a special type of stock that's sold by companies and acts more like a bond. Companies pay preferred stock holders a fixed dividend from earnings. Unlike with bonds, though, the company isn't obligated to pay the dividend if it doesn't have adequate earnings. If a company hits a tough patch, it can delay paying the preferred dividend until it regains its footing, after which it must pay the dividends it missed.

Preferreds have some advantages over bonds, though. Many preferreds give investors the option to convert their preferred stock into common stock. You might have the right to own a part of the company and enjoy the upside, rather than just collect a fixed interest payment. You can also buy preferred stocks through most online brokers.

Keep in mind, though, that many preferred stocks are *callable,* meaning a company can retire the shares by paying investors' money back, at any time. If that happens, you'll no longer receive the interest payments.

You can find out more about preferred stock at these Web sites:

- **Winans International:** (www.winansintl. com/Investment%20Products.htm) Winans International maintains an index that tracks the value of preferred stock, called the Winans International Preferred Stock Index. Scroll down the page and you can see a plot of the index at this Web site.

- **iShares:** (www.ishares.com/fund_ info/detail.jhtml?symbol=PFF) iShares offers an exchange-traded fund that tracks preferred stock. iShares' S&P U.S. Preferred Stock Index Fund (symbol PFF) lets you invest in a basket of preferred stocks. Check out Chapter 11 for more details on ETFs.

- **Income Investing Information:** (www. quantumonline.com) This site lets you search for preferred stock that might suit your needs. Just choose the All Preferred Stocks option from the Tables menu at the top of the page and you'll call up a new page with a list of all preferred stocks, their trading symbols, and interest rates. If you find one you're interested in, write down the trading symbol and buy it through your online broker. The site is free, but you must register to use it.

- **PreferredsOnline:** (www.epreferreds. com) This site provides news and quotes on preferred stocks, but it's not free. Subscriptions range from $10.49 for access for one day to $445 a month.

Part IV
The Part of Tens

The 5th Wave

By Rich Tennant

"Oh, look! Mr. Peepers just picked the very same mutual funds your investment software did!"

In this part . . .

No *For Dummies* book would be complete without a Part of Tens. This part is the place for you to find some of the information readers look for most when they dabble with online investing. Here I address ways to avoid the most common mistakes made by online investors and also highlight techniques to protect your financial and personal information online. Security is critical for online investors, who are passing very sensitive data over the (very public) Internet.

Chapter 17

Ten Top Mistakes Made by Online Investors

....

In This Chapter

▶ Finding out about common mistakes online investors make

▶ Avoiding the mistakes that can eat into your returns

▶ Getting answers to questions before you make a mistake

▶ Understanding that it's okay to make a mistake once

....

*W*hen people tell me they're afraid to start investing online, most of the time it's the fear of making a mistake that's holding them back. With its jargon, formulas, charts, and Wall Street slang, investing online can seem scary and intimidating. For some investors, the thought of managing their money by themselves is overwhelming. The fear of making a mistake and losing hard-earned money is too much to bear.

Calming these fears is what this chapter is all about. After answering thousands of e-mails sent to me by readers of my online *Ask Matt* column at USATODAY.com, I've heard it all. Most of the mistakes investors make can be neatly placed into ten categories, each of which I explain in this chapter. By reading about the common mistakes other online investors make, you'll probably think twice before committing them yourself. I discuss the ten most common mistakes, explain why they're made, and show you how to avoid them.

Buying and Selling Too Frequently

One of the greatest things about online investing is that it gives investors the power to buy and sell stocks whenever they want. Unfortunately, though, some investors turn this 24/7 access to their portfolios and stock trading into a liability.

Don't get me wrong; it's great that investors can check their portfolios whenever they want instead of calling a broker or waiting for a printed brokerage statement to arrive in the mail. It's just that constant access turns some investors into

✓ **Obsessive portfolio checkers:** These investors are constantly logging in to their online brokerage accounts and checking the value of their portfolios. And I mean constantly — often several times a day. This is a problem because it makes investors get overly concerned about the short-term swings in their stocks.

If the market falls 1% one day, these investors measure how much money they lost and start thinking about all the things they could have bought if they'd just sold the day before. Clearly, no one can have the foresight to sell ahead of a 1% downdraft, much less a 10% correction. But these obsessive investors start to take every $1 move in their portfolio personally.

Checking your portfolio's value online is fine, unless it starts to affect your judgment. If you find you're telling yourself you should have sold or bought because the market is up or down in a given day, you might be missing the point of investing.

✓ **Trigger-fingered investors:** These investors are so antsy that they can't help but trade. They buy and sell stocks in a flash, well, just because they can. Trigger-fingered investors figure commissions are so cheap that there's no harm in picking up shares of a stock, trying it out, and then dumping it if it doesn't work out. Trigger-fingered investors also seem to get a rush out of trading online, much like someone might get when pulling on the arm of a slot machine.

The trouble, though, is that these investors are hurting themselves more than helping. Not only are they paying more in taxes than they should, but they're setting themselves up for losses as they dump stocks they can't remember why they bought in the first place. Without an asset allocation plan in place, these investors are just haphazardly buying stocks and have no idea what their plan is. You can find out how to determine the perfect asset allocation for you in Chapter 9.

Letting Losers Run and Cutting Winners Short

Human nature, in some respects, is your worst enemy when investing online. Humans react in particular ways when faced with certain circumstances, but those reactions can work against you in investing. Two of those elements of human nature are defending bad decisions too long and cashing in on good decisions too early.

If you've ever been to Las Vegas, you've seen this before. Just walk over to one of the cash machines scattered on the casino floor, and you're sure to bump into people who lost all the cash they brought so they're pulling out another $500. These people figure they'll "win it all back" if they keep trying. The same thing, sadly, happens with some investors. Investors who buy an individual stock that collapses often hang onto it, figuring that "it will come back" because "it's a good company."

When you're buying individual stocks, it's critical that you cut your losses. Pick a percentage you're willing to risk and stick with it. You can use stop market orders or protective puts, both described in Chapter 5.

Other investors make the opposite mistake by cashing in winning stocks too soon. Say your asset allocation tells you to put 20% of your stocks in emerging markets, so you buy an emerging markets index mutual fund. If emerging markets soar in the following few weeks, but your emerging market index fund still accounts for 20% or less of your portfolio, you should resist the temptation to sell it all to lock in your gains. Instead, you should stick with your asset allocation. To understand how asset allocations can boost your returns and cut your risk, read Chapter 9.

The rule of cutting losses short applies to individual stocks. If you don't think you'll have the courage to sell individual stocks when they sink, you should instead invest in index mutual funds or exchange-traded funds (ETFs) that follow a broad stock market index, such as the Standard & Poor's 500. These investments are already diversified and less risky than individual stocks, so you don't have to worry so much about a 40% or greater decline.

Focusing on the Per-Share Price of the Stock

The fact that one stock is $2 a share and another is $500 a share tells you absolutely nothing about either stock. The $2-a-share stock might actually be more expensive than the $500-a-share stock because it either doesn't grow as rapidly, doesn't earn as much relative to its stock price, or is riskier.

A stock's per-share price is meaningful only if you compare it with something else. Typically, investors multiply the stock price by the stock's number of shares outstanding to get the company's *market value* or market capitalization. A stock's market value tells you whether a stock is small, medium, or large and gives you a good idea of its valuation. Chapter 9 explains why the size of a stock's market value is so important.

Don't be fooled into thinking it's better to own 1,000 shares of a $2 stock than owning 100 shares of a $20 stock. What really matters is the company's valuation and market value. Think of it this way: What's better, buying one reliable car for $8,000 or ten unreliable and broken-down $800 cars?

Failing to Track Risk and Return

For some reason, prudence vanishes when it comes to online investing. Many online investors, perhaps because it takes some effort and practice, don't take the time to see how much risk they're taking on to get the reward they're expecting from stocks they buy.

The biggest danger of investing without knowing your risk and return is that you risk not knowing whether you're doing more harm than good to your portfolio. You might be spending a great deal of time and effort buying individual stocks thinking the effort is worthwhile, but it might turn out you'd be better off buying and holding index mutual funds. Instead of burning hours looking at stock charts, you might be better off spending the time with your family, on hobbies, or at work.

Chapter 8 shows you the techniques of measuring your portfolio. You can find out how to calculate the returns and risk yourself or check out Web sites that will do it for you.

Taking Advice from the Wrong People

It's almost hard not to get stock tips. Turn on the TV. Talk to people sitting next to you on an airplane. Chat with other browsers in the financial section of the bookstore (unless they're reading *Investing Online For Dummies,* of course). Connect with other investors online. You'll constantly encounter people who are convinced such-and-such stock is going to take off and that you need to buy in now. Some of my readers have told me they've bought shares of retailers because employees told them to.

Here's my advice: Unless Warren Buffett is the guy sitting next to you on the airplane, you're better off politely nodding and wiping your memory clean of all the investing advice you get. Stick with your asset allocation plan.

You should also be cautious of advice you're getting from a financial advisor that you hire. The two things you should do when evaluating your advisors are

✔ **Use online broker screening tools.** You want to meticulously check to make sure the person giving you advice has the right licenses. Chapter 4 contains some online ways to check out your broker. You'll want to make sure you use The Financial Industry Regulatory Authority's BrokerCheck (www.finra.org). Just click the FINRA BrokerCheck link on the left side of the page and follow the directions. I give you additional tips on how to avoid scams in Chapter 18.

✔ **Track the advisor's performance.** You might not be making the calls in your portfolio, but you still want to make sure your advisor is getting you adequate returns for the risk you're taking. That also goes for any stock-picking newsletters or Web sites that promise to make you fabulously rich. Use the tools and techniques in Chapter 8 to make sure you're getting what you're paying for.

Trying to Make Too Much Money Too Quickly

The reason you invest is to make money. That's the American way. But as an investor, you need to appreciate that wealth is built over time as companies you've invested in expand their revenue and earnings. Generally speaking, stocks have returned about 10% a year. You can boost that 10% a bit to 13% or so with smart asset allocation and exposure to riskier types of stocks like emerging markets and small companies.

Some investors, though, just aren't satisfied with that. They chase after brand-new IPOs, pile into stocks that have been the market's leaders, and load up on penny stocks. These investors are typically the ones that get sucked into "get rich quick" e-mails, stock conferences, and other dubious stock promotion schemes that make only their promoters rich.

Sometimes things work out okay for these speculators, and they might buy shares of the right stock at the right time. But more often than not, these speculators suffer as the stocks whip around more than they expected. The volatility proves too much to bear, and the speculators buy and sell stocks at the wrong times. Before they know it, speculators are down 30% or more and then write to me on my online column asking what to do.

I suppose that if you limit your investment to a small amount, there's no harm. But for the bulk of your portfolio, you'll find much better success over the long term if you read Chapters 8 and 9 and find out how to track your risk and return.

Letting Emotions Take Over

It's happened to you before: You've fallen in love. No, I'm not talking about your spouse or significant other. I'm talking about your favorite stock. Everyone has had one. The stock you fall in love with is the one that you happened to buy at just the right time and have never lost money on. It might be the one that soars and always shows up on the "Top Performers" lists printed by magazines and Web sites. It's easy to be proud of a stock just like parents who see their kid's name in the paper for being on the Honor Roll.

The opposite happens, too. Say your asset allocation calls for you to own large-company stocks, you invest in them, and they do nothing. There you are, you own shares of big companies and watch your portfolio go sideways while your friends brag about the tiny upstarts and penny stocks they make a fortune on.

Periods of self-doubt and second-guessing account for many investors' worst decisions. These investors might be so blinded by their enduring affection for a stock they that proudly ride it down lower and lower. It's funny, but the love for the stock wears pretty thin by the time the stock is down 50% or more. What's the answer to this? Unless you're a robot or computer, you're stuck with your emotions. But you can stop these emotions from meddling with your portfolio by sticking with your asset allocation plan. Yes, I know this asset allocation stuff is getting repetitive, but trust me, it will protect you from yourself.

Emotions can burn you badly with investments that just keep going down. It's easy to get so fed up with certain stocks you can't bear to keep buying more. You curse at your asset allocation for ruining your portfolio. You might get so disgusted with stocks you either inquire about CDs from your local bank or start scanning the "new high" lists for stocks you think will be your ticket to riches.

If you let your greed for huge returns and fear of losses run your investment decisions, you can practically guarantee you'll buy and sell at the wrong time.

If you find that you're an emotional investor and take the market's movements too close to heart, you're probably a good candidate to invest in passive index mutual funds and exchange-traded funds. You can just buy these investments and let them ride, removing the temptation to tinker with your portfolio and almost guaranteeing you better results.

Looking to Blame Someone Else for Your Losses

No one likes to lose money on stocks. And everyone loses money on stocks from time to time. It's how you react to the losses that makes the difference. Some investors go on a witch hunt and start trying to track down anyone who might have mentioned a stock as a good buy, ranging from publications,

Web sites, friends, or the company's executives. These investors are generally the first in line to join securities class-action lawsuits and try to sue the company or executives.

Certainly there are cases of fraud, in the mold of Enron and Worldcom. These cases are regrettable because even investors who attempted to do their homework by studying the company's financials were misled. But if you just lost money because you bought a stock at the wrong time or overestimated the company's profit potential, you can only look to yourself. It's best to analyze what you did right, what you did wrong, and learn from it as opposed to playing an unproductive blame game.

Sometimes investors truly are wronged by companies' managements. In those cases, securities class-action lawsuits attempt to extract money for the shareholders. You can find out whether shareholders are suing a company by using Stanford Law School's Securities Class Action Clearinghouse (`http://securities.stanford.edu`). If there's a suit, you generally must fill out a claim form. You can find out how to fill out the form at Claims Compensation Bureau (`www.claimscompensation.com`). Just don't get your hopes up. Investors generally get pennies on the dollar even if the lawsuits are successful.

Ignoring Tax Considerations

Come tax time, each April, it's amazing the lengths taxpayers go to cut their tax bill by just a few bucks. Some go as far as to get married or have a child to pay less tax to Uncle Sam. But many of these same investors ignore or aren't aware of ways of investing that will save them thousands on taxes.

Uncle Sam offers extremely generous tax breaks for investors, if you just know how to take advantage of them. Tax breaks investors should never pass up on include

- **Lower tax rates for long-term capital gains:** If you can wait more than a year before selling winning stocks, you'll be much further ahead than investors who trade with no regard to taxes. By holding onto stocks for longer than a year, you usually qualify for long-term capital gains taxes, which in many cases are half what you'll pay if you sell stocks in a year or less.

- **Major tax breaks on education savings:** If you're trying to save for your child's college, you can let Uncle Sam help out. Special education savings accounts, such as the 529 plan, let you largely shield your money from taxes as long as it's used to pay for school.

Say you need to save $50,000 to pay for your kid's college. If you ignore the tax breaks available to you through educational savings plans like 529s, you might actually need to save $58,824. You'll need the extra $8,824 to pay the 15% long-term capital gains tax that might apply.

✔ **Major tax breaks on retirement savings:** Always take advantage of any retirement savings tax breaks you can get. Researching what's available to you should be the first thing you do when you start to invest. If your company matches contributions to a 401(k) or other profit-sharing plan, take advantage of it as soon as you can. If there's no such plan at your job, don't assume nothing is available to you. Many taxpayers are entitled to invest in a Roth IRA, which offers tremendous tax benefits, as described in Chapter 3.

Dwelling on Mistakes Too Long

It might sound funny to tell you to not think about investing mistakes in a chapter dedicated to mistakes, but it's important to not let a mistake in the past paralyze you. So, you bought a stock and rode it down too long before selling it. Don't linger on the mistake. Just don't do it again, and over time, you'll obtain the success in investing you're shooting for.

Chapter 18

Ten Ways to Protect Your Investments and Identity Online

*p*romising a big return to investors is kind of like waving red meat in front of a salivating tiger. Even educated investors can't help but bite when offered what seems to be a plausible chance at winning big-time returns. Investors' innate craving for that big score makes them easy targets for less-than-honest financial snake oil salesmen.

It's always been amazing to me how people are so careful about their money in everyday life but let their guard down then it comes to investing. The same people who clip coupons and shop at discount stores to save a few bucks will readily hand over their life's savings to a stranger with dubious qualifications selling questionable investments.

It's up to you to do your homework when checking into any investments. Online tools make it easier than ever to sniff out unscrupulous people hawking investment products. Unfortunately, though, the Internet is also a boon for the bad guys. E-mail lets fraudsters reach millions of users with the click of a button. Fraudsters can also glean basic information about you online, perhaps from your *blog,* or online diary, and craft a pitch that seems more realistic and personable. Keeping these things in mind, this chapter points out some of the main types of investments frauds and shows you how to dodge them.

Beware of Pyramid Schemes

When it comes to investment frauds, *pyramid schemes* are among the greatest hits. Organizers behind pyramid schemes try to convince investors to contribute money and tempt them with promises of a giant payout. That sounds like playing the lottery, I know. But what makes pyramid schemes so insidious is that they're based on a sham that eventually collapses.

Generally, pyramid schemes work like this: Six fraudsters send out e-mails to as many people as they can, each hoping to get six additional "investors." These initial promoters convince investors to sign up by telling them that if they contribute money, they'll get a 100% or greater return in just 90 days. If the six initial promoters are successful in lining up other participants, they pocket the money from the new investors. But, that's just the tip of the pyramid, so to speak. The 36 just-recruited investors are then instructed to get six more investors each, which brings the total number of investors in the scheme to 216. The scheme then continues, and each time more investors are brought in, the previous investors get their payout.

There's just one big problem: The pyramid collapses under its own weight. After 13 rounds of this pyramid scheme, for instance, more than 13 billion people are required to keep it going. That's impossible because it exceeds the world's population. So unless you think you can find six suckers on Mars or Jupiter to buy your stake of a pyramid scheme, you could end up losing your investment. The Securities and Exchange Commission provides helpful information on pyramid schemes at http://sec.gov/answers/pyramid.htm.

Pyramid schemes have a close relative: *multilevel marketing plans*. In a multilevel marketing plan, a company e-mails you with an offer to make you a distributor of its products — usually pills or medical devices — that promise miraculous benefits. These plans not only promise to pay commissions if you're able to sell the products, but also pay you if you find other distributors. The problem is that these are often based on pyramid schemes at www.ftc.gov/bcp/conline/pubs/invest/mlm.shtm. The Federal Trade Commission provides tips on how to avoid getting caught up in these plans. You should also always run a company through the Better Business Bureau's Web site (www.bbb.org) to make sure it's legitimate.

Just because a company is in the BBB database and doesn't have any complaints, that doesn't mean it's safe. The company could be new and looking for fresh victims. The BBB site, though, is a good place to start. It's a good idea to also run the owners' names through the SEC's Web site (http://sec.gov) to see whether there have been any prior run-ins with regulators.

Steer Clear of Ponzi Schemes

Ponzi schemes are some of the oldest frauds in the book. Ponzi schemes are a type of pyramid scheme with one key difference: All the "investors'" money goes to one person — the organizer of the fraud.

Ponzi schemes are pretty simple. The organizer sends out e-mails offering investors fabulous returns in a very short period of time. After the initial investors eagerly sign up, the Ponzi promoter takes a cut and then seeks a second round of investors. When the money comes in from the second round of investors, the Ponzi operator takes another cut but also returns a slice of the money to the first round of investors. Clearly, the first investors are ecstatic and eager to tell others about their great investment. Those testimonials play right into the Ponzi operator's hand, who keeps repeating the process until it falls apart.

Avoid Tout Sheets and Know Who You're Taking Advice From

There's no shortage of investment and stock-picking newsletters that claim to have the inside track on the stocks you need to buy now. But some of these newsletters, known in the trade as *tout sheets,* have nefarious intentions. Tout sheets are investment newsletters distributed for the sole purpose of hyping stocks with exaggerated or false information to stir up investors' interest. Tout sheet have proliferated due to the Internet, which makes distributing and promoting such things a cinch. (You can read more about investment newsletters in general in Chapter 15.)

Above all, you need to be perfectly sure an online newsletter is above board. Whenever considering subscribing to a newsletter or following its suggestions, you want to be 100% clear on whether the newsletter writer is paid by the companies to be a *tout.* Touts are hired by companies or shady brokerage firms to stoke interest in stocks by putting out glowing reports on the company based on exaggeration or lies. If the tout is successful in attracting investors and driving up the stock price, the company's executives and brokerage firm can then sell and pocket the quick profit.

The SEC is somewhat restricted in its ability to crack down on newsletters. The First Amendment allows anyone to make statements, including about stocks. The SEC can get involved, though, when the newsletter writers are paid for issuing misleading statements about a stock for personal gain.

The SEC (http://sec.gov/investor/pubs/cyberfraud/newsletter.htm) warns investors to be especially skeptical of online newsletters that vaguely say how they're paid. A statement like "From time to time, XYZ Newsletter may receive compensation from companies we write about," is a huge red flag, says the SEC. You should also avoid newsletters that say they're paid to promote stocks in tiny or hidden places in the newsletter.

Check up on newsletters, or any other stock promoter for that matter, by searching the following sites:

- **The SEC's Division of Enforcement page** (http://sec.gov/divisions/enforce.shtml) is a great site for all things fraudulent. You can click the Enforcement Actions link to see whether the newsletter you're looking at has been accused of wrongdoing by the SEC.

- **The SEC's Investment Adviser Public Disclosure page** (www.adviserinfo.sec.gov/IAPD/Content/IapdMain/iapd_SiteMap.aspx) is an excellent way to check up on "investment advisers." Many, but not all, professionals who dispense advice to investors are required to file Form ADVs with the SEC. The Form ADV contains information about the adviser or advisory firm, including any disciplinary actions. To access the site, just click the Investment Adviser Search link on the left side and follow the directions.

- **The North American Securities Administrators Association** (www.nasaa.org/QuickLinks/ContactYourRegulator.cfm) provides helpful information about securities crackdowns in various states. Just click your state in the 50-state map and the site will direct you to the appropriate state regulators that punish securities fraudsters.

- **Certified Financial Planner Board of Standards** (http://cfp.net) lets you quickly see whether someone who claims to be a Certified Financial Planner, or CFP, really is. Just click the SEARCH for a Certified Financial Planner Professional link on the navigation bar on the left side. Enter the person's last name, choose the state, and click the Search button.

Don't Fall for Investment Spam E-Mails

Open your e-mail box, and you're likely to find all sorts of offers. You'll see pitches selling Vioxx for next to nothing, ways to get Microsoft to write you a giant check, and hot tips on stocks about to take off.

Generally these *spam* e-mails, or unsolicited promotional e-mail messages, are all very similar. The e-mails masquerade as being legitimate reports from stock research firms or investors who are in the know that are passing along their tips out of generosity. The messages will talk about some major development that will move the stock by a huge amount in a short period of time.

And the e-mails generally pitch stocks with very low share prices that trade on lesser regulated markets, like the Pink Sheets.

If you get such spam, don't even read it. Trash that rotten spam immediately. They're almost always *pump-and-dump* schemes. They work like this: The fraudsters first pick a few lightly traded stocks and buy them up. After the promotional e-mail goes out, the fraudsters wait for gullible investors to buy shares and drive the stock price up. That's the *pump* part of pump and dump. Next, these investors sell their shares. That's the *dump*.

Sadly, many investors fall for these schemes. A study from Rainer Bohme and Thorsten Holz of the Dresden University of Technology and University of Mannheim (http://papers.ssrn.com/sol3/papers.cfm?abstract_id=897431) found stock prices do react to these e-mails, indicating investors are reading them and buying the stocks.

Don't think for a moment you can profit from these spam e-mails. Spam Stock Tracker (www.spamstocktracker.com) has tracked how investors would have done if they'd bought the stocks recommended through spam e-mails. The study found in just a year and a half, investors who bought the stocks suggested in the spam would have lost more than 90% of their money.

Don't fall for the e-mails from supposed Nigerian nationals hoping to transfer cash to the United States, either. They're scams called *advance fee frauds,* or *4-1-9* frauds after that section of the Nigerian penal code. Don't participate in these. The Secret Service (www.secretservice.gov/faq.shtml#faq15) provides information on these scams if you're interested.

Understand Loopholes Scammers Can Use

Before you invest your money in anything, your first stop should be the SEC's Web site at http://sec.gov. You should always find out whether there are any regulatory filings on the investment or person selling the investments.

If you're looking to buy a stock, for instance, you can download the company's regulatory filings as explained in Chapter 2. Companies with more than 500 investors and $10 million in assets must file statements with the SEC. Companies listed on major exchanges, such as the New York Stock Exchange and NASDAQ, must also file statements. If it's a broker or an investment newsletter you're interested in checking up on, you can follow the instructions in the section about that tells you how to research tout sheets.

If you're not able to turn up any filings, your defenses should go up. Scamsters know there are loopholes in SEC rules — originally designed to help small companies avoid bureaucratic red tape — that allow them to avoid filing potentially troublesome documents. You can read about these loopholes fully for yourself on the SEC's Web site (www.sec.gov/info/smallbus/qasbsec.htm) in the section titled, "Are There Legal Ways to Offer and Sell Securities Without Registering With the SEC?"

But to save you the trouble, below are summaries of the primary loopholes that may allow certain firms to avoid filing documents with the SEC:

- **Intrastate offerings** occur when a local business sells investments to residents of the state it primarily does business in. This is called the intrastate offering exemption.

- **Private offerings** take place when companies only sell investments to investors that have deep understanding of business and also provide financial information to these investors.

- **Regulation A** is an SEC exemption that kicks in when firms raise less than $5 million in a 12-month period. Regulation A allows companies to file paper statements called *offering circulars* with the SEC instead of making their information readily available online. Offering circulars contain limited information and can be hard to get because they're often filed only on paper in Washington D.C.

- **Regulation D** is a more common SEC exemption that applies to firms that meet a variety of requirements, including raising less than $1 million in a 12-month period or selling investments only to "accredited investors" who are very sophisticated. These firms need to file only a *Form D* with the SEC. A Form D offers just bare-bones information and provides few details other than the names of the company's owners. You can read more about Regulation D from at http://sec.gov/answers/regd.htm.

If you can't find a company on the SEC's Web site, call or e-mail the SEC (http://sec.gov/contact.shtml) to see whether paper forms are available. You should also contact your state's regulator, which you can find from The North American Securities Administrators Association (www.nasaa.org).

Familiarize Yourself with the Fingerprints of a Scam

There are only so many ways to rob a bank. Face it; most of the scams fraudsters use online and off generally fall into just a few categories, most of which are variants of pyramid or Ponzi schemes. Sure, there are twists, such as *affinity frauds* (http://sec.gov/investor/pubs/affinity.htm), where the scammers infiltrate a group of investors of a similar age, race, or hobby, gain the trust of the group, and then use the group members to promote the scheme to each other.

Still, a few common traits should set off alarm bells in your head:

- **Promises of guaranteed returns that seem abnormally large:** By reading Chapter 1, you know that stocks have returned roughly 10% average annual returns. If someone tells you he can get you a return of greater than 10% a year, you know the investment is riskier than stocks. So if the promoter says the returns are guaranteed or risk-free, you know something isn't right.

- **Pressure to act right now:** Perpetrators of frauds know they have to get your checkbook open now, or you might get cold feet and start thinking about the risks. If you're told you have to invest now or you'll miss out, you're better missing out on the "opportunity."

- **No documentation on paper:** Bad guys hate paper trails and try their best to avoid documenting anything. If you can't print out the information about an investment, you shouldn't invest in it. Proper investment proposals should be registered with regulators and come with a prospectus, an annual report, and other financial statements.

The SEC provides a list of other telltale signs of online frauds (`http://sec.gov/investor/pubs/cyberfraud/signs.htm`), which are worthwhile checking out.

Learn to Be an Online Sleuth

Scammers often reinvent themselves and try different scams until they get caught. If you're being pitched an investment or seminar, try to find out whether the person is working under an alias or has sold investments before. Get as much information as you can about the person, and use the Web search techniques described in Chapter 2 to see whether you can turn up more information.

It's also important to find out whether a regulator or private party has gone after a company or broker to recover funds. There are three main places to check:

- **The SEC's Investors Claims Funds** (`http://sec.gov/divisions/enforce/claims.htm`) is a list of all the companies that have been targeted by enforcement actions that resulted in funds being given back to investors.

- **The Securities Investor Protection Corporation** (`www.sipc.org/cases/sipccasesopen.cfm`) maintains a list of brokers that have gone out of business and are being liquidated. You'll also find instructions on how to fill out a claim form to make sure you get your money back.

✔ **The Stanford Law School Securities Class Action Clearinghouse**
(`http://securities.stanford.edu`) provides a free database
of companies that are being sued by investors for securities fraud.

Know How to Complain if You Suspect a Fraud

It might be embarrassing if you've been taken in by a fraud. But if you feel
that you've been had, it's critical that you let regulators know right away. The
sooner you can tip off the authorities, the greater the chance the fraudster
can be nailed and the better the chance of recovering money.

The SEC's Center for Complaints and Enforcement Tips (`http://sec.gov/
complaint.shtml`) allows you to fill out electronic forms to alert regulators
to a possible fraud. Give as much detail about the alleged fraud as you can to
help investigators who might decide to take your case.

Make Sure Your Computer Is Locked Down

You should always be concerned with computer security. Make sure you have
the proper software and other safeguards installed to protect your computer
from viruses and hackers. You have many options, including some offered by
the online brokers themselves. When you're online using a public wireless network service, such as those in Starbucks coffeehouses, you should be especially careful. You can read more about ways to lock down your computer in
Chapter 2.

But online criminals also use other low-tech methods to bilk investors. The
most common trick used is *phishing*, which is pronounced "fishing." In phishing
scams, the fraudster sends out millions of e-mails purporting to be from a bank
(say Citibank), a store (like Circuit City), a government agency (say the Internal
Revenue Service) or an online service (like PayPal or eBay). These e-mails are
carefully crafted to appear official and generally ask the recipients to click
a link to confirm or update personal information.

Here are a couple ways to protect yourself from these scams:

✔ **Log in routinely:** Log in to your bank, online broker, PayPal, and other
important accounts directly and routinely check the "messages section.
Generally, when these companies want to reach you, they leave a message
for you on the site.

✔ **Never click links in e-mails:** If you get an e-mail claiming to be from your online brokerage, assume it's a fraud. Don't click the link in the e-mail that claims to direct you to the Web site. Instead, manually enter the site's address into your browser or click the Favorite for the site that you set up.

✔ **Hover your pointer over the link:** If you want to know whether the e-mail is phishing for information, put your pointer over the link in the e-mail. Do *not* click the link, but look in the lower-left corner of the screen. You see the address the link wants to take you to. If it's not the complete address of the site it purports to be, you know instantly it's a fraud.

Be Aware of Online Sources for More Information

Scams are constantly evolving. It's up to you to be constantly vigilant and be aware the Internet is a perfect environment for people trying to fool you and take your money. That doesn't mean you should unplug your computer and give up on online investing. It's just that it's up to you to be aware of the potential risks.

Internet sources can help online investors understand how to protect themselves, including

✔ **The SEC's Web site** (http://sec.gov/investor/pubs/cyberfraud. htm) explains many of the common online investing frauds and gives detailed examples. If you're new to online investing, this site is very worthwhile and will make you more street-smart and aware of the dangers.

✔ **Fraud Discovery Institute** (www.barryminkow.com/index.html) is operated by Barry Minkow, a former fraudster convicted for being the mastermind behind the Zzzz Best "carpet-cleaning" business that bilked investors out of millions in the 1980s. Minkow is now a Christian minister and operates the Fraud Discovery Institute, which seeks to sniff out frauds in the making. In addition to serving up warnings of potential frauds, Fraud Discovery Institute is also a useful source that shows investors how frauds are detected and how to avoid them.

The Journal of Accountancy Online (www.aicpa.org/pubs/jofa/aug2001/wells.htm) steps investors through the process of how reading financial statements could have warned them of the Zzzz Best fraud ahead of time.

✔ **Investor Protection Trust** (www.investorprotection.org/upr/ initiatives.html) provides links to a variety of investor education materials. You can download a free course on how to avoid investment fraud at www.investorprotection.org/basics/06_Basics_ Unit4.pdf.

✔ **Investor's Watchdog** (www.investorswatchdog.com) helps investors teach themselves how to identify an investment scam before being taken in. Stories detail recent frauds and tips on how to smell a scam before it's too late.

Index

• B •

• *N* •